Charitable Gifts of Noncash Assets

2nd Edition

Bryan Clontz, MS, MSFS, Ph.D., CFP®, CLU®, ChFC®, CAP®, RICP®, AEP, CBP

Edited by Ryan Raffin, JD

Copyright © 2018 by The American College Press

All rights reserved. No part of this publication may be reproduced, distributed, or transmitted in any form or by any means, including photocopying, recording, or other electronic or mechanical methods, without the prior written permission of the publisher, except in the case of brief quotations embodied in critical reviews and certain other noncommercial uses permitted by copyright law. For permission requests, write to the publisher the address below.

ISBN-10:
ISBN-13:

The American College Press
270 S. Bryn Mawr Avenue
Bryn Mawr, PA 19010
http://www.theamericancollege.edu

Printed in the United States of America

With Gratitude to Our Funders

Commissioned by The Chartered Advisor in Philanthropy program at The American College of Financial Services, this book was generously funded by Leon L. Levy, CLU, RHU. Previously, Leon had funded Bryan Clontz, MS, MSFS, Ph.D., CFP®, CLU®, ChFC®, CAP®, RICP®, AEP, CBP as the inaugural Leon L. Levy Fellow in Philanthropy at The American College. Leon's purpose has been to advance the field of philanthropy by encouraging collaboration between financial, tax, and legal advisors, and nonprofit professionals. In that way, Leon is advancing the mission of the Chartered Advisor in Philanthropy program, funded by Sallie B. and William B. Wallace, through The American College of Financial Services. Thank you, Leon, Bill, and Sallie!

While this book covers technical financial, tax and legal aspects of noncash donations, it is not intended to provide any advice specifically to donors. As with any project of this complexity, errors, misinterpretations and dated or obsolete information are not only possible, they are nearly guaranteed. As always, seek additional resources and counsel when exploring noncash planning solutions for your donors and clients.

Table of Contents

Charitable Gifts of Noncash Assets
With Gratitude to Our Funders
Table of Contents i
Preface and Users' Guide v
Contributors xiii
Noncash Opportunities, Aggregate Market and Property Types xxxi
Donor Questions | Quick Take-Aways xlvii
Donor Questions | Identifying Charitable Passions and Noncash Giving Opportunities xlix
Donor Questions | Additional Resources lxiii
Key Noncash Gift Process Considerations lxv
Key Terms and Concepts lxix
General Regulations and Information lxxvii

Real Estate 1.1
Real Estate   Quick Take-Aways 1.2
Real Estate   Intermediate 1.5
Real Estate   Advanced 1.11
Real Estate   Additional Resources 1.29

C Corporations 2.1
C Corporations   Quick Take-Aways 2.2
C Corporations   Intermediate 2.5
C Corporations   Advanced 2.9
C Corporations   Additional Resources 2.22

S Corporations 3.1
S Corporations   Quick Take-Aways 3.2
S Corporations   Intermediate 3.5
S Corporations   Advanced 3.10
S Corporations   Additional Resources 3.25

Pass-Through Entities 4.1
Pass-Through Entities   Quick Take-Aways 4.2
Pass-Through Entities   Intermediate 4.5
Pass-Through Entities   Advanced 4.11
Pass-Through Entities   Additional Resources 4.23

Agricultural Assets 5.1
Agricultural Assets   **Quick Take-Aways** 5.2
Agricultural Assets   **Intermediate** 5.4
Agricultural Assets   **Advanced** 5.8
Agricultural Assets   **Additional Resources** 5.16

Life Insurance 6.1
Life Insurance   **Quick Take-Aways** 6.2
Life Insurance   **Intermediate** 6.4
Life Insurance   **Advanced** 6.9
Life Insurance   **Additional Resources** 6.19

Tangible Property 7.1
Tangible Property   **Quick Take-Aways** 7.2
Tangible Property   **Intermediate** 7.5
Tangible Property   **Advanced** 7.10
Tangible Property   **Additional Resources** 7.19

Mineral Interests 8.1
Mineral Interests   **Quick Take-Aways** 8.2
Mineral Interests   **Intermediate** 8.4
Mineral Interests   **Advanced** 8.9
Mineral Interests   **Additional Resources** 8.22

Vehicles 9.1
Vehicles   **Quick Take-Aways** 9.2
Vehicles   **Intermediate** 9.4
Vehicles   **Advanced** 9.8
Vehicles   **Additional Resources** 9.23

Virtual Currency 10.1
Virtual Currency   **Quick Take-Aways** 10.2
Virtual Currency   **Intermediate** 10.4
Virtual Currency   **Advanced** 10.8
Virtual Currency   **Additional Resources** 10.17

Intangible Assets ... 11.1
Intangible Assets **Quick Take-Aways** ... 11.2
Intangible Assets **Intermediate** ... 11.4
Intangible Assets **Advanced** ... 11.9
Intangible Assets **Additional Resources** ... 11.23

Life Income Assets ... 12.1
Life Income Interests **Quick Take-Aways** ... 12.2
Life Income Interests **Intermediate** ... 12.5
Life Income Interests **Advanced** ... 12.10
Life Income Interests **Additional Resources** ... 12.23

Appendix ... A.1
Appendix A:
Valuation, Appraisals, and Substantiation ... A.2
Appendix B:
Charitable Estate Settlement ... A.19
Appendix B:
Charitable Estate Settlement Additional Resources ... A.40
Appendix C: At Least a Day Late and Perhaps Many Dollars Short ... A.42
Appendix D: Unique Gift Annuity Planning Opportunities with S-Corp Stock and Real Estate A.55

Preface and Users' Guide[1]

By Phil Cubeta

Intended Audiences

This book is intended for several audiences:

1. Front line advisors: financial, tax and legal advisors who have clients whose assets go well beyond cash and public securities.
2. Nonprofit gift planners: fundraisers in major gifts, planned gifts, and principal gifts whose donors wish to give assets other than cash.
3. Technical experts: Lawyers, accountants, and back office staff at charities and financial institutions charged with determining how an asset may be used for a philanthropic purpose, or determining whether that asset should be accepted as a gift.

The Scope of the Opportunity

Today in gift planning we have an historic opportunity, if we can seize it through canny collaboration among professional advisors, national gift funds, local community foundations, single issue charities, and nonprofit gift planners.

Boomer business owners (think of them as The Rotarians) are reaching an age at which they must exit the business that has been their baby and their identity. As they exit, they are very good prospects for a charitable tool or gift, both to reduce tax upon sale of their appreciated business interests, and also to transition to a new way of life, post-exit, as community leaders. These can-do people, when they exit, want to do more than take their name off the trucks and their building, and put it on a gravestone. They want to go from "success to significance," set a good example for their heirs, and as one said to me, "make my last stand." They made their money in town, will die in town, and often want to give locally. They see giving generously, post-exit, as stepping up rather than stepping down, or stepping aside. They step up into leadership and set an example for their heirs.

As the case in point below shows, there are better and worse ways to exit a business and turn to philanthropy.

---

1. Phil Cubeta, MSFS, CLU®, ChFC®, CAP®, The Wallace Chair in Philanthropy at the American College of Financial Services.

A Case in Point: Todd, A Day Late

Todd (not his real name) came to our wealth transfer firm the day after he sold his business, a C corporation with zero basis, for $100 million. His capital gain was $100 million. Tax due was $20 million. He said, "Help me wipe out my $20 million tax bill." We helped him some, but the truth is he came to us at least one day too late.

Simplified Solution

Charitable planning for noncash assets, particularly for closely held business interests and commercial real estate, is one of the most complex areas of the tax code. Proper planning requires a team with at least a tax attorney, a CPA, a business exit specialist, a qualified appraiser, an investment advisor, and perhaps an insurance professional.

To see the value of proper planning, consider how Todd might have done better. Assume he gave half his firm to charity, say, in a donor-advised fund (DAF). What would be the effects?

- No capital gain on the half sold inside the DAF.
- A charitable deduction up to 30 percent of adjusted gross income, with five year carry forward, subject to whatever limitations may apply under the phaseout of itemized deductions. (Be thankful CPAs are happy to do these calculations.)
- Half sold outside the DAF, with the gain partly offset by the deduction for the part given to the DAF.

Note the effect on assets under management (AUM).
- $50 million new dollars under management in the DAF.
- $50 million (minus whatever residual tax is due) outside the DAF.

Note the effect on potential gifts from the DAF.
- $50 million new dollars that must and will go to a charity.
- A "charitable checkbook" from which the donor can recommend gifts to your organization.
- Alternatively, of course, Todd might have given half the stock in his business directly to a charity. But would they have accepted it? What about the land under the business? What if the firm had been an S corporation? A Limited Partnership? What if Todd had

owned antique cars, an apartment complex, timber interests, an oil and gas lease, intellectual property, crops in the field, livestock, or some other arcane asset that he wanted to give? How could the charity have researched such a gift? Until now, there has been no comprehensive guide.

How to Use This Book to Capitalize on this Historic Opportunity

Now, you, as a frontline advisor or gift planner, have a reference tool you can use to determine whether or not you have a good prospect for a gift asset. These resources should be valuable whatever assets the client has, no matter how complex or unusual. The book is designed to support a three step process.

First, with the particular asset in mind, you will turn to "the quick take-aways," written about that asset by Bryan Clontz, MS, MSFS, Ph.D., CFP®, CLU®, ChFC®, CAP®, RICP®, AEP, CBP. Bryan has worked on dozens, if not hundreds, of cases involving that asset.

Second, if the gift seems promising, you can read the "intermediate review," by Ryan Raffin, JD, writing in plain English, with you as either a front line advisor, or a gift planner in mind. The "review" will not make you an expert, but it will give you what you need to know to consult with the experts, such as the client's attorney or CPA.

Third, you will find the advanced, "advisor level" essay on that asset. Bryan Clontz, Ryan Raffin, and noted tax expert, Laura Peebles, CPA carefully chose these advanced essays. Their respective authors have updated the essays as of September 2016. These advanced treatises are designed for you, the front line advisor or nonprofit gift planner, to share with the client or donor's own tax and legal advisors. Your sharing the article will save them time, and will save the client money. The article will position you as a key resource on the client's planning team.

As you consider reaching out to the experts, also consider getting in touch with an intermediary or two. Today, some charities do, and many charities do not, accept gifts of noncash assets. They either will not accept them, or they may, but the process takes too long, and the deal falls through. Instead, advisors and nonprofits often detour the gift of the noncash asset through an intermediary, such as a national gift fund, religious foundation, or Bryan's own organization, Charitable Solutions, LLC. These organizations can work with you and with client advisors to accept the noncash asset, place it in a donor-advised fund, sell it, and then transfer the cash, at the donor's suggestion, to the nonprofit the donor loves.

Finally, if you as a nonprofit gift planner do work for an organization that can and will accept gifts of noncash assets, by all means, keep this reference tool at your fingertips. It can guide you, your in-house experts, your gift acceptance committee, and your business office, in garnering these potentially transformational gifts.

Developing a Pipeline of Noncash Asset Gifts

Accepting gifts of noncash assets assumes you have a pipeline of such gifts, and, sadly, most nonprofits today do not. Generally, as Bryan Clontz would agree, and as his case studies in this book suggest, these assets come from closely held business owners in transition as they exit their business. If you are a nonprofit gift planner, you more than likely have, in your own backyard, many such "millionaires next door," or "diamonds in the rough." To help them make a transformational gift is inherently a team effort. They need expert technical planning to build up the value of the firm prior to sale, to find a buyer, calculate how much they need post-exit to sustain their lifestyle, how much they wish heirs to ultimately receive, how to reduce taxes in favor of charity and children, when to give, and how best to give, with what asset to give, and through what tool or strategy. As complex as all that is, no gift will be consummated unless the nonprofit gift planner has stoked charitable passion, and built a vision for charitable impact in line with the donor's newfound charitable capacity.

A Case In Point: JD and Mary Riley

The courses I teach in the Chartered Advisor in Philanthropy program (CAP®) land on a Capstone Case, "The Riley Case." That case clearly demonstrates that without cross-disciplinary collaboration, for "gifts of noncash assets," we are vastly underserving our business-owning clients and donors.

JD and Mary, age 70, with three grown children, and seven grandchildren, own two S corporations, worth about $18 million, including the underlying real estate. Their total net worth is just shy of $22 million, with other major assets including a home, vacation home, and a ranch leased to JD's brothers. They have an IRA, and a small investment portfolio. What they do not have is cash. They live on $20,000 a month after tax. They give today about $30,000 a year, with $10,000 being their biggest gift, and several charities getting $5,000 each. They say they would like to leave their estate 75 percent to heirs, 25 percent to charity, and zero percent to estate taxes. They are also concerned about taxes on the sale of the business, which they plan to exit in 1–3 years.

Dave Holaday, ChFC®, CAP®, a nationally known financial planner, was asked to compute the Riley's philanthropic capacity, assuming they made tax-smart decisions, as they sold the business. Using a donor-advised fund or supporting organization for $5 million of the business, and a charitable lead trust at death, Dave computed that the Rileys could go from giving $30,000 a year to giving $450,000 a year until life expectancy, and a like amount for another 18 years after their death. All that without shortchanging any of their other goals.

Now here is the kicker: in surveys of top advisors, in presentations to estate planning societies, financial planning associations, and associations of philanthropic planners, over 75 percent of the advisors say that the plan is perfect with only one defect: The Rileys will not sign it. They will not sign, say these top advisors, because the plan is so complex, but more importantly because the family simply does not have enough charitable passion or purpose to justify $450,000 a year in giving. The fifteen-fold increase in giving would leave them speechless.

So why don't their charities build that vision? Reasons given include these: The Rileys today are just small-time givers, so why bother with them? The case will take too long to come together. Advisors may kill the deal. The funds may detour through a donor-advised fund before coming to the charity. The fundraiser has quotas, and the metrics often preclude investing time in people like the Rileys.

Yet, here we have a family who can give more than $10 million over time, starting soon, if and only if we collaborate across our sectors to do what is right. That is why the Chartered Advisor in Philanthropy (CAP®) program was created, and why this book was commissioned.

Chartered Advisor in Philanthropy

The Chartered Advisor in Philanthropy designation is a three course, Masters level curriculum, designed to bring professional advisors and nonprofit gift planners together to better serve their shared clients and donors. Many of these ideal CAP® clients and donors are successful business owners, transitioning to philanthropy as they exit their business. Study Groups for CAP® are springing up around the country, as advisors and nonprofit people meet to learn together, and then perform together. The potential for philanthropy and for our communities is staggering. Our business owning families will do more, and be more fulfilled, and our communities will do so much better, if we collaborate. If you are interested in learning more about CAP® and CAP® Study Groups, please go here[2], or call Elaine Gulezian at 610-526-1479. Together, we can take advantage of the historic opportunity in our own backyards.

---

2. https://www.theamericancollege.edu/designations-degrees/cap

Acknowledgments

By Bryan Clontz

I had the great fortune of stumbling into charitable planning when I was still in college. As a 22-year-old financial advisor, I will never forget trying to explain to my family exactly what charitable planning meant. I was finally able to make it clear to my mother with the following exchange:

"Mom, when you were growing up, I bet there was a person or family who were known to make gifts to local charities?" She said, "Yes, there were a few families that always seemed to be involved with anything happening in the community." "And I bet you thought it was great they were making contributions to help, and that they probably had a team of people helping them donate in the most tax-efficient way possible?" She said, "Yes, I am sure they had good planners figuring out all the possible loopholes." I said, "Okay stop… I am that person! I am part of that team!" It finally clicked.

Over the last two decades, my work has increasingly focused on the design, transfer, management and liquidation of noncash assets. Throughout my travels, I am frequently asked if there is one book that covers all things noncash, and if not, I should write one… clearly, easier said than done. Fortunately, I was deeply honored to be approached by The American College of Financial Services to produce a series of training materials in this space. Having served as the inaugural Leon L. Levy Fellow in Philanthropy, I was further humbled that Mr. Levy wished to fund this effort as well. This book is the culmination of a career of practical experience as well as a deeper review of the academic articles in this unique space. Rather than attempting to inadequately write the chapters myself, I thought the prudent approach would be to assemble a kind of noncash-dream-team from my friends who are experts in the field and subject matter experts on specific asset transactions. Ryan Raffin, my coeditor, deserves deep thanks for his excellent formatting and editing counsel through the text's iterations and did so with impressive stamina.

I must also say how much I have benefited from the friendship and guidance of Phil Cubeta over the last two decades both personally and professionally. I have never met anyone so deeply rooted in the essence of philanthropy and who can communicate and champion the cause so well. And from his perch at The American College, he inspires literally thousands of advisors and gift planners to encourage and excite donors to do more than they ever thought possible. The multiplying effect of this Johnny Appleseed-type approach is having a measurable impact on communities and causes now, but is also helping to generate personal legacies that may not have occurred but for his work. That is his true gift and purpose.

My greatest gratitude is reserved to the 15 individuals whom I cajoled into writing various chapters of this book. Amazingly, every person I asked agreed to participate in this effort. I invite the reader to review their accomplished biographical sketches in the following Contributors section.

Contributors

Bryan K. Clontz, MS, MSFS, Ph.D., CFP®, CLU®, ChFC®, CAP®, RICP®, AEP, CBP

>Book coeditor and author/coauthor, Quick Take-Away Sections - Chapters 1, 2, 3, 4, 5, 6, 7, 8, 9, 10, 11, and 12; Advanced Sections - Chapters 1, 6, 10;
>Appendix B - Charitable Estate Settlement
>Appendix C - The Top Seven Post-Transaction Creative Charitable Planning Ideas
>Appendix D – Unique Gift Annuity Planning Opportunities with S-Corp Stock and Real Estate
>Founder and President
>Charitable Solutions, LLC
>Jacksonville, Florida
>http://www.charitablesolutionsllc.com/
>bryan@charitablesolutionsllc.com
>404-375-5496

Mr. Clontz received a bachelor of science in business administration from the College of Charleston in Charleston, SC; a master's degree in risk management and insurance from Georgia State University in Atlanta, GA; and a master's degree in financial services as well as a Ph.D. in retirement and financial planning from the American College in Bryn Mawr, PA. He is a Senior Partner to Ekstrom Alley Clontz & Associates. He is the founder of the Dechomai Foundation, Inc. and the Dechomai Asset Trust. He is also the founder of the Emergency Assistance Foundation, Inc. Finally, he created the National Gift Annuity Foundation which is the largest national independent gift annuity platform.

Prior to founding Charitable Solutions, LLC in 2003, Mr. Clontz served as the Director of Planned Giving for the United Way of Metropolitan Atlanta, National Director of Planned Giving for Boys & Girls Clubs of America, and then as vice president of advancement at The Community Foundation for Greater Atlanta. He served from 2013–2014 as the Leon L. Levy Fellow in Philanthropy at The American College of Financial Services.

Mr. Clontz has given more than 2,000 presentations on charitable gift planning; been published in an international insurance textbook; and written more than two dozen articles in financial services and planned giving journals, including a planned giving manual entitled *Just Add Water*, which has sold more than 2,000 copies. He chaired the inaugural statewide Leave a Legacy Georgia!

campaign. He is the co-inventor of a proprietary CGA risk management process (LIRMAS—Life Income Risk Management Analytic Suite).

He serves on the Editorial Board of the Planned Giving Design Center (2000–current), the Advisory Board for the American College's Chartered Advisor in Philanthropy designation (2001–current), and the American Council on Gift Annuities' Research Committee (2003–current). From 2000–2005, Mr. Clontz served as a graduate adjunct professor for both personal financial planning and life insurance in the Department of Risk Management and Insurance at Georgia State University. He also served on the American Council on Gift Annuities' Rate Recommendation Committee (2003–2010) and the National Association of Charitable Gift Planners (formerly NCPG) Board (2007–2009).

Contributors

Ryan Raffin, JD

Book coeditor and author, Intermediate Sections - Chapters 1, 2, 3, 4, 6, 7, 8, 9, 10, 11, 12; Advanced Section - Chapter 10
Vice President, Non-Cash Assets and Research
Charitable Solutions, LLC
Denver, Colorado
http://www.charitablesolutionsllc.com/
ryanraffin@charitablesolutionsllc.com
574-339-5627

Mr. Raffin received a BBA in accounting from the University of Notre Dame, and a JD from the University of Iowa College of Law. He researches tax, legal, and compliance issues for Charitable Solutions, LLC, and is admitted to practice in Colorado and South Carolina. He has also developed and edited processes, programs, and marketing materials for The Emergency Assistance Foundation, Inc.

While in law school, he was a legal intern with the Iowa Governor's Office. He was also a member of the *Journal of Corporation Law* at the University of Iowa, and a research assistant focusing on economics, financial law, and constitutional law.

Turney Berry, JD

Author, Advanced Section, Chapter 2
Partner
Wyatt Terrant & Combs LLP
Louisville, KY
http://www.wyattfirm.com/
tberry@wyattfirm.com
502-562-7505

Mr. Berry received his BA and BLS in 1983 from the University of Memphis and his JD in 1986 from Vanderbilt University. He is the author or co-author of three Tax Management Portfolios: Estate Tax Deductions; Private Foundations—Self Dealing; and Taxable Expenditures. Articles by Mr. Berry have been published in *The ACTEC Journal, Trusts and Estates, The Journal of Taxation, Business First of Louisville,* and the *Louisville Courier-Journal.*

Mr. Barry is a Regent of the American College of Trust and Estate Counsel (ACTEC) and is Chair of the Charitable Planning and Exempt Organization Committee, a member of the Estate and Gift Tax Committee, the Program Committee, and the State Laws Committee. He is a Uniform Law Commissioner from Kentucky and has served on committees dealing with the Uniform Probate Code and new biology, Transfer on Death Deeds, Insurable Interests for Trustees, and Marital Agreements. He is a member of the Louisville Estate Planning Council, Kentuckiana Planned Giving Council, an adjunct member of the American Association of Life Underwriters, and is a member of the Legal Advisory Committee of the Council on Foundations.

Mr. Berry has been an Articles Editor of *The Tax Lawyer,* a past chair of the Louisville Bar Association Probate and Estate Planning Section, Adjunct Professor at Vanderbilt University, the University of Missouri, and the University of Louisville. Mr. Berry is Chair of the Center for Interfaith Relations, a Director of Actors Theatre of Louisville, a Director of Kentucky Opera, a Director of the Louisville Science Center, a member of Louisville Downtown Rotary, and past President of the Daily Bread Sunday School Class at Christ Church United Methodist in Louisville. He has previously served on a number of community boards.

Contributors

Phil Cubeta, MSFS, CLU®, ChFC®, CAP®

> Author, Preface and User's Guide
> Assistant Professor of Philanthropy
> Sallie B. and William B. Wallace Chair in Philanthropy
> The American College of Financial Services
> Bryn Mawr, Pennsylvania
> http://www.theamericancollege.edu/
> Phil.Cubeta@theamericancollege.edu
> 610-526-1319

Professor Cubeta's original training was in English Literature, Williams College, BA; Philosophy and Psychology, Oxford University, MA; and English Language and Literature, Yale, MA, MPhil. He also holds the Masters of Science in Financial Services (MSFS) from The American College. He is responsible for the Chartered Advisor in Philanthropy® (CAP®) curriculum at The American College.

Prior to joining The American College, Professor Cubeta served as Chief of Staff for The Nautilus Group, a service of New York Life Insurance Company providing estate, business, and philanthropic strategies to affluent clients through 200 of the company's top agents.

Essays by Professor Cubeta on philanthropy have appeared in *Nonprofit Quarterly*, Tracy Gary's *Inspired Legacies*, (Wiley and Sons: 2008); H. Peter Karoff, *The World We Want: New Dimensions in Philanthropy and Social Change* (Altimira Press: 2007); and Amy Kass, *Doing Well Doing Good: Readings for Thoughtful Philanthropists* (Indiana University Press: 2008). He has been quoted, or been the subject of articles, in *The New York Times*, *The Journal of Gift Planning*, *Lifestyles Magazine*, *Financial Planning*, and the *Financial Times*.

Professor Cubeta, along with Charles Collier of Harvard, was the 2012 Fithian Leadership Awardee from Advisors in Philanthropy. He received the 2012 "Power of the Purse Award," in the advisor category, from Dallas Women's Foundation. He serves on the Planned Giving Advisory Board for The Carter Center (established by Jimmy and Rosalind Carter).

Randy Fox

Coauthor, Advanced Section, Chapter 9
Founder
EzCharitable, LLC
Chicago, Illinois
https://ezcharitable.com
randyafox1@gmail.com
704-698-4055

A third-generation entrepreneur, Randy is a founder of EzCharitable, LLC, an online training resource for professional advisors who wish to expand their capabilities in philanthropic giving. EzCharitable has created original content that is useful for attorneys, financial advisors, and CPAs, all of which will facilitate better philanthropic advice for families of wealth. He is also currently the Editor in Chief of Planned Giving Design Center, a national newsletter for philanthropic advisors. In 2015 Randy was awarded the Fithian Leadership Award by the International Association of Advisors in Philanthropy.

Randy was a founding principal of InKnowVision, LLC, a national consulting and marketing firm that developed estate and wealth transfer designs for clients of exceptional wealth. During his tenure, more than three hundred families were served and more than $500 million was directed to philanthropic purposes. He served as director and faculty member of the InKnowVision Institute, which provided professional advisors with the advanced technical and interpersonal tools required to attract and work successfully with high net worth clients.

Contributors

Larry Garrison, PhD, CPA (inactive)

>Coauthor, Advanced Section, Chapter 9
>Emeritus Professor of Accountancy
>University of Missouri – Kansas City

Professor Garrison is a graduate of Central Missouri State University (BSBA), the University of Missouri-Kansas City (MSA), and the University of Nebraska-Lincoln (PhD). His research interests include the taxation of individuals and business entities.

Professor Garrison was a professor of accounting at the University of Missouri – Kansas City from 1986 until retiring in 2016. He is past president of the North American Accounting Society and the Missouri Association of Accounting Educators.

Professor Garrison has numerous publications in leading tax and accounting journals, including *The Journal of the American Taxation Association, The Tax Adviser, TAXES-The Tax Magazine, Practical Tax Strategies, The CPA Journal, Oil, Gas and Energy Quarterly, Journal of State Taxation* and *The Journal of Multistate Taxation and Incentives*. Garrison has twice received the UMKC Alumni Elmer F. Pierson Outstanding Teaching Award and is the recipient of the Outstanding Accounting Educator of the Year Award from the Missouri Society of Certified Public Accountants. He has also received the Chancellor's Award for Excellence in Teaching and the Governor's Award for Excellence in Education.

Joseph Hancock, JD, MBA

Author, Advanced Section, Chapter 8
Vice President & General Counsel
HighGround Advisors
Dallas, Texas
http://highgroundadvisors.org/
Joe.Hancock@highgroundadvisors.org
214-978-3394

Mr. Hancock holds a BBA from Baylor University and MBA and JD degrees from the University of Arkansas. He has practiced extensively in the area of charitable planned giving for the past 20 years, focusing on technical issues related to the research, drafting and implementation of all types of charitable gifts. From 1999 to 2002, he was Trust Counsel at the Children's Medical Center of Dallas.

Mr. Hancock's responsibilities include counseling with nonprofit organizations and prospective donors regarding matters of taxation, trust law, estate planning and administration, and charitable giving. He speaks frequently on topics related to estate and charitable planning. He is admitted to practice in Texas and Arkansas, and is a member of the North Texas chapter of the National Committee on Planned Giving.

Contributors

Christopher Hoyt, JD, MSA

Author, Advanced Section, Chapter 3
Professor of Law
University of Missouri – Kansas City
Kansas City, Missouri
http://law.umkc.edu
hoytc@umkc.edu
816-235-2395

Professor Hoyt received an undergraduate degree in economics from Northwestern University and dual law and accounting degrees from the University of Wisconsin. He teaches courses in the areas of federal taxation, business organizations, retirement plans and tax-exempt organizations. Previously, he was with the law firm of Spencer, Fane, Britt and Browne in Kansas City, Missouri.

Professor Hoyt is currently the chair of the American Bar Association's Committee on Lifetime and Testamentary Charitable Gift Planning (Section of Probate and Trust) and serves on the editorial board of *Trusts and Estates* magazine. He is a frequent speaker at legal and educational programs and has been quoted in numerous publications, including *The Wall Street Journal, Forbes, MONEY Magazine* and *The Washington Post*.

Russell James III, PhD, JD, CFP®

Author, Appendix 1 - Valuation, Appraisals, and Substantiation
Professor & CH Foundation Chair in Personal Financial Planning
Texas Tech University
Lubbock, Texas
http://www.encouragegenerosity.com/
Russell.James@ttu.edu
806-787-5931

Dr. James graduated, cum laude, from the University of Missouri School of Law, and also holds a Ph.D. in consumer economics from the University of Missouri. He is a professor in the Department of Personal Financial Planning at Texas Tech University. He directs the on-campus and online graduate program in Charitable Financial Planning. Additionally, he teaches Charitable Gift Planning at the Texas Tech University School of Law.

Previously, Dr. James worked as the Director of Planned Giving for Central Christian College in Moberly, Missouri for six years and later served as president of the college for more than five years. During his presidency the college successfully completed two major capital campaigns, built several new debt-free buildings, and more than tripled enrollment.

Dr. James has over 150 publications in academic journals, conference proceedings, and books. He has been quoted on charitable and financial issues in numerous national and international news sources. His research was profiled in The Wall Street Journal's *Smart Money Magazine*. While in law school, he was a member of the Missouri Law Review, and received the United Missouri Bank Award for Most Outstanding Work in Gift and Estate Taxation and Planning.

Contributors

Michael Parham, JD, LLM

Author, Advanced Section, Chapter 12
Senior Vice-President and Trust Officer
Poplar Trust, a division of The Bank of Fayette County
Collierville, Tennessee
https://www.thebank1905.com
mike@poplartrust.com
901-877-6810

Mike Parham is a Senior Vice-President and Trust Officer with Poplar Trust, a division of The Bank of Fayette County. Prior to joining Poplar Trust, he was the founding member of Parham Estate Law, a firm which limited its practice to estate planning and probate.

He has more than twenty-five years of experience as an attorney, receiving his law degree from the Vanderbilt University School of Law and a master of laws in Estate Planning from the University of Miami School of Law.

Mike is a Fellow in the American College of Trust and Estate Counsel. He is a former member of the Board of Directors of the Memphis Estate Planning Council, the Planned Giving Council for Greater Memphis and Hopeworks, Inc. From 1993 through 1998, Mike served as Director of Planned Giving for Freed-Hardeman University.

Laura Peebles, CPA

>Coauthor, Appendix 2 - Charitable Estate Settlement
>Partner, Charitable Solutions, LLC
>Senior Fellow
>Bloomberg BNA
>Washington, DC
>http://www.laurahpeebles.com/
>http://www.charitablesolutionsllc.com
>laura@charitablesolutionsllc.com

Ms. Peebles earned a bachelor of science degree in accounting (summa cum laude) from the University of New Orleans. She is a consultant on estate planning, tax, and philanthropic matters with Bloomberg BNA, and a partner with Charitable Solutions LLC. Previously, she was a director with Deloitte Tax for 16 years in the Washington National Tax office.

Ms. Peebles is the author of Bloomberg BNA Tax Management Portfolio 844, Estate Tax Credits and Computations and co-author of Portfolio 822, Estate, Gift, and Generation-Skipping Tax Returns and Audits. She has contributed to articles in *Bloomberg Wealth Manager, Journal of Gift Planning, Trusts & Estates Magazine, Estate Planning Magazine, Estates, Gifts and Trusts Journal, Journal of Accountancy, Planned Giving Today,* and *Planned Giving Design Center.* She has also been quoted in *NY Times, Forbes, U.S. News & World Report, Tax Adviser Magazine, Bloomberg Wealth Manager, Wall Street Journal, Business Week,* and Charity Channel.com.

Contributors

Philip M. Purcell, CFRE, MPA, JD

Author, Intermediate Section, Chapter 5; Advanced Section, Chapter 5
Vice President for Planned Giving, Ball State University Foundation
Consultant for Philanthropy, LLC
Adjunct Faculty
Indiana University Maurer School of Law and Lilly School of Philanthropy
Noblesville, Indiana
http://www.bsu.edu/
ppurcell@bsu.edu
765-285-7070

Professor Purcell received his BA degree from Wabash College (magna cum laude) and his JD and MPA degrees (with honors) from Indiana University. He teaches courses on law and philanthropy, nonprofit organization law, and planned giving as adjunct faculty for the Indiana University Maurer School of Law (Bloomington, IN) and Indiana University Lilly School of Philanthropy and The Fund Raising School (Indianapolis, IN).

Purcell is currently the Vice President for Planned Giving for the Ball State University Foundation and has served in development and gift planning positions for the Central Indiana Community Foundation, St. Vincent Hospital Foundation, and Rose-Hulman Institute of Technology. He has written articles on charitable gift and estate planning which have appeared in *The Journal of Gift Planning, Planned Giving Today, CASE Currents,* Planned Giving Design Center and other publications.

Professor Purcell is a member of the Tax Exempt Organization Advisory Council for the Internal Revenue Service (Great Lakes states), and serves on the Editorial Advisory Board for *Planned Giving Today*. He has served on the board of directors for the Partnership for Philanthropic Planning (past secretary), Planned Giving Group of Indiana (past president) and Association of Fundraising Professionals—Indiana Chapter (past president).

Gary Snerson, JD, MSF

Coauthor, Appendix 2 - Charitable Estate Settlement
Partner
Charitable Solutions, LLC
Miami, Florida
http://www.charitablesolutionsllc.com/
gary@charitablesolutionsllc.com
305-466-1029

Mr. Snerson received his bachelor's in science in business administration (cum laude) and MSF from Babson College. He earned his JD from Georgetown Law School and a master's of science degree in finance from the Carroll School at Boston College University.

For the past 15 years, Mr. Snerson served as the Senior Vice President of Estates and Special Investments at the Harvard Endowment. For 25 years prior to accepting his position at Harvard, he practiced law in Boston, Massachusetts and specialized in Estate Planning and Trust Administration. Mr. Snerson has taught numerous undergraduate and graduate courses in finance, law, negotiation and estate planning at institutions including Bentley University, Boston University, and Lesley University. He has spoken to numerous groups including the NEPGG, IMI Institute and the Ivy League Plus Planned Giving Group.

Contributors

Jay Steenhuysen, MA, MBA

Author, Identifying Charitable Passions and Noncash Giving Opportunities
Founder and President
Steenhuysen Associates
Seekonk, Massachusetts
http://www.steenhuysen.com/
jay@steenhuysen.com
508-336-4544

Mr. Steenhuysen holds a BA from Seattle Pacific University, an MA in theological studies from Gordon Conwell Theological Seminary, and an MBA from Pepperdine University. He provides consulting, training, and donor qualification services to leading nonprofit and charitable organizations, including The Nature Conservancy, Boston Children's Hospital, World Wildlife Fund, ACLU, Salvation Army, AARP Foundation and World Vision. With expertise in planned giving, major and principal gifts, and philanthropy advising, he has helped these organizations refine their gift planning programs to be more effective; has trained and coached major and principal gift officers; and has created programs to meet the needs of donors at all wealth levels.

Mr. Steenhuysen has been cited by Worth magazine as one of the nation's top resources for high-net-worth families seeking guidance in the practice of philanthropy. Since creating his Strategic Gifts (2003) and Philanthropy Coach (2005) training programs, he has taught over 1,000 fundraisers and allied professionals how to identify and discuss noncash gift opportunities with donors and clients.

Mr. Steenhuysen previously served as Managing Director of Philanthropy Services at myCFO. He developed Brown University's philanthropic planning program within the principal gifts department. He also served as the Principle Gifts Officer at World Vision, directed its Gift Planning Program and ran its Capital Campaign.

Mr. Steenhuysen twice served on the Board of the Partnership for Philanthropic Planning. He was Board Chair in 2014 and co-chaired the committee responsible for developing the PPP Leadership Institute.

Armen R. Vartian, JD

>Author, Advanced Section, Chapter 7
>Principal
>Law Offices of Armen Vartian
>Manhattan Beach, California USA
>http://www.vartianlaw.com/
>armen@vartianlaw.com
>310-372-1355

Mr. Vartian received his undergraduate degree from City University of New York (summa cum laude), and his JD from Harvard Law School. He has practiced commercial law since 1981, and is admitted to practice in the state courts of California, Illinois and New York, as well as federal courts nationwide.

From 1986–90, Mr. Vartian was Vice President and General Counsel to Heritage Capital Corporation. For eighteen years, Armen's monthly column, "Collectibles and Law," was published in *Coin World*, the leading numismatic trade newspaper. Armen currently writes a Chinese-language column for fortunechina.com on the subject of strategies for high-net-worth individuals. Armen is also the author of the foremost book on the legal aspects of collecting, *Legal Guide to Buying and Selling Art and Collectibles*.

Since 1992, Mr. Vartian has served as Legal Counsel to the Professional Numismatists Guild, and is currently Vice-Chair of the American Bar Association's Art and Cultural Property Law committee. From 2010–12, he served as Vice-Chair of the Editorial Board for the ABA's *Annual Review of Developments in Intellectual Property Law*. He was Editor-in-Chief of the *Harvard International Law Journal*. He has served as receiver and special counsel in cases involving art and collectibles, and as an expert witness to private clients in these areas.

Contributors

Dennis Walsh, CPA

Author/coauthor, Advanced Sections, Chapters 4 and 11
Vice President and Treasurer
The Deborah and Dennis Walsh Foundation
Greensboro, North Carolina
http://www.walshfdn.net/
nonprofitcpa365@gmail.com
336-285-6753

Mr. Walsh graduated from the University of Wisconsin. A licensed CPA, he is a member of the North Carolina Association of CPAs and the American Institute of CPAs. He completed the Duke University certificate program in nonprofit management, Leadership High Point 2008, and Leadership North Carolina Class XIX (2012).

Mr. Walsh has served the financial reporting, compliance, and planning needs of individuals, businesses, and exempt organizations for more than 30 years. Following a career in public accounting, he now volunteers as a consultant to religious workers and exempt organizations, focusing on financial management, legal compliance, and organizational development. Since 2003, he has been a consulting resource to hundreds of nonprofits and Christian workers across the country. His articles have appeared in multiple publications including the *Planned Giving Design Center, Journal of Accountancy,* and *Blue Avocado.*

Mr. Walsh served with the Not-for-Profit Committee of the NC Association of CPAs and has participated in nonprofit conference panels and workshops on finance and governance topics.

Jane L. Wilton, JD, LLM

>Coauthor, Advanced Section, Chapter 4
>General Counsel
>New York Community Trust
>New York City, New York
>http://www.nycommunitytrust.org/
>janewilton@nyct-cfi.org
>212-686-2563

Jane Wilton received her BA from Michigan State University (summa cum laude) and her JD from the University of Michigan School of Law. She holds an LLM in taxation from New York University Law School. She has been The New York Community Trust's General Counsel for more than two decades.

As counsel to The New York Community Trust, the community foundation for New York City, Long Island and Westchester county, Ms. Wilton is responsible for a broad range of legal issues relating to charitable contributions, board governance, donor-advised funds, unrelated business income tax, foreign grantmaking, commercial co-ventures, lobbying, and fiduciary duties of trustees and charitable corporations. She is an author and editor of The Trust's *Professional Notes* series; she also served as counsel to the September 11th Fund.

Prior to joining The Trust, Ms. Wilton was in private tax practice at a New York City law firm. She served as a member of the Legal Framework Work Group of the Panel on the Nonprofit Sector and she lectures on various subjects involving charities and planned giving.

Noncash Opportunities, Aggregate Market and Property Types

By Bryan Clontz

Noncash assets, for the purposes of this book, are all assets other than cash, publicly-traded stock, or mutual funds—said simply, illiquid assets.

The Opportunity: The larger the donor's wealth, the greater the likelihood of noncash holdings and the greater the proportion of the holdings relative to other assets. Interestingly, the majority of millionaires created their wealth through real estate or privately-held business interests, and they are nearly always the most charitably-inclined donors. From a planning perspective, these same interests are likely to have a very low tax basis and are therefore ideal for charitable planning opportunities. Yet over 90 percent of all charitable donations are cash donations because that is what fundraisers ask for—the smallest percentage asset on the balance sheet, the one that hurts the donor's lifestyle the most and the one that is nearly always the most tax inefficient.

My charitable tax mantra has long been—"Cash Bad, Everything Else Good!" Everything else is simply long-term capital gain assets that have the greatest appreciation. To be sure, many donors/clients have publicly-traded stock or mutual funds that may meet this criteria, but these assets also represent liquidity. After the 2008 financial meltdown, we all likely have a different definition of liquidity and its importance.

Combining all these assets, the aggregated value is estimated to be 4 to 6 times that of the entire stock market, yet 80 percent of these types of gifts are initially declined by charities.

The points above discuss one aspect of the noncash giving opportunity. Another important aspect is in the nature of the donor pool. The Baby Boomer generation is retiring in huge numbers; some 10,000 Americans in their 50s and 60s retire every day.[3]

And they are already predisposed to charitable giving. Over 40 percent of individual contributions come from Boomers, equating to about $62 billion.[4] Better yet, they are projected to transfer some

---

3. Kessler, G. (July 24, 2014), "Do 10,000 Baby Boomers Retire Every Day?," *The Washington Post*, https://www.washingtonpost.com/news/fact-checker/wp/2014/07/24/do-10000-baby-boomers-retire-every-day/.
4. Rovnet, M. (2013), "The Next Generation of American Giving," Blackbaud at 7, https://www.blackbaud.com/conf/prod/info/Next-GenAmericanGiving.aspx.

Charitable Gifts of Noncash Assets

$10 trillion in closely held business assets by 2025.[5] Further, a survey indicates that "pre-retirees" believe they will most miss the reliable income from work.[6] This opens the door for a conversation about income streams from planned giving vehicles such as charitable gift annuities and remainder trusts. The opportunity is clear: A wealthy, charitably-inclined generation, which is in the midst of a generational transition out of active business roles and is sensitive to the value of reliable income.

What follows is an environmental scan of the market overall, followed by some specific noncash types and finally a brief discussion of the opportunities.

The Market

- In nearly every survey, cash or cash equivalents represent the smallest portion of the overall balance sheet for high net worth individuals / major donors. The most current research suggests cash represents 7 percent of total high net worth assets in 2015.[7]
- The aggregate domestic stock market value as of 2017 was approximately $32.1 trillion.[8]
- The aggregate value of privately-owned US land (not government owned), as of the first quarter of 2018, is approximately $53.2 trillion.[9]

Most recently published IRS data has 2015 figures for individual noncash contributions. Total deductions for noncash contributions (excluding publicly traded stock) were $60.4 billion out of $221.9 billion in 2015, working out to 27 percent. Backing out the deduction amounts for cars, household, electronics, clothing, food, and other assets—leaving closely held businesses, real estate and art / collectibles—then it drops to approximately $40.9 billion. Out of $425.8 billion of total charitable gifts from all sources, this $40.9 billion is about 9.6 percent.

---

5. Beshore, B. (October 11, 2015), "Why Small Businesses Are Feeling an Economic Crunch," *Forbes*, http://www.forbes.com/sites/brentbeshore/2015/10/11/the-small-business-crunch/#2d62490d5dc7.
6. Merrill Lynch, "Giving in Retirement: America's Longevity Bonus," 2015, https://mlaem.fs.ml.com/content/dam/ML/Articles/pdf/ML_AgeWave_Giving_in_Retirement_Report.pdf.
7. Statista, "Asset allocation of high net worth individuals in the U.S. 2009-2015," http://www.statista.com/statistics/322581/hnwi-asset-allocation-usa/.
8. The World Bank, "Market Capitalization of Listed Domestic Companies (Current US$)," http://data.worldbank.org/indicator/CM.MKT.LCAP.CD.
9. The Federal Reserve, "Financial Accounts of the United States: Flow of Funds, Balance Sheets, and Integrated Macroeconomic Accounts, First Quarter 2016" Tables B.101, B.103, B.104 (August 14, 2018), https://www.federalreserve.gov/releases/z1/20180308/z1.pdf. See also Yglesias, M. (December 20, 2013), "What's All the Land in America Worth?," Slate, http://www.slate.com/blogs/moneybox/2013/12/20/value_of_all_land_in_the_united_states.html (describing how to calculate the value).

Total Charitable Contributions (Cash and Noncash, From All Sources Including Individuals, Corporations, and Bequests) in the United States, from 2003 to 2014.[10]

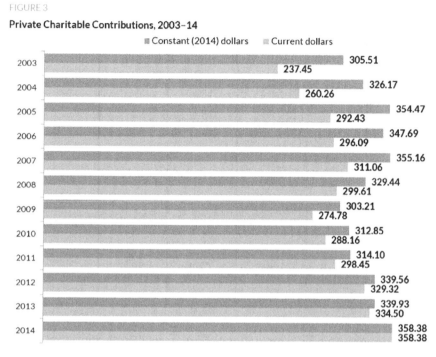

FIGURE 3
Private Charitable Contributions, 2003–14

Source: Giving USA Foundation (2015).

Note that the contribution amounts largely track overall U.S. economic performance in the years, before, during, and after the 2008 economic downturn. By 2014, the contribution amounts had returned to pre-recession levels.

A groundbreaking, first-of-its-kind paper by Russell N. James III indicates that nonprofit organizations accepting noncash gifts can experience significant growth in contributions. The paper analyzed data from over one million nonprofit tax returns filed between the 2010 and 2016 tax years. It found that when comparing 2010 and 2015, nonprofits receiving any type of noncash gift reported 50 percent growth in contributions. Conversely, nonprofits receiving only cash gifts reported only 11 percent growth. These trends held no matter the size of the organization (as measured by contributions in the base year of 2010).

---

10. McKeever, B. (October 9, 2015), "The Nonprofit Sector in Brief 2015: Public Charities, Giving, and Volunteering," Urban Institute, http://www.urban.org/research/publication/nonprofit-sector-brief-2015-public-charities-giving-and-volunteering.

5-year Total Fundraising Growth by Initial Level of Total Contributions

	$100,000 - 499,999	$500,000 - 999,999	$1,000,000 - 1,999,999	$2,000,000 - 2,999,999	$3,000,000 - 4,999,999	$5,000,000 - 9,999,999	$10,000,000+
Nonprofits reporting only cash contributions	56%	25%	14%	18%	0%	0%	26%
Nonprofits reporting any noncash contributions	137%	71%	60%	58%	48%	36%	35%
Nonprofits reporting any securities contributions	400%	176%	103%	94%	68%	50%	43%

Further, this growth appears to hold over 3-year periods as well, indicating that the 2010 and 2015 comparison is not anomalous.[11]

Years	Received cash only	Any noncash	Any securities
'10-'13	5%	34%	44%
'11-'14	1%	30%	42%
'12-'15	2%	30%	39%
'13-'16	0%	25%	33%

Taken together, these trends indicate a clear and powerful opportunity for nonprofits considering accepting noncash donations. It is very appealing to combine that opportunity for growth with the high proportion of donor assets that are in noncash form.

---

11. James III, R.N. (July 18, 2018), "Why Cash Is Not King in Fundraising," p.7, https://www.stelter.com/docs/webinars/CashNot-King-Handouts.pdf.

Individual Noncash Charitable Contributions: All Returns with Itemized Donations, by Donation Types, Form 8283, Tax Years 2003 to 2015

The following table below breaks down noncash charitable deductions by asset type from 2003 to 2015. Dollar amounts in billions. All information derived from statistics and tables available from the Internal Revenue Service's Statistics of Income at https://www.irs.gov/uac/tax-stats.

In analysis of noncash contributions, the IRS notes the following trends:

> "Over the years, taxpayer donations of corporate stock have consistently represented the highest amounts of donations. Clothing has accounted for the second largest share of donations in nearly every year since 2006; the sole exception was 2007 when taxpayers reported slightly larger noncash contributions for real estate, land, and easements. However, while the amount of clothing donations has remained consistent since 2006, the amounts deducted for corporate stock and real estate, land, and easements declined significantly between 2007 and 2009. Donations of corporate stock have almost recovered since that time, but donations of real estate, land, and easements have remained relatively low. In 2007, taxpayers reported $23.7 billion in corporate stock donations, and, together, the declines in 2008 and 2009 represented a 59.0-percent decrease since 2007. For 2010, stock donations rose 37.3 percent, followed by increases for 2011 (19.5 percent), 2012 (5.1 percent), and 2013 (17.7 percent)."[12]

---

12. Liddell, P. and Wilson, J., "Individual Noncash Contributions, 2013," IRS Statistics of Income Bulletin Summer 2016, 3, https://www.irs.gov/pub/irs-soi/soi-a-innc-id1611.pdf.

Charitable Gifts of Noncash Assets

Asset type	2015	2014	2013	2012	2011	2010	2009	2008	2007	2006	2005	2004	2003
Total charitable deductions	221.850	210.599	178.953	179.059	160.337	158.188	148.595	161.870	174.504	173.018	172.025	156.200	139.666
Stock, mutual funds, other investments	33.763	33.195	23.916	22.358	18.663	17.770	11.465	15.697	27.708	26.450	19.761	17.605	15.786
Real estate & easements	5.391	5.596	12.167	4.509	3.918	5.456	5.044	7.218	12.907	8.256	12.674	9.459	20.956
Art and collectibles	1.792	1.136	1.271	1.380	0.999	1.275	0.984	1.511	1.260	1.304	1.461	1.212	0.866
Subtotal	40.946	39.927	37.354	28.247	23.580	24.501	17.493	24.426	41.875	36.010	33.896	28.276	37.608
% of all deductions	18.46	18.96	20.87	15.78	14.71	15.49	11.77	15.09	24.00	20.81	19.70	18.10	26.93
Food	0.425	0.360	0.217	0.371	0.110	0.101	.091	.121	0.101	0.100	0.111	0.104	0.079
Clothing	15.549	14.492	9.867	9.381	9.050	8.327	7.608	7.940	7.759	6.298	7.085	6.349	5.831
Electronics	0.623	0.589	0.409	0.422	0.408	0.457	0.365	0.432	0.372	0.445	0.475	0.478	0.376
Household items	6.800	6.254	4.223	3.737	3.626	3.264	3.226	3.141	3.921	3.847	3.860	3.466	3.224
Cars & other vehicles	0.198	0.177	0.395	0.468	0.505	0.400	0.387	0.613	0.727	0.594	0.622	2.672	2.476
Other donations	1.799	1.596	3.719	4.289	3.576	2.313	1.779	2.686	3.907	3.017	2.964	2.178	1.477
Total noncash deductions	66.340	63.252	56.098	46.915	40.856	39.362	30.951	39.359	58.663	50.310	49.012	43.523	51.073
% of all deductions	29.90	30.03	31.35	26.20	25.48	24.88	20.83	24.32	33.62	29.08	28.49	27.86	36.57

Noncash Opportunities, Aggregate Market and Property Types

Comparing the total charitable contributions over this period to total deductions and specific noncash deduction amounts provide valuable insight. Consider the total charitable deductions and overall contribution numbers in the following data breakdown:

Asset type	2014	2013	2012	2011	2010	2009	2008	2007	2006	2005	2004	2003
Total charitable contributions	358.38	334.50	329.32	298.45	288.16	274.78	299.61	311.06	296.09	292.43	260.26	237.45
Total charitable deductions	210.599	178.953	179.059	160.337	158.188	148.595	161.870	174.504	173.018	172.025	156.200	139.666
% of donations deducted	58.76	53.50	54.37	53.72	54.90	54.08	54.03	56.10	58.43	58.83	60.02	58.82
Investments, real estate, art, & collectibles subtotal	39.927	37.354	28.247	23.580	24.501	17.493	24.426	41.875	36.010	33.896	28.276	37.608
% of all deductions	18.96	20.87	15.78	14.71	15.49	11.77	15.09	24.00	20.81	19.70	18.10	26.93
% of all contributions	11.14	11.17	8.58	7.90	8.50	6.37	8.15	13.46	12.16	11.59	10.86	15.84
Total noncash deductions	63.252	56.098	46.915	40.856	39.362	30.951	39.359	58.663	50.310	49.012	43.523	51.073
% of all deductions	30.03	31.35	26.20	25.48	24.88	20.83	24.32	33.62	29.08	28.49	27.86	36.57
% of all contributions	17.65	16.77	14.25	13.69	13.66	11.26	13.14	18.86	16.99	16.76	16.72	21.51

Charitable Gifts of Noncash Assets

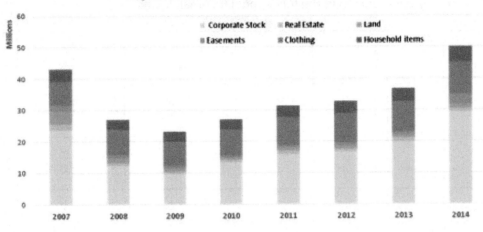

Source: Liddell, P. and Wilson, J., "Individual Noncash Contributions, Tax Year 2014," IRS Statistics of Income Bulletin, Summer 2017, 3, https://www.irs.gov/pub/irs-soi/soi-a-innc-id1507.pdf.

Noncash Asset Types

Here are the most common noncash donations (excluding personal household and clothing items).

Real Estate

    Residential, commercial or investment

    Encumbered or unencumbered

    Foreign or domestic

Privately-Held Interests

    C corporation stock

    S corporation stock

    Limited partnerships

    LLC interests

Restricted Stock

Section 144 and 145 stock

Tangible Personal Property

Art

Collectibles

Vehicles (i.e., cars, boats, planes)

Weird Stuff

Other assets that have been donated include:

Horses/livestock/crops

Gold bullion and other precious metals

Bitcoin and other virtual currencies

Foreign currencies or denominated bond

Intellectual property (e.g., patents, royalties and copyrights)

Mineral and resource interests (e.g., oil, gas, water, timber, clay rights)

Professional sports teams

Historical artifacts

Important Noncash Substantiation Requirements

IRS substantiation requirements are addressed in depth in Appendix A. However, given the importance of these considerations, a few points are worth emphasizing. Put simply, failure to comply with substantiation rules will mean no tax deduction for the donor.

The donee charity must provide a contemporaneous written acknowledgement for all gifts valued over $250. The charity need not put a value on the gift itself in the acknowledgement. Further, the IRS requires a qualified appraisal of deductions over $5,000 on assets other than cash or publicly traded stock.

The donor must file Form 8283 to properly substantiate this deduction and show that an appraisal occurred. The appraiser and a representative of the charity must sign the form—the charity need not agree to the appraised (and therefore deducted) value. All of this is to say that the burden of properly substantiating the deduction is on the donor, and that the appraisal is therefore also the donor's responsibility. However, the charity is responsible for reporting sale or disposition of the donated property if it occurs within three years. It must send Form 8282 detailing the sale to both the IRS and the donor.

Noncash Asset Considerations

Financial / Estate / Tax Planning Considerations for Top Ten Noncash Asset Contributions

Asset Type	Various Forms	Unique Issues and Potential Traps	Planned Gift Issues	Additional Comments
Real Estate Deduction: FMV	Residential, commercial, domestic or foreign, leasehold / life or remainder interest	Environmental liability, holding period management, accelerated depreciation, negative basis, debt (note "5-and-5 UBTI exception"), pre-arranged sale	Ideal for FLIP-CRUT, difficult for CRAT and CGAs because of marketability / liquidity	Real estate represents nearly 50% of privately held wealth, estimated at twice the entire stock market. Yet only 2% of all charitable gifts are real estate.
Closely-Held Stock Deduction: FMV	C-Corp or S-Corp	Thin to non-existent market, difficult valuation, self-dealing / inurement without independent appraisal, pre-arranged sale, S-Corp UBTI issues	Ideal for FLIP-CRUT, except S-corp, with no known liquidation event – other vehicles work for corporate redemption or market sale. S-corp to a CGA can be optimal for a life income gift.	Private company contributions are very popular prior to a market sale. S-Corp gifts to a trust charity are tax-effective prior to sale or to a corporation if held.
LLC Interests Deduction: FMV	Tax status may be corporate or partnership	Same as Closely-Held & characteristics of underlying assets & potential capital calls, multiple shareholders / assets difficult	Same as Closely-Held. LLC may donate illiquid asset directly for a charitable deduction flow-through.	Charities usually want the LLC interest for liability protection. Multiple owners may make asset donations difficult.
Partnerships Deduction: FMV	General, Limited or Operating	May be difficult to appraise, general partnership liability or negative basis, characteristics of underlying assets.	Limited partnerships are particularly good funding assets for Lead Trusts.	For LLCs and Partnerships, appraisal discounting may apply unless income approach is used.
Life Insurance / Annuities Deduction: Lesser of Adjusted Cost Basis or FMV	Paid-Up and Non-Paid Up Life Insurance – Variable or Fixed Deferred Annuities	Non-paid up policies, "Stranger-Owned" or premium financed, or gifts with policy loans are more difficult. Paid-up whole life policies work well. Annuities trigger gain upon transfer.	Life insurance is an excellent life-time or testamentary gifts (through beneficiary designation). Annuities are only attractive as testamentary gifts because of IRD.	Life insurance can be an excellent wealth replacement tool for any planned or outright gift. Premiums for charity-owned policies can be paid with appreciated property.
Mineral Interests Deduction: Varies	Oil / Gas Working or Non-Working Interests, Timber, Other Minerals	Valuation difficult, tax law very complex and state rules may govern (e.g., timber).	Difficult based on specific asset type and marketability but possible.	These assets are typically held in partnerships or LLCs so those rules apply as well.

Charitable Gifts of Noncash Assets

Asset Type	Various Forms	Unique Issues and Potential Traps	Planned Gift Issues	Additional Comments
Restricted Stock Deduction: FMV	Section 144 or 145	Appraisal requirement, lock-up period	Restricted stock can easily be used for just about every planned gift – but liquidity needs should be addressed with long lock-ups	Restricted stock should be coordinated with an experienced broker and company's SEC counsel.
Stock Options and ESOP Qualified Replacement Property Deduction: Varies	Qualified (ISOs) or non-qualified	"In-the-money" option transfers trigger gain to the donor at ordinary income rates at the time the charity sells the option (important for same tax year)	ISOs can be exercised, the underlying stock is held for over a year and then can be donated to charity	Qualified replacement stock from an employer retirement plan / ESOP can work well for both outright and planned gifts.
Collectibles/Art Deduction: Basis for non-related use / FMV for related use	Art, coins, antiques	Valuation, insurance, storage, transaction costs, complex structures like private operating foundations are sometimes used	Works fairly well for nearly all forms of planned gifts, but cost basis deduction is triggered upon sale. Testamentary gifts are ideal, but many donors prefer a lifetime gift and do not mind a lower income tax deduction if no related use.	Current law limits partial interest art gifts. Federal capital gains taxes remain at 28% - an extra tax benefit for tangible property donations for the gains exclusions plus the potential 3.8% net investment income tax.
Intellectual Property Deduction: Varies	Patents, royalties, copyrights, regardless of revenue produced	Valuation cost, disposition process	Work best as testamentary gifts to receive step-up in basis.	2004 Act reduced attractiveness of patent/royalty gifts with a deduction schedule.
Bitcoin/ Cryptocurrency Deduction: FMV	Bitcoin, Ethereum, Litecoin, other altcoins	Difficult to find qualified appraiser, charity may not have "know-how" to accept and sell.	Works well for most planned gifts – liquidity is extremely desirable given volatile cryptocurrency markets.	Unsettled legal and regulatory status. Extremely volatile markets. Vulnerable to hacking/theft.

Noncash Opportunities, Aggregate Market and Property Types

Gift Acceptance / Management / Disposition Considerations for Top Ten Noncash Asset Contributions

Asset Type	Liability / Cost Exposure	Risk Management / Due Diligence	Acceptance Issues	Staff Role	Disposition Alternatives
Real Estate	Environmental, UBTI, liens, IRS penalties, accident claims, up-front due diligence expense, holding or improvement costs, time-to-reward ratio, fiduciary risk	Indemnification letter, environmental audit, survey, BPO or appraisal, insurance, site inspection, assess property's history, develop sales plan - review all deeds, lease/rental agreements, inspection reports, donor should complete disclosure citing any issues, outsource to another charity specializing in real estate donations.	Conflicts of interest, valuation, self-dealing, implied, assignment of income issues or expressed restrictions	Tax substantiation, due diligence, change insurance / utilities, execute transfer documents, donor communication, audit preparation, manage disposition Note: Ideally, one person should project manage all illiquid assets.	1. Hold (not usually recommended) 2. Sell to private buyer (unrelated party) 3. Sell to related party (additional compliance) 3. List with broker
Privately-Held Stock / LLC / Partnerships	Capital calls, indemnification clauses, lack of control with minority gifts, UBTI and specific issues related to underlying property as well as reputational or community risk	Indemnification letter, independent appraisal, review financials if appropriate, develop sales plan, review all entity documents	Thin to non-existent market, difficult valuation, self-dealing without independent appraisal, S-Corp UBTI issues	Tax substantiation, due diligence, execute transfer documents, donor communication, audit preparation, put stock certificate or assignment document in safe. Check in with company annually for any material changes.	1. Sell back to entity 2. Sell in open market transaction 3. Sell to private unrelated buyer 4. Sell to related buyer 5. Initial Public Offering
Life Insurance / Annuities	Virtually none except as it relates to complex foundation-owned, charity-owned and investor owned contracts, or policies with loans.	Numerous reportable transactions require compliance with IRS regulations. Review the illustration or policy being considered and have a memo outlining the donor's premium paying responsibilities and the charity's options for non-compliance.	Work with agent to illustrate any non-paid up (universal or variable life policies) at 2% under the current crediting rate or guaranteed if greater.	Tax substantiation, due diligence, execute transfer documents, donor communication, audit preparation, manage policies annually to determine health. Put donor in contact with a qualified insurance appraiser.	1. Usually hold to death 2. Cash surrender to company 3. Reduce paid-up 4. Sell to life settlement companies
Mineral Interests / Intellectual Property	None other than potential capital calls and environmental / reputational issues assuming working mineral interests rather than royalty interests	More than any other asset, having a well-designed sales plan prior to acceptance is critical	Marketability, appraisals	Tax substantiation, due diligence, execute transfer documents, donor communication, audit preparation	1. Hold (not recommended unless strong income stream) 2. Sell via broker 3. Sell privately

Charitable Gifts of Noncash Assets

Asset Type	Liability / Cost Exposure	Risk Management / Due Diligence	Acceptance Issues	Staff Role	Disposition Alternatives
Restricted Stock / Stock Options	Post-contribution loss possibilities during restricted or holding period, process of removing the legend	Review all restrictions and option agreements, also consider including a put option to mitigate risk	None	Tax substantiation, due diligence, transfer documents, donor communication, audit preparation	Sell with broker as soon as restriction is lifted
Collectibles / Art	Post-contribution holding expenses, project management –reputational and potential provenance issues	Review history of collection, document with pictures and brief descriptions; discuss tax implications with donor prior to acceptance	Consult broker / appraiser / auctioneer to assess value and liquidation prior to acceptance	Tax substantiation, due diligence, execute transfer documents, donor communication, audit preparation, insurance, storage	1. Auction sale 2. Private buyer 3. Broker
Bitcoin/ Cryptocurrency	Loss of asset or sale proceeds during or post-contribution due to error, hacking, or theft.	Set up wallet and exchange account to securely accept, hold, and sell coins. Verify how coins will be sold and that USD can be withdrawn. Have donor send a small amount of coin as a test.	Appraisals, account/ wallet setup, sale process, security	Tax substantiation, due diligence, execute transfer, donor communication, audit preparation, manage disposition	1. Hold (not recommended) 2. Sell on exchange

YouTube Noncash Video Links

Complete playlist of Clontz videos: https://www.youtube.com/playlist?list=PLFANojJqNtDTgnsxU8UzI7dK0egD7uawS

1. Commercial Real Estate Contribution: https://www.youtube.com/watch?v=6I8TwHJfu_A
2. C Corporation Contribution: https://www.youtube.com/watch?v=GJ-oTXegT28
3. S Corporation Stock Contribution: https://www.youtube.com/watch?v=ze4gqHw1UHo
4. Ten Least Wanted Assets: https://www.youtube.com/watch?v=ftrxs1aaL0o
5. Crops and Timber Contributions: https://www.youtube.com/watch?v=OlhoHecftGE
6. Depreciated Asset Contributions: https://www.youtube.com/watch?v=OYnwLLaBTw8
7. Assisted Living: https://www.youtube.com/watch?v=614xlSyfKgg
8. Art and Collectibles: https://www.youtube.com/watch?v=tSJN0OKb0J0

Donor Questions | Quick Take-Aways

By Bryan Clontz

Below are quick take-aways on questions to ask potential donors in a broader planning context. This topic is based on Jay Steenhuysen's "Philanthropy Planning: What to Say and Do in the Room with your Donors/Clients to Explore and Document the Philanthropy Mission." For an in-depth examination adapted and excerpted from the article, see Identifying Charitable Passions and Noncash Giving Opportunities. For further details, see Donor Questions | Additional Resources.

Although most upcoming chapters address unique considerations and questions for specific types of noncash assets, this chapter deals specifically with the up-front questions. These questions are often necessary to assess the charitable outlook and receptivity of potential donors. Although they may seem directed at development or gift officers, any party to the gift-making process should consider these questions. This includes the potential donor's tax, legal, and financial advisors, and even the potential donor himself.

These questions, of course, are not comprehensive. However, they should work as a jumping-off point to develop the charitable conversation. Questioning skills are a balance between art and science, but always include the most important element—listening. With that in mind, general principles for conversations with potential donors include:

- Let the prospective donor's passions and interests guide the discussion.
- Base the questions you ask on the interests they show.
- Assess the potential donor's past charitable activities—cast a broad net to pull in all social, political, educational, religious, environmental, or scientific causes the donor supports or supported.
- Understand the prospective donor's balance sheet, particularly any noncash assets which might be suitable gifts.
- Similarly, try to evaluate the potential donor's current income, and need for future income.
- Evaluate the rough overall cost of completing the gift transaction.
- Determine what it will take for the donor to be satisfied with the gift - what are the donor's goals?

The core concept is that a good gift will not only be efficient from both economic and tax perspectives, but that it will also accomplish existing charitable goals. Of course, the parties to the gift must balance that against the charity's need to bring in gifts at the lowest reasonable cost. A gift officer or advisor should ask questions with those goals always in mind.

Fundraising Nugget

Jeff Comfort, a very successful gift planner formerly with Georgetown University and currently with Oregon State University, trains fundraisers on the art of the ask. He suggests a technique called the Four Ss—Story, Story, Story and then Shut Up. By aligning these brief stories to known or perceived donor interests, and then remaining silent, this allows the donor to expand or self-select a particular topic. Once the donor is excited and engaged around a specific area, then the gift planner / advisor can use many of Jay's questions to probe more deeply.

Donor Questions | Identifying Charitable Passions and Noncash Giving Opportunities[13]

By Jay Steenhuysen

Below is an in-depth examination on questions to ask potential donors. This topic is based on Jay Steenhuysen's "Philanthropy Planning: What to Say and Do in the Room with your Donors/Clients to Explore and Document the Philanthropy Mission." For quick take-aways on donor development, see Donor Questions Quick Take-Aways. For further details, see Donor Questions Additional Resources.

Charitable Giving – A Singular Opportunity to Use Assets in Lieu of Cash

There is no substitute for cash. It fuels our economic system and makes daily living and commerce possible. However, there's one place where using cash may not be the best use of resources. **Charitable giving is a singular opportunity to use noncash assets in lieu of cash to fund philanthropy goals.**

A 2016 study of nonprofit donors by Fidelity Charitable noted that two-thirds of respondents expressed a desire to give more to the causes they support.[14] Major Gift and Planned Giving Officers know that donors are inclined to give more when they can demonstrate to donors how a gift of noncash assets increases their philanthropy while also offering potential tax benefits. Now, thanks to the in-depth research of Professor Russell James III, J.D., Ph.D., CFP, there is empirical evidence that **giving noncash assets is a win-win for both the donor and the charity.**[15]

Professor James' groundbreaking work reveals that nonprofits receiving noncash gifts experience a much higher average growth in total fundraising dollars. His analysis of more than one million nonprofit tax returns filed from roughly 2010-2015 demonstrates that nonprofits receiving **only cash gifts** saw 11% average growth in total contributions over that time period. Those nonprofits reporting **any noncash gifts** saw average growth of 50%; while nonprofits receiving **noncash gifts of securities** experienced 66% average growth in total fundraising.

---

13. This chapter is an adaptation of Steenhuysen, J. (2012), "Philanthropy Planning: What to Say and Do in the Room with your Donors/Clients to Explore and Document their Philanthropy Mission," Partnership for Philanthropic Planning 7-9, http://my.pppnet.org/library/75938/1/NCPP12_Steenhuysen.pdf.
14. Overcoming Barriers to Giving; a survey conducted by Fidelity Charitable in June-July 2016 among 3,254 people who give to charity and who itemized charitable deductions on 2015 tax returns.
15. Professor Russell James III, J.D., Ph.D., CFP® - Cash is Not King in Fundraising: Results from 1 Million Nonprofit Tax Returns, Executive Summary available at http://bit.ly/2GYznFS.

This growth applied to nonprofit organizations at every fundraising level! Professor James' bold conclusion: "**Cash is not king in fundraising.**" With this fundraising growth trajectory in mind, nonprofits would be wise to consider how they might adapt their donor strategies to take full advantage of noncash giving.

The Gift of Assets Conversation Begins with Discovery

There are typically two ways the gift of assets conversation with a donor begins: 1) it is introduced by a nonprofit's Major Gifts Officer, or 2) as part of a broader discussion the donor has with an advisor about how to achieve maximum impact through philanthropy. Each of these conversations relies upon a set of questions specific to the task of discovery.

These are **not** the "technical" questions about particular assets provided in subsequent chapters in this book. They are the questions listed in this chapter that uncover a donor's charitable intent and noncash gift opportunities. **These discovery questions precede and set the stage for the detailed discussion about the gift of a specific asset.**

For the Major Gifts Officer, there are questions designed to encourage the donor to reveal his/her affinity for the organization and relevant financial information. For the philanthropy advisor, there are reflective questions designed to help the donor uncover personal giving patterns, and other personal and wealth information that informs his or her philanthropy objectives.

Why spend time exploring charitable passions with a donor? Because when a donor becomes more intentional about **why** they want to give and **who** they want to give to, they also become more intentional about **how** they want to give. Igniting a donor's charitable passion fuels a desire to make the largest possible gift – a gift that exceeds available cash resources and can only be made with a noncash asset.

Whether the conversation is conducted by the Major Gifts Officer or a trusted advisor, both approaches can be used effectively to propose a gift of noncash assets.

Better Together

One of the first steps nonprofits can take is to "break down the silos" that separate Major Gift and Planned Giving staff. Nonprofits can't reach their maximum donor potential unless these two groups learn how to work effectively together.

Each group employs a particular and different set of premises and skills when engaging with donors. For example, Planned Giving Officers focus on deferred gifts; value the longevity of the relationship; and are comfortable mastering the technicalities involved with planned gifts. On the other hand, Major Gift Officers focus on outright gifts; generally work with high capacity donors; are not limited by the longevity of the relationship; and are not familiar with the technicalities of deferred, blended, or complex gifts.

But these differences can become complementary!

Collaboration between Planned Giving Officers and Major Giving Officers results in bigger gifts – and those gifts are usually made with assets. When Planned Giving Officers and Major Giving Officers work together, it promotes both personal and organizational success – they are, simply, "better together." Planned Giving Officers are included in donor strategy discussions, raise larger deferred gifts, and receive more current gifts. Major Gift Officers raise larger gifts – from assets – and enjoy stronger relationships with more satisfied donors. For both, the job becomes more interesting!

With training and practice, fundraisers can learn how to conduct meaningful conversations about a donor's financial matters, wealth events, and life changes – strategic topics that they previously may have been unwilling to discuss or uncomfortable doing so. The key to making this work is providing Major Gift Officers with specific questions that can be used to open and expand the wealth conversation with donors.

The Art of the Question – Major Gift Officers

The following questions (and more like them) can be used by Major Gift Officers to develop and guide an ongoing donor conversation that leads to a gift of noncash assets. The questions can be used in several ways. For example, they can be used to structure a meeting where all of the topics are covered in a single meeting. Or they can be strategically used across several sessions of cultivation conversations.

Questions about Your Nonprofit/Charitable Organization

These questions help fundraisers understand the origins of the donor's affinity and support.

1. What inspired your first gift to us?
2. What do you like about our work now?
3. What were your first impressions of our organization?

4. What do you think is the most exciting thing we are doing?
5. What moves you most about our work?

Questions about Nonprofit/Charitable Organizations in General

These questions help fundraisers understand the donor's broader interests and how their organization fits into the donor's giving.

1. Do you support other organizations similar to ours?
2. May I ask which ones?
3. Do those organizations comprise the bulk of your giving?
4. What is important to you about those causes?
5. What do you hope to accomplish with your philanthropy?
6. How do you decide how much to give away each year?
7. What is the best charitable gift you've ever made?
8. Where do we fit into your overall giving?

Questions about Family

These questions help fundraisers understand the family dynamic as it relates to the donor's giving.

1. Does your family support the organizations that you support?
2. Tell me about your family:
    a. Marital/partner status?
    b. Children/grandchildren?
3. What do they do?

Questions about Income/Financial Resources

These questions help the fundraiser understand the donor's sources of income and cash flow.

1. What do you do?
2. If employee:
    a. What is your role at your company?

Donor Questions | Identifying Charitable Passions and Noncash Giving Opportunities

   b. What brought you to your company?
3. If owner:
   a. Tell me how you got started in your business?
   b. How are you involved in the day-to-day operations of the business?
   c. What are your long-term goals for the business?
   d. Will you always work as much as you do now?
4. If retired:
   a. What do you do with your time now that you're retired?
   b. What do you enjoy most about retirement?
5. Any special plans for the future?
6. What makes it possible for you to support our organization and others as generously as you do?

Questions about Professional Advisors

These questions help the fundraiser understand the two major concerns of high net worth individuals: the transfer of their wealth to future generations and the impact of taxes. These questions can help address their philanthropy plans and tax concerns.

1. Have you discussed your philanthropy goals with any of your professional advisors?
   a. If so, do you have any formal philanthropy plans in place?
2. Would you be interested in learning more about the superior tax benefits of funding your philanthropy plan with a gift of assets?
3. Do you fund (or have plans to fund) a Private Foundation or Donor Advised Fund?
   a. Why did you choose this platform?
   b. How do/will you use it?
   c. How do/will you involve your family?
   d. What are your goals for the foundation/fund?
   e. Will your Private Foundation/Donor Advised Fund outlive your generation?
   f. Have you thought about funding your foundation/fund with a gift of assets?

The Major Gift Officer's task is to ask the right questions, listen to the donor's answers, and know when to engage the technical experts for the deeper conversation about a gift of assets: "I don't know the answer to that question, but I know someone who does. Can I arrange a meeting to follow up?"

These discovery questions can be used to validate a donor's commitment to the organization's mission or identify the donor's interest in specific programs they care about. They also can be used to assess whether there are significant assets in the family; to discern if donors have made gifts of assets in the past; and to explore how they want to structure their philanthropy over the long-term. The resulting conversations can provide a deeper understanding of how donors developed their current interests and practice their philanthropy.

The Art of the Question – Philanthropy Advisors

When trusted philanthropy advisors – whether fundraisers or allied professionals – help donors discover the charitable purpose they want to accomplish through their giving, they are contributing to each donor's life in a profound and meaningful way. Thoughtful conversations can mean the difference between donors merely continuing a habit of giving or practicing proactive, intentional philanthropy that flows from the creation of a Giving on Purpose personal mission statement.

Advisors can prepare for and successfully guide these important conversations that reveal a donor's philanthropic priorities. This process can be taught, learned and practiced – eventually becoming an intuitive approach to donor engagement.

The Power of Story

Story has the power to supplement analytical thinking by getting to the heart of a donor's philanthropic impulses. Stories put the individual's facts in context and supply advisors with the raw material to assist donors in achieving their philanthropic goals.

As philanthropic advisors use the following questions to prompt key emotions and help donors put words to those emotions, they begin to unlock what really excites donors. You touch their passion – and passion helps you develop their purpose for giving, identify programs that fulfill that purpose, and ultimately, connect them with programs or organizations that match their passion.

Personal Charitable History

The donor's history of giving is very important. It helps advisors understand the context for a donor's experience with nonprofit/charitable organizations and causes, as well as the donor's personal philosophy. These factors can create preconceptions and attitudes which may help or hinder how the donor gives. They also can provide valuable insight about the donor's goals.

1. What types of organizations did you contribute to when you first began to make charitable contributions?
2. What personal factors molded your giving?
3. What environmental factors molded your giving?
4. What cultural factors molded your giving?
5. When you were young, was there anyone whom you considered a role model for giving?
   a. Who?
   b. Why?
   c. What was the impact of that relationship on you?
6. Is that person still a model for your giving today?
7. Do you feel that you are serving (or have served) as a philanthropic role model for others? For whom? In what way?

Family Philanthropic Activities

Just as individual giving history can be important to developing and planning the gift, so are family philanthropic activities. Given the nature of family wealth, philanthropy conversations can be an excellent opportunity to begin a discussion about values and giving across generations. When there is a family history of philanthropy, there is very likely agreement and support for the completion of the gift.

1. Have you involved your family in your philanthropy?
   a. If yes, please share some examples.
2. What are the most significant stories in your family's giving? How did those experiences impact you?

For spouses/partners:

3. Tell me about your shared charitable interests.
4. Have you ever had disagreements over charitable gifts? How did you resolve those disagreements? Were gifts ultimately made? What compromises were involved?

For parents:

5. How did you and your spouse/partner give before you had children?
6. Has having children changed that in any way?
    a. If so, how?
7. Do you involve your children in your giving currently?
    a. If so, why and how?
    b. If not, why not?
8. What sort of participation in giving do you feel is most important for the children?
    9. Have the children shared your interests as they have grown?
    c. If not, how are their interests different?
    10. If client's children are very young, ask: How do you plan to involve them?
    11. What is your hope for your children and their giving?

Family Volunteer History

Similar to family philanthropic history, this topic can give advisors an idea of the donor's active engagement in nonprofit/charitable endeavors. It can provide insight into a donor's enthusiasm for the gift and philanthropic outlook generally.

1. Did your parents volunteer?
    a. Tell me about those experiences.
    b. How did they impact you?
2. What were your early volunteer roles?
    a. How has that changed as you have aged?
3. Have you been involved in leadership roles?
    a. Describe those roles.
4. Do not limit thoughts exclusively to board involvement: What other active roles did you assume?
    a. Did those roles focus your talents on solving problems?
    b. Establishing new ventures?
    c. Dramatically enhancing programmatic effectiveness?
    d. Improving organizational efficiency?
5. Do your spouse/partner and/or children volunteer?
    a. What has been the impact, if any, of their volunteer experiences on you?

Grantee Selection

These questions begin to delve into the donor's history of gift-giving specifically. They are intended to evaluate donor experience and any resulting attitudes towards giving.

1. Tell me about some meaningful gifts that you have made.
2. What were your criteria for selecting these organizations?
    a. How did you research the organizations?
    b. How did you select the organizations? Based on:
        i. Mission?
        ii. Specific programs?

iii. Your relationships with people involved in the group?

iv. Were those relationships with someone who benefited from the charity?

   c. Did you personally benefit from the charity?

3. Did you initiate programs yourself?

   a. If so, what were they?

   b. What caused you to launch those programs?

Good Gifts

Here the questions evaluate what the donor wants to achieve and how to qualify a gift as a success. This will provide guidance on how to keep the donor engaged and satisfied going forward.

1. What is your definition of a "good gift?"

   a. How do you know when you have made a "good gift?"

2. Share a couple of examples of "good gifts" with me.

   a. Why did you feel they were good?

3. What process did you use to make "good gift" decisions?

4. What details did the organization provide to you as you considered making that gift?

5. Which details were most influential in making the decision?

6. What were the best parts of the gift?

   a. Outcomes achieved?

   b. Acknowledgments you received?

   c. Leverage of the gift?

   d. The fact that it served as an example for other potential donors?

   e. Which of these things were most meaningful to you in the gift process?

Giving Philosophy and Goals

Rather than looking back to the donor's history, these questions look forward and seek to understand what the donor hopes to accomplish in the future through giving.

1. Broadly speaking, what is your rationale for giving?

   a. Do you feel that any of the following was a factor in your rationale?

i. Giving back to those who gave to you?

ii. Making a difference in the world?

iii. Addressing a specific need that touched your life or the life of a loved one?

2. Do you recognize any element of luck, blessing, or grace in your professional success?

3. Have you ever made any gifts that you consider outside the normal pattern of your giving?

   a. If so, what and why?

   b. Why do you consider these gifts outside the norm?

   c. In retrospect, how do you feel about those?

After exploring these questions with the donor, a Philanthropy Advisor will be equipped to draft the donor's Giving on Purpose mission statement. The document is provided to the donor as a service; after review, reflection, and edits by the donor, it can be finalized and used to guide the donor's future philanthropy.

The next set of questions introduces the idea of using a gift of assets to fulfill the donor's philanthropic mission.

Accomplishing Philanthropic Goals

This conversation "drills down" to the specific gift that the donor has in mind. It probes timing, underlying assets, and family involvement.

1. What do you want to have accomplished through your philanthropy 20 years from now?

   a. What will you need to do ten years from now to ensure that your goals are met?

   b. Five years from now?

   c. In the next two years?

   d. This year?

2. When do you envision making your primary philanthropic contributions?

   a. Do you want to make a large gift now?

   b. Do you want the gift to be part of your estate plan?

3. Do you have the financial resources to accomplish your current and lifetime philanthropic goals?
    a. If not, what event will make it possible for you to achieve that goal?
4. Have you considered using a non-cash asset to fund the gift?
    a. Will you transfer that asset to charity?
5. Do any other family members need to be a part of this conversation?

When the questions listed above have been answered as thoroughly as possible, philanthropy advisors will have a clear picture of the donor's affinity for specific organizations/causes as well as the capacity to make a major or planned gift.

Asset Discovery

To move forward in identifying a specific asset, the conversation needs to continue with questions that gauge the donor's financial and estate plans, and tax concerns/benefits. There are many questions about assets, taxes, and financial implications of the gift that can be used. For example:

1. How has the volatility of financial markets impacted you?
2. Do you own shares in a company that experienced an IPO, merger, or stock buyback this year?
3. Do you have any major income-producing assets?
4. Have you ever made a gift of assets to a nonprofit/charitable organization?
a. If yes, what asset did you give?
5. Have you experienced any significant tax events this year that could be offset by a charitable deduction?
6. Would you like to receive superior tax benefits by making your charitable gift from assets?

This is by no means an exhaustive list of the questions that can be used to determine which gift of assets will provide the greatest value for the organization and the donor. The specific asset-focused questions and advice in the remainder of this book provide can guide the rest of the conversation and help fundraisers and philanthropy advisors close the gift.

Major and transformational gifts don't happen in a vacuum. They occur in the context of a donor's lifetime experience, financial resources, and a desire to use those resources to make a positive impact in the world. The stories that emerge in response to thoughtful discovery questions illustrate a donor's values and focus – but these stories may not rise in the natural course of conversation.

Skilled professionals who ask thoughtful, probing questions and listen carefully to the donor's replies create a space for the stories to be told. Working together, they can achieve a mutually beneficial conclusion. This discovery process is essential and should not be minimized or overlooked. It should always precede discussion about the specific kind of asset being considered for a charitable gift.

Charitable Gifts of Noncash Assets

Donor Questions | Additional Resources

Below are further details on questions to ask potential donors. This topic is based on Jay Steenhuysen's, "Philanthropy Planning: What to Say and Do in the Room with your Donors/Clients to Explore and Document the Philanthropy Mission." For quick take-aways, see Donor Questions | Quick Take-Aways. For an in-depth examination adapted and excerpted from the article, see Identifying Charitable Passions and Noncash Giving Opportunities.

For a discussion of developing ongoing conversations with prospective donors, see Foord, E. and Daniels, J. (2014), "It's All About Conversing with Donors," *Partnership for Philanthropic Planning,* http://my.pppnet.org/library/92861/1/FoordandDaniels_Final.pdf.

For a discussion of charitable estate planning questions from the financial planner or advisor's perspective, see Breiteneicher, J. (1996), "Advisor's Enthusiasm Helps to Shape Client's Charitable Role," *Trust & Estates,* http://www.toledocf.org/clientuploads/directory/PDF_Library/Advisor's%20Enthusiasm%20Helps%20To%20Shape%20Client's%20Charitable%20Role.pdf.

For tips on common gift planning hurdles, see Hays, J. (September 29, 2005), "The 7 Commandments of Planned Giving," *Partnership for Philanthropic Planning,* http://my.pppnet.org/library/000/000/d9/NCPGC05s12.pdf.

For an examination of the relationship between gift planners and professional advisors, see Blakesley, S. and Lampo, J. (Oct. 1, 2005), "What Do You Want From Me? Developing Working Relationships Between Nonprofit Gift Planners and Professional Advisors," *Partnership for Philanthropic Planning,* http://my.pppnet.org/library/000/000/ee/NCPGC05s30.pdf.

For analysis of developing blended gift opportunities from the gift officer's perspective, see Buderus, A.A. and Smith, G.P. (2013), "Blended Gifts, Eh? Making the Most of This Emerging Workhorse for Major & Planned Gift Officers," *Partnership for Philanthropic Planning,* http://my.pppnet.org/library/85123/1/NCPP13_Buderus%2CSmith.pdf.

For an in-depth look at the rationale behind ten key questions for donors, see Brovey, A.P. and Roenigk, P.L. (October 25, 2008), "'How Old Are You and Did You Know You Could…?' Initiating Planned Gift Discussions and Getting Answers to Key

Questions," *Partnership for Philanthropic Planning,* http://my.pppnet.org/library.htm?mode=view&did=3137&lid=5.

For tips on timing and preparing for the charitable conversation, see Nopar, K. (October 15, 2015), "Don't Wait; Have the Charitable Conversation with Clients Now," *Financial Advisor Magazine,* http://www.fa-mag.com/news/have-the-charitable-conversation-with-clients-now-23499.html?section=40.

Key Noncash Gift Process Considerations

By Ryan Raffin

This section quickly outlines the essential considerations common to the noncash donation process. Where the consideration involves an important concept or term, it will be briefly defined.

Due Diligence

Charity

1. What due diligence is necessary for this type of property beyond the charity's standard evaluation procedures?
2. Has the charity physically inspected the property?
3. What liability issues are associated with the property?

Donor

1. Does the charity have appropriate legal status, i.e. a 501(c)(3) public or private charity?
2. Does the charity have the sophistication to properly accept the gift or manage a deferred gift?
    - "Deferred gift" here meaning a planned giving vehicle like a charitable remainder trust, charitable gift annuity, or bequest.

Assignment / Transfer

1. What are the legal requirements for transfer of title or recording and are there any impediments to completing the gift?
    - Title and recording show official ownership, usually with a specific state where the property is located.
2. Would the gift to charity be an assignment of income?
    - "Assignment of income" is when the donor avoids recognizing gain from sale of property by donating it when receipt of income from that gain is practically certain to occur.
3. Is this a gift of all or substantially all the corporation's assets?
    - If the donor gives a significant proportion of closely held business assets, the IRS may require the donor to recognize gain on those assets.

4. If the gift is part of a bequest, will there be a probate process or estate tax?
5. Are there any restrictions on transfer, including easements or approval from other owners?

Valuation / Substantiation

1. Is the donation of an undivided portion of the entire interest in the property?
   - The gift must be some portion of the donor's whole interest in the property; for example, 50 percent of the donor's LLC interest is acceptable, but 50 percent of the donor's profits from the LLC interest is not acceptable under the partial interest rules.
2. What is the tax character of the property?
   - Is the donated property capital gain or loss property? If so, what is the holding period (long term or short term)? Could the property be considered inventory? Is the asset considered ordinary income? If the asset is tangible personal property, is it related to the donee's mission?
3. What is the fair market value of the proposed gift?
   - Every charity's acceptance guidelines are different but lower value assets many not be worth the effort and/or tax savings from the donation.
4. How will the donor obtain a qualified appraisal?
   - A qualified appraisal is necessary if the value of the donated property exceeds $5,000, and the appraiser must have relevant, verifiable experience and education.
5. Will the donor receive a deduction for the property? If so, will it be fair market value, adjusted cost basis, or another method?
6. If the charity obtained the property via bargain sale, what portion of the property is allocated to gift versus sale?
   - A bargain sale is a transfer of property to charity for below fair market value, resulting in part-gift, part-sale treatment, based on the difference between fair market value and actual sale price.

Holding Period

1. Will the property generate unrelated business taxable income (UBTI)?

- Income-generating property unrelated to the organization's charitable purposes can lead to tax on that income, with some exceptions for passive income such as rents, leases, royalties, etc.

2. Is the property debt-financed and generating income? If so, it may be subject to UBTI.
    - "Debt-financed" meaning that the donated investment property was purchased with borrowed money, or has an existing loan / mortgage, and produces debt-financed income as a result.

3. Does the charity have the ability to manage the asset? What sorts of personnel are required? What are the associated expenses?

4. Is the charity legally obligated to pay-in additional capital or to incur the liabilities and expenses of the donated property, if a closely held business or real estate?

5. What additional reporting requirements does the charity need to satisfy while it holds the property?

Liquidation

1. When will the charity be able to liquidate the property? If there are no legal restrictions on liquidation, should the charity liquidate it?

2. How will the charity find a buyer for the donated property?

3. Is there a pre-arranged sale organized prior to the donation?
    - A pre-arranged sale means the charity is legally obligated to sell the property to a third party, under a contract the donor executed, after it receives the donation and may result in the donor incurring capital gains tax.

4. If the charity sells the property within three years, does it need to complete Form 8282 for both the IRS and the donor?

Key Terms and Concepts

By Ryan Raffin

Below are brief definitions for key terms and concepts used throughout this book. Where appropriate, we have included links and references to additional information. For more general charitable laws and regulations, see **General Regulations and Information**.

A **split interest gift** is a planned giving vehicle whereby the donor retains some interest (financial or otherwise) in the gifted property or proceeds from its sale. The nonprofit gets the other portion of the property, and the donor typically receives a tax deduction for that portion. A common type of split interest gift discussed in this book is the **deferred gift**, where the nonprofit does not receive its portion of the gift until after some period of time has passed, often the donor's lifetime. Important split interest planned giving vehicles include:

- The **charitable remainder trust**, where the donor retains a present income interest for a term of years or life, and the charity receives a remainder interest. It is the most common deferred gift discussed in this book. Payments can be a fixed dollar amount (a charitable remainder annuity trust) or a fixed percentage of trust assets (a charitable remainder unitrust). A CRAT makes regular payments to the donor in a set dollar amount (at least five percent of the initial fair market value of the assets). A CRUT makes regular payments to the donor in a set percentage of the principal as valued on a certain day each year (at least five percent of the trust, as valued on an annual basis). The donor receives an immediate tax deduction for the present value of the remainder—that is, the difference between the amount paid and the actuarially-determined present value of the annuity payments.

    "CRT Primer," Planned Giving Design Center, http://www.pgdc.com/calculation-center/charitable-remainder-trusts/crt-advisor-information (last visited July 27, 2016).

- The **charitable gift annuity**, which is technically an annuity contract that the donor purchases from the charity. The donor provides some amount of money in exchange for regularly scheduled payments to one or two named individuals for the balance of their lives. The donor receives an immediate tax deduction for the present value of the remainder—that is, the difference between the amount paid and the actuarially-determined present value of the annuity payments.

    Fox, R.A. (August 14, 2014), "Charitable Gift Annuities," Planned Giving Design Center, http://www.pgdc.com/pgdc/charitable-gift-annuites.

- The **charitable lead trust**, which is the inverse of a charitable remainder trust. Here, the charity receives income from the property for a term of years (or lifetime of some living person the trust agreement names), and the donor or heirs receive it afterwards. Payments can be a fixed dollar amount (a charitable lead annuity trust) or a fixed percentage of trust assets (a charitable lead unitrust). The advantage of a properly designed charitable lead trust is that it can allow for favorable estate tax treatment. Availability and amount of income tax deduction depends on the structure of the trust.

    Peebles, J. (August 27, 2015), "A Practical Look at Charitable Lead Trusts, Part 1 of 3," Planned Giving Design Center, http://www.pgdc.com/pgdc/practical-look-charitable-lead-trusts-part-1-3.

    IRC § 664 (charitable remainder trusts)

    Treas. Reg. § 1.170A-6 (charitable lead trusts)

    Treas. Reg. § 1.170A-1 (charitable gift annuities)

Assignment of income occurs when the taxpayer donates appreciated capital assets, and there is some right to receive income from those appreciated assets. In that case, the IRS will disregard the donation and require the taxpayer to recognize capital gain on the assets, as if the taxpayer had sold the assets personally and was simply donating the proceeds. Typically, this occurs when the owner of a closely held business agrees to sell the company, and donates a portion of his shares prior to completion of the sale. Since the taxpayer is nearly certain to receive income, the IRS states that he cannot avoid it by assigning it to another.

Similar to assignment of income, a **pre-arranged sale** involves a quid pro quo agreement (formal or otherwise). For example, a donation conditioned on the nonprofit's use of the proceeds to complete another transaction with the donor. More common is a case where the charity signs some agreement to sell before receiving the assets. In these cases, the IRS will characterize the transaction instead as the donor's realization of capital gain and subsequent donation. Even if there is a right of first refusal, so long as the charity is not compelled to sell the asset, there will not be a pre-arranged sale.

> Kallina II, E.J. and Temple, P. (October 14, 1995), "How Far Is Too Far? The Prearranged Sale and The Palmer/Blake Conundrum," Planned Giving Design Center, http://www.pgdc.com/pgdc/how-far-too-far.
>
> *Palmer v. Commissioner*, 62 T.C. 684 (1974), aff'd on other grounds, 523 F.2d 1308 (8th Cir. 975); *Blake v. Commissioner* [83-1 USTC 9121], 697 F.2d 473 (2d Cir. 1982), aff'g 42

Key Terms and Concepts

TCM 1336 (1981); *Ferguson v. Commissioner,* 108 T.C. #14 (1997) (assignment of income doctrine)

A corporation (either S or C status) which donates **all or substantially all** of its assets to charity will recognize gain or loss on the property. "Substantially all" is loosely defined, but 70 to 80 percent of assets is often enough to trigger gain recognition. Additionally, courts have also focused on the business's ability to continue its operations after the donation.

> Peebles, L.H., (May 17, 2005), "A Hidden Trap for Generous Corporations," Planned Giving Design Center, http://www.pgdc.com/pgdc/hidden-trap-generous-corporations.

> Treas. Reg. § 1.337(d)-4(a)(1) (gain recognition for transfer of "all or substantially all" corporate assets)

An **easement** is a permanent restriction on the use of real property. In the nonprofit realm, it is most often seen as a qualified conservation easement. The restriction reduces the value of the property, and the donor receives a corresponding tax deduction as a result. These easements are put in place to preserve environmental, historical, or recreational real property.

> Fox, R. (February 3, 2016), "Ease-ment Does It," Planned Giving Design Center, http://www.pgdc.com/pgdc/ease-ment-does-it.

> IRC §§ 170(f)(3), 170(h) (partial interests gifts and qualified conservation contributions)

A donation must be an **undivided portion of the entire interest** in most cases. This means that the donor generally cannot carve out only some rights in the property, but must give a portion of all of their interest. For example, an owner of mineral development rights could not donate only right to net profits. The gift must be a "full slice" of the interest.

> Newman, D.W. (September 30, 2015), "Charitable Gifts of Real Property," Planned Giving Design Center, http://www.pgdc.com/pgdc/charitable-gifts-real-property.

> Treas. Reg. § 1.170A-7(b)(1)(i) (undivided portion of entire interest requirement)

A gift of a **partial interest** in property is where the donation is not an undivided portion of the entire interest. Here, the donor is giving some specific portion of her rights to the nonprofit donee, and retaining others. For example, the donor might give the charity a remainder interest in her farm, while retaining the right to live on and use the farm for her lifetime. Generally, these gifts are not deductible, but there are some important exceptions, such as the example here and others discussed in this book.

Charitable Gifts of Noncash Assets

> James III, R. (March 30, 2016), "Gifts of Partial Interests, Part 1 of 3," Planned Giving Design Center, http://www.pgdc.com/pgdc/10-gifts-partial-interests.
>
> Rev. Rul. 76-331, 1976-2 C.B. 52 (partial interest rule and retained mineral rights)

An important factor for donors is the **tax character** of donated property. First, the property is either an ordinary income asset or capital asset. If the property is the type that the donor sells in his normal business, it is an ordinary income asset. If the property is held and not for sale in the ordinary course of business, it is a capital asset. If the capital asset has been held a year or less, it is short-term capital gain property. If the capital asset has been held for more than a year, it is long-term capital gain property.

> James III, R. (October 7, 2015), "Visual Planned Giving: An Introduction to the Law and Taxation of Charitable Gift Planning," Chp. 5: Valuing Charitable Gifts of Property, parts 1 and 2, http://www.pgdc.com/pgdc/5-valuing-charitable-gifts-property-part-1-2; http://www.pgdc.com/pgdc/5-valuing-charitable-gifts-property-part-2-2
>
> IRC §§ 1221 – 1223 (character of property)

A **qualified appraisal** is an assessment of property value by a certified professional with experience in valuing the type of property at hand. For certain types of asset with values over $5,000, the IRS requires the taxpayer to obtain a qualified appraisal. This information must be submitted with the donor's itemized charitable deductions.

> IRS Publication 561 (April 2007), Determining the Value of Donated Property, https://www.irs.gov/publications/p561/index.html.
>
> Treas. Reg. § 1.170A-13(c) (appraisal requirements)

A **bargain sale** is where the donor gives the property to the donee nonprofit in exchange for some consideration worth less than the fair market value of the donated property. This consideration can be cash, but can also be other property. Essentially, the bargain sale is part-gift and part-sale, so the donor receives a tax deduction only for the gift portion and must recognize gain (but not loss) on the deemed sale portion.

> Hoffman, M.D. (May 10, 2011), "Bargain Sales," Planned Giving Design Center, http://www.pgdc.com/pgdc/bargain-sales.
>
> Treas. Reg. § 1.1011-2 (bargain sale regulations)
>
> Rev. Rul. 67-246, 1967-2 C.B. 104 (part-gift, part-sale treatment for bargain sales to charity)

Key Terms and Concepts

Unrelated business taxable income (or "UBTI") is the income which a tax-exempt organization derives from trade or business which is not substantially related to its exempt purposes. A corporate nonprofit will pay tax at ordinary corporate rates on any UBTI. Further, excessive UBTI may put the nonprofit at risk of losing its tax-exempt status entirely.

Further, **debt-financed income** can give rise to UBTI. Debt-financed property which generates income qualifies. This means that unpaid debt the nonprofit incurs in order to acquire or make improvements to property held for investment or not used in its exempt purpose will lead to tax on income that same property generates.

> Rice, D. (May 10, 2016), "Bashing UBIT to Bits," Planned giving Design Center, http://www.pgdc.com/pgdc/bashing-ubit-bits.
>
> IRS Publication 598 (January 2015), Tax on Unrelated Business Income of Exempt Organizations, https://www.irs.gov/publications/p598/.
>
> IRC § 512 (unrelated business taxable income)
>
> IRC § 514 (debt-financed income)

A **capital call** is a common provision in partnership and LLC operating agreements. Investors are required to pay in capital over a number of years. Nonprofits holding these interests may or may not be exempt.

> Mayer Brown, "Addressing UBTI Concerns in Capital Call Subscription Credit Facilities," November 2012, https://www.mayerbrown.com/files/Publication/8d5b0f8f-a76f-44b4-9141-6016dd2dddf7/Presentation/PublicationAttachment/3f2293fb-e97a-41d0-beea-6221271df252/Addressing_UBTI_Concerns_in_Capital_Call_Subscription_Credit_Facilities_Moulton_Fi.pdf.

An **excess benefit** is an economic benefit a nonprofit provides to an insider. The IRS levies an excise tax for any excess benefit the nonprofit gives to certain disqualified persons. That benefit is the amount above the fair market value of goods or services those disqualified persons provided. A disqualified person is one in position to significantly influence the affairs of the organization, including the family members of such persons.

> Walsh, D. (May 23, 2013), "Reasonable Compensation: A Section 4958 Primer," Planned Giving Design Center, http://www.pgdc.com/pgdc/reasonable-compensation-section-4958-primer.
>
> IRC § 4958 (taxes on excess benefit transactions)

Inurement occurs when a tax-exempt organization's income goes to the benefit of a private individual or organization. Any unjust enrichment for a private party may be sufficient. If the IRS finds inurement, it may revoke the organization's tax-exempt status.

> IRS Overview of Inurement/Private Benefit Issues in IRC 501(c)(3) (1990), https://www.irs.gov/pub/irs-tege/eotopicc90.pdf
>
> Treas. Reg. § 1.501(c)(3)-1(c)(2)

Self-dealing occurs when there is a direct or indirect transaction between a private foundation and a disqualified person. As above, disqualified persons are persons, entities, or family members with significant influence on the private foundation. The IRS imposes an excise tax depending on the amount involved in the transaction.

> Disqualified person: IRC § 4946
>
> Self-dealing: IRC § 4941
>
> Newman, D.W. (July 14, 1999), "Dealing with the Self-Dealing Rules," Planned Giving Design Center, http://www.pgdc.com/pgdc/dealing-self-dealing-rules.

The **adjusted basis** of property is the net cost of the property after making certain tax adjustments. Most commonly, this is the cost paid for the property. However, it may also be increased by capital improvements, or decreased for any depreciation deductions previously taken.

Conversely, **fair market value** is the price that the property would sell for on the open market. The sale must be an arm's length transaction between two reasonably informed parties, voluntarily engaging in the sale.

> Adjusted basis: IRC §§ 1012, 1016
>
> Fair market value: *U.S. v. Cartwright,* 411 U.S. 546, 551 (1973)
>
> James III, R. (October 7, 2015), "Visual Planned Giving: An Introduction to the Law and Taxation of Charitable Gift Planning," Chp. 5: Valuing Charitable Gifts of Property, parts 1 and 2, http://www.pgdc.com/pgdc/5-valuing-charitable-gifts-property-part-1-2; http://www.pgdc.com/pgdc/5-valuing-charitable-gifts-property-part-2-2

Passive income is excluded from unrelated business taxable income. This income includes dividends, interest, royalties, and rent. Essentially, revenue the tax-exempt organization derives from investment holdings will generally not be taxable.

> IRC § 512(b)

Rev. Rul. 76-331, 1976-2 C.B. 52 (partial interest rule and retained mineral rights)

In some cases, the tax-exempt organization must put donated property to a **related use** for the donor to receive a tax deduction. If the donee organization's use of the property is unrelated to its exempt purposes, no deduction is available. This rule applies only to donations of tangible personal property.

> IRS Publication 526 (2015), "Charitable Contributions," https://www.irs.gov/publications/p526/ar02.html.
>
> Treas. Reg. § 1.170A-4(b)(3) (related use definitions)

Tax-exempt organizations can be classified as a **public charity** or a **private foundation**. Public charities receive at least a third of their support from the general public. Private foundations, meanwhile, do not rely on funding from the public, and are often supported by small groups of wealthy donors, typically families.

> IRS Exempt Organization Operational Requirements: Private Foundations and Public Charities (April 22, 2016), https://www.irs.gov/charities-non-profits/eo-operational-requirements-private-foundations-and-public-charities.
>
> IRC §§ 501 (public charities), 509 (private foundations)

General Regulations and Information

Below is a listing of general charitable laws and regulations. For brief definitions for key terms and concepts used throughout this book, see **Key Terms and Concepts.**

IRC § 170 (specific donation and income tax deduction rules)

IRC § 2055 (charitable deductions from the estate)

IRC § 2522 (allowing a charitable deduction for gifts)

Treas. Reg. § 1.170A-1(c) (general valuation principles)

Treas. Reg. § 1.170A-13(b) (nonprofit noncash gift substantiation requirements)

Treas. Reg. § 1.6050L-1 (regulations on donee's disposition of gifted assets)

IRS Notice 2012-52, 2012-35 I.R.B. 317, Charitable Contributions to Domestic Disregarded Entities (charity may use a disregarded entity which it controls to receive gifts)

IRS Form 8282, Donee Information Return (donated property substantiation form)

IRS Form 8283, Noncash Charitable Contributions (donor declaration of noncash contributions)

Rev. Proc. 90-32, 1990-1 C.B. 546 (sample charitable remainder annuity trusts)

Rev. Proc. 2005-55, 2005-34 I.R.B. 367 (sample inter vivos charitable remainder unitrust)

Rev. Proc. 2007-46, 2007-29 I.R.B. 102 (sample testamentary charitable lead annuity trust)

Rev. Proc. 2008-46, 2008-30 I.R.B. 238 (sample testamentary charitable lead unitrust)

Joint Committee on Taxation, "Present Law and Background Relating to the Federal Tax Treatment of Charitable Contributions (JCX-4-13)," February 11, 2013, https://www.jct.gov/publications.html?func=startdown&id=4506 (discussing and analyzing history, policy, data, and possible future proposals relating to the charitable deduction)

Congressional Research Service, "Tax Issues Relating to Charitable

Contributions and Organizations (7-5700)," January 24, 2013, http://www.pgdc.com/pgdc/crs-reports-tax-issues-relating-charitable-contributions-and-organizations (examining current legislative issues relating to charities and the charitable deduction)

Chapter 1
Real Estate

- Quick Take-Aways
- Intermediate
- Advanced
- Additional Resources

Real Estate Quick Take-Aways

By Bryan Clontz

Below are quick take-aways on gifts of real estate. Real estate topics are based on the following paper I co-authored with Dennis Bidwell, "Converting Real Estate Wealth to Gifts—Opportunities and Challenges." For quick take-aways on gifts of real estate, see Real Estate Quick Take-Aways. For a review based on that article, see Real Estate Intermediate. For an in-depth examination adapted and excerpted from the article, see Real Estate Advanced. For further details, see Real Estate Additional Resources or cross reference to the asset's ownership entity (e.g., LLC, Limited Partnerships, etc).

As an asset class, real estate has both the advantages and disadvantages of familiarity. Although a vast proportion of the nation (and world's) wealth is in real estate, it is often perceived as a difficult asset to donate. Below is an overview of the advantages, disadvantages, and possible wrinkles of real estate donations.

Advantages of donations of real estate include:

- Real estate is often highly appreciated in value, in particular when commercial property has been depreciated, meaning a large fair market value deduction for donors.
- Donated real estate may create significant revenue for the charity on sale.
- Since real estate is such a commonly-held asset, there is a large pool of potential donors.
- Laws and regulations governing real estate sale and ownership are readily available and generally clear.
- Real estate can be an excellent outright major gift or used to fund flip charitable remainder unitrusts or income producing real estate for charitable lead trusts.

Disadvantages of donating real estate include:

- Real estate might create UBIT for the nonprofit organization if it is operating an active business or if it generates debt financed income, which may also create immediate gain recognition to the donor under bargain sale rules.
- Charities must develop and follow comprehensive screening procedures to avoid marketability, environmental, and legal issues.
- Gifts of real estate can be costly and time-consuming if the charity does not have internal or external experience with the process.

- Real estate is generally not a good funding asset for charitable gift annuities or charitable remainder annuity trusts.

Wrinkles in the process to consider include:

- Everyone must know his/her role, from internal evaluation and screening to the final sale.
- It is important to have a clear memo of understanding with the donor, which will be a roadmap for completing the gift.
- Communicating the willingness to accept gifts of real estate is essential.
- Experienced internal staff or external professionals (e.g., real estate brokers, legal counsel, real estate appraisers and environmental assessors) are essential.
- Nonprofit risk tolerance and the internal process and infrastructure should be a guiding principle when evaluating potential gifts.

Discovery Questions

Donor Questions

1. What is the donor trying to accomplish with the gift (e.g., can't sell property, concerned about liability/tenant issues, wants to take advantage of hot real estate market without recognizing capital gains)?
2. What is the value of the real estate and how was that determined (e.g., appraisal, brokers opinion, opinionated brother-in-law)?
3. How is the property owned and where is it located?
4. Is there any debt, how much, and when was the mortgage placed on the property? Any other encumbrances?
5. What is the property's present use (and past use if known)?
6. Are there any unique aspects that we should be aware of (e.g., tenants, leases, liens, repair issues, title problems, etc.)?

Advisor Questions

1. What is the current adjusted tax basis?
2. If the property was held for investment, was straight-line or accelerated depreciation used?

3. Is there an executed legally binding contract to sell the property?

Charity Questions

1. Is the effort and risk worth the expected benefits (i.e., is the juice worth the squeeze)?
2. Has the screening and due diligence process identified any potential problems and can the risks be mitigated?
3. Is there the necessary expertise to accept gifts of real estate in a timely way?
4. Should indirect gift acceptance be considered, like using external third party foundations or supporting organizations to receive the asset?
5. Is there a clear liquidation plan to maximize the sales proceeds as soon as possible?

Real Estate Intermediate

By Ryan Raffin

Below is a review on gifts of real estate. Real estate topics are based on the following paper Bryan Clontz co-authored with Dennis Bidwell, "<u>Converting Real Estate Wealth to Gifts – Opportunities and Challenges</u>." For quick take-aways on gifts of real estate, see <u>Real Estate Quick Take-Aways</u>. For a review based on that article, see <u>Real Estate Intermediate</u>. For an in-depth examination adapted and excerpted from the article, see <u>Real Estate Advanced</u>. For further details, see <u>Real Estate Additional Resources</u> or cross reference to the asset's ownership entity (e.g., LLC, Limited Partnerships, etc).

This review of charitable gifts of real estate has five parts, and begins with a discussion of real estate tax treatment. It then examines risk scenarios and assessment. Next, it turns to a number of different challenges and solutions, followed by a brief summary of direct and indirect gifts of real estate. Finally, the review concludes with an overview of current, deferred, and life income gift structures.

Despite being a common type of asset (probably more so than any other in this book), real estate is underdonated. 24 percent of the country's private wealth is in real estate, yet it represents 4 percent of all charitable gifts. This considerable disparity makes sense. Real estate is complex, illiquid, time-consuming, and difficult both to manage and transfer. At the same time, it can be extremely valuable for charities who accept the property, and very satisfying for donors. The primary challenge is simply that charities are not asking donors to consider real estate gifts, and donors are therefore unaware real estate can be a possible donation.

Real estate gifts can backfire—environmental problems, expensive improvements, low curb appeal, and high management costs are just some of the issues that can arise. However, with proper screening and inspection, these risks can be managed or even eliminated. Indeed, many nonprofits do just that, with a real estate survey of nonprofit organizations showing that 13 percent of respondents receive over 10 percent of their total gifts in real estate form. The most efficient charitable gifts tend to come from low cost basis, high capital appreciation assets—so real estate is perfectly suited to effective planned giving.

Review Part 1: Real Estate Tax Treatment

The obvious solution for charities is for donors to sell the property and donate the proceeds. For donors, this would likely result in long-term capital gain treatment, meaning a maximum 20 percent federal tax rate (25 percent for unrecaptured Section 1250 gain) plus 3.8 percent net investment income tax, plus any applicable state taxes. This is likely not an appealing result for donors, since they have to pay taxes on money they are planning to give away.

Donating the real estate will generally lead to a better tax outcome. Gifts of long-term (meaning held over a year), unencumbered real estate to qualified public charities allow a deduction of the greater of fair market value or adjusted cost basis, up to 30 percent of adjusted gross income (AGI). The IRS allows taxpayers a five year carry-forward for any unused deduction amounts. The same gift to a private foundation gets the lesser of fair market value or adjusted cost basis, up to 20 percent of AGI—much less appealing, except in testamentary transfers where the property receives a stepped-up basis. Any transferred debt on the property results in adverse tax consequences under IRS bargain sale rules.

Any income the donated real estate generates can create a tax headache for the charity receiving it. This unrelated business taxable income (UBTI) leads in turn to unrelated business income tax (UBIT). For example, UBTI will arise from a donated property that generates income, such as a golf course. UBTI can also result from debt-financed income (see the IRS's discussion on IRC Section 514). Two exceptions to UBTI exist. The first is the so-called "old and cold" property, where debt is placed on the property over five years before the donation and the donor has owned the property for more than five years. The second is where the charity is bequeathed encumbered real estate.

Clearly, existing real estate debt is a big tax hurdle for nonprofits. The best strategies for addressing encumbered real property involve the help of the donor in either paying off or reassigning the security interest. The possibility of UBTI is certainly one of the thornier issues that charities face when investigating prospective gifts of real estate.

Review Part 2: Risk Scenarios and Assessment

Charitable organizations may be becoming more receptive to donations of real estate. This section lists different gifts involving real estate and the accompanying difficulty and level of risk to the accepting charity. It is intended only to be a general guide—the main take-away should be that charities need formal acceptance policies based on existing risk tolerance.

Easiest:
- Outright gift of local residential property, free of debt and with buyers readily identifiable

Easy:
- Outright gift of local commercial or agricultural property
- FLIP-CRUT gift of residential property

Medium:
- Gifts of partial interests
- Installment sales
- Real estate gifted to multiple charities
- Nonlocal property
- Real estate under contract for sale
- Real estate without an easily identifiable buyer

Hard:
- Multiple interests in the real estate
- Real estate located in a different country
- Multiple tenants in the property
- Real estate that would trigger UBTI (as discussed above)

Stay away:
- Real estate with existing environmental or legal issues
- Donation involving more than three layers of entities (i.e., real estate held by an LLC, owned in turn by a partnership)

Review Part 3: Challenges and Solutions

The section above illustrates the various possible gift structures, and the accompanying differences in level of complexity. Given that proposed gifts are often more than just a simple plot of land or a house, what are some commonly perceived challenges to accepting these gifts? Just as importantly, what are some possible solutions for those issues? This section breaks down perceived problems and suggests ways to effectively address them.

1. Real estate gifts are too time-consuming. An effective up-front screening procedure is necessary to avoid considerable time investment without a completed gift. A quick

information-gathering form or conversation can save time and effort by screening out high-risk gifts at the outset.

2. Tax and legal complexity. Identifying these issues is half the battle—investigate the property in more depth. A gift officer talking through the various possible problems with the donor is probably the best way to complete the due diligence. Based on the results, it may be necessary to engage outside counsel.

3. Environmental concerns. A notorious, but overblown, concern with donated real estate is environmental hazards or liabilities. The simple solution is to have a qualified professional perform an environmental assessment. Although this may cost the organization anywhere from $1,000 to $2,000, it is a necessary precaution. Also consider environmental liability insurance, if the policy is appropriate for nonprofits.

4. Management and holding period concerns. This is a "once bitten, twice shy" scenario for donee charities. Assessing potential gift acceptance problems is not enough—charities must consider the maintenance, management, and other holding costs. These post-closing issues need evaluation before gift acceptance, and the donee should develop a plan to address them. The charity, as the new owner, should expect to receive calls for maintenance issues from the tenants unless it hires a property manager.

5. Market and liquidity concerns. Similar to maintenance and management, market and liquidity issues appear for charities who already own the real estate, but can be avoided by thorough planning before closing. If a buyer is easily found, then there is no issue. Similarly, a real estate broker can assess the marketability and value of the property, so the nonprofit is not left holding an unsellable property. The donee organization must complete IRS Form 8282 if the property is sold or disposed of within three years of acquisition.

6. Internal acceptance processes. If the nonprofit has never considered accepting real estate gifts, it likely will have no framework for deciding whether or not to accept. Conversely, if it has a real estate acceptance program or policy, it is much more likely to successfully accept and liquidate donated real estate. Plans and people in place to assess the proposal and implement next steps are essential. Many, if not most, real estate opportunities require a timely response.

7. Benefit-cost analysis. All gifts come with a cost, and real estate—even the simplest transaction—is no exception. A minimum gift value helps establish a baseline on whether the proposed gift is worth the nonprofit's effort. It should develop a formula for estimating the cost and time versus the value of the gift. A simple multiplier may

work, or a calculation of net present value. Many minimums are in the $50,000 to $250,000 range.

8. Getting to closing on a complicated real estate gift. Once the donee organization evaluates a gift, and takes necessary precautions, what is left to do? If it wants to accept the gift, the parties should put everything in writing. The timeline, expectations, and responsibilities of everyone involved should be clearly stated in an acceptance letter or memorandum of understanding which all parties read and accept. Not only will this put everyone on the same page, but it can be used as a roadmap for completing the gift.

9. No one offers gifts of real estate. The best real estate gift policies and procedures are useless if a nonprofit gets no donation inquiries. To optimize the program, charities should emphasize their ability to receive real estate in communications to constituents and potential donors. Further, when researching donors, the organization should make special note of real estate holdings that show potential. Correspondingly, potential donors and their agents should make note of charities that advertise their acceptance of real estate gifts (including completed gifts with third-party charities).

Review Part 4: Direct and Indirect Gifts of Real Estate

There are various options for accepting other than a binary yes or no—transfer of ownership is not the only way to complete the gift. A small but not insignificant proportion of nonprofits utilize a supporting organization to receive the property. They can also employ more complex, risk-reducing legal strategies, such as creating a put option, utilizing an agent, or working through an LLC. Finally, the nonprofit can outsource the gift to another public charity which will liquidate the real estate within a donor-advised fund.

Sometimes use of different legal strategies or external organizations can be a more effective manner of completing a real estate gift. This is important when considering the goal of maximizing net contributions and minimizing risks and costs. Most importantly, this allows a charity to capture a gift (indirectly or by risk mitigated means), that it would otherwise decline in its traditional gift acceptance process.

Review Part 5: Current Gifts, Deferred Gifts, and Life Income

A current gift in this context means that the nonprofit donee will receive the donated land in the present, even if the gift is structured as a charitable lead trust. Lead trusts are often utilized as a way for those with very large estates to transfer their real estate assets to younger family members. However, donee nonprofits may not want property that does not generate any revenue.

Deferred gifts flip the script. These typically involve gifting real estate after the donor's death, and are commonly structured either as a bequest, transfer on death deed, or gift of a remainder interest in a personal residence or farm. In these cases, the donor retains lifetime use, and after transfer, the charity is free to use or sell the land as it sees fit.

Life income plans combine elements of current and deferred gifts. Often taking the form of either a charitable remainder trust or gift annuity, these involved the donor transferring the real estate to a nonprofit in exchange for a stream of income. Charitable gift annuities are contracts, while charitable remainder trusts are, as the name indicates, trusts (with either a percentage-based unitrust payment model, or an annuity payment model). In either variation, the charity will usually sell the land to meet its payment obligations, and the donor will receive an income tax deduction for the gift portion of the land (since the IRS treats the portion which is exchanged for the income stream as a "sale").

Conclusion

Real estate is certainly the most commonly-owned asset class discussed in this book, and yet is also relatively infrequently donated. Despite being a highly lucrative asset for nonprofits, many shy away from it due to perceived risks and complexity. Although there are certainly challenges (including aspects like UBTI, environmental problems, holding period and property management concerns, etc.), none of these are necessarily preclusive. Proper policies, assessment, and planning can avoid many of these issues from the outset. If those steps are taken, then real estate becomes a much less daunting type of gift for charities to accept.

Real Estate Advanced[1]

By Dennis Bidwell and Bryan Clontz

Below is an in-depth examination of gifts of real estate. Real estate topics are based on the following paper I co-authored with Dennis Bidwell, "Converting Real Estate Wealth to Gifts – Opportunities and Challenges." For quick take-aways on gifts of real estate, see Real Estate Quick Take-Aways. For a review based on that article, see Real Estate Intermediate. For an in-depth examination adapted and excerpted from the article, see Real Estate Advanced. For further details, see Real Estate Additional Resources or cross reference to the asset's ownership entity (e.g., LLC, Limited Partnerships, etc).

This section looks more closely at the magnitude of the real estate gift opportunity, reviews the types of real estate assets and the various structures through which they are owned, examines key issues and challenges faced by organizations that seek and accept real estate gifts, and reviews various mechanisms for receiving real estate gifts.

Real Estate: The Opportunities

The nonprofit world is increasingly aware that most donors have more of their wealth in real estate than in any other asset type. In fact, about 24 percent of the nation's private wealth (combining both household and nonprofit assets) is in real estate, compared to 23 percent for equities and mutual funds, 21 percent in pension funds and life insurance reserves, and just 9 percent in cash and equivalents.[2] Other data points which show the potential of real estate gifts are as follows:

- The total amount of U.S. privately-held real estate is approximately $25 trillion. Interestingly, nonprofit organizations own $3.3 trillion of real estate.[3] Worldwide, real estate represented 60 percent of the total wealth in 2015.[4]

- The total value of all U.S. publicly-traded stocks (NYSE, NASDAQ, etc.) is approximately $32 trillion.[5]

---

1. This chapter excerpts and adapts Bidwell, D. and Clontz, B. (2008) "Converting Real Estate Wealth to Gifts – Opportunities and Challenges," The Journal of Gift Planning, 3rd Quarter, http://charitablesolutionsllc.com/wp-content/uploads/2014/04/Converting_Real_Estate_Wealth_to_Gifts_Journal_of_Gift_Planning.pdf.
2. Federal Reserve, Balance Sheet of Households and Nonprofit Organizations, June 7, 2018, https://www.federalreserve.gov/releases/z1/20180607/html/b101.htm.
3. Id.
4. Savills, "World Real Estate Accounts for 60% of All Mainstream Assets," January 25, 2016, http://www.savills.com/_news/article/105347/198559-0/1/2016/world-real-estate-accounts-for-60--of-all-mainstream-assets.
5. See https://www.world-exchanges.org/home/index.php/statistics/annual-statistics.

- The IRS reported that for the 2014 tax year, real estate only represented 0.06 percent of the number of total noncash charitable donations and 4 percent of the value of all noncash charitable deductions. By comparison, corporate stock was over 48 percent of the value.[6]

- In 2004, total real estate gifts were $3.1 billion from more than 25,000 donors, with 36,000 distinct contributions and an average gift over $85,000 (the average was $172,000 for gifts exceeding $5,000). This represented slightly more than one percent of total 2004 giving. In 2003, approximately the same number of donors made contributions of real estate, but the total was nearly double, amounting to $6 billion in contributions (these amounts exclude conservation easements). Interestingly, closely held stock gifts were more than $15 billion in 2004, or five times all real estate donations in that year.[7]

Conservation Easements

A few words about conservation easements may be valuable. Generally speaking, only qualified conservation 501(c)(3) organizations - typically land trusts - and governmental bodies or agencies will accept "gifts" of conservation easements. These easements are essentially a donation by way of permanent restriction on the use of land or structures. They are an exception to the partial interest rule, where no deduction is available for gifts of less than an entire interest.

The owner(s) of the real property enter into a contract with the conservation organization agreeing to limit the use of the property in perpetuity (the easement). In doing so, the owner(s) bind themselves and all future owners to the use limitation specified in the easement contract. This can sharply limit the fair market value of the property, particularly if the limitation is on commercial development, and so the owner is entitled to a deduction equal to the decline in value. Further, the owner may exclude the property, up to a certain amount, from his or her estate for tax purposes.

Stated simply: These figures show that the total value of all privately-held real estate is approximately equal to that of the entire publicly-traded stock market, yet represents four percent of all charitable gifts. Why, if 24 percent of the nation's private assets are in real estate, has so little of this real estate come to nonprofits as gifts? Certainly much of the disparity between the amount of real estate wealth in the country and its share of total giving has to do with the backgrounds and comfort zones of development personnel. Real estate has traditionally loomed as a very different, more complicated, less liquid asset, requiring expertise gift officers often do not develop.

Real estate gifts often have risks and complications, and the classic real estate donation "horror stories" will reinforce those existing preconceptions. There can be no doubt that these stories, shared among colleagues at other institutions, help to perpetuate the belief that real estate gifts tend to be "more trouble than they are worth."

---

6. Liddell, P. and Wilson, J. (2017), "Individual Noncash Contributions, Tax Year 2014," Internal Revenue Service, https://www.irs.gov/pub/irs-soi/soi-a-innc-id1707.pdf.
7. See http://www.irs.gov/pub/irs-soi/04innoncash.pdf.

Real Estate

On the other hand, many institutions have stories (usually less well-circulated) of successful real estate gifts that proved extremely lucrative while being very satisfying to the donor. Many non-profit organizations have enjoyed great success in attracting real estate gifts as part of their development operations. Of 590 respondents to the National Committee on Planned Giving's recent Survey on Real Estate Gifts (NCPG Survey),[8] 74 (12.8 percent) reported that in the last three years more than 10 percent of the total gifts to their organization, in dollar terms, have come in the form of real estate gifts. Indeed, 38 respondents (6.6 percent) reported receiving more than 15 percent of their total contributions in the form of real estate gifts.

Real Estate Taxation Summary: From the Perspective of the Donor and the Charity

Real estate comes in many types, and each type has a number of ownership forms. The various real estate types and forms of ownership can create an array of tax consequences. For the purposes of this section, remember: if the most efficient charitable gift nearly always comes from the lowest adjusted cost basis, highest capital appreciation property held for the long-term, then real estate is clearly tailor-made for charitable giving.

If the owner sells real estate, the general real estate taxation rules are as follows:

1. The owner can receive long-term capital gains tax treatment on real estate held more than one year. Under current tax rates, this would generally equate to either 15 or 20 percent federal tax plus any applicable state income tax. To the extent the donor had a negative adjusted cost basis in the property, the IRS generally taxes any recapture at capital gains tax rates as well. Do note that it is particularly important to seek specific tax counsel for the gift the donor is considering.

2. If the owner has any unrecaptured depreciation Section 1250 gain in the property, the income tax rate is 25 percent.[9]

3. If the owner used an accelerated depreciation schedule, then the IRS generally taxes any recapture beyond straight-line depreciation amounts at ordinary income rates.[10]

---

8. See Bidwell, D. (October, 2008), "Charitable Gifts of Real Estate – Findings from a National Survey," *Journal of Gift Planning*, http://www.bidwelladvisors.com/wp-content/uploads/2009/07/Charitable-Gifts-of-Real-Estate-Findings-from-a-National-Survey-by-Dennis-Bidwell.pdf.
9. See Taxpayer Relief Act of 1997.
10. For an excellent discussion on the technical aspects of depreciation and charitable gifts, see "Real Estate Depreciation Issues for Charitable Contributions and Charitable Remainder Trusts" by Tom Wesley, CPA published on the Planned Giving Design Center - http://www.pgdc.com/pgdc/article/2002/02/real-estate-depreciation-issues-charitable-contributions-and-charitable-remainder-trusts

4. If the owner had furnished the property, the IRS would tax any gain on tangible personal property at 28 percent federal tax plus any applicable state income tax.

If the owner instead donates real estate, the general charitable income tax deduction rules instead are as follows:

1. Charitable gifts of long-term, unencumbered real estate to a qualified public charity allow the donor to receive a deduction of fair market value. The deduction is limited to 30 percent of adjusted gross income with a five-year carry-forward.

2. The same donor giving piece of real estate to a private foundation would receive a deduction based on the lesser of the fair market value or the adjusted cost basis. Regulations limit the deduction to 20 percent of adjusted gross income limitations with a five-year carry-forward. Note that real estate may be conducive to the testamentary funding of a private foundation to the extent the property receives a stepped-up basis, but there may still be liquidity issues as well as an annual valuation (both for the required payout).

3. Regulations reduce any charitable income tax deduction dollar for dollar for any ordinary income element of the gift.

4. If the real estate has any debt—recourse or nonrecourse—the donation will trigger bargain sale rules (as well as a sale to charity for below market value). This results in part-gift and part-sale treatment. To determine the indebtedness the donor realizes, the formula is: Cost Basis x Selling Price (Acquisition Indebtedness in this case)/Fair Market Value = Basis Allocation. Then Selling Price − Basis Allocation = Taxable Gain. The charitable income tax deduction is the Fair Market Value − Selling Price. For a complete explanation see IRC Section 1011(b).

From the charity's perspective, the main tax issue is unrelated business taxable income (UBTI), which gives rise to unrelated business income tax (UBIT). The charity can trigger this treatment if the real estate represents an unrelated business (e.g., a golf course), or if the property has debt financed income.

There are two exceptions to this UBTI rule. The first is debt financed income where the debt was placed on the property more than five years prior to the donation and the donor owned the property for at least five years. This is known as the "old and cold" exception. In this case, the charity has ten years to dispose of the property before it triggers any UBTI. The second exception is where the donor bequeaths encumbered property to the charity. The IRS allows ten years to dispose of the property before UBTI applies.

As it relates to charitable remainder trusts, keep in mind that any UBTI the trust realizes post-January 1, 2007 results in a 100 percent excise tax. While certainly harsh, it no longer automatically disqualifies the trust, so relatively small amounts of UBTI now represent new planning opportunities under the right set of facts.

Remember that there are a number of planning strategies to reduce or eliminate real estate debt for both outright or deferred gifts. The simplest solution is for the donor to pay off the debt. The donor can also try to arrange for a release of the security interest and then can place the debt on a different property. Or, the donor can obtain a bridge loan to pay off the debt, or a margin loan on a securities portfolio, prior to making the transfer. And finally, the charity can buy the debt encumbered proportional interest from the donor and then subsequently sell its interest to recoup the investment.[11]

Real Estate Risk Continuum

Charitable organizations are increasingly receptive to real estate gifts. In the NCPG Survey, 22 percent of respondents said they were more receptive to such gifts in recent years, compared to only four percent who said they were less receptive. However, the perceived risks and complexity of accepting real estate gifts causes many organizations to devote the bulk of their development resources to the pursuit of cash, securities and retirement fund assets.

What follows is a risk continuum for various kinds of real estate contributions. Clearly, each charity will have its own risk tolerance level with various real estate scenarios, but the continuum can be excellent starting point for gift acceptance discussions, policy drafts and risk management strategies. Donors will also find the continuum applies in terms of the real estate gift's potential headache. The following 20 real estate cases are subjectively ranked from 1, being the least complex/risky, to 5, the most complex/risky.

Level One

1. Outright gift of local residential property or LLC/limited partnership interests with no debt and a nonbinding "buyer-in-the-wings."

---

11. These strategies come from Charitable Business Planning – The Sole Proprietorship, Crescendo's Gift Law Pro Article of the Month.

Level Two

2. FLIP-CRUT gift of local residential property or LLC/limited partnership interests with no debt and a nonbinding "buyer-in-the-wings."

3. Outright gift of local commercial or agricultural property, or LLC/limited partnership interests with no debt and a nonbinding "buyer-in-the-wings."

Level Three

4. Outright gift of partial interest in undivided real estate.

5. Outright gift of nonlocal residential or commercial property (LLC/limited partnership/fee simple) with no debt and no "buyer-in-the-wings."

6. Any real estate transaction where donor wishes to make multiple donations to multiple charities.

7. Charitable gift annuity the donor funds with real estate.

8. Real estate charitable installment bargain sale.

9. Any residential or commercial property the owner has listed for sale for more than one year, or has listed several times for sale in the recent past, or has lowered the price several times.

Level Four

10. Operating partnership units from UPREIT exchange.

11. General partnership interests with real estate.

12. Any non-U.S. real estate.

13. Charitable gift annuity issued for retained life estate.

14. Commercial property with multiple tenants or apartment complexes.

15. Charitable remainder annuity trust fund with real estate.

16. Asset donation from a business entity with multiple owners.

Gifts of Timeshares

From a tax perspective, a timeshare is simply an undivided fractional interest in real estate. For this reason, the IRS allows the donor of a timeshare to take a charitable deduction of fair market value. This is one area where difficulty arises—the fair market value of a timeshare in an arms-length transaction is often de minimis.

Another problem with gifts of timeshares is that charities are typically unwilling to accept an asset with limited market value but considerable maintenance fees. Many nonprofits specifically exclude timeshares in their gift acceptance policies for this reason. A nonprofit may be happy to accept the use of a timeshare for a week (as an item in a charity auction, for example), but this is not an ownership interest, nor is it eligible for a deduction.

Plus, it is important to note that virtually no timeshare has ever increased in value so it is better for the donor to sell it directly.

Level Five

17. Any real estate donation that triggers unrelated business taxable income (UBTI)—operating business or acquisition indebtedness.

18. Any real estate donation with environmental issues.

19. Any real estate donation with legal issues.

20. Any real estate donation involving three or more layers of entities.

Of course, a charity can (and should) determine its own risk tolerance for various types of real estate and then can develop acceptance policies, legal structures, and referral relationships for anything the charity is uncomfortable accepting.

Real Estate: Challenges and Solutions

What holds these donations back? Below are a number of perceived challenges in accepting real estate gifts, and emerging best practices for addressing and overcoming them.

1. Real estate gifts are too time-consuming: Many charities commit a great deal of staff time and resources to exploring proposed real estate gifts, only to conclude after many months that they do not wish to accept the gift. This can be very off-putting to the donor prospect, and can reinforce the belief that real estate gifts just take too long.

   As a best practice, a charity should divide the real estate screening process into two stages, aiming for a balance between donor-friendliness and the very real need to gather extensive information. The first stage—designed to be minimally time-consuming for charity and donor, at least initially—aims at gathering enough essential information about the property and the prospect in order to render a relatively quick (one to two weeks) decision on whether to reject the gift out of hand or to begin intensive due diligence procedures. The donor can typically gather this data in one or two phone calls or personal visits, with a Real Estate Gift Data Sheet guiding the gift officer to collect essential information about the proposed gift.

   The charity should combine the basic information it collects with informal inquiries of local real estate brokers as to general market conditions for a property of the sort the donor proposes as a gift. That data is generally sufficient to render an initial Go/No Go decision, i.e., determining whether the proposed gift is worthy of further examination, or whether the donor should be told, before more of anyone's time is wasted, that this gift does not hold promise. Such an approach helps a charity devote its scarce staff and consultant resources to only promising gifts, and does not lead on prospective donors.

2. Tax and Legal Complexity: After the nonprofit's representatives decide to seriously consider the real estate gift—generally stopping far short at this stage of actually committing to accept—then the more labor-intensive (for donor prospect and charity) work of due diligence begins. At this time a detailed questionnaire will gather more extensive information about environmental issues, property operating costs, leases, etc. Even here, a gift officer should generally work with the prospect to complete the questionnaire and gather information, as opposed to mailing it and asking for its completion in two weeks. Donor friendliness at this stage can make all the difference in the world.

   Generally, most real estate gifts which nonprofits process are relatively straightforward. However, issues raised in the course of due diligence can be daunting: pre-arranged sales (Palmer/Blake/Ferguson cases);[12] unrelated business income tax;[13] concerns related to legal documents and agreements; self-dealing; private inurement; and excess benefit audits are among the potential obstacles. Generally, experienced internal staff along with both pro-bono and retained counsel can sufficiently navigate these issues.

   It is not uncommon for the donee organization to retain an attorney operating in the vicinity of the gift property to review existing deeds, mortgages (if any), and title work and to commission a title search. This same attorney may often handle the legal closing of the gift acceptance (recording of deeds, purchasing of title insurance, etc.) on the organization's behalf, and to render similar services upon resale of the property.

3. Environmental Concerns: Often most charities cite this as the primary reason they are uncomfortable with real estate, but this concern is typically overblown. Engaging an environmental appraiser to complete a Phase I environmental appraisal is usually a rather quick way to determine any issues.

   First, a representative of the charity should visit the land to conduct a site inspection.[14] Touring the property with the donor can be helpful to learn about the history of the land and any potential issues. As an example for farms in particular, disposal of fertilizer on an area of land over a prolonged period of time can result in the potential for environmental remediation or clean up. Furthermore, run-off of fertilizer can result in contamination of flowing or standing bodies of water.

---

12. For an excellent overview of prearranged sale issues, see "How Far is Too Far? The Prearranged Sale and the Palmer/Blake Conundrum" by Emanuel Kallina, II and Philip Temple - Planned Giving Design Center http://www.pgdc.com/pgdc/article/1999/07/how-far-too-far.
13. The treatise on UBTI is *The Tax Law of Unrelated Business for Nonprofits* by Bruce Hopkins, John Wiley & Sons (2005).
14. Thanks to Phil Purcell for the comments in this paragraph.

The Phase I environmental assessment should identify anything at all problematic with regard to environmental hazards. The assessment thoroughly reviews public fire and safety records, interviews existing and previous owners, and conducts a physical inspection of the property. In order for the charity to be in control of this important investigation, and to assure that a qualified environmental engineer or the equivalent conducts a quality review, it is important for the nonprofit to arrange for and pay for this service. This is a critical step in protecting the organization from exposure to environmental liability. The fees for a Phase I assessment (typically in the range of $1,000 to $2,000 for most properties) are dollars well spent in the interest of completing a gift with minimal risk. If a Phase I assessment suggests the need for further explorations in a Phase II assessment, donor and charity may elect to share the payment responsibility. It may be appropriate in some instances for the charity to delay commissioning the Phase I while awaiting other elements of the due diligence.

To ask the prospective donor to pay for a Phase I assessment can be quite off-putting, and does not make any more inherent sense than asking the donor prospect to pay for the organization's title insurance. Both services—environmental assessment and title insurance—protect the donee organization's balance sheet, and are thus appropriate financial obligations of the charity.

In some instances, the charity might purchase environmental liability insurance. However, the expense of such policies has generally limited their use to large commercial transactions, rather than charitable transactions. Such policies generally are in effect for a maximum of ten years (sometimes with renewal options), with a large premium payable up front.

4. Management and Holding Period Concerns: Internal management concerns are usually based on either risk or responsibility aversion. Frankly, too many development officers close gifts without involving the business office soon (or often) enough in the process. The business or finance department is usually responsible for organizational risk management, and if a gift goes bad, they can be blamed. The business office's memories of bad experiences are much longer than those of most development officers.

Development officers should also consider that property management work often means increased responsibilities in the "other duties as assigned" category for the business office. For example, it is critically important to know who is responsible for changing the property insurance, managing the landscaping, paying the water bill, renewing leases, paying the property tax, etc. Many business officers feel ill-equipped to perform these functions because of their lack of real estate knowledge, or a lack of staff time. And while there may be plenty of time during the summer, there may be less or no time available during audit season or year end.

5. Market and Liquidity Concerns: Most charities want to sell the property as soon as possible for the highest price possible. Hence, independent assessment of the marketability and value of the property is a critical component of due diligence. The donee organization should, at the very least, seek its own opinion of value and marketability from a qualified local broker or other real estate professional. This need not be a full-blown and fully documented (and expensive) real estate appraisal, since this is ultimately the responsibility of the donor. The charity can often obtain an opinion of value, and an informal report of how the subject property is positioned in relation to current market trends, for $500 to $1,000. This is an important and worthwhile expenditure, as the charity needs to make its own estimate of likely sales price and likely holding period prior to the time of sale. These are critical pieces of information leading to the ultimate decision as to whether to accept the gift property and, if so, subject to what terms and conditions.

6. Charity's Internal Process: While environmental concerns receive most of the attention, the reality is that the charity's internal acceptance process, if one even exists, is by far the biggest culprit in keeping a charity from receiving real estate gifts.

    The NCPG/PPP Survey provides solid evidence that the most successful real estate gift programs have in place clear policies and procedures regarding the acceptance of real estate gifts. The purpose of such policies and procedures is generally to establish what sorts of real estate assets and what sorts of real estate gift structures the institution will and will not accept. Further, they should clarify exactly who does what—gift planning office, treasurer's office, general counsel, outside counsel, real estate office—in moving a potential gift through the process.

    In addition to policies and procedures, many charities have created gift acceptance committees for any unusual gifts. Unfortunately, the charity usually populates these committees with knowledgeable, successful professionals who always seem to be on vacation whenever a new gift opportunity arises. Most charities find it very difficult to get a quorum within three to four weeks, and by that time donor relations can become strained. Further, many charities will have someone from both the development and the finance/business offices doing some of the internal due diligence to prepare the report for the gift acceptance committee. Having a single point person for this due diligence helps ease confusion about who is responsible for stewarding the gift.

7. Benefit-Cost Analysis: Even with the best legal counsel, the most comprehensive internal process and the cleanest gift possible, the charity should still decline some

gifts. The best example of this would be a very small parcel of property or a time-share. At some point, nearly every charity will accept one time-share (which is nothing more than a fractional ownership interest in real property). And then after putting in 100-plus hours on what was supposed to be an easy donation, the net proceeds check of $841.39 will eventually arrive. A quick approach to screening is the Pi rule: multiply how much internal work you think it will take and how long you think the property will be on the market and multiply by Pi, or 3.14.

A policy on gift minimums applying to various real estate gift structures is an important part of the Go/No Go analysis. One increasingly popular approach is to establish a gift minimum using an estimated net present value basis. This method projects the likely amount in current dollars, net of all estimated costs in assessing and closing the gift, and net of projected payments (life income payments or bargain purchase amount). This approach allows for one yardstick against which to measure outright gifts, life income gifts, retained life estates, bargain sales and the like. It allows for the complexity of a gift—as it projects in likely staff, legal, consulting and due diligence costs—to be accounted for when estimating the true value to the institution of the prospective gift. Such real estate gift minimums tend to run from $50,000 to $250,000.

8. How do we actually close a complicated real estate gift? Once the charity has completed its due diligence investigations, assessed the benefits and risks, and gathered other necessary information, officials at the nonprofit organization can make an informed decision on whether to accept the proposed gift. It is generally helpful to communicate this decision in a gift acceptance letter or memorandum of understanding.

   This letter or memorandum should detail any outstanding information or documents, describe the alternative gift structure that the parties may have agreed to, and outline the terms, conditions, and responsibilities of the various parties and their attorneys. Often, the charity will ask the donor to countersign this letter as acknowledgment of his/her understanding of the terms upon which the gift may proceed, and in order to manage the donor's expectations as to timetable and financial results of the gift. Sometimes, in more formal versions of such a document, the charity will include environmental indemnification language for the donor's review and signoff. This letter can also serve as a "roadmap" detailing how the various parties—donor's attorney, real estate broker, various staff and consultants at the nonprofit, nonprofit's local counsel—will coordinate with one another to get to the successful closing of the gift.

9. But no one ever calls us to suggest they give us a piece of real estate: No amount of internal procedures, thorough due diligence process and capacity to manage legal and

tax complexity will be of any use if no one is inquiring about real estate gifts. Though a charity may get some "cold" calls proposing real estate gifts, the institutions that report high level of such inquiries—and a high level of resulting gifts—are the ones that effectively communicate their interest in real estate donations. When discussing any major or planned gift with constituents, friends, or prospects, the charity should list real estate as a funding option. Any donor materials should also include the willingness to discuss real estate gifts in various forms. Donor research should include information about real estate holdings, so that the charity can initiate conversations with prospects who own multiple pieces of real estate and otherwise have the ingredients that make up a promising real estate gift prospect.

Real Estate: Capturing More Gifts Directly and Indirectly

When marketing for real estate gifts, too many charities think the only way to receive the gift is to accept it directly. If they choose to decline the gift, they get nothing and have a disappointed donor. What follows is a new approach to noncash gift acceptance involving four levels of what could be called acceptance triage. The objective is to receive as many gifts as possible, while limiting risk; retaining the maximum net proceeds and keeping the donor as happy as possible. Below are four approaches to real estate gift acceptance:

Option 1—This is the traditional method of accepting real estate. Donor brings property to charity; charity completes due diligence and accepts property. Charity is on the chain of title and attempts to sell the property for the highest price possible as soon as possible.

Option 2—From the NCPG Survey on Real Estate Gifts, approximately ten percent of the respondents had created separate corporations or trusts to receive real estate. Almost always, a supporting organization is the structure that those respondents employed.

Option 3—These are the various legal strategies to reduce risk. See "Minimizing Risk Through Alternative Structures for Charitable Gift of Real Estate" for more on these strategies.[15]

Option 4—There are numerous public charities that can receive real estate, sell it within a donor-advised fund, and then allow the donor to grant some or all of the net proceeds to the charity of his or her choice (subject to the charity's grant-making and donor-advised fund policies). So rather than declining a gift, or creating additional legal structures, community foundations and

---

15. See Kallina, E. (2008), "Minimizing Risk Through Alternative Structures for Charitable Gift of Real Estate," Journal of Gift Planning 14.

some national donor-advised funds can receive the property and take on all the aforementioned challenges directly. Generally, the total charitable fee these advised funds charge is between one and five percent of the proceeds. Since these organizations handle a large volume of real estate gifts, the charity can "outsource" many gifts that may be too complex, too risky or require a decision too quickly so that it still receives the gift proceeds of 95 to 99 percent indirectly.

As the charity uncovers real estate opportunities, it should consider the traditional straight acceptance as just one way to receive the gift. More often than not, three different real estate prospects might require three different "tiered" approaches of directly or indirectly receiving the gift. Remember, the goal is to maximize net real estate contributions while minimizing risks and internal direct/indirect costs. And perhaps most importantly, to stop declining gifts that otherwise could have been accepted.

Current Gifts[16]

A gift of an undivided interest in land is a percentage of every right the donor holds, for the entire term donor owns. This gift may decrease the overall fair market value of the remaining property given the split ownership. This type of gift qualifies for income, gift/estate tax deductions and escape of capital gains tax.[17] This type of gift plan is helpful where a gift of 100 percent of the land would exceed the donor's deduction limit. Rather, the gift can be spread over time.

Charitable lead trusts can be a valuable gift planning techniques for land and other property when the circumstances are right. Payments from a lead trust are made to one or more charities in either a unitrust or annuity trust format.[18] These trusts do not require a minimum payout percentage and may make payments for life or any term of years. At the end of the payment term, the remainder or residual may be paid to the donor (reversionary trust) or loved ones chosen by donor (nonreversionary). Inter vivos or lead trusts established during life offer no step-up in basis of the land received for heirs, whereas a testamentary lead trust permits a step up in basis when the heirs inherit the assets.

A key consideration for land donated to a charitable lead trust is to determine ahead of time whether the land will be sold with the cash funding the lead trust payments. If the trustee does not sell the land, with the intent that loved ones ultimately inherit the land from the lead trust, then it

---

16. The "Current Gifts," "Deferred Gifts," and "Life Income Plans" sections courtesy of Phil Purcell.
17. See IRC § 170(f)(3)(B)(ii) and § 2522(c)(2).
18. IRC §§ 2055(e)(2)(B) and 2522(c)(2)(B).

must produce income from leasing or agricultural production to fund the lead trust payments to charity. A qualified nongrantor lead annuity trust leverages attractive savings on gift and estate tax for the ultimate transfer to loved ones. On the other hand, a qualified grantor lead trust can generate a significant income tax deduction for high income years. The IRS provides sample forms, annotations and alternate provisions for inter vivos and testamentary grantor and nongrantor charitable lead annuity trusts and unitrusts.[19]

Deferred Gifts

Bequests in a will or revocable living trust are the most popular form of planned gift. These gifts are popular since they are usually revocable. Donors can specifically bequeath land to a charity by reference to its legal description or perhaps a mailing address. Of course, prior to acceptance upon the death of the donor, the charity must conduct due diligence pursuant to its policies and procedures as explained above. An alternative to a bequest in a will or trust is a transfer on death (TOD) or pay on death (POD) deed that may be allowed pursuant to applicable state law.

Another type of deferred gift of land is the irrevocable gift of a remainder interest in a personal residence or farm with a life estate retained by the donor. The donor retains a life estate and donates the remainder interest. This technique is available for a principal residence, vacation home, condominium, co-operative. The gift can include fixtures but not equipment, furnishings, or crops. When calculating the present value of the remainder interest for the charitable deduction, the donor discounts the value to reflect depreciation and factors in a salvage value.[20]

This technique is particularly helpful where the donor wants to use the property for life but charity wants to ultimately use the property or sell value property to fund its programs. As Adjusted Federal Rate (AFR) decreases, the income tax charitable deduction value increases for this technique. The donor and charity must sign an agreement stipulating respective rights and responsibilities relative to property tax, insurance, and maintenance. It must also address the potential for subsequent leases, sales, or gift of the donor's remaining life estate interest.

Life Income Plans

Charitable remainder trusts and charitable gift annuities may both be considered for gifts of land.

---

19. Rev. Proc. 2007-45 and 2007-46; Rev. Proc. 2008-45 and 2008-46.
20. IRC § 170(f)(3)(B).

Real Estate

A charitable gift annuity is a contract between the donor and the charity. The donor contributes assets such as land and the charity provides fixed and guaranteed income for one or two lives per the terms of the contract. The American Council on Gift Annuities recommends payout rates of return which leave an average 50 percent ultimate residual for the charity.[21] If land is donated, then either the charity may sell the land to fund the annuity or it may draw from its budget or endowment to fund the annuity payments. A deferred payment gift annuity can permit time for the charity to sell the land to fund the annuity as well. An income tax deduction subject to the 30 percent of AGI limit is available for long-term property. Capital gain is ratably spread over life expectancy if the donor is the annuitant.[22] If donor is not the annuitant, a portion of the capital gains tax is owed immediately. The balance of payments is taxed as a combination of ordinary taxable income and tax-free return of principal.

Charitable remainder trusts are tax-exempt trusts that allow the donation of highly appreciated property, such as land, that the trustee may then sell without payment of capital gains tax. The cash proceeds can then be invested in a diversified and personalized portfolio to earn income for the named beneficiaries. The trust can either pay a unitrust or annuity trust format. An annuity trust pays a fixed dollar amount determined by multiplication of the stated fixed percentage (5 percent or more) by the value of assets donated to trust. No additional gifts are allowed. If the donor gives real estate to an annuity trust either it must produce income to satisfy the fixed payment amount or the land must be sold to invest the cash to fund the annuity payments.

The unitrust format pays a fixed percentage (at least five percent) of the trust value, paying from income and principal (standard unitrust) or paying from the lesser of the fixed percentage amount or net income (net income unitrust or net income with make-up unitrust). The net income format is attractive for gifts of land since this allows time to sell the land to fund the payment obligation. However, the standard unitrust format is popular as it allows for maximizing income payments over time through a total return investment strategy. As a result, a popular option for gifts of land is the flip unitrust. This trust "flips" from a net income type unitrust to a standard unitrust after the land sells. The qualified appraisal when the property is donated to the trust determines the value of the donor's income tax deduction. However, since the trust is a net income type, no income need be paid until the trust sells the land and receives cash. Once it reinvests the sale proceeds, the trust "flips" and now is a standard unitrust paying a fixed percentage from income and principal.[23]

---

21. IRC § 170(f)(3)(B).
22. See American Council on Gift Annuities at www.acga-web.org.
23. Reg. § 1.664-3(a)(1)(i)(c).

All charitable remainder trusts require the calculated income tax deduction to be at least ten percent of the value of the donated assets at the time of transfer to the trust. Annuity trusts require an additional test that the potential of exhaustion of the trust be five percent or less. The IRS provides sample "safe harbor" charitable remainder unitrust and annuity trust documents, including the flip provision.[24]

Conclusion

Given the enormous wealth in the private real estate market, and the fact that real estate can be the ideal asset from a charitable income tax perspective, clearly it should represent a much greater share than two to three percent of total contributions. Most importantly, if charities confidently market real estate gifts and "shake the proverbial tree," they can handle almost any kind of "fruit" that falls directly or indirectly using a multitude of risk management strategies. In the end, the donor will be happy from both a giving and a tax perspective and the charity will receive more and larger contributions because of a sound real estate marketing/acceptance program designed on their unique risk tolerance.

---

24. Rev. Proc. 2003-54 to 60; Rev. Proc. 2005-52 to 59.

25 Questions for Gifts of International Real Estate[25]

Sometimes a donor will approach a charity with a potential real estate gift that is located outside of the United States. Thankfully, this detail is usually one of the first things mentioned about the property. But what other questions should the charity ask to determine if the proposed donation is a good fit, or even possible?

In addition to the normal questions any charity asks as part of its standard real estate due diligence, it should be sure to ask the questions below. This is a brief overview, and charities should investigate and request further details from donors as necessary. It may be wise to consult with legal experts both in the United States and abroad.

Basic Questions

1. Where, specifically, is the property located?
2. If there is a language barrier, how will the charity manage that?
3. What is the address of the property?
4. Where does the donor reside?
5. How long has the donor owned the property?
6. Is the property occupied?

Legal and Tax Questions

7. Can U.S. entities legally own real estate in the foreign country? If so, is there tax the U.S. entity must pay the foreign country to transfer the proceeds of the sale to the U.S.?
8. How is the property currently owned? If the property is owned by a foreign entity can a U.S. entity own the stock or other ownership right in that entity?
9. Does the donor have an attorney in the foreign country? Can that attorney assist with the donation and sale? Does the attorney speak English and is he or she familiar with real estate transactions and foreign ownership of real estate?
10. How would the charity own the property?
11. Would the charity need to register with a foreign government body or agency? If so, what information would it need to provide and what would be the cost?
12. Would it need to form a new entity (such as a single-member LLC or local equivalent)? If so, what is the process and cost?

---

25. Thanks to Gary Snerson for his comments and feedback on this section.

13. What are the tax implications of accepting the property? Are there transfer taxes? What are the property taxes?

14. Will the donor be able to find a qualified appraiser who can complete the IRS Form 8283? If the appraiser cannot sign the 8283, is the appraiser recognized by a qualified U.S. appraiser who will review and certify that the appraisal is sufficiently qualified for the U.S. appraiser to sign the 8283?

Holding and Management Questions

15. Does the donor have a property manager?
16. Is there a local contact who can coordinate access, inspections, and repairs as necessary?
17. Does the donor have a preferred realtor who can list the property?
18. What are market conditions like for property of this type?
19. Will insurance be necessary and how will it be obtained?
20. What property maintenance, if any, is required?
21. How will foreign expenses be paid?

Sale Questions

22. How will the charity transfer/deed the property to the (presumably foreign) buyer?
23. What is the escrow and title process like in this country?
24. How will the funds be transferred back to the charity?
25. How will any post-closing bills and taxes be paid?

Real Estate Additional Resources

Below are further details on gifts of real estate. Real estate topics are based on the following paper I co-authored with Dennis Bidwell, "Converting Real Estate Wealth to Gifts – Opportunities and Challenges." For quick take-aways on gifts of real estate, see Real Estate Quick Take-Aways. For a review based on that article, see Real Estate Intermediate. For an in-depth examination adapted and excerpted from the article, see Real Estate Advanced. For further details, see Real Estate Additional Resources or cross reference to the asset's ownership entity (e.g., LLC, Limited Partnerships, etc.).

For a technical analysis of real estate donation transactions, see Newman, D.W. (September 30, 2015), "Charitable Gifts of Real Property," Planned Giving Design Center, http://www.pgdc.com/pgdc/charitable-gifts-real-property.

For a discussion of real estate gift administration (particularly trusts), see Prosser, T. (October 15, 2014), "Are You Prepared for the Recovery in Real Estate Gifts?," *Partnership for Philanthropic Planning*, http://my.pppnet.org/library/92847/1/Prosser_FINAL.pdf.

For results and analysis of a survey on this topic, see Bidwell, D. (October, 2008), "Charitable Gifts of Real Estate – Findings from a National Survey," *Journal of Gift Planning*, http://my.pppnet.org/library/000/000/2c/s3.pdf.

For a gift acceptance policy with a particular emphasis on gifts of real property, see New York Agricultural Land Trust (October 22, 2009), "Policy on Gifts, including the Receipt, Ownership, Sale and Transfer of Marketable Assets," http://www.nyalt.org/NYALT%20Gift%20Acceptance%20Policy-APPROVED-10-22-09.pdf.

For IRS discussion on conservation easements, see *Conservation Easement Audit Techniques Guide* (January 3, 2012), https://www.irs.gov/businesses/small-businesses-self-employed/conservation-easement-audit-techniques-guide#_Toc124.

IRC §§ 170(f)(3), 170(h) (partial interests gifts and qualified conservation contributions)

IRC § 514 (debt-financed property)

Rev. Rul. 79-326, 1979-2 C.B. 206 (installment method bargain sale of real property to charity)

Charitable Gifts of Noncash Assets

Rev. Rul. 85-99, 1985-2 C.B. 83 (valuation in light of restriction on use)

Internal Revenue Manual 4.48.6 (July 1, 2006), "IRS Real Property Valuation Guidelines" (IRS policy on land valuation)

Ivey v. Comm'r, TC Memo, 1983-273 (combined value of multiple real estate gifts)

Douglas v. Comm'r, TC Memo, 1989-592 (timing of transfer for deduction purposes)

Irby v. Comm'r, TC Memo, 139 T.C. 14 (2012) (real estate donation case involving bargain sale, conservation easement, appraisal, and substantiation issues)

Chapter 2

C Corporations

- Quick Take-Aways
- Intermediate
- Advanced
- Additional Resources

C Corporations Quick Take-Aways

Below are quick take-aways on gifts of C corporations. C corporation topics are based on Turney Berry and Jeffrey Thede's "Giving the Business to Charity: Charitable Planning with Closely Held Businesses," and Turney Berry's "Charitable Planning with Closely Held Businesses." For quick take-aways on C corporation gifts, see C Corporations Quick Take-Aways. For a review based on the articles, see C Corporations Intermediate. For an in-depth examination adapted and excerpted from the articles, see C Corporations Advanced. For further details, see C Corporations Additional Resources.

Compared to gifts of other types of business entities, donations of C corporation stock are relatively simple. Distinguishing features are liability insulation, double taxation, and no unrelated business taxable income issues. Below is an overview of the essential advantages, disadvantages, factors to consider, and questions to ask.

Advantages of donations of C corporation shares include:

- The C corporation will often buy back the donated stock from the nonprofit (the so-called "charitable bailout" or "charitable redemption").
- Stock can be donated before an employee or outside investor purchase, merger or acquisition, or initial public offering (IPO).
- The stock can fund outright donations as well as planned giving vehicles like flip charitable remainder unitrusts.
- Closely held C corporations may donate business assets directly.
- Redemptions in exchange for promissory notes often include guaranteed interest income.

Disadvantages of donating C corporation shares include:

- Self-dealing rules are complex, and often come up where private foundations or charitable remainder trusts are part of the transaction.
- Prearranged redemptions may attract audits—nonprofits cannot be obligated to surrender shares.
- For gifts during mergers, assignment of income rules may prevent an effective donation.
- C corporation stock may not be a good funding asset for charitable gift annuities, charitable lead trusts, or charitable remainder annuity trusts unless there is a quick liquidation or there are large consistent dividends.

Wrinkles in the process to consider include:

- Generally, the more entities and transactions involved, the hazier the overall tax situation.
- The C corporation can donate appreciated assets without recognizing gain (though this becomes a de facto donation from each shareholder proportionally), but not if the assets comprise "all or substantially all" of the business.
- If the donation involves stock (or assets) held in charitable lead trusts, the grantor may be able to restructure the trust's terms, but the nonprofit cannot be paid less than it is owed.
- Charities are subject to the Shareholders Agreement as well as potential representations and warranties to investors or company acquiring the stock.

Discovery Questions

Donor Questions

1. What is the donor trying to accomplish with the gift?
2. What is the value of the stock and how was that determined (e.g., appraisal, 409A valuation, recent transactions)?
3. What is the total percentage of stock that the donor owns when combined with all related entities (probing if the excess business holding issue will apply)?
4. Legally, who or what owns the shares?

Advisor Questions

1. What is the current tax basis per share?
2. Do the governing documents allow charitable transfers, and if so, what is the process?
3. What is the likely exit plan for the charity (e.g., will sale be for cash, note, stock or some combination)?
4. Does the advisor have an estimate of what a qualified appraisal will cost (this expense can vary greatly and can be an impediment to smaller donations)?
5. If a corporate asset donation is being explored, would the size trigger the "substantially all" liquidation tax?
6. Are there any self-dealing issues with a donation to a charitable remainder trust, private foundation, or donor-advised fund?

Charity Questions

1. Is the effort worth the expected benefits (i.e., is the juice worth the squeeze)?
2. Has the screening and due diligence process identified any potential problems and can the risks be mitigated (primarily this will occur in the Shareholders Agreement or reps and warranties)?
3. Is there the necessary expertise to accept gifts of private stock in a timely way?
4. Should indirect gift acceptance be considered, like using external third party foundations or supporting organizations to receive the asset?
5. Is there a clear liquidation plan to maximize the sales proceeds as soon as possible?

C Corporations Intermediate

By Ryan Raffin

Below is a review on gifts of C corporations. C corporation topics are based on Turney Berry and Jeffrey Thede's "Giving the Business to Charity: Charitable Planning with Closely Held Businesses," and Turney Berry's "Charitable Planning with Closely Held Businesses." For quick take-aways on C corporation gifts, see C Corporations Quick Take-Aways. For a review based on the articles, see C Corporations Intermediate. For an in-depth examination adapted and excerpted from the articles, see C Corporations Advanced. For further details, see C Corporations Additional Resources.

This review of charitable gifts of C corporation stock has seven parts, and begins with an overview of C corporation donations and the charitable bailout or redemption generally. Next, it turns to transfer considerations, then prearranged redemptions and assignment of income issues. Following this is an examination of redemption for a promissory note. A discussion of gifts by the C corporation itself is the sixth part, and the review concludes with a look at charitable lead trusts.

C corporation stock is a relatively simple type of asset to donate when compared to other business entity interests. Unlike partnership interests, LLCs, or S corporation stock, there are no questions of liability or UBTI. Another distinction is that the C corporation is taxed at the entity level—meaning no pass-through of income. Despite that disadvantage, the relatively straightforward donation process makes C corporation stock an appealing gift.

Review Part 1: C Corporation Donations Overview

C corporation stock that produces significant dividends or is highly appreciated can lead to a significant tax bill for owners. As a result, owners of closely held C corporations may donate stock to avoid taxes and receive an income tax deduction. Nonprofits are typically happy to accept these gifts if there is an upcoming dividend or it can easily find a buyer.

From the donee's perspective, it typically wants to avoid holding the stock for an extended period. The potential buyers are often limited to the corporation itself, a business acquiring the corporation, and other shareholders. This is both because there is a limited market for closely held shares on the open market, and because these donations often occur in the larger context of some business transition for the corporation.

Review Part 2: The Charitable Bailout

Most gifts of C corporation stock are structured as "charitable bailouts." This transaction is where the donor gives the stock to the nonprofit, and the corporation proceeds to redeem the stock, leaving the nonprofit with cash in hand, the donor happy with the gift, and the corporation having made a tax-free redemption. The income tax benefits are the driving factor for the gift structure, but can also result in a gift-tax-free shift of ownership and control of a closely held corporation as part of a succession plan.

With a charitable bailout, both the gift and the redemption are tax-free, and the corporation can dispose of some accumulated cash. If the gift is made to a private foundation or charitable remainder trust, the redemption will be considered self-dealing unless it complies with the corporate adjustment exception. That exception requires a redemption offer at fair market value for all shareholders. Gifts made to donor-advised funds generally follow a similar path, using an independent appraisal process, to ensure the sale to a related or disqualified party is at fair market value.

Review Part 3: Transfer Considerations

As with other closely held businesses, it can be complicated to transfer ownership interests. Nonprofit donees should review governing documents to understand any restrictions on transfer (both on gift acceptance and on sale). They should also examine any possible liabilities—representations and warranties particularly. Donors should be aware that standard appraisal and substantiation requirements apply, but that lack of marketability and minority interest discounts may reduce the gift's value.

Review Part 4: Prearranged Redemptions and Assignment of Income Issues

Donors often make charitable gifts, including those of C corporation stock, to obtain a tax advantage for an upcoming event or transaction. However, this can cause timing problems—sometimes it is too late to avoid realizing capital gains by giving the stock away. The assignment of income doctrine states that taxpayers who earn or create a right to receive income are taxed on that income, if the receipt of income is practically certain to occur. This is true even if the taxpayer transfers the right to the income before receiving any of it.

Also significant is prearranging the redemption. A closely held business redeeming stock from a donor-stockholder's private foundation may get special IRS scrutiny. Initially the Service said that in such circumstances, the proceeds of stock redemption are taxable income to the donor when the donee nonprofit is legally bound or compelled to surrender shares for redemption.

However, this "bright line" rule became increasingly hazy with time. For example, a case where the charity's proceeds from redemption were used to buy the donor's yacht at an inflated price was held to be essentially a donor's sale of stock and subsequent donation of the yacht. The quid pro quo of the yacht purchase in exchange for the donation-then-redemption may be a key distinction here. After a series of court decisions, a general rule for corporate stock bailouts emerged. If there is a binding agreement, or some quid pro quo transaction, and the donee nonprofit is obliged to sell the shares back, the IRS will characterize the transaction as a taxable sale and donation of the proceeds.

Review Part 5: Redemption for a Promissory Note

Another common feature of these donations is redemption of stock in exchange for a promissory note from the C corporation. In the case of redemption from a private foundation or charitable remainder trust, the specter of self-dealing can arise if it is considered a loan from a private foundation to a disqualified corporate entity. Although the Service initially approved such a redemption under the corporate adjustment exception, it later reversed course. It is important to note that the self-dealing issues do not apply for direct gifts to public charities.

A redemption in exchange for a promissory note would be allowed, if approved, under the probate exception. That exception allows a private foundation's interest in property held by a decedent's estate or revocable trust (the note here) if certain criteria are met, including but not limited to trustee's control over the property, sale price, and probate court approval.

Another way to avoid impermissible self-dealing is by using an LLC to hold the note. The IRS has approved this use in recent rulings. The LLC is structured so that there are nonvoting units which are distributed to the foundation or charitable trust. This allows the foundation or trust to receive the proceeds of the note, but avoids self-dealing due to the lack of control.

Review Part 6: Gifts By the C Corporation

In some cases, it is better to consider gifts of C corporation assets, if the closely held corporation is holding highly-appreciated, nonproductive property. This can be either an outright gift, or to a charitable remainder trust (which C corporations may establish). However, unlike individuals, C corporations can only deduct charitable contributions up to ten percent of taxable income.

As a cautionary note, donations of "all or substantially all" corporate assets to a tax-exempt entity or charitable remainder trust require the donating corporation to recognize gain on those assets. This determination largely depends on the circumstances, including factors such as percentage of assets transferred, types of assets retained, and purpose of remaining assets, among others. The test seems to be whether the corporation can continue its business following the donation. If the C corporation chooses to create a charitable remainder trust for the appreciated assets it donates, those assets may later be sold without recognition of gain.

Review Part 7: Charitable Lead Trusts

A charitable lead trust can hold C corporation stock, which can work very well. Since the lead distributions are made to the designated nonprofit, the CLT can deduct income in those amounts, avoiding double taxation. Further, CLTs can be used to minimize transfer and estate taxes when shifting wealth to younger generations in wealthy families. The CLT can also direct its distributions to a family-controlled foundation or donor-advised fund if the donors so desire.

The IRS heavily taxes charitable trusts with excess business holdings, meaning disqualified persons own a fifth or more of the voting stock and the CLT owns more than 2 percent. The CLT has five years within which to dispose of excess holdings. Self-dealing taxes and taxable expenditure rules still apply, but the CLT can avoid taxes on excess business holdings if the value of the income interest is 60 percent or less of the initial value of the entire trust property.

Since CLTs often run for decades, changes to the business or family naturally may occur. The IRS has allowed modification of CLT terms in some cases, where there is no disadvantage to the nonprofit donee. Instead, when the underlying CLT assets have appreciated unexpectedly, the excess can be used to make all distributions early, or to restructure the agreement.

C Corporations Advanced

By Turney Berry and Jeffrey Thede

Below is an in-depth examination on gifts of C corporations. C corporation topics are based on Turney Berry and Jeffrey Thede's "Giving the Business to Charity: Charitable Planning with Closely Held Businesses," and Turney Berry's "Charitable Planning with Closely Held Businesses." For quick take-aways on C corporation gifts, see C Corporations Quick Take-Aways. For a review based on the articles, see C Corporations Intermediate. For an in-depth examination adapted and excerpted from the articles, see C Corporations Advanced. For further details, see C Corporations Additional Resources.

Unlike charitable gifts of partnership or LLC interests or S corporation stock, gifts of C corporation stock generally are straightforward and do not involve the phantom income, unrelated business income, and donee liability problems discussed in other chapters.

Overview of C Corporation Donations

A successful, closely held C corporation can lead to a significant tax bill for either dividend-receiving owners, or the C corporation subject to the accumulated earnings tax. C corporations do not receive pass-through tax treatment (like a partnership would, for example), so owners are taxed on dividend income they receive from the business. Similarly, an owner facing the sale or transfer of a C corporation would be subject to capital gains tax on appreciated corporate stock. In either case, the owner may be able to avoid that tax burden by donating some or all of his or her stock.

Donating stock in a closely held C corporation is appealing in many cases because it achieves charitable objectives while improving the donor's tax position. Not only are capital gains or dividend taxes avoided, donations of stock held for over one year to public charities may be eligible for income tax deductions for the fair market value of the stock. Public charities like these donations when there are either dividends to be paid, or an easily-arranged sale of the donated stock.

The owners of the C corporation (including the donor) typically will not want a charitable organization influencing business affairs, and charities similarly do not want to get involved in such a business—particularly when the corporation produces little dividend income. Therefore all parties involved in the transaction are typically eager to minimize the holding period.

In the case where the nonprofit sells the donated stock, there are usually only a few possible buyers. This is because it is often difficult to find a buyer for closely held stock on the open market. Instead, the buyers are typically limited to the corporation itself (a corporate redemption), an acquirer in a merger or acquisition, or a new/existing shareholder. The new or existing shareholder may be a family member—this is one way the C corporation donation can be part of a family business succession plan.

Charitable Bailout

In any case, since the corporation is closely held, the donors are likely to be in a good position to ensure that the donated stock is purchased, so that the donee receives cash it can use for its charitable purposes. Since the nonprofit is tax-exempt, it will not typically be subject to capital gains tax. If the corporation is redeeming the shares (a charitable bailout), it allows a tax-free distribution of excess cash the corporation has accumulated.

The bailout is another way to put succession plans into effect. If the donor's successors (often children) already owned some interest in the business, the corporate redemption will increase their proportionate holding in the business. This transfer is achieved free of any transfer taxes (gift or estate).

This charitable bailout means that both the charitable gift and the subsequent redemption would be completely income tax free, and the corporation would be able to "bail out" its accumulated cash. In the case of gifts to a private foundation or charitable remainder trust, the redemption must comply with the "corporate adjustment" exception to the self-dealing rules. That exception requires that 1) the corporation offers the redemption to all shareholders on the same terms, 2) the offer is a "bona fide offer," and 3) redemption price is not less than fair market value.

Transfer Considerations

There are some relevant transfer factors for both the donor and nonprofit donee alike once the planning is complete. The nonprofit should review corporate governing documents, particularly shareholders' agreements, to understand any restrictions or approvals on both the initial donation and the charity's eventual sale of the stock. If the nonprofit's holdings in the company will be part of a sale to or merger with a third party, it may be required to make representations and warranties, potentially exposing itself to liability. For this reason, it might seek indemnification from the donor.

For the donor, there are the same appraisal and substantiation requirements as with other asset types. As mentioned above, the lack of marketability may reduce the value of the gift. Further, minority interests are usually discounted as well. These valuation discounts will affect the donor and the selling nonprofit.

Prearranged Redemptions and Assignment of Income Issues

As discussed above, upcoming taxable events often prompt charitable gifts. For example, an owner in the process of selling a business may wish to make a gift of stock to charity to (a) obtain a charitable income tax deduction to offset income the sale generates, and (b) avoid the capital gain income that the owner would have realized as taxable income if he or she still held the stock at the time of the sale. The latter objective frequently triggers issues in connection with timing. Similar issues also arise frequently with gifts of real estate or other assets. The question is, at what point in the sale process is it too late for the donor to avoid the realization of capital gain income by giving the asset to charity?

Under the anticipatory assignment of income doctrine, the IRS will tax a taxpayer who earns or otherwise creates a right to receive income on any gain he or she realizes from that right if, based on the realities and substance of events, the receipt of income is practically certain to occur, even if the taxpayer transfers the right before receiving the income. The related step transaction doctrine similarly prevents a taxpayer from escaping taxation by collapsing a series of substantially linked steps into a single overall transaction.

After a series of court decisions, a general rule for corporate stock bailouts emerged. If there is a binding agreement, or some quid pro quo transaction, and the donee nonprofit is obliged to sell the shares back, the IRS will characterize the transaction as a taxable sale and donation of the proceeds. Courts have repeatedly looked to whether the nonprofit has a binding obligation to sell—this is the "bright line" rule of Palmer v. Commissioner and Rev. Rul. 78-197. Although the IRS has, at times, attempted to collapse all transaction steps into a single donor sale, courts have sided with taxpayers and insisted that the presence of a redemption obligation remains the test.

Redemption for a Promissory Note

Redemptions from a public charity may be for cash or in exchange for the corporation's promissory note. In the case of redemption from a private foundation or charitable remainder trust, a continuing question is whether and under what circumstances the redemption can be for a note, because loans from a private foundation to a corporate disqualified person are impermissible self-dealing. Private Letter Ruling 9347035 approved an installment redemption under the corporate adjustment exception to self-dealing. However, several years later, the Service revoked that ruling in Private Letter Ruling 9731034. The answer thus appears to be a resounding "no."

It is clear that a redemption in exchange for a promissory note of a disqualified person is permissible if a court approves as part of the probate exception. The probate exception states that a transaction relating to a foundation's interest in property, which an estate holds (or a revocable trust becoming irrevocable upon a grantor's death), is permissible if the following applies:

- The personal representative or trustee either
    - has a power of sale with respect to the property,
    - has the power to reallocate the property to another beneficiary, or
    - is required to sell the property under the terms of any option subject to which the estate or trust acquired the property
- Such transaction is approved by the court having jurisdiction over the estate or trust (or the foundation).
- Such transaction occurs before the IRS considers the estate terminated for federal income tax purposes, under the rules of Treasury Regulation section 1.641(b)-3 (or in the case of a revocable trust, before it is considered subject to IRC section 4947).
- The estate or trust receives an amount that equals or exceeds the fair market value of the foundation's interest or expectancy in such property at the time of the transaction, taking into account the terms of any option subject to which the estate (or trust) acquired the property.
- The transaction either
    - results in the foundation receiving an interest or expectancy at least as liquid as the one it gave up,
    - results in the foundation receiving an asset related to the active carrying out of its exempt purposes, or
    - is required under the terms of any option which is binding on the estate (or trust)

Many private letter rulings approved redemption for a note, but without comment on whether subsequent note payments similarly would not be self-dealing. The answer should be that payments are permissible, and certainly that result is within the spirit of the rulings.

There are rulings approving the distribution of an existing note under the probate exception. In Private Letter Ruling 200729043, for example, a decedent's revocable trust received notes of a disqualified person upon liquidation of a corporation. The trustee proposed allocating the notes to the share of a private foundation. The Service ruled that the private foundation's receipt of the notes would not be an act of self-dealing. None of these rulings involved a redemption or other "transaction" in the estate or trust that would be part of the probate exception, but instead merely addressed a discretionary allocation of an existing note. For that reason, some planners take little comfort from them, and particularly in light of the recent rulings approving the use of an LLC to receive and hold notes of a disqualified person.

Gifts by the Corporation

Although most of the focus is on charitable gifts of interests in closely held businesses, sometimes it makes sense to consider a charitable contribution by the business entity. This can be a particularly effective strategy for gifts of highly-appreciated, underproductive assets, whether outright to a charitable organization, or to a term-of-years charitable remainder trust for the benefit of the business entity. Based on the very broad definition of "person" contained in IRC section 7701(a)(1), the Service has ruled that C corporations, S corporations, or partnerships may establish charitable remainder trusts of this nature.

Unlike individual taxpayers, C corporation contributions are deductible up to only ten percent of the corporation's taxable income, which they must compute without regard to certain special deductions for corporations (under IRC sections 241, 243-247, and 249), any net operating loss carrybacks (under section 172), and any capital loss carrybacks (under section 1212(a)(1)).

Corporations making large charitable contributions must be careful not to violate the "new" regulations under IRC section 337, which continue the repeal of the General Utilities doctrine. The new regulations were generally effective as to transfers of assets occurring after January 28, 1999. Under these regulations, a taxable corporation is legally required to recognize gain or loss upon the transfer of "all or substantially all of its assets to one or more tax-exempt entities." With certain exceptions, the rule also applies in the event of "a taxable corporation's change in status to a tax-exempt entity." It specifically applies to transfers both to tax-exempt organizations and charitable remainder trusts.

The determination of whether a corporation has transferred "substantially all" its assets looks to all the facts and circumstances under the general rules of IRC section 368(a)(1)(C). The Courts generally have considered a variety of factors in determining whether a corporation has transferred substantially all of its assets. These include the corporation's percentage of assets transferred, the types of assets retained, the purpose for the retention of assets, and the liabilities of the corporation prior to the transfer.

A business entity's creation of a charitable remainder trust can enable sale of contributed appreciated assets with no capital gains cost. An illustrative ruling is Private Letter Ruling 200644013. In that ruling, an S corporation proposed to contribute appreciated real property to a 20-year term charitable remainder unitrust. The Service ruled that there would be no built-in gain recognition upon either the contribution to the trust or the trust's sale of the property within the 10-year recognition period.

Contributions to Charitable Lead Trusts

A charitable lead trust (CLT) can be set up with C corporation stock as its underlying assets. The CLT will need to pay tax on any income it received, even if that income is not distributed. For closely held businesses, the double taxation at both entity and CLT levels is noteworthy. However, the IRS allows an income tax deduction on amounts the CLT then distributed to nonprofits.

Families with significant wealth may consider using charitable lead trusts to minimize transfer taxes as that wealth shifts to younger generations. When that wealth derives from C corporation holdings expected to appreciate in value, the family can structure the lead trust in such a way as to reduce estate taxes. Further, the CLT can direct distributions to a family foundation for additional influence or control over the use of the funds (although if the donor controls the foundation, the trust assets will be included in the grantor's estate).

The IRS heavily taxes charitable trusts with excess business holdings. Generally, holdings are excessive if disqualified persons own 20 percent (35 percent where a third party has effective control) or more of the voting stock of incorporated business and the CLT owns more than 2 percent. The CLT has five years within which to dispose of excess holdings. Nevertheless, caution is advised when funding a CLT with interests in a closely held business. While the taxes on acts of self-dealing and taxable expenditures will still apply, the taxes on excess business holdings and jeopardizing investments do not apply if, at inception, the value of the charitable "income interest" is 60 percent or less of the initial value of the entire trust property. The regulations define "income interest" to include a guaranteed annuity or a unitrust amount.

Since donors often design charitable lead trusts with the long-term in mind, unexpected changes to their business or families can have resulting impact on the CLTs. The IRS has ruled that in some cases, grantors can modify the terms of their CLT. For example, these can involve early termination or extension of the term with early distribution.

The IRS has allowed early termination when the closely held business underlying the CLT merged with a publicly held company, meaning the CLT received easily liquidated stock and dividends far in excess of the annuity amount. The grantor and trustees attempted to prepay the amounts owed and dissolve the trust. The IRS allowed this arrangement since the distributions were made for the charitable purposes originally intended, and since no disqualified person would receive any additional benefit. The key factor is that the prepayment was of the entire remaining amount without discount—so essentially the only change was to the timing and lifespan of the CLT.

In another case, the donors used appreciated trust assets to extend and restructure the CLT. The agreement stated that the trustee was to distribute all assets exceeding 110 percent of the remaining obligations to the remainder beneficiary, and the annuity would be extended such that the remainder interest would be close to zero. The IRS ruled this modification was allowable, and that it was not subject to penalties for self-dealing, early termination, nonexempt assets or purposes.

Charitable Giving with ESOPs

Small business owners almost inevitably consider how their business will continue after they are no longer involved. Often, these thoughts occur with the specter of significant capital gains taxes looming. What is the best way to address these concerns? One possibility for charitably-minded owners is to consider integrating an employee stock ownership plan with gifts to a nonprofit organization.

What Is an ESOP?

An employee stock ownership plan (ESOP) is a type of qualified retirement plan. Its core premise is that the primary assets are the stock of the corporation which adopts the plan. Closely held companies whose owners are retiring or otherwise engaging in succession planning often consider an ESOP as an option. ESOPs receive favorable treatment under the law, both in terms of tax treatment and allowable structure.

ESOPs are qualified deferred compensation plans where over half of the plan's assets are invested in the corporation's own stock.[1] Like other types of qualified deferred compensation plans, employers get a tax deduction, and employees get tax-deferral. Employers make deductible cash contributions to fund the plan. Those contributions either pay directly for the newly issued stock, or repay loans which were used to purchase stock. The latter aspect is unique to ESOPs – they are the only qualified retirement plan which can borrow money.[2] Typically, as the loan is repaid, stock is released to participating employees.

Qualified Replacement Property

ESOPs can be very appealing for ownership. When they sell their stock in the company, they may defer or eliminate capital gain recognition by reinvesting the proceeds over into "qualified replacement property" (QRP).[3] By making a section 1042 election, the taxpayer is able to purchase domestic corporate securities as QRP.

The time period for buying the QRP under 1042 is from 3 months before the ESOP sale to 12 months after.[4] The taxpayer then will not pay any capital gain until they sell the QRP. Of course, if the taxpayer holds the QRP until death, any heirs will take the QRP with a stepped-up basis.[5] However, note some significant restrictions to make an effective 1042 election. Among other requirements, the taxpayer must be selling "best common" stock held for over three years, and the ESOP must after the sale hold at least 30% of the company's stock.[6]

S corporations, as is often the case, have special rules. ESOPs can hold S corporation stock, and are even exempt from paying unrelated business income taxes on corporate earnings.[7] However, a major hurdle is that S corporation stockholders are not eligible to make the 1042 election.[8] One way around this is giving up the S corporation election and converting temporarily back to C

---

1. Wells Fargo Institutional Retirement and Trust, "A Look at the Good, the Bad, and the Ugly of an Employee Stock Ownership Plan" at 2 (2016), http://www.kinnearfamilywealth.wfadv.com/files/60140/good-bad-ugly-esop.pdf
2. Id.
3. Vira, D. (2015), "Section 1042: A Guide to Qualified Replacement Property," UC San Diego,
4. Id.
5. Wells Fargo Institutional Retirement and Trust at 4.
6. Diamond, L.H. (July 28, 2016), "Coupling ESOPs with Charitable Remainder Trusts, Part 1 of 2," Planned Giving Design Center, http://www.pgdc.com/pgdc/coupling-esops-charitable-remainder-trusts-part-1-2.
7. Internal Revenue Code § 512(e).
8. Diamond, "Coupling ESOPs, 1 of 2."

corporation status. After the five year waiting period, the company can make the S corporation election again.[9]

Charitable Options with ESOPs

With that background information in mind, consider the broader charitable scenario. A closely-held business owner considering retirement with two common impulses in mind – to avoid a sizeable tax bill and to give something back to the employees that helped build the company. Since long-term owners of closely-held business interests typically have large capital gains, the tax question frequently looms large. Similarly, business succession is a big issue, and aside from family members, ownership often considers how longtime employees might be involved as well. Given those two parallel concerns, combining tax-reducing charitable contributions with ESOPs makes sense.

There are two primary ways to make a charitable gift in tandem with an ESOP. First, the small business owner can create an ESOP, buy QRP with the proceeds from selling the business' stock to the ESOP, and then donate the QRP. Second, it can donate the small business stock directly to the charity before creating the ESOP. This latter option can incorporate planned giving, particularly a charitable remainder trust, charitable gift annuity or donor advised fund. Below is an investigation of these options.

Direct Donation of Qualified Replacement Property

A direct donation to charity of QRP is an intuitive option. Since QRP defers capital gain recognition, if the donors are selling all or a portion of their interest, they will have taxable gains. Those gains are often significant, since, as described above, the QRP takes a carryover basis from the original closely-held stock.

In this case, the donors should consider donating QRP (whether a direct donation or split interest gift) to offset the gain. A direct donation may be the simplest option. Standard tax rules will apply in this case, and the donor may have better options which still include a charitable component if the donor needs some form of income stream. Those options are discussed in more depth below.

---

9. Id.

Donate QRP to Planned Giving Vehicle

Planned giving vehicles can be an appealing option for donors who want to retain an interest in the gift or need income. These can take the form of charitable gift annuities, remainder trusts, or even lead trusts. Since the QRP must be domestic corporate securities, these can (but need not necessarily) be liquid, publicly traded securities. In that case, a charity should be easily able to accommodate those gifts.

The advantage of donating QRP in a planned giving context is that the deferred capital gains are at least partially eliminated for donated stock. Better still, the planned giving vehicle can generate regular income for the donor (or a person of their choosing). This means that the donation not only mitigates the tax impact, but it also can provide income which might substitute for the planned QRP income stream. Below, gifts to CRTs are discussed in more depth.

Donate QRP to a Charitable Remainder Trust

Donating QRP to a charitable remainder trust is a particularly appealing option. QRP can be donated without triggering capital gains, and the donee charitable trust can sell the QRP tax-free due to its exempt status.[10] This means the CRT can invest as it sees fit, which can accommodate the donor's income needs. Typically, the CRT's reinvestment obviates the need for a variant like a NICRUT, NIMCRUT or Flip-CRUT. Note that QRP assets can be donated to fund a charitable gift annuity as well.

The CRT funded with QRP can lead to comparable or even greater personal wealth on a long enough timeline, when compared to a 1042 election and holding QRP. Payments to the lifetime income beneficiaries can reach this threshold over 20 or 30 years. Consider a 10 million dollar closely held C corporation, which a married couple, both 45 years old, own in its entirety. As is often the case with closely held businesses, the stock is highly appreciated, with a basis of nearly zero. They are considering an ESOP for 100% of the company's stock. Below, see the results when QRP is donated to a CRUT.

QRP assets to charity	$10,000,000
CRUT term	Two lives

---

10. Diamond, L.H. (July 28, 2016), "Coupling ESOPs with Charitable Remainder Trusts, Part 2 of 2," Planned Giving Design Center, http://www.pgdc.com/pgdc/coupling-esops-charitable-remainder-trusts-part-2-2.

C Corporations

CRUT payout rate	5%
CRUT rate of return on diversified assets after sale of QRP	8%
August 2018 7520 discount rate	3.4%
Present value of remainder / 2018 charitable deduction	$1,407,500
Tax savings in 37% bracket	$520,775

Assume the 8% rate of return holds throughout the life of the trust, and that at least one of the couple lives for the full projected 50 years. Under these assumptions, the trust will produce $500,000 in income to the lifetime beneficiaries in the first year, and due to reinvestment of the additional income, will grow principal over time. At the end of the 50 year period, the annual payment is nearly $2 million, and the principal which the charity will receive as remainder beneficiary is nearly $41 million. Even with a shorter projected lifespan, the deduction, income, and remainder can all grow to significant amounts.

Donating Closely Held Stock Before ESOP Formation

Rather than rolling the closely held stock over into QRP, a charitably-inclined taxpayer might simply donate the closely held stock to charity or a charitable vehicle. Then, the charity will sell the stock to the company's new ESOP. If the donation has an income element for the donors, the sale to the ESOP can be structured to accommodate that.

Why would this be a better option than donating QRP? Often, this is best when a 1042 election is not possible, so the charitable QRP route is simply a no-go. This can occur when the shareholder is a C corporation or non-resident alien, or if the shareholder has held the stock for between one and three years.[11] Practical planning reasons for the direct gift abound, including a simple desire to invest sale proceeds in assets other than domestic corporate securities. This option also may be better if, after the sale, the ESOP will not own at least 30% of the stock, or if the donors or their family will participate (as buyers) in the ESOP.[12]

Regardless of the reason, it is important to note that the charity or charitable vehicle cannot be legally bound to sell to the ESOP. Nor can the ESOP be compelled to buy the shares at a

---

11. Diamond, "Coupling ESOPs, 2 of 2."
12. Id.

pre-arranged price.[13] Additionally, valuation may be discounted for a donated minority interest, meaning a smaller deduction.[14]

Donate Closely Held Stock to a Charitable Vehicle

Rather than contributing QRP to a CRT, an alternative is to donate closely-held stock directly to charity or to some other type of charitable vehicle. This may be a more intuitive option than buying QRP and then donating it, although it has some disadvantages. The core concept is that the charity or trust will sell the closely held stock back to the ESOP.[15]

It is important to design the gift with future cash flow/liquidity projections in mind. For example, CRUT options like NICRUT, NIMCRUT, and Flip-CRUT may all be viable. This is particularly true when the CRT payment will come due before the ESOP is in place and the closely held stock has yet to sell to the ESOP. Even if the sale to the ESOP occurs in multiple stages, the NIMCRUT (or Flip-CRUT from a NIMCRUT) may be a good option. The makeup feature will allow repayment of the unitrust amounts that would have been due had the net income been sufficient.

Imagine another 10 million dollar C corporation, which a married couple owns in entirety. They are considering an ESOP for the entire company, but know that the sale to the plan would not occur for 3 years. They are both 60 years old in this case, and the stock again is highly appreciated. They can donate all their stock to a NIMCRUT, retain their positions and salary until the NIMCRUT sells to the ESOP, and still receive a significant tax deduction (with carryforward).

Closely held stock to charity	$10,000,000
NIMCRUT term	Two lives
NIMCRUT payout rate	5%
NIMCRUT rate of return on diversified assets after sale of closely held stock	8%
August 2018 7520 discount rate	3.4%
Present value of remainder / 2018 charitable deduction	$2,768,700
Tax savings in 37% bracket	$1,024,419

---

13. Clarkson, C.J. and Jacobsen, S. (2015), "Investing After You Sell Your Business to an ESOP," National Center for Employee Ownership, https://www.bernstein.com/Bernstein/Email/InvestingAfterYouSell.pdf.
14. National Center for Employee Ownership, "The Virtues of Using ESOPs with Charitable Contributions," https://www.nceo.org/articles/esops-charitable-contributions.
15. Gillis, M., "Succession and Exit Planning for the Privately-Held Business," Davenport, Marvin, Joyce & Co. 41, http://www.dmj.com/uploads/Succession-and-Exit-Planning-for-the-PrivatelyHeld-Business.pdf.

As with the QRP example, an 8% return would produce significant growth in income and principal over a period of time. After 34 years, it would grow from an initial $627,000 in annual income to over $1.45 million. The principal would increase to nearly $30 million. Principal would decline slightly in the first few years, but would rebound and begin significant growth by the end of the first decade.

Conclusion

The mechanics of ESOP transactions can be very complex, but nonetheless can be very appealing. The core asset is, fundamentally, the closely held business interest, and as such, is very advantageous for charitable giving. Since these interests are often highly appreciated, the opportunity for a deduction can be very valuable.

Two common charitable routes for closely held interests in a larger ESOP transaction are donating qualified replacement property and direct donation prior to the sale to the ESOP. Both allow the donors to escape capital gains on sale. Further, either route can be configured with a life income element.

C Corporations Additional Resources

Below are further details on gifts of C corporations. C corporation topics are based on Turney Berry and Jeffrey Thede's "Giving the Business to Charity: Charitable Planning with Closely Held Businesses," and Turney Berry's "Charitable Planning with Closely Held Businesses." For quick take-aways on C corporation gifts, see C Corporations Quick Take-Aways. For a review based on the articles, see C Corporations Intermediate. For an in-depth examination adapted and excerpted from the articles, see C Corporations Advanced. For further details, see C Corporations Additional Resources.

For an analysis of C corporation gifts in the context of the increasingly popular corporate inversion, see Fox, R. (August 19, 2014), "Charitable Gifts of Stock to Avoid Forced Gain Recognition When Shares Are Exchanged in Corporate Inversions," Comm. Fdn. of Broward, http://www.cfbroward.org/cfbroward/media/Document-Library/Richard-Fox.pdf.

For a discussion of charitable remainder trusts as a vehicle for C corporation philanthropic and succession planning, see Ackerman, J. (September, 2009), "The CRT Stock Redemption Strategy for Philanthropic and Business Succession Planning," *Journal of Gift Planning,* http://my.pppnet.org/library/000/000/1a/s1.pdf.

For a discussion of charitable bailouts, see Annino, P.M. (September 21, 2015), "Charitable bailouts can save your C corporation clients big on taxes," *Journal of Accountancy,* http://www.journalofaccountancy.com/newsletters/2015/sep/charitable-bailouts-can-save-c-corp-clients-taxes.html.

For an examination of possible misuse of C corporation stock donations, see Yermack, D. (2008), "Deductio Ad Absurdum: CEOs Donating Their Own Stock to Their Own Family Foundations," University of Southern California Finance and Business Economics Seminar Series, http://www.usc.edu/schools/business/FBE/seminars/papers/F_10-10-08_YERMAK-Gifts.pdf.

Treas. Reg. § 1.337(d)-4 (transfer of corporate assets to a tax-exempt entity)

Treas. Reg. § 1.170A-13 (special appraisal requirements and exceptions)

Rev. Rul. 78-197, 1978-1 C.B. 83 (charitable bailout outlined)

Private Letter Ruling 200024052 (June 19, 2000) (IRS approves bailout of stock in exchange for a note under probate exception)

Rauenhorst v. Comm'r, 119 TC 157 (2002) (court affirming the continuing validity of the bailout arrangement)

Blake v. Commissioner, 42 T.C.M. 1336 (1981), aff'd on different grounds, 697 F.2d 473 (2d. Cir. 1982) (court denying deduction where the redemption was conditioned on a subsequent purchase of donor's personal property)

Ahmanson Foundation v. U.S., 674 F.2d 761 (1981) (valuation and deduction issues with bequests of closely held corporate stock)

Chapter 3
S Corporations

- Quick Take-Aways
- Intermediate
- Advanced
- Additional Resources

S Corporations Quick Take-Aways

By Bryan Clontz

Below are quick take-aways on S corporation gifts. S corporation topics are based on Christopher Hoyt's "Charitable Gifts by S Corporations and Their Shareholders: Two Worlds of Law Collide," and "Charitable Gifts by S Corporations: Opportunities and Challenges." For quick take-aways on S corporation gifts, see S Corporation Quick Take-Aways. For a review based on the articles, see S Corporations Intermediate. For an in-depth examination adapted and excerpted from the articles, see S Corporations Advanced. For further details, see S Corporations Additional Resources.

Generally, the best asset to donate is appreciated capital gain property, but Subchapter S corporation stock is a potential exception. A charity pays unrelated business income tax (UBIT) on its gain from selling S corporation stock. Thus the charity has to pay income tax on precontribution gain, post-contribution gain, and any allocated income during the holding period. One solution can be for the S corporation stock to be donated to a public charity-sponsored donor-advised fund in trust form. Another option is for the business itself to donate assets.

Advantages of donations of S corporation shares include:

- The stock of an S corporation might be valuable, based on the underlying corporation assets.
- A donation to a public charity in trust form can mitigate up to 60 percent of the UBIT.
- Donating the assets from the corporation will allow the charitable deduction to flow through proportionally to all shareholders.
- Donors may contribute S corporation stock as an outright gift or for a charitable gift annuity.
- There are more S corporations than C corporations and LLCs combined.

Disadvantages of donating S corporation shares include:

- The donor's income tax deduction may be less than the stock's appraised value if there are so-called "hot assets" or other ordinary income elements.
- The charity must pay tax on its share of S corporation income for every day it owns the stock, and on gain from the sale of the stock after taking the donor's carryover tax basis.
- If S corporation stock is donated to a charitable remainder trust, 100 percent of the UBIT is taxable making it a very inefficient gift.

Wrinkles in the process to consider include:

- It may be more efficient for the S corporation to donate assets, however a large shareholder base may make this unwieldy, since each shareholder would have to agree on the charity. A solution can be donor-advised funds created for each shareholder proportionally.
- It is important that the Shareholders Agreement has an equalization clause so the charity receives distributions to pay the unrelated business tax.

Discovery Questions

Donor Questions

1. What is the donor trying to accomplish with the gift?
2. What is the value of the stock and how was that determined (e.g., appraisal, 409A valuation, recent transactions)?
3. What is the total percentage of stock that the donor owns when combined with all related entities (probing if the excess business holding issue will apply)?
4. Legally, who or what owns the shares?

Advisor Questions

1. What is the current tax basis per share?
2. Do the governing documents allow charitable transfers, and if so, what is the process?
3. What is the likely exit plan for the charity (e.g., will sale be for cash, note, stock, or some combination)?
4. Does the advisor have an estimate of what a qualified appraisal will cost (this expense can vary greatly and can be an impediment to smaller donations)?
5. Are there any "hot assets" which will trigger the ordinary income reduction rules on the deduction?
6. Does the donor want to use a public charity sponsoring a donor-advised fund to mitigate UBTI?
7. What is the expected after-tax cash flow from the stock (cash distributions less UBIT paid)?

Charity Questions

1. Is the effort worth the expected benefits (i.e., is the juice worth the squeeze)?
2. Has the screening and due diligence process identified any potential problems and can the risks be mitigated?
3. Is there the necessary expertise to accept gifts of private stock in a timely way?
4. Should indirect gift acceptance be considered, like using external third party foundations or supporting organizations to receive the asset?
5. Is there a clear liquidation plan to maximize the sales proceeds as soon as possible?
6. Is the charity comfortable making quarterly UBIT estimated tax payments and then calculating and filing the 990-T return?

S Corporations Intermediate

By Ryan Raffin

Below is a review on S corporation gifts. S corporation topics are based on Christopher Hoyt's "Charitable Gifts by S Corporations and Their Shareholders: Two Worlds of Law Collide," and "Charitable Gifts by S Corporations: Opportunities and Challenges." For quick take-aways on S corporation gifts, see S Corporation Quick Take-Aways. For a review based on the articles, see S Corporations Intermediate. For an in-depth examination adapted and excerpted from the articles, see S Corporations Advanced. For further details, see S Corporations Additional Resources.

This review of charitable gifts of S corporation stock has six parts, beginning with an overview. The second part discusses the three bad things that happen when S corporation stock is donated to charity. Next is the best way to structure a charitable gift of S corporation stock. Following this is a brief update on recent statutory changes. Obstacles for corporate gifts are examined next, before concluding with a point-by-point discussion of other issues to consider.

Without proper planning, gifted S corporation stock can lead to greater tax liability for a charity than if the donor had sold it and donated the proceeds. Unlike C corporations, S corporations that meet IRS eligibility requirements will not pay income tax at the corporate level. This avoids the classic C corporation double taxation, on both the entity and on dividends. As a result of this favorable tax treatment, it has become a popular form of business entity. Over four million S corporations exist, with over seven million shareholders.

Review Part 1: Overview

Generally, charities prefer to sell contributed stock rather than holding it. Two reasons for this are 1) the desire to liquidate the asset and use the proceeds, and 2) held stock usually will not conform with the charity's existing investment profile and policy. Unfortunately, S corporation stock is often difficult to sell. Typically, the possible buyers are the corporation itself, other shareholders, or a third-party acquiring the entire business. Often, there is an informal understanding that the corporation will redeem the donated stock. This is appealing for shareholders, since they get a deduction.

Donations of S corporation stock were not allowed until 1998, when Congress allowed tax-exempt charities to own such shares. This means that two sets of laws apply—those governing tax-exempt status, and those governing S corporation status. With so many technical rules, it is easy to make a mistake that can have serious tax consequences. For example, some charitable lead trusts can own

S corporation stock, but charitable remainder trusts cannot. Ineligible shareholders can cause the corporation to lose its Subchapter S status, although these transactions can often be undone.

Since S corporation financial transactions flow through to shareholders, the S corporation itself can make the donation, meaning the charitable income tax deduction will be claimed on the shareholder's tax return. There is no need for the shareholder to contribute stock to obtain a charitable tax deduction when the corporation's gifts can produce these tax benefits to the shareholder, often at less cost since there is no need to have the stock's value appraised. This also helps the charity avoid unrelated business income tax (UBIT) liability on income from the S corporation stock or gain from sale of that stock.

Review Part 2: Three Bad Things Happen When S Corp Stock Is Donated to a Charity

Tax law provides that three bad things happen when a donor gives appreciated S corporation stock to a charity:

1. The donor's tax deduction is usually less than the appraised value of the stock.

    The tax deduction for S corporation stock is more like a donated partnership interest than a gift of C corporation stock. This means that donors are subject to "hot asset" rules, which determine the amount of ordinary income versus capital gain that partners have when they sell their interests. As a result, the corporation may pay more money to redeem the stock than the shareholder was able to deduct.

2. For every day that the charity owns the stock, the charity must report its share of income as unrelated business taxable income (UBTI).

    The charity is taxed on its portion of that S corporation income, including passive investment income the S corporation generates, such as interest or capital gains. This attributable income is reflected on the K-1 return and is taxable whether it is distributed or not.

3. Whereas normally a charity does not have UBTI when it sells stock from its investment portfolio for a profit, a sale of appreciated S corporation stock will trigger a UBIT liability.

    In fact, the tax liability for a charity can often be greater than the donor would have incurred had the donor sold the stock—individuals are subject to a 20 percent maximum rate on long-term capital gains, but corporate charities pay UBIT at ordinary rates of up to 21 percent.

Review Part 3: The Best Way to Structure a Charitable Gift

Despite the adverse tax treatment described above, there are still unique ways to structure charitable gifts from S corporations and their shareholders. This is because in most cases, only one or two shareholders own an S corporation. They dominate every aspect of the business' operations, and therefore, can select the best asset to donate—either the donor's stock or specific corporate assets.

In most cases, both the donor and the charity will usually benefit if the corporation contributes assets, rather than if the shareholder contributes stock. The shareholder claims the tax benefit with either type of gift. General advantages of a gift by the S corporation itself follow:

- The lack of marketability problem does not apply to gifts of corporate property, unlike stock. Essentially, fair market value is higher for both the donor's deduction and the charity's sale.

- Other assets the S corporation owns will not reduce the value of donated property.

- Charitable gifts of property can avoid the "built-in gains tax" (for C corporations that convert to S corporations). Although appreciated property which the corporation sells or distributes is subject to the tax, property that it donates outright is not.

- Charities are not subject to UBIT on income from contributed property (unless debt-financed or active business interests) or on gain from sale, unlike with S corporation stock.

- Charitable remainder trusts (CRTs) can receive and hold S corporation assets, but not stock. Asset gifts are good for both corporate donors and shareholders. The tax deduction flows to the latter, and the IRS does not tax the charity on gains from sale of the property, meaning more cash in the CRT.

Review Part 4: Recent Statutory Changes

S corporation donations of appreciated property used to have tax disadvantages compared to those of partnerships or LLCs. The 2015 PATH Act made permanent a tax provision that encourages S corporations to donate appreciated assets. The shareholder can claim a charitable income tax deduction for the full value of the property by the S corporation, even if that value exceeds the shareholder's basis in stock. The Tax Committee Report gives a good example:

"Thus, for example, assume an S corporation with one individual shareholder makes a charitable contribution of stock with a basis of $200 and a fair market value of $500. The shareholder will be treated as having made a $500 charitable contribution ... and will reduce the basis of the S corporation stock by $200. This example assumes that basis of the S corporation stock (before reduction) is at least $200."[1]

Review Part 5: Obstacles for Corporate Charitable Gifts

Complications may prevent either an S corporation from making a gift of assets or a shareholder from claiming a charitable income tax deduction. These are as follows:

- If any other shareholders oppose the charitable gift, it may be difficult to donate corporate assets. One possible solution is to establish a corporate donor-advised fund, which would allow shareholders to recommend grants to different public charities.
- The S corporation's assets may not be useful or valuable to charity, for example, inventory or equipment.
- The charitable income tax deduction might be limited for shareholders with a low basis. This is a common outcome, since nearly one third of S corporations report operating losses.
- The IRS treats donations of "substantially all" of S corporation assets as a liquidation. This triggers an income tax liability as if the corporation sold its assets to an unrelated buyer. The definition of "substantially all" is unclear, but 80 percent of assets usually qualifies. In these cases, the S corporation recognizes a gain as if on sale.
- Accrual-method C corporations can deduct charitable pledges in that year as long as it pays the pledge within the first 2½ months of the next year. Cash-method shareholders of S corporations cannot deduct an S corporation's charitable gifts until it actually makes the gift.

Review Part 6: Other Issues to Consider

Other factors that the charity, all advisors, and the donor(s) should consider follow:

    A. When are cash and property distributions taxed as UBIT?

    B. Low basis of S corporation stock can cause problems.

---

1. Joint Committee on Taxation, Technical Explanation of H.R. 4, "The Pension Protection Act of 2006," JCX-38-06 (Aug. 3, 2006) at page 271.

S Corporations

C. Tax issues for S corporation with losses.

D. Is municipal bond interest subject to UBIT?

E. Can an S corporation's charitable contributions reduce UBIT?

F. Does S corporation income keep or lose its character for UBIT?

G. What if the charity and S corporation have different fiscal years?

H. Tax issues if S corporation was once a C corporation.

I. Private foundation as an S corporation shareholder.

J. Inadvertent termination of S corporation status.

K. What if an S corporation becomes a C corp, or vice versa, while the charity owns stock?

L. Does the installment sales method apply when a charity sells its S corporation stock in exchange for the buyer's promissory note?

S Corporations Advanced[2]

By Christopher Hoyt

Below is an in-depth examination on S corporation gifts. S corporation topics are based on Christopher Hoyt's "Charitable Gifts by S Corporations and Their Shareholders: Two Worlds of Law Collide," and "Charitable Gifts by S Corporations: Opportunities and Challenges." For quick take-aways on S corporation gifts, see S Corporation Quick Take-Aways. For a review based on the articles, see S Corporations Intermediate. For an in-depth examination adapted and excerpted from the articles, see S Corporations Advanced. For further details, see S Corporations Additional Resources.

If donors and charities do not properly plan a transaction, more tax can be paid when a tax-exempt charity owns and sells S corporation stock than if the contributing donor owns and sells it. This counterintuitive result frustrates Congressional policies of encouraging charitable gifts and having charities devote resources to charitable purposes. With over four million S corporations and over seven million shareholders, the transactions could affect many parties.

Two Ways Corporations Are Taxed: Subchapter C and Subchapter S

The tax laws provide two alternative ways of taxing corporations. The general rule is that a corporation is subject to the corporate income tax under Subchapter C of the Internal Revenue Code (C Corporation).[3] There is another option available to a corporation that has fewer than 100 shareholders: it can file an election with the IRS to be taxed under Subchapter S of the Internal Revenue Code (S corporation), provided that it meets the eligibility criteria.[4]

---

2. FREE DOWNLOADS OF COMPREHENSIVE ARTICLES: This outline is an abbreviated version of two comprehensive articles that go into great detail about the laws governing charitable gifts made by S Corporations and by S corporation shareholders. You can locate and download .pdf copies of these two articles with a simple Google search: SSRN S corporation charity. The articles are as follows:
   #1 - Charitable Gifts of S Corporation Stock:
   Charitable Gifts by S Corporations and Their Shareholders: Two Worlds of Law Collide; —*ACTEC Law Journal*, Vol. 36, pp. 693-768, Spring 2011, http://ssrn.com/abstract=1926693.
   #2 - Charitable Gifts Made by S Corporations:
   Charitable Gifts by S Corporations: Opportunities and Challenges—*ACTEC Law Journal*, Vol. 36, pp. 477-515, Fall 2010, http://ssrn.com/abstract=1926717.

3. IRC § 11.
4. IRC §§ 1361 and 1362.

S Corporations

Except for three unusual situations, an S corporation does not pay income tax. Instead, the IRS taxes corporate income directly to the shareholders.[5] The principal advantage of this tax treatment is that a shareholder can avoid the double taxation of income that often occurs with a C corporation (the IRS taxes corporation income first, and then shareholder dividends). After the Tax Reform Act of 1986 made the taxation of S corporations more attractive than that of C corporations, small businesses embraced S corporations.

Charitable Gifts of Stock: The Charity's Perspective on Gifts of Stock

Most charities prefer to sell donor-contributed stock rather than hold it. First, they want to apply the proceeds—or with an endowment, apply the investment income—to charitable purposes. Second, a large block of donated stock will usually not conform to the charity's investment policy. The charity prefers to diversify, and put the proceeds in its investment pool.

The charity can easily accomplish this with a gift of publicly traded stock which it can sell on the stock market. By comparison, stock of closely held businesses have an extremely limited market. The potential purchasers are usually only the corporation, the shareholders, or a possible purchaser of the entire business. A common strategy has been for the shareholder to contribute closely held stock with an informal understanding that the corporation will redeem the stock in the future. As long as the agreement does not compel the charity to sell the stock to the corporation at the time of the gift, the IRS is agreeable with this arrangement.[6]

This arrangement had great appeal to shareholders. First, the shareholder was able to claim a charitable income tax deduction on his or her personal return for the gift of stock. Second, it was the corporation's cash that went to the charity to redeem the stock. This was a much better tax arrangement than if the corporation paid a taxable dividend to the shareholder and the shareholder gave the cash to the charity. As a result, this redemption-after-gift arrangement was a popular way for small business owners to make large charitable gifts.

Charitable Gifts of Stock: Why Legislation Was Needed

What changed this paradigm of redemption-after-gift was the decline in the number of closely held C corporations, many owners of which converted to S corporations. Between 1986 and 1993, the number of C corporations experienced an average annual decline of 3.2 percent whereas the

---

5. IRC § 1366.
6. Rev. Rul. 78-197.

number of S corporations grew at an annual rate of 13 percent. Even today, over 90,000 C corporations convert to Subchapter S status every year.[7]

This trend posed a challenge to charities, since the tax law prohibited them from owning stock of an S corporation. Until Congress changed the law, only individuals, estates and certain trusts were eligible to be shareholders. If an ineligible shareholder, such as a charity, ever acquired stock of an S corporation, the corporation lost its S corporation tax status and converted into a taxpaying Subchapter C corporation. Charities witnessed a major source of charitable gifts drying up as small business owners converted their corporations to Subchapter S status. They and others lobbied Congress to add charities to the list of eligible shareholders and it granted their wish: beginning in 1998, charities could own stock of S corporations.[8]

Charitable Gifts of Stock: A Charity Can Be A Shareholder, But A Charitable Remainder Trust Cannot

With so many technical rules, it is easy to make a mistake that can have serious tax consequences. For example, whereas some forms of charitable lead trusts can own S corporation stock,[9] a charitable remainder trust cannot.[10] When an ineligible shareholder acquires S corporation stock, the corporation loses its Subchapter S status and becomes a Subchapter C corporation.[11] The IRS has been very generous to forgive inadvertent mistakes and allow shareholders to undo such transactions,[12] but obviously all parties would have been better served if the parties had never made the mistake in the first place.

---

7. Luttrell, Kelly, "S Corporation Returns, 2003", *IRS Statistics of Income Bulletin,* Spring, 2006, pp. 91-165, computed from Table 1 at p. 105.
8. IRC § 1361(c)(6).
9. A charitable lead trust that is not a grantor trust can elect to be an Electing Small Business Trust (ESBT). Treas. Reg. § 1.641(c)-1(k), Example (4).
10. A charitable remainder trust is not listed as an eligible shareholder in IRC §§ 1361(b)(1), 1361(c)(2) or 1361(c)(6), and, unlike a charitable lead trust, it is specifically prohibited from qualifying as an Electing Small Business Trust (ESBT). IRC § 1361(e)(1)(B)(iii). The Service also concluded in a revenue ruling that a charitable remainder trust could not qualify as a Qualified Subchapter S Trust (QSST) under § 1361(d). Rev. Rul. 92-48, 1992-26 I.R.B. 7.
11. IRC § 1362(d)(2)(A).
12. Section 1362(f) provides that if the Secretary determines that there was an inadvertent termination of an S corporation, and if all affected parties work to restore S corporation status and make adjustments to income as if the corporation had never terminated, then, notwithstanding the terminating event, the corporation shall be treated as never having lost its S corporation status. The legislative history instructs the IRS to be liberal in granting waivers. S. Rep. No. 640, 97th Cong., 2d Sess. 12-13 (1982), 1982-2 C.B. 718, 723-24; H.R. Rep. No. 826, 97th Cong., 2d Sess. 12 (1982), 1982-2 C.B. 730, 735. As can be seen from the many waivers for transferring S corporation stock to IRAs, the IRS has been very generous in granting inadvertent termination relief.

Charitable Gifts of Stock: Charity's Mistake—To Structure S Corp Gifts Like the C Corp Gifts

Once Congress enacted the law, many charities approached small business owners ready to make the same redemption-after-gift transaction that had been popular with closely held C corporations. What many people were not aware of was that they could often accomplish better results by structuring the gift in a manner that the law had always permitted: have the S corporation contribute some of its appreciated assets rather than have the shareholder contribute some of his or her stock.

Recall that the advantage of the redemption-after-gift strategy with a C corporation was that the shareholder obtained a charitable income tax deduction for the gift of stock even though the corporation ultimately made the cash payment to the charity. This two-step process of redemption-after-gift is not necessary for S corporation shareholders. Unlike a C corporation, an S corporation's financial transactions flow through to the shareholder's tax return. Thus, if an S corporation makes a simple cash gift to a charity, the shareholder will claim the charitable income tax deduction on the individual's tax return.

As a result of this tax treatment, there is no need for the shareholder to contribute stock to obtain a charitable tax deduction. The S corporation's gifts can produce these tax benefits to the shareholder, often at less cost since there is no need to pay for an appraisal of the stock's value. The charity also benefits from a corporate gift, since it will not have to pay UBIT. By comparison, when a shareholder of the S corporation contributes stock, a charity has a UBIT liability for the income attributable to the days and/or years that it was a shareholder of an S corporation as well as a UBIT liability for the gain on the ultimate sale of the stock.

Three Bad Things Happen When S Corp Stock Is Donated to a Charity

By way of background, normally the best way to structure a large charitable gift is to contribute appreciated stock or real estate to a public charity. The donor gets the double tax benefit of an income tax deduction for the appreciated value of the property, and also avoids recognizing the taxable gain that would have occurred on sale of the property. Donors are aware of this and often make large gifts shortly before the sale of their corporation or real estate. However, the tax laws provide that three bad things happen when a donor contributes appreciated S corporation stock to a charity:

First Bad Thing: The Donor's Tax Deduction Is Usually Less Than the Appraised Value of the Stock

Congress made the tax deduction for a gift of S corporation stock comparable to a gift of a partnership interest rather than a gift of Subchapter C corporation stock. Consequently, the law requires a donor to reduce the deduction by the amount of ordinary income that the donor would recognize if the S corporation liquidated its assets (that is, the portion of a hypothetical gain from selling inventory, assets subject to depreciation recapture, and other ordinary income assets). For most donors, this adjustment does not significantly affect the amount of the charitable tax deduction.

The last sentence of Section 170(e)(1) (relating to income tax charitable deductions for contributions of ordinary income and capital gain property) states, "For purposes of applying this paragraph in the case of a charitable contribution of stock in an S corporation, rules similar to the rules of Section 751 shall apply in determining whether gain on such stock would have been long-term capital gain if such stock were sold by the taxpayer." Congress therefore imported the "hot asset" rules, which determine the amount of ordinary income versus capital gain that partners have when they sell their partnership interests, to charitable gifts of S corporation stock. By comparison, when a shareholder sells S corporation stock instead of contributing it to a charity, the partnership hot asset rules that apply to the sale of a partnership interest do not apply to the sale of stock. Instead, the IRS classifies all of the gain as capital gain. The partnership hot asset rules only apply to a charitable donation of S corporation stock and not a sale.

This may cause the corporation to pay more money to redeem the stock than the shareholder was able to deduct. For example, assume that a shareholder owns 100 percent of an S corporation and that the shareholder makes a charitable gift of stock that appraisers value at $100,000. Also assume that the corporation holds $5,000 of ordinary income assets attributable to the stock, so that the IRS reduces the charitable tax deduction for the stock gift to $95,000. If the S corporation redeems the stock from the charity in an arm's-length transaction, the corporation would have to write a check for the entire value of $100,000. The charity should not sell the stock for anything less than its value.

From a tax perspective, it would have been much better for the example S corporation to have simply made a cash gift of $100,000 to the charity. The full $100,000 charitable tax deduction would flow through to the shareholder's return, rather than just $95,000, and the parties would have avoided the costs of a qualified appraisal. Of course, if the shareholder's basis in the stock is very low—for example, less than $100,000—then the corporate gift could produce less tax benefit to the donor than would a gift of stock.

Second Bad Thing: For Every Day That the Charity Owns the Stock, the Charity Must Report Its Share of the Corporation's Income as Unrelated Business Taxable Income (UBTI) and Must Pay the Unrelated Business Income Tax (UBIT)

The tax treatment is worse than a comparable gift of a partnership interest. A charity does not pay UBIT on its share of a partnership's passive investment income, such as interest or capital gains, but it will have to pay UBIT on such income earned by an S corporation. In 2003, nearly 20 percent of all S corporation income was from such investment sources.

Third Bad Thing: Whereas Normally a Charity Does Not Have UBTI When It Sells Stock from Its Investment Portfolio for a Profit, a Sale of Appreciated S Corporation Stock Will Trigger a UBIT Liability

Normally an exempt organization excludes from the computation of UBTI any capital gains earned from the sale of corporate stock.[13] However, with regard to the sale of S corporation stock, Section 512(e)(1)(B)(ii) overrides this exemption: "notwithstanding any other provision of this part... any gain or loss on the disposition of the stock in the S corporation shall be taken into account in computing the unrelated business taxable income of such organization."

In fact, the tax liability incurred by a charity can often be greater than the tax liability that the donor would have incurred had the donor sold the stock. Whereas individuals are subject to a maximum federal tax rate of only 15 percent on their long-term capital gains, incorporated charities receive no tax break for long-term capital gains and pay UBIT at ordinary corporate rates, which can be as high as 21 percent. Thus, if there is a $100,000 gain, the shareholder would have paid only $15,000 federal tax on the sale but the charity that receives the stock as a gift must pay a tax as high as $35,000! By comparison, a charity that is a trust rather than a corporation can pay the same low 15 percent rate as the donor.

---

13. IRC § 512(b)(6).

The Best Way to Structure a Charitable Gift

Overview

Despite these three negative consequences, an optimist will observe that S corporations and their shareholders can structure charitable gifts in a multitude of ways that are not possible in many business settings. This is because in most cases just one or two shareholders own the entire S corporation, and therefore dominate every aspect of the business' operations. Thus the parties can select the best possible asset for a charitable gift, whether it is the shareholder's stock or specific corporate assets. They can also select the best charitable beneficiary.

What are the best ways for a shareholder of an S corporation to structure a charitable gift? The answer depends on many factors, including whether the corporation will continue as a going concern or if the gift is made in contemplation of an imminent sale of the business or the death of the controlling shareholder.

In most cases both the donor and the charity will usually benefit if the corporation contributes some of its assets rather than if the shareholder contributes stock. With either type of gift, the shareholder claims the tax benefit. Either the shareholder will deduct the shareholder's gift of stock or the shareholder will deduct the corporation's gift, since an S corporation's financial transactions flow through to the shareholder's personal return. The principal advantage from having the S corporation make the charitable gift is that the three negatives above will not apply. Regulations will not reduce the donor's income tax deduction and the charity will usually not pay UBIT when it owns or sells a gift it received from a corporation.

The tax planner should therefore first explore whether such a gift is possible. Does the corporation have cash or appreciated property that it could contribute to a charity? In many cases the corporation might not have any assets that are suitable for a charitable gift so that a shareholder's gift of stock may be the only viable option.

Advantages of Gift By Corporation—In General

1. A lack of marketability discount does not reduce a charitable deduction for a gift of corporate property (e.g., real estate), as a shareholder's gift of stock would be. That is, potential buyers may value the corporation's real estate at its full worth. Conversely, appraisers will often value the stock of any closely held business at less than the value

of the corporation's underlying assets, because of the difficulty of selling a minority interest in a closely held business.

2. As explained above, the value of any other assets that the S corporation owns does not reduce the charitable income tax deduction for a gift of corporate property. By comparison, the income tax deduction for a charitable gift of S corporation stock will usually be less than the appraised value to reflect any "ordinary income" assets that the S corporation might have.

3. A charitable gift of property can avoid the "built-in gains tax" of Section 1374. When a Subchapter C corporation becomes a Subchapter S corporation, the conversion triggers a special tax, if the corporation disposes of any appreciated property that it owned on the date of conversion—whether by sale or distribution to the shareholders—within ten years of that date. Such a disposition will usually trigger both a taxable gain to the shareholders under the Subchapter S rules and a Section 1374 income tax liability to the corporation based on the value of the property on the conversion date. The built-in gains tax is by far the most frequent and largest of the three corporate taxes that S corporations pay. Therefore it was a significant development when the IRS concluded in a private letter ruling that an outright charitable gift of such property within ten years of the conversion date would not trigger such tax.[14] There is no comparable IRS pronouncement on the consequences of a donor's deferred charitable gift of such property, such as a contribution to a charitable remainder trust.

4. A charity is not subject to UBIT on the income of the S corporation's contributed property such as real estate (unless it was "debt-financed") or on the gain from its sale, whereas a charity will have to pay UBIT taxes when it holds and sells stock of a profitable S corporation and

5. Although a charitable remainder trust (CRT) cannot receive or hold S corporation stock, it can receive and hold corporate assets, such as real estate. Such a CRT is usually for a term of years (e.g., 20 years) rather than for the life of an individual.

Having the corporation contribute real estate or other appreciated property to a CRT, and then the CRT selling the real estate, could be beneficial to both the corporation and shareholder. First, the charitable income tax deduction from the gift of real estate would flow through to the shareholder's individual returns. Second, since a CRT is tax-exempt, it will not pay any tax on the gain when it sells the real estate. It can thereby retain greater cash for investment to produce greater annual cash flow to benefit the S corporation, which the S corporation can then distribute to the

---

14. Private Letter Ruling 200004032 (Jan 28, 2000).

shareholder. In oversimplified terms, the charitable remainder trust would issue a check payable to the corporation and the corporation would simply endorse the check to the shareholder. The S corporation would report income from the charitable remainder trust on its return and, in turn, would then appear on the shareholder's personal tax return.

There are three important situations when the S corporation laws can cause problems for a corporate gift to a charitable remainder trust. First, it is important that the term of the charitable remainder trust be a fixed number of years rather than a term measured by the life of a shareholder. According to one private letter ruling, it could be an income tax disaster if an S corporation establishes a charitable remainder trust that will last for the life of a shareholder.[15] Second, as explained above, there is no guidance from the IRS about the impact of a contribution of property that might be subject to the Section 1374 built-in gains tax. Perhaps the transaction would trigger tax liability; perhaps not. Finally, under certain circumstances—most likely when the corporation liquidates its assets—the investment income from the charitable remainder trust could trigger a corporate tax and could cause the corporation to involuntarily convert from a Subchapter S corporation to a Subchapter C corporation.[16]

Incentive for S Corporations to Donate Appreciated Property

Since 2006, charitable gifts by S corporations qualify for the same favorable income tax treatment that currently applies to such charitable gifts made by partnerships and limited liability companies (LLCs). Until this law was enacted, such gifts by S corporations were subject to a comparable tax disadvantage. Normally the prime situation for obtaining a tax benefit from a charitable gift of appreciated property is to make the gift shortly before its sale, but this strategy does not work well with a gift of S corporation assets. Rather than incur the cost of an appraisal for a gift of appreciated property, it may be easier for the corporation to sell its assets and then make a cash gift.

Example: Assume that an S corporation with only one shareholder is about to sell all of its assets. The corporation has $1 million of assets with a cost basis of $400,000, which if sold would produce a $600,000 gain. Assume that the shareholder's stock has the same numbers: $1 million value and $400,000 basis. If the corporation sold all of its assets and the gain was taxed to the shareholder, the basis in the stock would increase to $1 million ($400,000 + $600,000 taxable gain). Thus, when the corporation distributes the $1 million cash proceeds to the shareholder in liquidation, the shareholder would not recognize a gain upon liquidation. The shareholder could then make a

---

15. Private Letter Ruling 200203034 (Oct. 18, 2001).
16. IRC §§ 1375 and 1362(d)(3).

charitable cash gift of $100,000 and claim a $100,000 charitable income tax deduction. The end result would be $600,000 of taxable gain and a $100,000 charitable tax deduction.

Charitable Gift Under Prior Law: Rather than sell all of its assets, the corporation might make a charitable contribution of some of its appreciated property before the anticipated sale. Among the corporation's assets is appreciated real estate with a value of $100,000 and a cost basis of $20,000. To claim a charitable tax deduction for a gift of the real estate, the corporation would have to pay for a qualified appraisal. If the corporation donates the real estate to a charity before the sale, the shareholder could deduct a $100,000 charitable gift but has to reduce his or her basis in his/her stock by the full $100,000—from $400,000 to $300,000. When the corporation sells the remainder of its assets for $900,000, the corporation will recognize a gain of $520,000 ($900,000 sale price minus the remaining $380,000 basis that the corporation has in its assets).

The problem was that when the corporation liquidates and distributes the $900,000 cash, the shareholder will have to recognize a taxable gain of $80,000. This is because the shareholder's stock basis is only $820,000 (original $400,000 minus $100,000 charitable deduction plus $520,000 taxable gain). Thus the shareholder will ultimately recognize the same $600,000 taxable gain ($520,000 when corporation sells assets plus $80,000 on liquidation) that the shareholder would have recognized had there been no charitable gift of property at all. It would be simpler to sell the assets and give cash. By comparison, if a partnership or an LLC made the same gift, the $20,000 cost basis reduces the owner's basis in the partnership interest or LLC interest rather than the appreciated $100,000 market value. In that case, there would indeed be a tax advantage to a gift of appreciated property before its sale.

New Law After 2006: The S corporation would have parallel treatment to the LLC or partnership: the $20,000 cost basis reduces the shareholder's basis in the stock, rather than the appreciated $100,000 market value and there would indeed be a tax advantage to a gift of appreciated property before its sale. The shareholder would only recognize a $520,000 gain when the remaining assets are sold. The following sentence was added at the end of Section 1367(a): "The decrease under Subparagraph(B) by reason of a charitable contribution ... of property shall be the amount equal to the shareholder's pro rata share of the adjusted basis of such property. The preceding sentence shall not apply to contributions made in taxable years beginning after December 31, 2014."[17] [As amended by the Protecting Americans from Tax Hikes Act of 2015]

---

17. IRC § 1367(a).

Charitable Gift by S Corporation Built-in Gain (Section 1374) Property to a Charitable Remainder Trust (CRT): The IRS ruled that a CRT's sale of the contributed property within the recognition period does not trigger the Section 1374 tax.[18] However, it is possible that future distributions from the CRT to the S corporation could trigger the Section 1374 built-in gains tax if (under the four-tier system that applies to CRT distributions to donors) part of the CRT distribution included long-term capital gain.[19]

Obstacles For Corporate Charitable Gifts

There are several complications that could prevent a corporation from making a charitable gift of its assets or prevent a shareholder from claiming income tax deductions for the corporation's gift. In that case a shareholder's gift of stock might be the primary charitable giving opportunity. These obstacles are as follows:

1. If there are other shareholders who do not want to make a charitable gift to a particular charity, this lack of consensus may limit the shareholder who is advocating a charitable gift to giving her or his stock. One solution when there are shareholders with diverse charitable interests is for the corporation to establish a corporate donor-advised fund. A donor-advised fund is a grant-making account at a community foundation, Jewish federation, national donor-advised fund, or other sponsoring organization where donors recommend grants from the fund to other public charities. The corporation can divide its donor-advised fund into subaccounts that will allow each shareholder to recommend grants to the public charities that each shareholder wants to support.

2. The S corporation might not have any assets that are attractive to the charity (e.g., the only assets are equipment and inventory) so that stock will be the main option.

3. The charitable income tax deduction could be limited for shareholders who have a low tax basis in their S corporation stock. For example, if an S corporation informs a shareholder that her deduction for the corporation's charitable gifts is $20,000, but the

---

18. Private Letter Ruling 200644013 (June 21, 2006) (donation of IRC § 1374 built-in gain property to a 20-year FLIP-CRUT).
19. In Private Letter Ruling 200644013 (June 21, 2006), an S corporation that owned, leased, and managed residential and commercial real estate proposed to donate three parcels of real estate to a 20-year FLIP-CRUT. The property was Section 1374 built-in gain property that it had owned during its years as a C corporation. The contribution to the CRT and the CRT's subsequent sale of the contributed property were expected to occur within the ten-year recognition period. The Service ruled that the S corporation would not have a recognized built-in gain upon its contribution of the real estate to the CRT or upon the CRT's disposition of the real estate. The Service concluded that the S corporation also would not have recognized built-in gain when it received Tier 1 ordinary income from the CRT. However, the Service concluded that the S corporation "will have recognized built-in gain under section 1374 to the extent the unitrust amounts received by Company during the Recognition Period are characterized as capital gain under section 664(b) because of the Trust's disposition of the Real Estate."

shareholder only has stock with a basis of $12,000, the shareholder will be limited to a $12,000 deduction that year. If a shareholder has a very low basis in his or her stock, then a gift of the stock may be the only way for the shareholder to get a charitable tax benefit. With nearly one third of S corporations reporting operating losses, it is very common for a shareholder to have a low basis.

4. If an S Corporation donates "substantially all" of its assets to a charity, the corporation will be treated as if it had liquidated. This will trigger an income tax liability as if the corporation had sold its assets to an unrelated buyer.

   The definition of what constitutes "substantially all" is not clear. Contributing 80 percent or more of its assets to charity will probably trigger the liability. Some are concerned that contributing just a majority of the assets (over 50 percent) may be enough to cause problems. Consequently, the most generous gift that a shareholder can make—a gift or bequest of the entire corporation—poses serious tax challenges to a charity. When the S corporation distributes assets to the charitable parent corporation—even assets that could be considered charitable, such as a valuable painting for display to the public—the S corporation will recognize a taxable gain on the distribution as if the asset had been sold to a buyer and there will be no offsetting charitable income tax deduction.[20]

5. Although an accrual-method corporation can usually deduct a charitable pledge in the year it makes the pledge as long as it pays the pledge within the first 2½ months of the next year, cash-method shareholders of S corporations will not be able to deduct an S corporation's charitable gifts until the corporation actually makes the gift.

Alternate Donation Opportunities

A donor-advised fund (DAF) is a separately named fund that is held by a larger charity where a donor may recommend grants from the fund to eligible charitable recipients.[21] The governing body can accept or reject each recommendation, although they usually follow the donor's recommendation whenever the proposed recipient is an eligible public charity.

Although classified as public charities, DAFs are subject to private foundation excess business holdings tax, and must dispose of any donated S corporation stock within five years (or ten years with

---

20. § 1371(a) provides that an S corporation is subject to the same tax laws as a C corporation unless there is a specific S corporation law that is in conflict. Generally, a C corporation that distributes appreciated property to shareholder must recognize a taxable gain as if the property was sold, whether the distribution is made by an ongoing corporation (§ 311(b)(1)) or in liquidation (§ 336(a)).
21. IRC § 4966(d)(2)(A).

an extension).[22] Also, self-dealing rules for DAFs prohibit paying a donor/substantial contributor (or a related person)[23] for services,[24] but a property sale with a donor is permissible for cash (but not a loan) if it meets the general excess benefit standards for public charities.[25]

A DAF holding S corporation stock is still subject to UBTI rules. However, if the DAF is organized as a trust, it will be taxed at trust rates rather than corporate rates.[26] As a result, it can mitigate the UBTI burden when holding donated S corporation stock. Although the taxable income threshold for the highest marginal tax rate is much lower for trusts (only $8,350), long-term capital gains are taxed at only 20 percent.[27] This capital gains advantage is very appealing for highly appreciated S corporation stock. Further still, if the DAF makes charitable grants to other public charities, any capital gains tax would be reduced by 60 percent given the 990T UBIT return allows for a full deduction for charitable contributions limited to 60 percent of AGI. So the net long term federal capital gains tax would be just 10 percent. Similarly, any recognized ordinary income would be at half the maximum rate as well (currently, 18.5 percent vs. 37 percent).

Another option is funding a charitable gift annuity with S corporation stock. Ideally using the trust form again for the favorable capital gains treatment, a CGA can be used in lieu of an ineligible remainder trust.[28] As with other CGA agreements, the donor (or their named beneficiary) gets an income interest and a deduction for the charitable portion of the gift. Since UBTI rules still apply, the trust should liquidate the S corporation at its soonest convenience.

Checklist for a Charity When it Is Offered a Gift of S Corp Stock

    A. Charitable Purpose. If donor intends to make a restricted gift (e.g., scholarships only, endowment only), are the donor's charitable purposes acceptable?

    B. Stock as an Investment

---

22. IRC § 4943(e).
23. The prohibition against a payment for services generally applies to any donor to any DAF. IRC §§ 4958(c)(2), 4958(f)(7) and 4966(d)(2)(A)(ii).
24. IRC § 4958(c)(2)(A).
25. The special rules contained in IRC § 4958(c)(2) (c)(3) for donor-advised funds supporting organizations only apply to a "grant, loan, compensation, or other similar payment." See, for example, Private Letter Ruling 200821024 (May 23, 2008), which involved a donation of closely held stock to a DAF that the parties expected would be redeemed by the corporation in a manner similar to that described in Rev. Rul. 78-197, 1978-1 C.B. 83. The Service did not expressly address potential excess benefits tax issues under IRC § 4958.
26. Horwood, R.M. (2012), "Unlocking Your Donors' Noncash Treasure Chests," Partnership for Philanthropic Planning, http://my.pppnet.org/library/75955/1/NCPP12_Horwood.pdf.
27. Id.
28. Id.

S Corporations

1. What is the nature of the business and its prospects for profitability?
2. What is the stock worth?
3. When will the charity likely sell it?
4. During the time that the charity will own the stock, what is the expected after-tax cash flow from the stock? The after-tax cash flow will be the cash distributions from the S corporation minus the UBIT.

C. Should Donor's Recognition or Benefits Be Adjusted for Anticipated UBIT?

1. Should donor get credit in a major campaign for the full appraised value of the stock or only for the anticipated net amount after UBIT?
2. If a charitable gift annuity will be issued, should the payments be reduced since there will be less cash after the stock's sale because of the UBIT?

D. State Law Issues

1. Can charity own stock under state law?
2. Is there a state UBIT?

E. UBIT Concerns

1. Will gift be made to a charitable trust or an incorporated charity? If a charity has a choice, determine which type of entity will pay the least amount of UBIT.
2. What is donor's adjusted tax basis in the stock? If donor does not know, looking at the balance sheet of the corporation's income tax return may be a way to estimate the basis. Donor's tax basis is important because of the following reasons:
    a. It affects the gain or loss upon the sale of stock.
    b. It affects whether cash distributions from S corporation are taxable or tax free.
    c. It affects whether an S corporation's losses will be deductible or not.
3. What is the projected taxable income or losses of the corporation? How much UBIT will the charity have to pay while it holds the stock? Examine the Schedule K-1 that the donor received from the S corporation.
4. What are the projected cash and property distributions to the charity? See Line 20 of Schedule K-1.
    a. Cash distributions?
    b. Expected Amounts?
    c. Sufficient to pay UBIT?

    d. Any extra for charitable purposes?
 5. Distributions taxable or tax free?
 6. Timing of distributions to meet quarterly UBIT payments when due?
 7. Property distributions?
 8. A distribution of appreciated property could trigger tax. Are any such distributions planned in the near future?
    a. Will the charity have to file UBIT Form 990-T return (required if gross UBTI is over $1,000)?
    b. Will the charity have to make quarterly UBIT estimated tax payments (required if tax due for any year over $500)?
F. Administrative Requirements if Gift Is Accepted
 1. Charity must sign donor's Form 8283 (qualified appraisal) to acknowledge receipt of gift of stock. The donor should know that unlike gifts of other kinds of stock, the tax deduction for donated S corporation stock is often less than the appraised value.
 2. Charity should send donor a "contemporaneous written acknowledgment" that contains the language necessary for the donor to claim a charitable income tax deduction.
G. Sale of Stock
 1. Obtain evidence of the sale of the stock for its fair value (e.g., a recent appraisal).
 2. Send Form 8282 to the IRS and the donor if property is sold within three years.
 3. Charity must pay UBIT on the gain from the sale of S corporation stock.

S Corporations Additional Resources

Below are further details on S corporation gifts. S corporation topics are based on Christopher Hoyt's "Charitable Gifts by S Corporations and Their Shareholders: Two Worlds of Law Collide," and "Charitable Gifts by S Corporations: Opportunities and Challenges." For quick take-aways on S corporation gifts, see [S Corporation Quick Take-Aways](). For a review based on the articles, see [S Corporations Intermediate](). For an in-depth examination adapted and excerpted from the articles, see [S Corporations Advanced](). For further details, see [S Corporations Additional Resources]().

For a discussion on the possible pitfalls of donated S corporation stock, see Zaragoza, D. (February 28, 2012), "Charities, S Corporations and UBIT: Why a Charitable Gift of S Corporation Stock May Not Be the Best Option," LexisNexis, https://www.lexisnexis.com/legalnewsroom/estate-elder/b/estate-elder-blog/archive/2012/02/28/morrison-foerster-llp-charities-s-corporations-and-ubit-why-a-charitable-gift-of-s-corporation-stock-may-not-be-the-best-option.aspx?Redirected=true.

For a discussion of how nonprofits should hold S corporation stock, see Peebles, L. (1999), "Tax Saving Opportunities for Charities Owning Subchapter S Stock," Planned Giving Design Center, http://www.pgdc.com/pgdc/article/1999/10/tax-savingopportunities-charities-owning-subchapter-s-stock.

For analysis of an IRS ruling on S corporation gifts, see Hoyt, C. (March 3, 2008), "Service Issues Favorable Guidance Regarding Gifts of Appreciated Property by S-Corporations," Planned Giving Design Center, http://www.pgdc.com/pgdc/service-issues-favorable-guidance-regarding-gifts-appreciated-property-s-corporations.

For examples and analysis of S corporation charitable transaction, see Newman, D.W. (2011), "Gifts of S Corporation Assets," Partnership for Philanthropic Planning, http://my.pppnet.org/library/60433/1/NCPP11_Newman%28rev%29.pdf.

For analysis of IRS positions on S corporation donations, see Joseph P. Toce, Jr. et al, *Tax Economics of Charitable Giving* 10-13 – 10-16 (2003).

IRC § 1367(a) (adjusted basis rules for contributions by the S corporation)

IRC § 512(e) (unrelated business taxable income rules relevant to S corporation interests)

IRC § 170(e)(1) (donors recognize "hot asset" gain on contributed S corporation stock)

Rev. Rul. 92-48, 1992-1 C.B. 301 (CRTs not allowed to own S corporation stock)

Rev. Rul. 08-16, 2008-11 I.R.B. 585 (example and analysis of an S corporation making a gift)

IRS Notice 2004-30, 2004-17 I.R.B. 1 (donations of nonvoting S corporation stock)

Private Letter Ruling 200326039 (donation of S corporation assets with multiple entities)

Private Letter Ruling 200644013 (June 21, 2006) (donation of built-in gain property to a CRT)

Alli v. Comm'r, TC Memo, 2014-15 (January 27, 2014) (S corporation donation with appraisal problems)

Chapter 4
Pass-Through Entities

- Quick Take-Aways
- Intermediate
- Advanced
- Additional Resources

Charitable Gifts of Noncash Assets

Pass-Through Entities Quick Take-Aways

By Bryan Clontz

Below are quick take-aways on gifts of pass-through entities. Pass-through entity topics are based on Dennis Walsh's "Navigating the Charitable Transfer of a Partnership Interest: A Primer," and Jane Wilton and Nicole Spooner's "Considerations in Making Charitable Gifts of Interests in Pass-Through Entities." For quick take-aways on gifts of pass-through entities, see Pass-Through Entities Quick Take-Aways. For a review based on the articles, see Pass-Through Entities Intermediate. For an in-depth examination adapted and excerpted from the articles, see Pass-Through Entities Advanced. For further details, see Pass-Through Entities Additional Resources.

Interests in pass-through entities can make for appealing donations. They can be both strong income producing assets for charities, and a tax bargain for donors. These entities are often structured as either partnerships or limited liability companies.

Below is an overview of the advantages, disadvantages, considerations, and essential questions when considering accepting gifts of pass-through interests. Also highlighted are unique aspects of both partnerships and LLCs.

Advantages of donations of pass-through interests include:

- The IRS does not tax income at the entity level (pass-through treatment), particularly appealing for charities who receive interests in passive investment entities and are afforded the UBTI exception.
- Pass-through donations can be structured in a number of ways, depending on the donor's goals, the form of the entity, and the charity's desired use.
- Partnership and LLC interests can be used to fund most every kind of planned gift assuming no debt or other active business income which may generate UBTI and a clear and quick exit strategy.

LLC Features to Note:

- Limited exposure to potential liability to third parties in most cases.
- LLC operating agreements are more likely to require capital contributions from members.
- In some cases, LLCs may elect to be taxed as a corporation.

Partnership Features to Note:

- Interests often come with a share of the partnership's liabilities.
- Partnerships may not have a formal partnership agreement.
- State partnership law is uniform, unlike LLCs.

Disadvantages of donating pass-through interests include:

- Calculation of different elements of the interest can be quite complex (including basis, hot assets, passive losses, and more), meaning valuation is often complicated as well. This impacts the charitable transfer, reporting requirements, and the nonprofit's eventual sale of the interest.
- The partnership or operating agreement can restrict transferability of the interest, which can also limit marketability of the interest when the charity decides to liquidate.
- Similarly, pass-through interests often have a limited market on sale—typically only the original donor, the entity itself, and other partners or members.
- Pass-through entities can generate unrelated business taxable income, either by virtue of its normal, active business income-generating activities or through debt-financed income.
- A gift of a pass-through entity with debt will trigger bargain sale rules.
- Gifts of unique pass-through entities or property, like carried interests, can be extremely complex and are sometimes subjected to legislative or tax changes.
- Some of these interests can include capital calls or other liability exposures (i.e., general partnership interests).

Discovery Questions

Donor Questions

1. What is the donor trying to accomplish with the gift?
2. What is the value of the pass-through entity and how was that determined (e.g., appraisal, recent transactions)?
3. Is there any debt?
4. Legally, who or what owns the interests?

Advisor Questions

1. What is the current tax basis (and is the partnership basis negative)?
2. Does the operating or partnership agreement allow charitable transfers, and if so, what is the process?
3. What is the likely exit plan for the charity (e.g., will sale be for cash, note, stock or some combination)?

4. Does the advisor have an estimate of what a qualified appraisal will cost (this expense can vary greatly and can be an impediment to smaller donations)?
5. If an asset donation is being explored, will all owners/partners agree on the size of the gift and the charity?

Charity Questions

1. Is the effort worth the expected benefits (i.e., is the juice worth the squeeze)?
2. If the interest is in a partnership, is it a limited partnership interest? Otherwise charity is at risk for the partnership's liabilities.
3. Has the screening and due diligence process identified any potential problems and can the risks be mitigated (primarily this will be capital calls which can be found in the partnership or operating agreement)?
4. Is there the necessary expertise to accept gifts of pass-through entities in a timely way?
5. Should indirect gift acceptance be considered, like using external third party foundations or supporting organizations to receive the asset?
6. Is there a clear liquidation plan to maximize the sales proceeds as soon as possible?

Pass-Through Entities Intermediate

By Ryan Raffin

Below is a review of gifts of pass-through entities. Pass-through entity topics are based on Dennis Walsh's "Navigating the Charitable Transfer of a Partnership Interest: A Primer," and Jane Wilton and Nicole Spooner's "Considerations in Making Charitable Gifts of Interests in Pass-Through Entities." For quick take-aways on gifts of pass-through entities, see Pass-Through Entities Quick Take-Aways. For a review based on the articles, see Pass-Through Entities Intermediate. For an in-depth examination adapted and excerpted from the articles, see Pass-Through Entities Advanced. For further details, see Pass-Through Entities Additional Resources.

This review of charitable gifts of interests in pass-through entities has seven parts in total. The first part discusses asset considerations, and the second reviews bargain sales. Third is a valuation discussion, while fourth is an examination of holding considerations. Following that are sale and transfer considerations. The final two parts discuss planned giving vehicles and miscellaneous other considerations.

Although cash and publicly-traded securities are the most common asset classes for donors to contribute to charity, interests in closely held businesses can be attractive gifts as well. Pass-through entities, such as limited liability companies (LLCs) and partnerships, are a form of closely held business, and gifts of these interests have unique considerations.

Owners of these interests are referred to as members for LLCs and partners for partnerships. In either case, they may wish to donate all or part of their interest to a nonprofit. Gifts or sales of a pass-through entity interest present both tax and estate planning opportunities for donors. They also can provide valuable income for the receiving charities. However, like many classes of assets, they come with unique considerations that require special preparation and planning.

Transfers of pass-through interests present special issues for both the donor and the nonprofit. For this reason, the two parties should work together to make the process go as smoothly as possible. Some methods of making the transfer that should be considered include outright gift, bargain sale, asset donations, and gift of proceeds from sale.

Review Part 1: Asset Considerations

The Internal Revenue Service allows for a tax deduction equal to the fair market value of the donated property—in this case, the LLC or partnership interest. The IRS allows this deduction provided it is "long-term capital gain property," meaning capital assets held for over a year. Because the activities and assets of the entity are attributed to the partner, his or her pro rata share of various assets will reduce the benefit of the charitable deduction.

Further, for the donation to be deductible, it must be an undivided portion of the entire interest. This means that the donation must be a proportionate share of everything, not solely a donation of the share of distributions for example. A good way to think of this is that the donation must be a "full slice" of the donor's partnership or LLC interest. Note that the capital structure of most investment advisory partnerships were created for solid business reasons, and while they specifically may not have "full slices", these types of entities may still be donated effectively.

Items that the parties need to calculate are as follows:

- Adjusted basis—Regulations limit recognition of loss or deduction to adjusted basis and amount at risk. The share of partnership liabilities is added to the donor's basis to calculate adjusted basis. Note for donations the partnership that the amount of a partner's loss limitation is reduced by the share of tax basis in donated property.
- At-risk amount—The amount is increased to the extent the donor is personally liable for entity debt (less of a factor, therefore, for LLCs).
- Passive activity losses—For partners who did not at all times materially participate in the business's activities, unrecognized losses may present an issue. Tax benefits are foregone to the extent that such losses are allocated to the gifts. The benefits of the suspended losses are instead added to the donee's carryover basis.
- Hot assets—The presence of hot assets, as defined in Section 751, will impact both the character of gain on sale (if any), and the allowed deduction amount. Hot assets are unrealized receivables, appreciated inventory, and Section 1245 and 1250 property to the extent of depreciation recapture. Gain on the sale of such property is ordinary income and the donor's deduction, to the extent attributable to such property, will be limited to the partnership's basis in the assets.
- Relief of debt—Relief of donor debt due to transfer of the interest is also treated as amount realized. If that debt was part of the at-risk amount, then the benefit was either already received via past deductions or will be offset against the remaining basis allocable to a sale. This treatment generally applies to debt inside the partnership allocated to the donor, even if the donor is not personally liable for the debt.

Review Part 2: Bargain Sale

A bargain sale is the transfer of the interest to the charity by sale for below fair market value. In this case, the IRS prescribes part-gift, part-sale treatment, so that the difference between actual sale price and fair market value is a gift. Further, the donor's basis must be prorated between the portions gifted and sold. This means that the basis on the sale portion is proportionate to the basis on a fair market value sale.

Ordinary income and capital gain must be proportionally allocated using the same method in a bargain sale. Essentially, the sale portion of the transaction is a "smaller" version of what a normal fair market value transaction would be. However, no loss is recognized if the proceeds are less than the proportion of basis in the sale.

Review Part 3: Valuation

For outright gifts or bargain sales, the value of the interest is key to determining the allowable deduction. As discussed above, the parties must know the total value of the transferred interest in order to allocate the value and basis between the sale and gift portions for a bargain sale. Since there is rarely a market for minority closely held business interests, the value can be difficult to determine. If the donor acquired the interest through a broker, that route can be pursued again.

In the more likely case where there is no market for the interest, valuation is harder. IRS Revenue Ruling 59-60 is the defining methodology for valuing closely held interests, and should at least be consulted. Further, if the value exceeds $5,000, the donor needs a qualified appraisal (although the cost of such an appraisal may be prohibitive for small donations).

Review Part 4: Holding Considerations for the Charity

Unrelated business taxable income (UBTI) is often relevant to gifts of pass-through entities. A non-profit member or partner is allocated a share of gains, income, losses, and deductions. This income may be UBTI, depending on the nature of the underlying business activities. Debt-financed income will also give rise to UBTI. Charities should either not accept UBTI-generating member interests, or should verify that it generates cash distributions sufficient to pay the resulting tax liability.

Another factor which charities should consider is the possibility of capital calls. LLC operating agreements in particular may require that members commit to future capital contributions.

Nonprofits will generally not accept an interest—whether in an LLC or partnership—which requires payments by the charity. For a similar reason, a charity is unlikely to accept a general partnership interest because of the attendant liability for the entity's debts.

The IRS requires the business to disclose certain transactions, with harsh financial penalties for nondisclosure, even for participating charities. These transactions are ones that have the potential for tax avoidance or evasion. The donation itself may not be an issue, but later business transactions (even if the charity is not actively involved) may require disclosure. Those transactions will be legally attributed to the member charity.

Review Part 5: Sale Considerations

As with other asset types, the nonprofit should determine its exit strategy before accepting. A general policy is best. Will it hold all donated interests, sell all donated interests, or decide based on the attributes of the specific entity in question? Closely held businesses usually have a limited resale market—potential buyers include other partners or members, the entity itself, an acquiring firm, or the original donor.

Partnership or operating agreements may control conditions of a sale or transfer of an interest. Even if the agreement is silent, state law will govern. These agreements and laws can often require the assent of the other owners—clearly, both the donor and charity must verify if the transfer needs approval. Logically, the more owners there are, the more difficult it will be to get approval. This restriction may apply both on donation and on sale.

If subsequent sale of an interest by the charity to a third-party is prearranged as part of the donation, there must not be any legal obligation to carry out such a sale. If the sale does not meet these requirements, the IRS may disregard the donation, and instead it may be classified as an assignment of income to the charity—meaning the donor must recognize any long-term capital gain. Further, if the sale occurs within three years of receiving the interest, the nonprofit must file Form 8282 with the IRS and send a copy to the donor.

Review Part 6: Planned Giving Vehicles

If the donor desires an income stream rather than simply making an outright gift, there are different ways to structure the planned giving vehicle. Charities should approach anything that guarantees an annual income stream with caution. A charitable remainder annuity trust is one example, since it is unlikely that the LLC or partnership will produce a guaranteed distribution stream which can be used to pay the donor. A charitable gift annuity has similar concerns, although either can be done if the nonprofit has a buyer in mind.

However, a charitable remainder unitrust (CRUT) may be an appealing option, with important caveats. Partnership debt or liabilities may result in the donor recognizing gain. Note that if the interest is held in a CRUT, the income must be passive and not debt-financed to avoid UBTI. A net-income-with-makeup CRUT (NIMCRUT) might work. In most states, under some variation of the Uniform Principal and Income Act, trust agreements can define what qualifies as "income" for distribution to beneficiaries.[1] One of the problems with a CRT holding a partnership is that the partnership may pass through income to partners without making a distribution. A NIMCRUT solves this problem by including "only partnership distributions, not the actual items reflected on the partnership Schedule K-1 the trust received."[2]

Review Part 7: Other Considerations

A number of other considerations are worth mentioning. These are as follows:

- The business entity itself may consider donating assets to the charity. This transaction would proportionally lower the basis of each member by the corresponding donation amount. If the property is long-term capital gain property, the proportional lowering of basis preserves the benefit of the fair market value deduction without recognition of appreciation.

- Publicly traded partnerships are uncommon, but worth mentioning. As the name implies, they are readily available on securities or secondary markets, easing valuation and marketability concerns. However, they receive corporate tax treatment unless 90 percent or more of its income is "qualifying income"—generally passive investment or capital gain income. The trade-off then is the advantage of easier valuation and marketability versus double taxation rather than normal pass-through treatment.

- Real estate investment trusts (REITs) are corporations that own and manage a portfolio of real property and mortgages. REITs receive deductions for dividends paid, meaning investors are taxed only on their resulting income—similar to partnership tax treatment. Charities should investigate a potential REIT gift carefully, since it may generate

---

1. Phillips, M.S. (March 31, 2014), "Coordinating Charitable Trusts and Private Foundations for the Business Owner: Complying With UBIT and Self-Dealing Rules," The Tax Adviser, http://www.thetaxadviser.com/issues/2014/apr/clinic-story-05.html#sthash.m3V-J32Ff.dpuf.
2. Id.

UBTI in the event of debt-financed income—unless the entity has a UBIT blocker. Further, the terms of the REIT may not even allow a charitable gift to begin with.

- Carried interests and potential changes to laws governing their tax treatment are another unique wrinkle. A carried interest is an ownership interest granted in exchange for services and in lieu of a capital contribution. Current laws treat carried interests as capital assets, meaning they qualify for favorable capital gains tax rates (note that the holding period for capital gains treatment is three years, starting in 2018). However, proposals abound to alter this treatment so that at least a portion of the interest would be ordinary income. Effectively, this would reduce the value of the deduction. Both donors and charities should keep themselves apprised of these possible legislative changes.

Conclusion

Donors with well-planned current or deferred gifts or bargain sales of their partnership interests can create estate and income tax advantages for themselves. This transfer of interest can also be valuable as both an asset and an income-stream for the nonprofit. However, the donor and nonprofit alike need to consider factors such as the transferred basis, liability exposure, transferability restrictions, and numerous other tax issues. These factors can affect how the gift is structured, and the resulting tax benefits to the donor.

They can also be make-or-break factors for the charity, who may not want to accept an asset that opens them up to considerable future expenses or other contingent liabilities. Further, the charity should consider the ongoing administrative costs, and the difficulty of disposing of the asset should the need arise. UBTI, capital calls, and reportable transactions are all unpleasant surprises to the unprepared charity. Pass-through interests such as partnerships are simple on their face, but come with a host of possible tax complications. Since this is the case, careful analysis and planning is almost always required before making the go-ahead decision to donate.

Pass-Through Entities Advanced[3]

By Dennis Walsh, Jane Wilton, and Nicole Spooner

Below is an in-depth examination on gifts of pass-through entities. Pass-through entity topics are based on Dennis Walsh's "Navigating the Charitable Transfer of a Partnership Interest: A Primer," and Jane Wilton and Nicole Spooner's "Considerations in Making Charitable Gifts of Interests in Pass-Through Entities." For quick take-aways on gifts of pass-through entities, see Pass-Through Entities Quick Take-Aways. For a review based on the articles, see Pass-Through Entities Intermediate. For an in-depth examination adapted and excerpted from the articles, see Pass-Through Entities Advanced. For further details, see Pass-Through Entities Additional Resources.

This section addresses the tax considerations for charitable contributions using closely held businesses or alternative investments structured as "pass-through entities." For the most part, these are limited partnerships or limited liability companies (LLCs) that have not chosen to be taxed at the entity level as Subchapter C corporations, but instead "pass through" each partner or member's allocable share of net income or gain.[4]

For an individual holding an interest in a business or investment entity taxed as a partnership, a charitable transfer can create an attractive planning opportunity while providing welcome support to a favored charity. A transfer may take the form of an outright gift, a sale followed by donation of the proceeds, or part gift, part sale as needed to satisfy the charitable, estate, and succession objectives of the donor.

In the case of an interest in an active business, the donors can usually optimize the tax benefit of a charitable donation at a time when the entity is performing at or near its historical high, especially if it is likely to be bought out. A fair market value deduction that captures enterprise value and untaxed appreciation of tangible assets can result in greater tax savings than the contribution of the proceeds of a sale of the business interest or from the liquidation of its underlying assets.

But the transfer of a pass-through interest poses special challenges for both a donor and recipient charity. The parties must exercise great care to avoid inadvertent consequences and attain the desired charitable benefits.

---

3. This chapter excerpts and adapts Walsh, D. (January 26, 2011), "Navigating the Charitable Transfer of a Partnership Interest: A Primer," Planned Giving Design Center, http://www.pgdc.com/pgdc/navigating-charitable-transfer-partnership-interest-primer, and Wilton, J. and Spooner, N. (June 2010), "Considerations in Making Charitable Gifts of Interests in Pass-Through Entities," The New York Community Trust Professional Notes, http://www.nycommunitytrust.org/ProfessionalAdvisors/ProfessionalTaxEstatePlanning-Notes/UnusualCharitableGifts/GiftsofInterestsinPass-throughEntities/tabid/555/Default.aspx
4. Owners of interests in LLCs are referred to as members.

General Rules

The IRS considers gain from the sale or exchange of a pass-through interest to be gain from the sale of a capital asset.[5] The contribution of property to a qualifying charity is deductible at fair market value, except for gain that would not be long-term capital gain if the owners sold the property at its fair market value on the date it was contributed.[6] However, the IRS generally limits the deduction for long-term capital gain property contributed to a private foundation, other than an operating foundation, to the lesser of fair market value and cost or other basis of the property.

Subchapter K of the Internal Revenue Code (the "Code")[7] contains an extensive set of rules that govern partnership taxation (including entities taxed like partnerships such as LLCs). Under Code Section 702(b), the character of any item of income, gain, loss, deduction, or credit included in a distributive share from entity activities is determined as if such item were realized directly or incurred in the same manner as incurred by the entity.[8]

It should be noted that most charities will not accept a general partnership interest; the for-profit activity generally is inconsistent with a charitable mission, and may place charitable assets at risk for the liabilities of the partnership. Even the acceptance and disposition of a limited partnership of LLC interest may impose an undue burden on the charity and its staff.

Deduction Considerations

Generally, fair market value of an interest ordinarily will be the difference between the donor's share of the fair market value of entity assets and his share of liabilities, whether recourse or nonrecourse. This section discusses the various factors affecting the value of the interest.

Undivided Interest—Under the partial interest rules, the IRS only allows a charitable deduction if the donor of a pass-through interest gives his or her entire interest in the property or an undivided portion of that entire interest to charity. A gift of an undivided portion of an interest must include a pro rata share of all attributes of the interest in the entity, such as capital, allocation of income and expense, and distributions.

---

5. IRC § 741 (2002).
6. IRC § 170(e)(1) (2015); Treas. Reg. § 1.170A-1(c)(1) (2008).
7. All "Code" references are to the Internal Revenue code of 1986, as amended, and all "Treas. Reg. Section" references are to the regulations promulgated thereunder.
8. IRC § 702(b) (2003).

Relief of Debt—If the transfer of an interest results in a donor being relieved of any debt, it is treated as an amount realized. While the relief of debt does not provide any immediate consideration to a donor, the elimination of a liability improves the donor's economic position. In addition, if the debt was part of the donor's at-risk amount, he or she has either received an equivalent tax benefit from past entity deductions or will receive an offsetting deduction of such remaining basis allocable to a sale.[9]

Recognition of Loss—Before application of the passive loss limits (discussed below), the IRS initially limits recognition of any item of loss or deduction to the donor's adjusted basis and then to the amount at risk. These amounts may be different if the nature of the entity, nonrecourse debt (other than qualified nonrecourse debt), or a loss-limiting agreement act to limit personal liability.

Hot Assets—Another important consideration in evaluating a gift or sale is an exception to the Section 741 rule that gain recognized on a partnership or LLC interest is gain from the sale of a capital asset. The presence of Section 751 "hot assets" in the entity will affect the donor's character of gain recognized from a sale as well as the allowable amount of a charitable contribution of the interest.

Hot assets include unrealized receivables, inventory items that have appreciated to a fair market value exceeding 120 percent of their inside basis, and Section 1245/Section 1250 property to the extent of depreciation recapture. Gain realized from a transfer of such property treated as a sale is ordinary income. The donor reduces the amount of a charitable contribution deduction by the amount of any ordinary income that he/she would realize if the property had been sold at fair market value on the date contributed.

Passive Losses—Donors who have not at all times materially participated in any trade or business activities of the entity should calculate unrecognized losses with respect to such activities as a result of the passive loss limitations of Section 469. If passive losses are present, the tax benefit will be forfeited to the extent allocable to a gift.[10] Instead, the donee organization must add suspended losses allocable to a gift to its carryover basis.

Bargain Sale

Assuming that there is no receipt of cash or other consideration, and that there is not relief of any amount of partnership debt, the donor would not realize any amount from the donation. But when

---

9.   IRC § 752(d) (1954).
10. IRC § 469(j) (2014).

the donor receives consideration from the donee organization and the total amount realized is less than the fair market value of the interest, the IRS classifies the transfer as a bargain sale.

In such case, the transaction is a partial gift and a partial sale. The donor subtracts the total amount realized from the fair market value of the interest, and the difference is considered a gift.

However, regulations prohibit a sale between a private foundation and a "disqualified person," as defined in Section 4946(a), as an act of self-dealing. Further, they provide that a sale of stock or other securities by a disqualified person to a private foundation in a bargain sale is treated as an act of self-dealing regardless of the foundation's amount paid.[11]

The bargain sale provisions of Section 1011(b) limit the amount of basis allocated to the portion of the interest sold. The donor must prorate his or her basis in the pass-through interest, along with any suspended passive losses, between the gift and sale portions. The basis for calculating gain must bear the same ratio to the total basis that the amount realized from sale bears to the total fair market value of the interest. Donors may not recognize any loss if the amount realized is less than the basis allocated to the sale portion.[12]

The donor-seller must separately allocate ordinary income and capital gain realized on a bargain sale to the sale and gift portions as well. The amounts which a seller would realize on a fair market value sale of the entire interest are allocated between the sale and gift portions based on the ratio that the fair market value of the sale and gift portions each bear to the fair market value of the entire interest.[13] Examples of the allocation of basis, calculation of recognized gain, and reduction of a charitable contribution as the result of a bargain sale or an ordinary income element are available in Treas. Reg. Section 1.1011-2(c).[14]

Timing of Charitable Contribution

The limited partnership agreement or, in the case of an LLC, the LLC operating agreement generally governs the admission of a new partner or member. Where the agreement is silent, state law will control. For example, the substitution of a new partner may require consent of both the new partner and the existing partners. Under a typical limited partnership agreement, the contribution

---

11. Treas. Reg. § 53.4941(d)-2(a)(1) (1995).
12. Treas. Reg. § 1.1001-1(e)(1) (2007).
13. Treas. Reg. § 1.170A-4(c)(3) (1994).
14. Treas. Reg. § 1.1011-2(c) (1994).

of a partnership interest would not be effective until the charity accepts and the general partner consents.

Factors That May Affect a Charity's Willingness to Accept a Gift of a Pass-Through Interest

Unrelated Business Income Tax: Although generally exempt from tax, charities pay tax on their unrelated business taxable income (UBTI), which is net income they derive from any trade or business that is not substantially related to the charity's exempt purpose. As a result, if a charity becomes an owner in a pass-through entity that operates an unrelated trade or business, the charity will include in UBTI its share of the entity's income or gain derived from any unrelated trade or business, regardless of whether that entity distributes cash. In addition, under the debt-financed income rules of Code Section 514, UBTI also may arise as a result of the business's indebtedness. A charity is unlikely to accept an interest that will produce UBTI unless it gets assurances that it will receive sufficient cash distributions to pay the resulting tax liability.

Because hedge funds often raise money through borrowing, they are likely to produce UBTI as a result of the debt-financed income rules. To enable charities to invest in alternate investments such as hedge funds without incurring significant tax liabilities, U.S. hedge funds commonly create foreign corporations called "blocker corporations." Through these entities, charities can invest in limited partnership hedge funds without incurring UBTI. The dividends that charities receive from these foreign blocker corporations are not subject to the debt-financed income rules and are not UBTI. Many charities include hedge funds in their portfolios, investing through foreign blocker corporations.

A donor who wishes to contribute a limited partnership interest in a hedge fund to charity may want to consider whether the interest can be converted to an interest in the offshore blocker corporation before donating the interest to charity. However, if the donor himself/herself contributes his or her interest to a non-U.S. blocker corporation, he/she will recognize gain under Code Section 367 and face IRS reporting obligations as well. If the charitable recipient were to contribute the hedge fund interest to a foreign blocker corporation, it likely would have gain that would be treated as debt-financed UBTI.

Other Potential Liabilities: Partnership and LLC operating agreements commonly include provisions for capital calls. This is particularly true in venture capital or private equity funds where investors pay in their capital commitments over a period of years. A charity receiving a contribution of an interest will want assurance that it will not be subject to any capital call provisions.

Tax Shelter Restrictions: Regulations require that investors in certain tax shelters and "reportable transactions" disclose their participation in those transactions. A reportable transaction is any transaction where information must be included with a return or statement because IRS has determined that the transaction is of a type that has a potential for tax avoidance or evasion.

The failure to include information about a reportable transaction is subject to penalties. In the case of a charity, the penalty is significant: $50,000 for a reportable transaction and $200,000 if the reportable transaction is one that IRS has publicly identified (known as a "listed transaction").

Before accepting a gift of an interest in a closely held business, particularly an interest in a business structure with multiple layers, a charity will want to assess the activities of the entity at each level. Regulations will attribute the organization's transactions to the charity if it accepts the interest. The charity may want representations from the business that it is not engaged in any reportable or listed tax shelter transactions.

Other Considerations

Transferability: Partnership and LLC interests generally are not freely transferable. The contributing owner and the charity will want to confirm that all requirements for transfer under the partnership or operating agreement are met.

Valuation: A contribution of an interest worth more than $5,000 will require a written appraisal from a qualified appraiser, unlike the case of a contribution of publicly traded securities.

Publicly Traded Partnerships: Under Code Section 7704, a publicly traded partnership (PTP) is a partnership whose interests are traded on an established securities market or are readily tradable on a secondary market. A PTP gets corporate tax treatment unless 90 percent or more of its gross income in the current taxable year and each preceding year is "qualifying income." For this purpose, qualifying income includes interest, dividends, real property rents, gain from sale or disposition of real property, and gain on sale or disposition of a capital asset held for production of such income. If 90 percent of a PTP's gross income is qualifying income, the PTP is taxed as a partnership. A PTP that the IRS taxes as a partnership may raise UBIT issues for a charity, although generally speaking, the enumerated types of income do not constitute UBTI unless debt financing is involved.

If the PTP units are worth over $5,000, a donor will need to evaluate whether the contribution of those interests requires a qualified appraisal. Although a qualified appraisal is not required for a gift of "publicly traded securities," that term is limited to the stock of corporations. Units of a PTP which the owners treat as a corporation under Code Section 7704 are arguably equivalent to publicly traded stock of a corporation. However, the applicability of the qualified appraisal rules to those units is unclear. Additionally, the Tax Cuts and Jobs Act of 2017 makes the Section 199A deduction available to PTPs, so donors should consult their advisors to determine the impact of a donation.

Contribution of Assets by the Business Entity: Instead of an individual donating his/her interest to charity, the business itself can donate assets to charity. Each owner's basis in their interest decreases by the corresponding share of the organization's basis in the property contributed, because charitable deductions are separately allocated to and deductible by the owners under Code Section 702. The IRS has noted that, for long-term capital gain property, limiting the basis deduction to the share of the organization's basis in the assets preserves the intended benefit of providing a deduction for the fair market value of appreciated property without recognition of the appreciation. Note that the donation will reduce a partner's loss limitation under section 704(d) by the amount of the partner's share of basis in the donated property.

REITS: A real estate investment trust (REIT) is a corporation that owns and manages a portfolio of real estate properties and mortgages. Like mutual funds, the law entitles REITs to a deduction for dividends paid and generally are subject to tax only on undistributed income. As a result, investors in REITs are generally subject to only a single level of tax with respect to their investments and, as such, resemble partnerships. A REIT interest may or may not be a suitable charitable gift. Although the income a charity receives from a REIT is treated as dividend income, it may in rare cases generate UBTI because of debt financing. However, regular dividend distributions from REITs, as well as gain from a disposition of a REIT interest, are exempt from the UBTI rules. A donor interested in contributing his or her REIT interest to charity should determine whether the REIT's activities might have negative tax consequences for the charity. The donor should also refer to the REIT's prospectus to determine whether the charitable contribution would be permissible in the first instance. As with PTPs, the Section 199A deduction is available to REITs, so donors should consult their advisors to determine the impact of a donation.

Carried Interests: A carried interest in an LLC or partnership refers to an interest in the entity's profits received in exchange for services, typically without any capital contribution by the provider of those services. Under current law, the carried interest gets capital asset treatment after a three-year holding period and as such is subject to favorable capital gains tax rates upon sale or realization. This rule has become controversial, particularly for carried interests of investment managers of hedge funds and private equity or venture capital funds. However, "qualified capital interests"—meaning capital a service member or partner invests on the same terms as other capital investments in the organization—would still enjoy favorable treatment as a capital asset.

Donors considering contributing a carried interest to charity should consult with their tax advisors and the charity about the possible tax consequences.

Planning Illustration

The following case illustrates the federal tax issues discussed thus far. For the past ten years Bob, age 60, has been a partner of XYZ, a general partnership engaged in a business activity. He does not materially participate in the business activities of XYZ. Bob has adjusted gross income of $200,000, a federal marginal tax rate of 24 percent, and files jointly with his spouse. Bob's current contribution ceiling for capital gain property donated to a qualifying organization other than a private foundation is therefore $60,000 ($200,000 x 30 percent).[15]

Bob estimates the fair market value of his interest in XYZ to be $50,000. He reasonably expects XYZ to continue annual income distributions of approximately seven percent, or $3,500. Bob's adjusted basis and amount at risk in XYZ is $26,000. He has $4,000 of suspended passive activity losses with respect to XYZ. He is personally liable for $5,000 of XYZ debt. His interest includes $3,000 of Section 751 hot assets.

Bob wants to provide for ABC, a 501(c)(3) public charity, by donating his interest but is unsure of the tax implications of such a transfer. He is undecided whether to donate the entire interest, sell it to a third party and then contribute the cash proceeds, offer it for sale to ABC at a bargain price, or take no current action. Assume for illustration purposes that ABC is willing to accept an interest in a general partnership (unlikely in most circumstances). Bob has asked you for help determining his best course of action.

Scenario A – Outright gift of the entire interest to ABC

Scenario B – Sale to a third party for $50,000 in cash and contribution of the proceeds to ABC

Scenario C – Bargain sale to ABC for a cash price of $10,000

---

15. IRC § 170(b)(1)(C)(i) (2015).

Pass-Through Entities

	A		B		C	
Sale and gift elements:						
Value of interest	$50,000		$50,000		$50,000	
Amount realized:						
Cash received	-		$50,000		10,000	
Relief of debt	5,000		5,000		5,000	
Amount realized & sale	5,000	10%	$55,000	100%	15,000	30%
Gift element & gift %	$45,000	90%			$35,000	70%
Tax effect of sale element:						
Amount realized	$5,000		$55,000		$15,000	
Basis of partnership interest (1)	2,600		26,000		7,800	
Gain realized	$2,400		$29,000		$7,200	
Gain recognized:						
Ordinary income (hot assets) (2)	300		3,000		900	
Long-term capital gain (3)	2,100		26,000		6,300	
Total gain recognized	$2,400		$29,000		$7,200	
Tax:						
Ordinary income (25%)	72		720		216	
Capital gain (15%)	315		3,900		945	
Total tax on sale	$387		$4,620		$1,161	
Passive loss recognized (4)	$400		$4,000		$1,200	
Tax savings (25%)	96		960		288	
Tax effect of gift element:						
Gift	45,000		50,000		35,000	
Less allocated ordinary deduction (5)	2,700		-		2,100	
Charitable contribution deduction	$42,300		$50,000		$32,900	
Tax savings (25%)	$10,152		$12,000		$7,896	
Net cost of gift:						
Value of interest	50,000		50,000		50,000	
Less cash received	-		(50,000)		(10,000)	
Plus cash contributed	-		50,000		-	
Plus tax paid on sale element	387		4,620		1,161	
Less tax saved on passive loss	(96)		(960)		(288)	
Less tax saved on gift element	(10,152)		(12,000)		(7,896)	
Net cost of gift	$40,139		$41,660		$32,977	

Step 1 – Determine the separate sale and gift elements. The resulting percentages will be used to allocate basis, long-term capital gain, and ordinary income where the bargain sale rules apply.

Step 2 – Calculate the separate tax effect of the sale and gift elements.

Step 3 – Summarize the results to determine the net cost of the gift:

    (1) $26,000 x sale percentage

    (2) $3,000 x sale percentage

(3) Total gain realized less ordinary income recognized

(4) $4,000 x sale percentage

(5) $3,000 x gift percentage

Comparing Outcomes

Although scenario A involves an outright gift with the donor receiving no cash, the $5,000 relief of debt is treated as an amount realized on sale and triggers application of the bargain sale rules.

In scenario B, it is assumed that the buyer would be willing to pay fair market value for Bob's share of net assets and in addition assume contingent liability for his share of XYZ debt. In practice the total consideration from the buyer at the time of purchase will of course depend upon assessments of the financial strength and future earning capacity of the entity.

In scenarios A and C, if ABC prefers to liquidate the interest immediately instead of carrying it for future cash flow, it may be possible for XYZ to liquidate the interest subsequent to the donation, while preserving Bob's deduction on the appreciated value of his share of long-term capital gain assets.

Alternatively, if XYZ initially liquidates Bob's interest and he then contributes the cash proceeds to ABC, he will lose the benefit of a charitable deduction on such untaxed appreciation. However, this may result in the initial transfer to ABC being disregarded under the assignment of income doctrine, and treated instead as a taxable liquidation of Bob's interest. To avoid this, there must be no legally binding obligation among the parties to carry out a subsequent liquidation.[16]

Comparing scenarios A and B, if Bob does not consider the added tax savings from an outright gift to be substantial, he might prefer instead to give ABC the cash realized from a fair market value sale of the entire interest to a third party. This would save ABC the costs incident to disposition or ongoing administration of the asset.

In addition, the greater the proportion of hot assets represented in a partnership interest, the less will be the added tax benefit of an outright gift as opposed to sale to a third party and contribution of the proceeds. Unlike long-term capital gain, no charitable deduction is allowable on an ordinary income element.

---

16. Rev. Rul. 78-197, 1978-1 C.B. 83

This alternative may also be more attractive where the sum of the adjusted basis (or at-risk amount if less) plus any suspended passive losses is in excess of the fair market value of the interest (i.e. the interest is depreciated). Significantly, recognition of suspended passive losses occurs where the entire interest is disposed of in a fully taxable transaction; that is, one in which any gain or loss realized is fully recognized.

In such case, regulations free up suspended passive losses for deduction in addition to any remaining basis in the interest. Depending on the amount of suspended passive losses, unrecovered basis, and marginal tax rate of the donor, the resultant added tax saving can reduce the gift's net cost.

As scenario C illustrates, a bargain sale can provide a good deal of planning flexibility and may be attractive to the charity where the purchase price is nominal in relation to expected cash flow. ABC would expect to realize an annual return of 35 percent, with its income distributions from XYZ of $3,500, divided by its investment of $10,000. In addition, a donor may combine cash it receives in a bargain sale with current tax savings to provide for wealth replacement as discussed next.

A fourth scenario would be for Bob to retain ownership of the interest, contribute cash distributions from XYZ to ABC, and revisit this analysis from time to time as circumstances change.

Wealth Replacement

Where donor objectives warrant, consider the use of life insurance to replace wealth lost to the estate as a result of a charitable transfer.

Building on the example, at age 60 Bob's life expectancy is 25 years.[17] Further, assume that Bob will be able to realize a similar investment yield of seven percent over the long term. And for simplicity assume that the underlying assets of XYZ are not of a nature that will further appreciate in value.

Accordingly, the future value of the forfeited year-end XYZ income distributions of $3,500 over Bob's life expectancy is approximately $237,000. Adding this amount to the $50,000 value of the interest Bob replaced, his total insurance requirement is $287,000.

---

17. IRS Publication 590-B, Appendix B, Table I.

Bob is in good health and has an insurance quote of a guaranteed annual premium of $1,335, payable at the beginning of each policy year, for a suitable universal life policy with a death benefit of $287,000. In scenario C, cash flow from his immediate net tax savings of $7,355 combined with the bargain sale proceeds of $10,000, totaling $17,355, exceeds the present value of the insurance premiums paid over his life expectancy, $16,600.

Thus, if Bob elects the bargain sale alternative, he will provide ABC with a high-yielding asset and stands a reasonable likelihood of fully restoring wealth otherwise lost to his estate as a result of the charitable transfer.

Conclusion

A well thought out gift or sale of a partnership or LLC interest may create an income tax and estate planning opportunity for a transferring partner as well as vital support for a preferred charitable organization. But such an interest carries special issues that the parties must explore in advance in order to capture maximum tax benefit and avoid unintended outcomes. They should consider any costs incident to transfer and ongoing administration as part of this analysis.

Planners can also aid the charity in the exercise of its stewardship by alerting principals to important concerns before accepting this type of gift, such as unrelated business income tax and transfer of liabilities. If the entity has certain types of property, the donor may not be able to take the full fair market value as a deduction, which may defeat the purpose of donating the interest. If the pass-through entity could generate more than insignificant amounts of UBTI from its assets or activities, the charity may not want to accept the interest. Therefore, before contributing such an interest to charity, the charity and donor alike must thoroughly understand the pass-through entity's structure and should become familiar with its governing documents and activities. They should also have a conversation in order to better understand the charity's needs and possible limitations around such a contribution.

Pass-Through Entities Additional Resources

Below are further details on gifts of pass-through entities. Pass-through entity topics are based on Dennis Walsh's "Navigating the Charitable Transfer of a Partnership Interest: A Primer," and Jane Wilton and Nicole Spooner's "Considerations in Making Charitable Gifts of Interests in Pass-Through Entities." For quick take-aways on gifts of pass-through entities, see Pass-Through Entities Quick Take-Aways. For a review based on the articles, see Pass-Through Entities Intermediate. For an in-depth examination adapted and excerpted from the articles, see Pass-Through Entities Advanced. For further details, see Pass-Through Entities Additional Resources.

For an examination of the IRS applying close scrutiny to a donation of a partnership interest, see Fox, R. (March 19, 2015), "Chief Counsel Advice Applies Substance-Over-Form Doctrine in Disallowing Deduction for Charitable Contribution of Partnership Units," Planned Giving Design Center, http://www.pgdc.com/pgdc/cheif-counsel-advice-applies-substance-over-form-doctrine-disallowing-deduction-charitable-cont.

For advice on charities considering accepting gifts of LLC interests, see Sangster, C.B. and Buckley, S.C. (2010), "Gifts of LLC Interest," *Journal of Gift Planning,* https://connect.wels.net/AOM/Subsidiaries/foundation/Leadership%20Resources/Educational%20Resources/Partnership%20for%20Philanthropic%20Planning%20Papers/Gifts%20of%20LLC%20Interest.pdf.

For a discussion of LLC transfers and basis, see Ellentuck, A.B. (May 31, 2008), "Handling Gifts and Bequests of LLC Interests," *The Tax Adviser,* http://www.thetaxadviser.com/issues/2008/jun/handlinggiftsandbequestsofllcinterests.html.

For an example of a college's policies towards acceptance of privately held securities, see Duke University, "Frequently Asked Questions: Privately Held Securities," https://dukeforward.duke.edu/ways-to-give/gift-planning/gift-plans/outright-gifts/faqs-privately-held.

Treas. Reg. §§ 1.170A-13(c)(iv)(F)-(G) (requirements for partners' tax documentation of appraisal)

Rev. Rul. 75-194, 1975-1 C.B. 80 (tax treatment for donation of limited partnership liabilities)

Rev. Rul. 96-11, 1996-1 C.B. 140 (partnership's donation of partnership assets and effect on bases in respective interests)

Private Letter Ruling 9533014 (IRS ruling favorably on the donation of a partnership interest to a CRUT)

Private Letter Ruling 201012050 (IRS ruling on self-dealing when donating LLC interests)

Private Letter Ruling 201435017 (IRS ruling on potential UBTI for a charity receiving an LLC interest)

Estate of Petter v. Comm'r, 653 F.3d 1012 (9th Cir. 2011) (court approves defined-value clause for LLC gift)

Chapter 5
Agricultural Assets

- Quick Take-Aways
- Intermediate
- Advanced
- Additional Resources

Agricultural Assets Quick Take-Aways

by Bryan Clontz

Below are quick take-aways on gifts of agricultural assets. Agricultural asset topics are based on Phil Purcell's "Gifts of Agricultural Assets." For quick take-aways on gifts of real estate, see Agricultural Assets Quick Take-Aways. For a review based on that article, see Agricultural Assets Intermediate. For an in-depth examination adapted and excerpted from the article, see Agricultural Assets Advanced. For further details, see Agricultural Assets Additional Resources.

Agricultural assets go beyond crops alone—they can include livestock, equipment, and any attached land. This asset class is often highly regulated, and contributions can be very complex as a result. This section discusses the advantages, disadvantages, factors to consider, and questions to ask when considering a gift of agricultural assets.

Advantages of donations of agricultural assets include:

- Versatile asset class that allows flexible giving—donors can contribute crops, livestock, and equipment with or without accompanying land.
- There is often an active market for the donated assets (farmers regularly sell commodities like crops and livestock, and regularly purchase farming equipment).
- Many deferred giving options, including life-income generating planned giving vehicles and retained life estates.
- Bargain sales and conservation easements are also possible avenues for giving.

Disadvantages of donating agricultural assets include:

- The charity's subsequent sale of assets may lead to unrelated business taxable income.
- Donors will generally only enjoy a full fair market value tax deduction if the charity puts the assets to a related use.
- Maintaining the assets while finding a buyer may be burdensome and expensive (for example, feeding livestock).

Wrinkles in the process to consider include:

- Due diligence is important for this asset class, including site inspection, environmental review, and marketing analysis.

- The charity will need a way to store, administer, insure, or otherwise manage the assets after the gift transaction is complete.
- The donor's use of the property can impact the tax deduction available (inventory versus property used in the business) in addition to the charity's intended use.

Discovery Questions

Donor Questions

1. What is the donor trying to accomplish with the gift?
2. What is the asset's value and how was that determined (e.g., appraisal or recent transactions)?
3. Legally, who or what owns the asset?

Advisor Questions

1. What is the current tax basis in the asset and is it ordinary income or long term gain?
2. What is the likely exit plan for the charity (e.g., auction, private sale, commodities broker)?
3. Does the advisor have an estimate of what a qualified appraisal will cost?
4. Is the asset business or farm inventory?

Charity Questions

1. Is the effort worth the expected benefits (i.e., is the juice worth the squeeze)?
2. Has the screening and due diligence process identified any potential problems and can the risks be mitigated?
3. Is there the necessary expertise to accept gifts of agricultural assets in a timely way?
4. Should indirect gift acceptance be considered, like using external third party foundations or supporting organizations to receive the asset?
5. Is there a clear liquidation plan to maximize the sales proceeds as soon as possible?
6. Can the charity use the assets as part of its charitable mission?
7. How will the charity manage or administer the assets while sale is pending?

Agricultural Assets Intermediate

by Phil Purcell

Below is a review on gifts of agricultural assets. Agricultural asset topics are based on Phil Purcell's "Gifts of Agricultural Assets." For quick take-aways on gifts of real estate, see Agricultural Assets Quick Take-Aways. For a review based on that article, see Agricultural Assets Intermediate. For an in-depth examination adapted and excerpted from the article, see Agricultural Assets Advanced. For further details, see Agricultural Assets Additional Resources.

This review of charitable gifts of agricultural assets has five parts in total. The first defines the relevant terms and government positions and publications. Next is an overview of different gift considerations. The third part looks at deferred gift opportunities. Finally, the review concludes with particular attention to the unique aspects of land and timber gifts.

Review Part 1: Definitions and Government Positions

Agricultural assets represent significant potential for philanthropic support of important charitable causes. As of the 2012 census of agriculture, there were 2.1 million farms in the U.S., covering an area of 914 million acres with an average of 434 acres per farm.[1] In 2014, total farm production of crops was estimated at $136.4 billion.[2]

Agricultural assets primarily include land, crops, livestock, and equipment. Gift planning with these agricultural assets presents many unique issues and opportunities. Planning options depend on the assets available for donation, as well as the personal financial and philanthropic goals of the prospective donor.

Regardless of the type of agricultural asset which the donor contributes, valuation remains a very important consideration. The IRS and Congress are increasingly concerned about the over-valuation of noncash gifts for the purposes of claiming charitable tax benefits. Therefore donors and their counsel are advised to carefully follow the rules.

If the sale price is significantly less than the charitable deduction the donor claimed on IRS Form 8283, then this could be a "red flag" for an IRS audit. See Appendix A on valuation considerations

---

1. United States Department of Agriculture (May 2014), "US Census of Agriculture, 2012," Table 1, https://www.agcensus.usda.gov/Publications/2012/Full_Report/Volume_1,_Chapter_1_US/usv1.pdf.
2. 2015 USDA-NASS reports, "Crop Values - 2014 Summary," www.usda/current/CropValuSu/CropValuSu-02-24-2015_correction.pdf.

for more details on substantiation and appraisal rules. A special rule for crops is that cost-basis donors may deduct the cost of growing donated crops, but it must be in the year the crops were grown.

Real estate is land and generally what is erected on, growing on, or affixed to land. A gift of real estate qualifies the donor for an escape of potential capital gains tax so long as the donor did not legally obligate the charity to sell the property in a prearranged sale. See Chapter 1 on real estate donations for a discussion of land gift considerations.

Review Part 2: Gift Planning Considerations

Crops, livestock, and some equipment are considered ordinary income property in the hands of a farmer, since these assets are used in the farmer's business. This means that the charitable deduction for outright gifts is limited to the lesser of fair market value or cost basis—almost always resulting in a cost basis deduction. Previously depreciated farm equipment receives largely the same treatment, with some recapture provisions.

Unharvested crops held for more than one year are long-term capital gain property, along with the land they are attached to. A donation of both the crops and attached land together would therefore qualify for a deduction of appraised fair market value. However, if the unharvested crops are donated without the land, the donation receives only ordinary income treatment. Nonprofit donees should note that if they harvest the crops for sale, they will be subject to UBTI on the proceeds.

A donation of crop shares from a passive landlord will trigger income tax recognition under the assignment of income doctrine. This is because those shares are typically a right to receive income. Conversely, a farmer who participates in production of farm assets and contributes crop shares will not recognize income and may even get a fair market value deduction.

Livestock most commonly includes cattle, hogs, horses, mules, donkeys, sheep, goats and other mammals, while poultry is not included. This distinction is important, because livestock held for draft, dairy breeding, or sporting purposes can get long-term capital gain treatment if held for 12 or 24 months (depending on the animal). A donation of such livestock would therefore qualify for a fair market value deduction. Otherwise it is ordinary income property as described above. Nonlivestock animals are tangible personal property subject to standard related use rules.

Agricultural equipment also receives tangible personal property treatment. This equipment is typically not business inventory (unless the donor is also in the business of selling farm equipment). It too is subject to related use rules reducing the donor's deduction in many cases to cost basis.

While the charitable deductions may be limited, the avoidance of income tax can be attractive to farmers. Similarly, the donation may positively impact the farmer's eligibility for certain government subsidies. As a result, the charity and donor must execute deeds of gifts and receipts that properly document the gift prior to sale. The eventual bill of sale should show the charity owned and sold the assets.

Review Part 3: Deferred Gifts

Donors may make deferred gifts of crops, livestock, and equipment with a will or trust bequest. The unlimited estate tax charitable deduction does not require application of the reduction rules for valuation of these assets as does the income tax deduction. Life income plans such as charitable remainder trusts and gift annuities may appeal to some donors. The donor reduces his or her charitable deduction value due to the type of property as with outright giving, but the opportunity to use these assets to fund additional retirement income that is either fixed or not may be attractive. The trust or charity's sale can avoid income tax recognition at that time by the donor. The IRS taxes payments made to the beneficiaries or annuitants.

Charitable lead trusts can leverage significant income or estate tax savings. They require careful planning, but can represent gifts of significant magnitude. Deferred gifts such as bequests in a will or trust are the most popular form of planned gift due to their simplicity and revocability that offers ease of planning. In addition, transfer on death deeds are increasingly popular deferred giving techniques. A final, unique deferred gift is donation of a remainder interest in a farm or residence subject to a retained life estate. The donor receives a current income tax deduction, plus the right to live on or use the property for donor's life and a spouse as well.

Life income plans such as charitable remainder trusts and gift annuities represent popular planning options for gifts of farm and forest land. For example, a flip charitable remainder trust offers the advantage of a current income tax deduction, but a later sale when the price is right. Then the trust "flips" to a standard unitrust to maximize long-term income and growth potential. Gift annuities also offer a current income tax deduction and fixed lifetime payments that may even be deferred allowing time for the property to sell.

Livestock can be placed in a charitable remainder unitrust—a variant sometimes called a "rawhide unitrust." As with other livestock donations, ordinary income treatment is the norm. Donors receive a cost of goods sold deduction when the trust sells the assets, but the main benefit comes in shifting that taxable income to the trust. The trustee must avoid fattening any livestock it holds before sale—this would trigger UBTI.

Review Part 4: Land Gifts

Gifts of farmland can include outright gifts, bargain sales, life income arrangements (i.e., gift annuities and charitable remainder trusts), charitable lead trusts, bequests, gift of remainder interest with retained life estate, and conservation easements. Each technique requires unique planning considerations and robust gift acceptance policies and procedures, especially for real estate. These policies should address due diligence considerations such as site inspections by staff, environmental review, marketing analysis, building inspections, title review, and deed. For further discussion of these policy considerations, see Chapter 1 on gifts of real estate.

A conservation easement represents a permanent restriction on the use of real property pursuant to a qualified conservation purpose. Examples of land or structures that qualify for easement protection include farmland, forests, wetlands, open space, and historic buildings. The charity owns a right to enforce and protect the qualified conservation purpose. The easement restriction passes to future owners of the property by sale, gift, or other transfer. The income tax deduction for an easement gift is the difference between the value of the easement property before the donation and after the donation.

Review Part 5: Timber Gifts

Gifts of timber or forest land tend to be the most complex. They combine the long term aspects of mineral interests with the harvest and management concerns of agriculture. Relevant factors include the age of the stand, thinning, harvest, transport, and organizing the logging effort. Nonprofits will have fewer concerns if the donor has already harvested the timber, in which case it will be more like other forms of tangible personal property.

Forest land's unique attributes affect its suitability for certain gift formats. Gifts involving annuity streams (gift annuities and charitable remainder annuity trusts) are difficult unless the timber is ready for sale. Charitable remainder unitrusts (including flip and net income variants) are better suited if the forest land still needs harvesting. Conservation easements exist specially for assets like forest land, so donors and nonprofits should consider if they are appropriate given the parties' respective goals.

Agricultural Assets Advanced

by Phil Purcell

Below is an in-depth examination on gifts of agricultural assets. Agricultural asset topics are based on Phil Purcell's "Gifts of Agricultural Assets." For quick take-aways on gifts of real estate, see Agricultural Assets Quick Take-Aways. For a review based on that article, see Agricultural Assets Intermediate. For an in-depth examination adapted and excerpted from the article, see Agricultural Assets Advanced. For further details, see Agricultural Assets Additional Resources.

Gifts of agricultural assets are a unique class in that they literally grow. Donors will typically give crops and timber after the assets have already been harvested. Livestock gifts have special considerations for charities resulting from their unique upkeep. Another unique feature of agricultural assets is a significant level of legislation at both federal and state levels—so donors, nonprofits, and advisors should ensure they are up-to-date with current law.

Land represents an important agricultural asset for gift planning purposes. Any charitable organization considering the acceptance of land should follow some important policies and procedures. For example, liability for environmental contamination can be "strict and several," applying to the charitable organization should it hold title even for a brief period of time.[3] Both federal and state environmental laws and regulations apply. See the discussion in Chapter 1 for an in-depth discussion on gifts of land.

Valuation of Noncash Gifts

Regardless of the type of agricultural asset that is donated, valuation is a very important consideration. The charity that receives the donated asset is not responsible for the valuation of the gift for tax deduction purposes. In fact, the IRS only requires the charity's gift receipt or written acknowledgment to "describe" (not value) the donated property.[4] Failure to follow the rules for gift receipts can result in denial of the charitable deduction.[5]

Cash-basis taxpayers making gifts of crops have some special rules for calculating the charitable deduction. The cost of growing the gifted crops is deducted as a business expense, but only in

---

3. See Comprehensive Environmental Response, Compensation and Liability Act (CERCLA). 42 U.S.C. § 1906 et seq.
4. See IRS Publication 1771.
5. See Durden v. Commissioner, T.C. Memo. 2012-140 (May 17, 2012).

the year the crops were grown.[6] This deduction should be taken on the donor's return in Schedule F, "Profit or Loss from Farming."[7] Regardless of when the crops were grown, the donor avoids including the revenue from sale in taxable income.

Gift Planning with Crops, Livestock and Equipment: Techniques

Similar to planning with land, there are many ways to plan gifts of crops, livestock and equipment. The same three broad categories of gift techniques are those that help the charity now (current use gift), help the charity later (deferred use gifts), and gifts that pay income. Each of these techniques will require consideration of unique planning issues and opportunities. In particular, since the IRS considers crops, livestock, and equipment to be business inventory and/or personal property, the tax benefits are very different than with gifts of land. And, as a result, the use of some planning techniques will be less popular and more complex.

Current Gifts

Current gifts of crops, livestock, and equipment require special consideration given their tax treatment. In general, crops, livestock, and some equipment are a form of personal property that is considered ordinary income property of the farmer. The IRS taxes ordinary income property at the owner's ordinary income tax rate rather than the capital gains tax rate when it is sold.

The charitable deduction rules in this context are as follows: An outright gift of ordinary income property, unlike capital gain property discussed above, is subject to a reduction rule that generally limits the deduction to the lesser of fair market value and cost basis. Crops and livestock can be ordinary income property if held as business inventory. Other types of ordinary income property include tangible personal property such as depreciated equipment or machines—the taxpayer recaptures prior depreciation deductions as ordinary income upon a sale. For example, if the donor has depreciated real property including buildings in excess of straight-line depreciation, then all or a portion of the excess depreciation will be recaptured as ordinary income if the property is sold at a gain. Of course, any property the owner holds for less than the long-term capital gains holding period is ordinary taxable property when sold.

---

6. Patrick, G.F. (December 2011), "Income Tax Management for Farmers in 2011," Purdue Univ. pp. 22 – 23, http://www.agecon.purdue.edu/extension/programs/tax/2011_INCOME_TAX%20MANAGEMENT_FOR_FARMERS.pdf.

7. Locher, J. (April 21, 2011), "Increasing Charitable Yields with Bushel Gifts," farmdoc daily, Department of Agricultural and Consumer Economics, University of Illinois at Urbana-Champaign, http://farmdocdaily.illinois.edu/2011/04/increasing-charitable-yields-w.html.

Two types of cost and expense are not to be treated under any section of the Code as resulting in any basis for the contributed property. These are 1) any costs and expenses which the taxpayer treats as part of the cost of goods sold of the crops for the year of contribution, and 2) any such costs and expenses which are properly deducted under Section 162 or other section of the Internal Revenue Code (Code).[8] The regulations offer two examples of the application of this rule.

First, as Example 5 in the regulations:

> "In 1970, C, a farmer using the cash method of accounting and the calendar year as the taxable year, contributed to a church a quantity of grain which he had raised having a fair market value of $600. In 1969, C paid expenses of $450 in raising the property which he properly deducted for such year under Section 162. Under Section 170(e)(1)(A) and paragraph (a) of § 1.170A-4, the amount of the charitable contribution in 1970 is reduced to zero ($600–[$600–$0]). Accordingly, C is not allowed any [charitable] deduction under Section 170 for the contributed property."[9]

And the second example states the following:

> "The facts are the same as in Example 5 except that the $450 expenses incurred in raising the contributed property were paid in 1970. The result is the same as in Example 5, except the amount of $450 is deductible under Section 162 for 1970."[10]

Unharvested crops and the land it grows on that the owner holds for more than one year are collectively long-term capital gain property. The length of time for which the donor holds the crop, as distinguished from the land, is immaterial relative to the determination of the holding period for long-term consideration. As discussed above, a charitable deduction for a gift of the land along with the unharvested crops (i.e., noncash property) is based on appraised fair market value of the land and crops on the date of contribution—subject to a 30 percent of AGI deduction limitation.

If the recipient charitable organization that receives the donated property later harvests the crop for sale, then the income from the harvested crops may be unrelated business income when the charitable organization sells the assets.[11] A gift of unharvested crops without the land is consid-

---

8. Reg. § 1.170A-1(c)(4).
9. Reg. § 1.170A-1(c)(4), Example 5.
10. Reg. § 1.170A-1(c)(4), Example 6.
11. IRC § 512. Determining unrelated business taxable income (UBTI) is a three-part test: (1) The income must be from a trade or

ered a gift of a futures contract, i.e., ordinary income property. Therefore the IRS limits the donor's deduction for a gift of unharvested crops to cost basis.

As explained above, regulations limit a gift of harvested crops to cost basis, plus consideration for costs of goods sold, which may mean no charitable deduction value at all. However, there is potential tax benefit to the donor in the saving of income taxes by avoidance of potential income on the sale of the crops, as well as avoidance of the related self-employment tax. Furthermore, a gift of crops will not count as income in potential government subsidy payment limitation calculations.[12] Therefore it is very important that the donor transfer title to the harvested crops to the charity before the sale at auction, contract, or other means takes place. The donor should use a signed deed of gift and receipt for the noncash gift from the charity to document this donation prior to sale. And the bill of sale should document that the charity owned and sold the crops.

A landlord who has nonmaterial participation in the production of crops may want to donate crop shares (i.e., right to receive the crop). In that case, a gift of the crop shares triggers income tax recognition at the time of contribution per the assignment of income doctrine.

A charitable contribution deduction is available for the gift that may offset in part or whole the income tax liability.[13] On the other hand, a farmer who has material participation in the production of the crops and who contributes crop shares may do so without income recognition. Sharecroppers who contribute crops may receive a deduction for their fair market value.[14]

Livestock includes cattle, hogs, horses, mules, donkeys, sheep, goats, fur-bearing animals, and other mammals. Livestock does not include poultry, chickens, turkeys, pigeons, geese, other birds, fish, frogs, reptiles, etc. Livestock the owner holds for draft, dairy breeding, or sporting purposes may be long-term capital gain property if held (i) for 24 months or more from the date of acquisition in the case of cattle or horses, or (ii) for 12 months or more from the date of acquisition in the case of such other livestock. Therefore a charitable contribution of qualified livestock to a related use public charity may qualify for full fair market value deduction.[15] Otherwise, livestock may be

---

business (i.e., selling of goods or performing of services); (2) The activity must be regularly carried on (i.e., with frequency and continuity); and (3) The activity must not be substantially related to charity's exempt purpose or mission. IRS Form 990-T is used to report UBTI. And see IRS Publication 598, Tax on Unrelated Business Income of Exempt Organizations at www.irs.gov.

12. Rev. Rul. 55-138; White v. Broderick, 104 F.Supp 213, 41 A.F.T.R. 1253 (D. Kan. 1952); Campbell v. Prothro, 209 F.2d 331, 45 A.F.T.R. 131 (5th Cir. 1954).
13. Rev. Rul. 75-11; Private Letter Ruling 8415030 (January 6, 1984).
14. Thompkins v. U.S. (S.D. Ill. 1977).
15. Reg. § 1231.

deemed ordinary income property as inventory and thereby the IRS limits taxpayers to a cost basis deduction as explained above. Other animals that are not livestock will be considered tangible personal property subject to the "related used" charitable reduction rule discussed below.

Agricultural equipment such as tractors, combines, trucks and so forth, as well as animals that are not livestock as discussed above, are tangible personal property. Assuming that the donor is not in the business of selling such equipment or livestock, then the asset is likely not inventory. However, a different "reduction rule" applies to tangible personal property that is not deemed inventory. In this case, the "related use" reduction rule applies. Pursuant to this rule, the donor's income tax charitable deduction is limited to the lesser of fair market value and cost basis if the recipient charity sells or puts the property to an "unrelated use."[16] The regulations require the taxpayer to provide proof that the charity is in fact putting the property to a related use, or that it is reasonable to anticipate that the property will not be put to an unrelated use.[17] For example, property donated for a charity auction is deemed (per se) an unrelated use.

A donor must recapture part of the charitable contribution deduction by including it in income if all the following statements are true:

1. The donor gave tangible personal property with a claimed value of more than $5,000, and the deduction is more than the cost basis in the property.
2. The organization sells, trades, or otherwise disposes of the property after the year it was contributed but within three years of the contribution.
3. The organization does not provide a written statement (such as on IRS Form 8282, Part IV), signed by an officer of the organization under penalty of perjury, that either
    a. certifies its use of the property was substantial and related to the organization's purpose, or
    b. certifies its intended use of the property became impossible.

Therefore the charity should explain the related use in the gift receipt letter and, if applicable, accurately complete and sign IRS Form 8282, sharing a copy with the donor as required, to protect the donor's claim of a fair market value deduction.

Gifts of natural resources are also possible. These gifts include oil, gas, timber, water and mineral interests. State and federal laws may apply to define whether the particular resource is deemed

---

16. IRC § 170(e)(1)(B)(i).
17. Reg. § 1.170A-4(b)(3)(ii).

real or personal property, as well as whether it is tangible or intangible personal property. These determinations can impact the charitable deduction value as described above. However, there is no charitable deduction if the donor contributes land but retains mineral interests as the IRS would consider this an impermissible partial interest gift.[18] On the other hand, if the natural resource is the only interest the donor owns, such as in the case of royalty interests, then a tax deduction is allowed. Issues relating to gifts of royalties are discussed in more depth in Chapter 8 on gifts of mineral interests.

Timber Gifts

Gifts of timber or forest land generally are even more complex than mineral rights. They combine the long term outlook of oil and gas with the growth and harvesting of agriculture. Generally speaking, the older the donated stand is, the more valuable it will be. This is because older trees are larger, and an older stand will have a higher proportion of older trees.[19] However, long term forest management and expertise is required. Relevant factors include whether the land has been properly thinned, harvesting and transport, and logging negotiation and monitoring.[20]

Of course, if the owner harvests the timber and then donates it, many of these issues will already have been handled. In that instance, it will be more like other forms of donated tangible property. However, natural hazards such as fire should be considered in all cases.[21]

Charities should also proceed with caution if the donor wishes to receive an income stream in exchange for the donated timber or forest land. The assets will need to be sold to meet the payment obligations of the planned giving vehicle, meaning that there can be significant hurdles for a charity trying to convert the gift into cash. For this reason, annuity obligations in particular, such as charitable gift annuities or charitable remainder annuity trusts, are ill-suited to this asset type.[22] Conservation easements are well-suited to forest land in some circumstances, so charities and donors should consider whether the forest land may be a good candidate for such treatment.[23]

---

18. Rev. Rul. 76-331.
19. Ward, P.L. and Straka, T.J. (October 2012), "Forestland and Timber Donations: Challenging Management Opportunities for Foundations," 2 *Open Journal of Forestry* 257, 258-59, http://file.scirp.org/pdf/OJF20120400010_63270182.pdf.
20. Id. at 261-62.
21. Id. at 263.
22. Siegel, W. et al (2009), "Estate Planning for Forest Landowners: What Will Become of Your Timberland?," U.S. Dep't of Agriculture – Forest Service 53, http://www.srs.fs.usda.gov/pubs/gtr/gtr_srs112.pdf.
23. Id. at 54.

Deferred Gifts

As explained above, bequests in a will or revocable living trust are the most popular form of planned gift. These gifts are popular since the donor may usually revoke them. Crops, livestock, and equipment can be specifically bequeathed to a charity by reference and description. Of course, prior to acceptance upon the death of the donor, the charity must conduct due diligence to assure the asset is appropriate to accept. Interestingly, the estate tax charitable deduction is not subject to the reduction rules. Therefore regulations value a testamentary bequest of tangible personal property or inventory at its fair market value without regard to charity's use of the property.[24]

Life Income Plans

Crops and livestock can be donated to a charitable remainder trust.[25] In Private Letter Ruling 9413020, a farmer donated beans and slaughter cattle to a charitable remainder trust. The Service held that the charitable deduction valuation was limited to the lesser of fair market value or cost basis pursuant to IRC Section 170(e)(1). In this case, that amount was zero, because the farmer had earlier deducted the costs of raising the cattle and crops as a business expense under IRC Section 162. Even though the IRS ruled for a reduced charitable deduction, the donor avoided or deferred income taxation when the beans and cows were sold from the trust. The trust would not produce taxable income for the beneficiaries when the trustee sold the donated farm assets. Rather, only as the trust made payments would beneficiaries owe income tax. In addition, the donor avoids self-employment tax on proceeds from the sale.

Livestock placed in a charitable remainder unitrust are sometimes referred to as "rawhide trusts."[26] The IRS treats these agricultural assets as tangible personal property, meaning the assets get ordinary income treatment (since they are usually business inventory for the farmer). Transfer of the livestock into trust results in a deduction for cost of goods sold once the trust sells them. Since farmers often have a low adjusted basis in these assets, the charitable income tax deduction is frequently minimal. The real benefit is bypassing the taxable income which the assets would otherwise create on sale. An important consideration for all parties is that the trust must not violate UBTI rules by fattening the livestock to increase their value (this would be an active, unrelated business endeavor).[27] Instead, the trustee should feed the livestock a "maintenance" diet.

---

24. IRC § 2055.
25. Private Letter Ruling 8119009 (February 10, 1981); Private Letter Ruling 9413020 (December 22, 1993).
26. Crescendo Interactive, GiftLaw Pro, "4.3.3 Tangible Personal Property Unitrust," http://www.wwcgift.org/giftlaw/glawpro_subsection.jsp?WebID=GL1999-0001&CC=4&SS=3&SS2=3
27. Private Letter Ruling 9413020 (December 22, 1993).

Agricultural Assets

If crops, livestock or equipment is donated for a charitable gift annuity, regulations also limit the deduction to the lesser of fair market value or cost basis. Again, the donor must take into account whether or not he or she had earlier deducted the costs of raising the cattle and crops as a business expense under IRC Section 162.[28] Regardless of the reduced charitable deduction, farmers may like the fixed payment opportunity of the gift annuity at a high rate based on age, as well as the avoidance of self-employment tax on the charity's subsequent sale of the donated assets.

---

28. IRC § 170(e)(1). See also Private Letter Ruling 9413020 (December 22, 1993).

Agricultural Assets Additional Resources

Below are further details on gifts of agricultural assets. Agricultural asset topics are based on Phil Purcell's "Gifts of Agricultural Assets." For quick take-aways on gifts of real estate, see Agricultural Assets Quick Take-Aways. For a review based on that article, see Agricultural Assets Intermediate. For an in-depth examination adapted and excerpted from the article, see Agricultural Assets Advanced. For further details, see Agricultural Assets Additional Resources.

For a discussion of factors farmland owners might consider, see McBride, E. (April 7, 1999), "Accepting and Retaining Gifts of Farmland," Planned Giving Design Center, http://www.pgdc.com/pgdc/accepting-and-retaining-gifts-farmland.

For a discussion of gifts of grain specifically, see Locher, J. (April 21, 2011), "Increasing Charitable Yields with Bushel Gifts," farmdoc daily, Department of Agricultural and Consumer Economics, University of Illinois at Urbana-Champaign, http://farmdocdaily.illinois.edu/2011/04/increasing-charitable-yields-w.html; and Hoff, G. (October 5, 2011), "Charitable Contributions of Grain," farmdoc daily, Department of Agricultural and Consumer Economics, University of Illinois at Urbana-Champaign, http://farmdoc-daily.illinois.edu/2011/10/charitable-contributions-of-gr-1.html.

For examples and an overview of the effects of various gift transactions, see Patrick, G.F. (December 2011), "Income Tax Management for Farmers in 2011," Purdue Univ. pp. 21 – 23, http://www.agecon.purdue.edu/extension/programs/tax/2011_INCOME_TAX%20MANAGEMENT_FOR_FARMERS.pdf.

For an examination of possible charitable avenues for retiring ranchers and farmers, see Hays, J. (October 29, 2015), "Donor-Centered Philanthropic Solutions for Retiring Farmers and Ranchers," *Journal of Gift Planning*, http://my.pppnet.org/library/93304/2/Hays-%20Donor%20Centered%20Philanthropic%20Solutions.pdf.

Treas. Reg. § 1.170A-14 (conservation easements)

Treas. Reg. § 1.170A-7(b)(4) (remainder interest in a farm)

Rev. Rul. 55-138, 1955-1 C.B. 223 (double deductions for donated farm inventory not allowed)

Private Letter Ruling 8415030 (crop share donations)

Private Letter Ruling 201315031 (nonprofit's operation of a ranch in accordance with its charitable purposes)

Sheppard v. U.S., 361 F.2d 972 (Ct. Cl. 1966) (approving taxpayer's donation-then-redemption of interest in racehorses)

Chapter 6

Life Insurance

- Quick Take-Aways
- Intermediate
- Advanced
- Additional Resources

Life Insurance Quick Take-Aways

by Bryan Clontz

Below are quick take-aways on gifts of life insurance. Life insurance topics are based on my article, "Charitable Gifts of Life Insurance: The Lone Ranger or Black Bart." For quick take-aways on gifts of life insurance, see Life Insurance Quick Take-Aways. For a review based on that article, see Life Insurance Intermediate. For an in-depth examination adapted and excerpted from the article, see Life Insurance Advanced. For further details, see Life Insurance Additional Resources.

Below is a macro overview of the pros and cons when it comes to donating life insurance.

Advantages of donations of life insurance include:

- It is a simple way to capture a fixed contribution, by donating either an existing or new policy, or using a beneficiary designation.
- A donor may have little cash on hand, but has an unneeded policy with the specific cash value she wishes to contribute.
- The donor is able to fund the gift on an installment sale but knows the gift will be complete whenever death occurs at the exact targeted amount.
- Donor can give appreciated property to charities to tax efficiently fund the premiums.
- Aside from a direct donation, life insurance can be used with major outright, life income or estate gifts to tax efficiently replace donations for their heirs.

Disadvantages of donating life insurance include:

- The deduction allowed from the donated policy is the lesser of the fair market value or the adjusted cost basis of the policy (assuming no capital gain element in the policy).
- Tax law always changes, and creative donations of insurance today may not have the same benefits in the future—a number of past insurance programs did not meet initial expectations.
- Many charities either do not accept insurance donations or require specific policy characteristics, like age minimums or life expectancy to maximize the donation.
- The two most powerful tax advantages of life insurance, tax free cash value build up and the tax free death benefit, are not needed by the charity.
- Assuming the donor lives to life expectancy and premiums were instead invested in the charity's endowment and could earn greater than 5–6 percent over time, it is likely the charity would receive a larger benefit. Clearly, the converse would be true with a premature death or poor endowment investment performance.

Wrinkles in the process to consider include:

- If the donated policy has value over $5,000, a qualified appraisal is needed.
- If the policy has an outstanding loan, this will likely be deemed a personal benefit contract under the charitable reverse split dollar legislation, and no deduction is allowed in addition to triggering bargain sale rules.
- If the donor had previously agreed to pay the premiums on the policy, and stopped, there is increased risk of lapse, plus additional administrative and donor relations considerations.

With donations of life insurance to public charities, consider the questions below.

Discovery Questions

Donor Questions

1. What is the donor trying to accomplish with the gift?
2. What is the current policy cash value?
3. Does the donor intend to keep paying premiums or will the charity surrender the policy?

Advisor Questions

1. What is the policy's current adjusted tax basis?
2. Are there any loans?
3. Is the donor aware that the policy's deduction is the lesser of fair market value or adjusted basis?
4. Are there any surrender charges?

Charity Questions

1. Is the effort worth the expected benefits (i.e., is the juice worth the squeeze)?
2. Assuming the charity is not going to immediately surrender the policy for the cash value, does the donor understand the options the charity may use if premiums are not paid timely?
3. Is there the necessary expertise to accept and manage gifts of insurance?
4. Would the charity be better off financially investing the cash value and future premiums in the endowment?

Life Insurance Intermediate

by Ryan Raffin

Below is a review on gifts of life insurance. Life insurance topics are based on my article, "Charitable Gifts of Life Insurance: The Lone Ranger or Black Bart." For quick take-aways on gifts of life insurance, see Life Insurance Quick Take-Aways. For a review based on that article, see Life Insurance Intermediate. For an in-depth examination adapted and excerpted from the article, see Life Insurance Advanced. For further details, see Life Insurance Additional Resources.

This review of the different ways life insurance can be used to give to charity has four parts. It starts with a discussion of simple transactions, and then proceeds to more complex gifts. The third part examines gift strategies that are more situational and less clear-cut. Finally, the review concludes with an overview of considerations that apply regardless of the structure of the gift.

As a planned gift, life insurance's flexibility is both a strength and a weakness. The donor and charity may structure the donation in any number of ways, with varying degrees of complexity. A gift of life insurance can be a simple way for the donor to guarantee the charity an eventual fixed payment. However, it can also include wrinkles relating to premium payments, annuities, policy sales in the secondary market, premium financing, etc.

Review Part 1: Keeping It Simple

The simplest and most intuitive transactions are usually best, such as cut-and-dried donations of a policy. The donor can designate the charity as beneficiary, but this is revocable and therefore provides no charitable income tax deduction. This is an appealing option for its ease and flexibility. The allocation can be a percentage of the total benefit, or a specific dollar amount. Unlike many other planned gifts, there is usually no need for an attorney, accountant, or other financial professional.

A more tax-advantaged, but still simple, alternative is donating the policy. The policy owner assigns all rights in the policy to the charity (or charities). She receives an income tax deduction of the lesser of the policy's fair market value or cost basis. The charity must hold all ownership rights to the policy. Who pays any additional premiums due will depend on negotiations between the donor and the charity, as well as the policy's structure. Slightly more complex is the charity purchasing a policy on the donor, using funds the donor provides (depending on state regulations on insurable interests).

Wealth replacement strategies can also utilize life insurance to facilitate more or larger donations. Donors may donate all or a portion of the estate as an outright, life income, or estate gift. Heirs receive the "replacement" benefits of a life insurance policy. Typically, the donor's irrevocable life insurance trust owns the policy so the proceeds are received tax free. This can be a very flexible strategy, because the donor can increase the size of the gift or adjust the policy as needed. A simple option is buying a policy with a fixed bequest target for heirs (i.e., $4 million death benefit providing $1 million to each of four children), with the donor's entire estate then donated to charity (although this simplicity may not be ideal for tax or estate planning purposes).

Another option for charities is gift annuity reinsurance. This strategy has the charity purchasing insurance to match its contractual liability on its gift annuities. This shifts the investment and longevity risk of the annuity to the insurer, and allows the immediate remainder to be used currently or invested more aggressively in the endowment.

Review Part 2: Getting Tricky

More complex transactions generally have bigger risks, and can lead to occasionally contentious interactions between charities and the insurance industry. Vanishing premium universal life insurance was the trendy strategy in the late 1980s and early 1990s. When actual interest rates were lower than illustrations projected, the premiums did not vanish. Tens of millions in life insurance death benefits were lost, angering donors and nonprofits alike. This frustration reoccurred in the late 1990s with charitable reverse split-dollar life insurance. There, donors made a deductible donation to the charity, the charity purchased a policy, and part of the death benefit went to the family estate, trust or heirs.

Other creative approaches still exist today. Prior to the crash of 2008, some charities would engage in interest rate arbitrage called premium financing by borrowing money at rates expected to be less than the policy would earn. The policy's benefit and cash value were collateral, and the charity would eventually pocket any leftover amount after paying back the loan. In essence, this was "free" insurance to the charity. However, many of these structures collapsed when banks started calling in loans during the financial crisis. With credit scarce, refinancing the loans was difficult, if not impossible. Newer versions of premium financing generally have longer financing terms and other structural changes to mitigate interest rate risk.

"Dead pools" were another questionable strategy. Best known for corporate use, the idea was that a charity would take out a group policy on a large number of donor lives—typically over one thousand in total. The charity borrows money to pay for the premiums, collect tax-free death benefits, grow the cash value of the policies, and then deduct the cost of interest. Congress significantly curtailed this strategy for corporations in the Pension Protection Act of 2006. Nonprofits can still utilize this strategy, if it can gather enough insurable lives. Even so, the optics can be off-putting to charities, regulators, and even donors whereby promoters are seeking to "rent" or "lease" donors for a small fee.

A second type of "donor rental" scheme uses Charitable/Foundation/Stranger/Investor Owned Life Insurance. Regardless of the type of insurance, these strategies were usually structured the same way. The promoters helped charities find high net worth donors that would allow the charities to take out policies on their lives. The charity paid the premiums (usually through premium financing), and sold the policy. The downside was that the insured donors did not typically realize that the charity was taking out large policies rendering them "overinsured," so they had difficult securing more personal insurance for estate or business liquidity needs.

Nonprofits, donors, and insurers did not receive these donor "rental" programs well. The promoters would collect their fee no matter the result, but the nonprofits and donors got only minimal benefits, if any, for the risk they were taking on. The insurance industry also takes a dim view of these strategies—even saying they have no business purpose and can be actively harmful, and in some cases, has sought to nullify the transactions.

Review Part 3: Ambiguous Strategies

Not all strategies have a "good" or "bad" feel to them. Some approaches are less clear-cut, and unsurprisingly, these tend not to be the simplest plans.

Life settlement is one such process. In this case, a charity sells a qualifying insurance policy—usually with a death benefit over $1 million, in-force for at least 2 years, with an insured over 70 years old, and a life expectancy between 2 and 10 years. The insured must also release all medical records to the broker / buyer. Bids are made based on cash value, death benefit, insured's age and health, and the type of policy, and represent a 10 to 14 percent internal rate of return (often 16 to 20 percent after the 2008 crash). Despite the complexity, estimates put the secondary market for life insurance at $200 billion. Charities who do not want to hold the policy due to the risk, cost, or headache of administration might therefore consider this option.

Another strategy is life insurance/annuity underwriting arbitrage. Here, the charity takes a donor between 70 and 85 years old with a nonterminal health issue, and has a number of life insurance carriers submit bids for a large policy (say, $5 million). Then the charity asks the same carriers to bid on an immediate annuity in the same amount. Then it selects the insurance policy with the longest life expectancy, and the annuity with the shortest. This means the premiums are lower than the annuity payments, so the charity keeps the difference. In some scenarios, this equates to a six to ten percent guaranteed rate of return no matter when death occurs.

Gifts of life insurance may also be combined with charitable remainder trusts (CRTs). CRTs can own life insurance policies, with the primary purpose of providing additional income to the surviving income beneficiary after the death of the first income beneficiary. Additionally, the IRS recently ruled privately that charitable remainder annuity trusts (CRATs) can own immediate annuities. This allows the CRAT to essentially reinsure its liability by transferring longevity and investment risk for a portion of the assets. These new options may be appealing as they guarantee an income stream or fixed death benefit, rather than relying purely on market-based investments.

Review Part 4: Issues to Consider

As with nearly every kind of estate and financial planning, careful preparation can prevent many problems. Life insurance, in particular, benefits from advance planning and communication, since most nonprofits do not have robust Gift Acceptance Policies for life insurance. Informal, verbal, or handshake agreements are typically recipes for disaster—a formal Memo of Understanding is essential to setting expectations from the start.

Another issue with life insurance donations is the IRS appraisal requirement. The Pension Protection Act of 2006 made clear that for any donated policy valued over $5,000, the donor must obtain a "qualified appraisal." Indeed, in 2007, the Journal of Accountancy stated:

"The questions of appraiser qualification and responsibility remain an area of concern for the IRS due to a long history of valuation problems dealing with gifted life insurance. Life insurance can be prone to incorrect valuation because of the plethora of types of policies available, ownership and beneficiary issues and misunderstanding of valuation methods of how to apply fair market valuation principles."[1]

Improper appraisals and substantiation have resulted in the IRS disallowing deductions if the appraiser was not properly qualified. For this reason, failing to properly obtain an appraisal can lead to unhappy donors and nonprofits.

---

1. Breus, Alan, "Life Insurance: What's It Worth? And Who Says?," *The Journal of Accountancy,* http://journalofaccountancy.com/Issues/2008/Jan/LifeInsuranceWhatsItWorthAndWhoSays.htm.

It can be challenging for nonprofits to manage the donated policy as well, especially if it is unexperienced at receiving gifts of life insurance. The nonprofit should have someone with expertise evaluate whether to accept the gift, and review its past and current performance. Risk disclosure is essential. Nonprofits must also determine who is getting paid (and how), and who will be performing critical pre- and post-gift functions.

Options to address situations where the donor no longer will pay premiums—or for underperforming policies—are: the charity surrenders the policy for the cash value, sells the policy (as in life settlement), takes a reduced death benefit paid-up policy, makes premium payments on its own, or simply does nothing. Not only is it wise to decide on a strategy in advance with the donor, the charity should have internal policies on how it makes these decisions.

Additionally, a staff person should organize any required annual statements, coordinate information for audit and FASB reporting purposes, ensure outstanding premium payments are being made, and monitor any material changes (i.e., life insurance company ratings drop, new policy loans, negative changes in assumptions).

Conclusion

Charitable gifts of life insurance are a broad category of planned giving, at least in terms of how the gifts are structured. The simpler structures are usually better, depending on the experience and goals of the parties involved. More complex gifts that involve arbitrage or remainder trusts can be successful as well, but require advanced planning. In cases of strategies that resemble dead pools or involve "renting" donors, an abundance of caution is the best approach. Even once the structure is settled, there are still potential hurdles like payment of future premiums, monitoring policy performance, and obtaining a qualified appraisal. Nonetheless, the flexibility of life insurance as a donated asset has strong appeal, and charities may wish to develop solid policies and procedures to confidently receive these gifts.

Life Insurance Advanced[2]

by Bryan Clontz

Below is an in-depth examination on gifts of life insurance. Life insurance topics are based on my article, "Charitable Gifts of Life Insurance: The Lone Ranger or Black Bart." For quick take-aways on gifts of life insurance, see Life Insurance Quick Take-Aways. For a review based on that article, see Life Insurance Intermediate. For an in-depth examination adapted and excerpted from the article, see Life Insurance Advanced. For further details, see Life Insurance Additional Resources.

Life insurance is one of the most mercurial of gift planning vehicles. To some, it is an elegant and simple way to capture a fixed amount that exactly matches the donor's intent. To others, it is a complex way to book gifts now that result in no eventual gift, potential litigation and/or never-ending management problems.

This discussion is not intended to take one position or the other. Rather, it is a survey piece intended to discuss and explain each of these three distinct categories—"Tried and True," "Black and Blue," and "It's Up to You." These sections are followed with a "Things You Must Do" section, where critically important pre- and post-gift acceptance issues will be covered.

"Tried and True"

When life insurance policies are donated to charity, boring is nearly always best. Why would a donor want to do this? She may have a policy she no longer needs, or a specific dollar amount she wishes to contribute no matter what happens. Or she may have more insurance than she currently wishes for her beneficiaries, or she may wish to provide more to her beneficiaries, should she choose to give away some assets. Or finally, the charity itself may wish to use insurance to protect itself against the premature death of a major donor or perhaps to cover its liability for a gift annuity. Here are some brief, but not all-inclusive, options.

1. **Existing Policy Donation**—A simple process where the owner of the insurance policy absolutely assigns all rights in the policy to the public charity. Because life insurance is ordinary income property, the IRS limits the deduction to the lesser of fair market value or adjusted cost basis. The policy may be paid-up, where no additional premiums are due. Or non-paid up, which means someone will need to make additional premiums.

---

2. This chapter excerpts and adapts on Clontz, B. (2011), "Charitable Gifts of Life Insurance: The Lone Ranger or Black Bart," Partnership for Philanthropic Planning, http://my.pppnet.org/library/60439/1/NCPP11_Clontz.pdf.

Nugget #1: If the policy's value is greater than $5,000, a qualified appraiser must complete a qualified appraisal of the policy to substantiate the gift on Form 8283.[3]

Nugget #2: If the policy has an outstanding loan at the time of gift, it may eliminate the entire deduction, because of a private benefit classification under the charitable reverse split-dollar legislation.[4]

2. **New Policy Donation**—A simple process where the donor makes a donation to a charity, which in turn, takes out a new policy on the donor's life. The charity, from the outset, is the owner and beneficiary. The donor may specify how she wishes the charity to use the proceeds. Regulations entitle the donor to an income tax deduction for the donation made to the charity. Note that under state law, an insurable interest must be present at the time the policy is issued. Some commentators have suggested that if a donor has never made a gift before, making an unrestricted contribution to the charity can help create an insurable interest prior to taking out the new policy.

Nugget #3: A tax-optimal way of making this donation would be with long-term appreciated property to get the full fair market deduction for the donation, and then to use the proceeds to fund the insurance.

Nugget #4: While administratively burdensome, having the donor make the donation directly to the charity is the cleanest process. The charity can then make the premium payment. If the donor makes the premium payments directly, it may have the unintended consequence of reducing the deduction limitation to 20 percent of AGI, since it would be a gift "for the benefit of" rather than "to" the charity. Further, the audit trail is usually much easier to follow.

3. **Beneficiary Allocation**—If the donor wishes to make a revocable gift, she can simply fill out a new beneficiary form with a specific allocation—percentage or dollar amount—for the charity. An example, "I wish to designate my husband, Chad Brown, for 95 percent of the benefit, and Charity ABC for 5 percent." Of course, the donor may revoke the designation at any time, and therefore no income tax deduction would be available (though she may derive some estate tax benefits depending on how the policy was owned).

Nugget #5: This is the easiest, possible way of getting a charity's board members into its Legacy Society. They can do this with an individual policy or even group term life from work. It takes very little time, and does not involve an attorney like a codicil. Additionally, through a percentage allocation, any socio-economic background

---

3. IRS Publication 561 (April 2007), Determining the Value of Donated Property, https://www.irs.gov/publications/p561/index.html.
4. IRC § 170(f)(10).

can participate without economically harming heirs. For example, one percent of a $100,000 policy is $1,000, but that might only represent 1/5th of 1 percent of the total estate. So there are really no excuses that a Board member could use to rationally exempt herself from participating—at least while on the Board.

4. **Wealth Replacement**—The donor's irrevocable life insurance trust (ILIT) typically owns the policy, rather than the charity. Nonetheless, this strategy may create a much larger gift than the donor originally imagined. It can also get a donor comfortable enough to even make the gift in the first place. Charities should be very comfortable with the structure and placement of wealth replacement, and how to integrate it into a charitable giving plan.

    Nugget #6: For some reason, when charities hear "wealth replacement," they immediately think of charitable remainder trust applications. This is like only using a back-hoe to build sand-boxes—an incredibly powerful and broad concept applied in a narrow space. The applications of wealth replacement are as powerful, if not more so, for straight bequests, gift annuities, major outright gifts, and, in particular, for qualified plans / IRA bequests.

    For example, with IRAs, a donor can take the minimum distribution, pay the tax, and then use the net to pay premiums on a life insurance policy. At death, the tax-disadvantaged retirement plan flows to charity, with no tax loss, and the insurance replaces the retirement balance for her heirs tax-advantaged way (assuming it was structured properly). During retirement, the donor would always have access to the full account if needed for lifestyle or emergencies. And from a planning perspective, wealth replacement does not always mean exactly the same value as the donation. It can be increased or decreased based on the donor's wishes.

    Nugget #7: Wealth replacement has also become an elegantly simple estate plan for some families. For many, estate planning is viewed as an expensive, complex and ever-changing process. And, this does not take into account the estate asset fluctuation over time. Some donors / clients have grown tired of the process and have devised a very straight-forward solution. Rather than always trying to follow estate planning rules, asset prices, vehicles, etc.—they simply say, "I want Johnny, Suzie and Timmy to get $2 million each. My wife and I will buy a survivorship life insurance policy for $6 million. Any assets we have not used during life will go to charity. Done." This may not be optimal from a tax or estate planning perspective, but some clients are choosing the certainty and simplicity over the uncertainty and complexity.

5. **Gift Annuity Reinsurance**—This is an insurance policy (an immediate annuity) the charity purchases to match the contractual liability for one or a group of gift annuities.

This kind of insurance can benefit the charity by shifting the longevity and investment risk to the insurance company. In this way, the charity may immediately release the difference creating a known amount at a known point in time, instead of a self-insured unknown amount at an unknown point in time. To be clear, the unknown amount may certainly be larger or smaller on a present value basis, depending on the mortality and investment experience of the gift annuity. This immediate surplus can be used for current pressing needs, or invested more aggressively in the endowment over time.

Nugget #8: Charities should follow IRC Section 170(f)(10) which exempt charity-owned annuities only to the extent that the contract matches the terms of the CGA contract in terms of the timing and amount of the liability. If this is not the case, the policy may not qualify under the law. Some recent, private letter rulings have ruled positively for a lifetime annuity with a premium refund, or for a period certain so long as the benefits and frequency match the gift annuity.[5]

"Black and Blue"

Generally, anything with a catchy name, acronym, or more than four boxes on a flow chart is a recipe for potential trouble. Insurance and charities have had a very turbulent relationship over the years. In the late 1980s and early 1990s, it was vanishing premium universal life insurance. But the premiums did not vanish, as interest crediting rates dropped, literally tens of millions of dollars of life insurance were lost and charities and their donors were furious. Then came charitable split-dollar life insurance in the late 1990s. This is where a donor made a donation, took a deduction and then the charity-owned policy provided a portion of the death benefit into a family trust or to heirs. In 1998, Congress passed legislation outlawing the structure. This led to more upset charities and donors. Then came LILAC (Life Insurance Life Annuity Contracts), which involved very large donor groups and combined life insurance and annuity contracts.

Here is a brief overview of the more popular charitable insurance programs in the last decade.

1. **Premium Financing**—This strategy had the charity borrowing money from a third-party lender at a rate lower than the projections indicated the policy would earn—in essence, interest rate arbitrage. The lender took a collateral interest in the policy for both the death benefit and cash value, and the charity got whatever was left over. This was "free" insurance, since the charity did not have to put any money into the contract and just needed to find a donor(s) where they had an insurable interest. Planners

---

5. Private Letter Ruling 200847014 (April 9, 2008); Private Letter Ruling 200852037 (September 30, 2008).

should note that there are nearly a dozen permutations of these structures and every one is a bit different in design.

Nugget #9: This financing was very popular in the early 2000s and more than a few charities participated (see the T. Boone Pickens Plan at Oklahoma State—Athletics Dept. Lawsuit).[6] However, illustrations are simply projections based on assumptions which are all but certain to be wrong. Interestingly, most experts thought the plans would buckle if short-term rates ever spiked quicker than the policy crediting rate—the so-called, inverted short-term yield curve. Instead, the plans actually started sinking in 2008 when banks started calling in loans and lines of credit given the financial system's cash crunch. The policies had not existed long enough to build up enough equity, and while everyone assumed there would be another bank to refinance the notes, very few were successful. And those that were, had to pay the price in higher interest rates, new expenses, commissions, etc.

2. **Dead Pools**—The idea was that if a charity could get a large enough amount of donor lives, usually 1,000 or more, they purchase a blanket group policy because they had an insurable interest. Note this is exactly the same structure corporations used until the Pension Protection Act of 2006 significantly curtailed it. In some cases, the employees did not even know their employers had insured them (so called "dead peasants" or "janitors insurance").[7] The companies would borrow the money for the premiums, collect death benefits tax free, grow the cash value on their balance sheets tax free, and then deduct the borrowing cost interest.

Nugget #10: If anyone approaches a charity because they need an intermediary with an insurable interest, to, as Steve Leimberg says "rent / lease the donors" in exchange for a small projected variable sum, the charity should proceed with caution.

3. **CHOLI, FOLI, IOLI and STOLI**—These plans, CHOLI (Charitable Owned Life Insurance), FOLI (Foundation Owned Life Insurance), STOLI (Stranger Owned Life Insurance), and IOLI (Investor Owned Life Insurance) all share the same general structure. The charity was to select a few very high net worth donors who would allow the charity to take out an insurance policy on their lives. The charity could provide the premium payments, though usually it was premium financed (see above), and then the idea was to sell the policy to another person (usually STOLI) or as a securitized block of lives (usually IOLI).

---

6. Strom, S. (February 12, 2010), "University and Pickens Sue Over Fundraising Plan," *N.Y. Times*, http://www.nytimes.com/2010/02/13/education/13oklahoma.html?_r=0.
7. For a discussion of the continuing use and criticism of such practices, see Gelles, D. (June 22, 2014), "An Employee Dies, and the Company Collects the Insurance," *N.Y. Times*, http://dealbook.nytimes.com/2014/06/22/an-employee-dies-and-the-company-collects-the-insurance/.

Nugget #11: Again, this model was a "rent our donor base"-approach but insurance owners here usually focused on a few select lives. Promoters sold it as free insurance for the charity, and as an added enticement, the insured donor was usually able to direct five percent or so of the death benefit to the charity. Many donors did not realize that the policies were usually quite large and therefore used up much of their insurance capacity. That means that if the person had $20 million in assets, she might be able to get $20 million or so of insurance. But if Alma Mater U took out a $20 million policy on her, and then she later realized she had a need for additional insurance, insurers may decline her due to limited additional capacity. Carriers may deem her to be "over-insured" even though she was not receiving any direct benefit from the charitable policy.

Perhaps there may be some scenario where these kinds of plans may work. However, when many in the insurance industry believe these strategies have no business purpose, can harm the companies themselves, and are bad policy, planners should think twice about these programs.

It's Up to You

Most gift planners tend to be in either the "insurance is bad" or "insurance is good" camp. The last two sections attempted to draw a bit of a line between good and bad, perhaps fairly or unfairly. This section will outline strategies which are a bit more ambiguous.

1. **Life Settlement**—This is where a charity sells an insurance policy in the secondary market. As mentioned, the intent of selling the policy when it is originally issued can create a number of problems. Usually this is done after two years to clear the incontestability clause. But from time to time, charities may receive large policies from donors who do not wish to continue paying premiums, or charities may have owned a policy for a long time and now the donor cannot pay the premiums.

    Charities should understand the process of settlement. First, the policy must qualify—usually that means an insured donor at least 70 years old, owns a $1 million policy and has a life expectancy between 2–10 years. Ideally (for the settlement process), the donor has had a severe decline in health after the insurer issued the policy. Second, the insured must agree to release all records to a third-party broker or directly to an institutional buyer. Third, the buyers calculate their bids from the cash value, donor's age/health, death benefit, type of policy, quality of company, minimum required premiums, etc.

Before the 2008 economic downturn, these bids were usually calculated at a 10 to 14 percent internal rate of return.[8] Of course, one policy could deviate significantly from that rate which is why investors securitized/bundled many of these policies into the financial markets. After 2008, much of the funding has dried up and now investors are looking for rates between 16–20 percent in some cases. Still, estimates are that donors sell approximately $2 billion of life insurance death benefit annually into the secondary market.

Nugget #12: If the donor can no longer make premium payments, and the facts / policy meets the conditions, should the charity just keep the policy and pay it with other funds? Rather than giving the investor 10–20 percent, it would seem prudent to retain that asset.

But some charities have a policy against fronting the money for premiums, or do not want the risk of a single policy, or do not want the hassle of on-going administration, or the donor may want to see the charity use the money while she is still alive. Hence, selling the policy in the secondary market may make sense.

2. **Life/Annuity Underwriting Arbitrage**—This strategy has been around since the late 1990s. The idea is that the charity takes a high-net-worth donor, usually between 70–85 years old, and who has some non-major health issue (i.e., prostate cancer in remission from ten years ago, managed diabetes, etc.). Then, it asks 15 or so life insurance carriers to bid on a $5 million life insurance policy. The charity then asks the same carriers to bid on a $5 million immediate annuity that is medically underwritten (these policies have higher payouts based on a shorter life expectancy). Interestingly, the life underwriting might show anywhere from a 10 to 20 year life expectancy since different companies have different experience with various maladies, as does immediate annuity underwriting. Then, the charity picks the life insurance company that has the longest life expectancy, and the immediate annuity carrier with the shortest life expectancy—hence the hedged spread.

The hypothetical math would work like this:

$5 million in premium for the immediate annuity	Annual payout of $700,000
$5 million life insurance policy	Annual premium of $400,000
Net Annual Cash Flow	$300,000

---

8. That is, if the donor died when actuarially expected, and the policy performed as the investor expected, then that investor would earn the targeted annualized rate of return.

Net Lifetime Guaranteed Rate of Return is six percent ($300,000 / $5,000,000). When the donor dies, the immediate annuity stops, but the life insurance pays off the full $5 million—the entire original principal.

Nugget #13: If designed correctly, the return can provide close to a risk-free bond equivalent return. Charities have used it for an endowment fixed alternative, in CRATs and in CLATs. Hence there are a number of interesting applications, but the entire solution relies on getting enough of an underwriting spread between two different insurance carriers to achieve a fixed rate of return worthy of the effort.

3. **Life Insurance in CRTs**—There are several private letter rulings that allow a CRT to own a life insurance policy. The charity/trustee can fund these with either existing policies or can issue new ones. The primary reason this is done is to provide a spike in income to the surviving income beneficiary after the first death.

   And a more recent ruling has allowed a CRAT to purchase an immediate annuity.[9] This could have a number of uses for CRATs, in particular, where they wish to transfer the longevity and investment risk for a portion of the assets, while still making the guaranteed payout (in essence, reinsuring the liability).

   Nugget #14: Using life insurance inside of a CRT is a challenging proposition in terms of administration, valuation, etc. But these issues are not insurmountable if it provides a specific solution for the client. Still, it is a rare planning technique.

   The recent Private Letter Ruling for immediate annuities inside of CRATs could open up better income planning in that area. Given the recent decade's investment performance, many CRATs are underwater already, and some have already exhausted or are projected to exhaust. This will provide a tool for donors / trustees who need a guaranteed income stream to minimize the exhaustion probability.

4. **Annuity Donations**—Both fixed and variable annuities may be donated to charities. But as an ordinary income asset (like life insurance), regulations limit the deduction to the lesser of fair market value or adjusted cost basis. However, unlike life insurance, any embedded gain inside the policy is accelerated at the time of the assignment or transfer. So practically speaking, while doable, it usually does not make much sense. It is usually best to simply surrender the policy for cash, and then contribute the net proceeds as a cash contribution (or alternatively, a long-term appreciated capital asset).

---

9. Private Letter Ruling 201126007 (December 15, 2010).

Nugget #15: If the donor gives the annuity policy to charity prior to surrender, it still must have a qualified appraisal to substantiate the deduction if the value is greater than $5,000.

5. **Life Insurance as an Investment/Asset Class**—In recent years, some insurance thought-leaders have challenged people to reconsider how they view life insurance. Not only does permanent insurance provide risk management protection, it also provides guaranteed growth in cash values and a death benefit. Life insurance, in many ways, is a vastly under-appreciated asset. It grows income tax-free. The death benefits are usually income tax-free, and owners can easily remove it from their estates using an Irrevocable Life Insurance Trust.

    Further, while a tax-free four to six percent rate of return to life expectancy used to seem paltry in the late 1990s, the more recent market environment has shown the benefits of a slow but steady return. So for many people who need life insurance protection for various reasons, re-calibrating their thinking to include permanent policies as a fixed income asset class alternative is reasonable.

    The challenge, however, lies with the application of this concept to charities. Nonprofits are already tax-free, so the three key insurance benefits are immediately lost. Most are not dependent on any specific donor who needs life insurance. The question is, barring early death (which no one can predict), are there better fixed income investment alternatives? And since life insurance companies are investing nearly all of their general account assets in institutional bonds, charities can access these same markets through institutional money managers.

Things You Must Do

Like most planning, the parties can avert many of the future problems on the front-end. This is especially true with life insurance as most charities' Gift Acceptance Policies are not robust enough. Most importantly, the donor and charity should always have a Memo of Understanding, an expectation-setting step that will alleviate any future misunderstandings.

Gift Acceptance Challenges and Solutions: Key Questions

Policy Management—One staff person must be responsible for policy acceptance and stewardship. Does the policy meet the original guidelines for acceptance? Was the policy conservatively designed? Was there an expectation the donor would pay up the policy quickly? How is the policy performing?

Policy Under-Performing—What if the policy is not meeting expectations—can the donor increase premiums? Or can the charity exchange the policy for another? Note that charities should be very careful about replacing the policy, as this can just put the new policy in worse shape—new commissions/expenses, surrender period, etc. But in some instances, mortality rates have dropped markedly and newer policies can be much more competitive than older policies, so an external review every five years or so can be advantageous.

Donor Stops Premium Payments—This scenario must be covered in the Memo of Understanding. A charity has five primary options:

1. Surrender the policy for the cash value.
2. Sell the policy in the secondary market (life settlement).
3. Take a reduced paid-up policy.
4. The charity can keep paying for the policy (but perhaps will change the beneficiary to the operating or unrestricted fund).
5. Do nothing and let the policy run out of money in due time. In many cases, the servicing agent may be able to help discuss the options.

Policy Valuation / Substantiation—The staff person responsible for the insurance portfolio should coordinate the annual policy statements for FASB purposes, and should also make sure the organization is accurately substantiating premium payments in the donor's acknowledgement letter.

Critical Questions—The charity should never hesitate to ask for all potential risks to be disclosed. It should always ask for references, in particular for institutional programs. Always ask who gets paid exactly what, when and under what circumstances. If they are not willing to disclose the moving parts with full transparency, the organization is correct to question motives.

Life Insurance Additional Resources

Below are further details on gifts of life insurance. Life insurance topics are based on my article, "Charitable Gifts of Life Insurance: The Lone Ranger or Black Bart." For quick take-aways on gifts of life insurance, see Life Insurance Quick Take-Aways. For a review based on that article, see Life Insurance Intermediate. For an in-depth examination adapted and excerpted from the article, see Life Insurance Advanced. For further details, see Life Insurance Additional Resources.

For wealth replacement and life settlement strategies, see Brietstein, J. (March 9, 2004), "Innovative Strategies for Using Life Insurance in Charitable Giving," Planned Giving Design Center, http://www.pgdc.com/pgdc/innovative-strategies-using-life-insurance-charitable-giving.

For examples of policies which a college or other organization's planned giving department might apply, see Willock, G.E. (October 2010), "Philanthropic Planning with Life Insurance," Partnership for Philanthropic Planning, https://connect.wels.net/AOM/Subsidiaries/foundation/Leadership%20Resources/Educational%20Resources/Partnership%20for%20Philanthropic%20Planning%20Papers/Philanthropic%20Planning%20with%20Life%20Insurance.pdf.

For a high-level discussion of life insurance donations from the charity's perspective, see Leimberg, S.R. and Zipse, R.L. (2008), "Life Insurance and Charitable Planning: How to Stay on the Right Side of the Comfort Line in the (Quick) Sand," *Journal of Gift Planning*, 2nd Quarter 2008, 11, http://my.pppnet.org/library/000/000/8c/NCPGJv10n3s2.pdf.

For a look at different types of life insurance in the gift planning context, see Abramson, E.L., "Evaluating Creative Planned Giving Scenarios Involving Life Insurance Part 1: An Introduction to Life Insurance Products," *Journal of Gift Planning,* 2nd Quarter 2004, 47, http://my.pppnet.org/library/000/002/24/NCPGJv8n2s2.pdf; and "Evaluating Creative Planned Giving Scenarios Involving Life Insurance Part 2: Premium Financed Life Insurance," *Journal of Gift Planning,* 3rd Quarter 2004, 13, http://my.pppnet.org/library/000/002/22/NCPGJv8n3s3.pdf.

For an example of a college's internal policy on acceptance of life insurance gifts, see Northwestern University Office of Alumni Relations and Development (December 1, 2009), "Policy on Acceptance and Management of Gifts of Life Insurance," http://my.pppnet.org/library/51159/1/Northwestern_Policy_on_Gifts_of_Life_Insurance.pdf.

IRC §§ 79(a) – (b) (group-term life insurance and donations thereof)

IRC § 170(f)(10) (charitable split-dollar arrangements)

IRC § 6050V (reporting requirements for nonprofits acquiring certain life insurance contracts)

Private Letter Ruling 9110016 (requirement that the policy owner have an insurable interest)

IRS Form 8921, Applicable Insurance Contracts Information Return (form for reporting nonprofit's qualifying life insurance transactions)

U.S. v. Ryerson, 312 US 260 (1941) (determining deduction amount for donated policy)

Tuttle v. U.S., 436 F.2d 69 (2d Cir. 1970) (conditions which reduce deduction for donated policy)

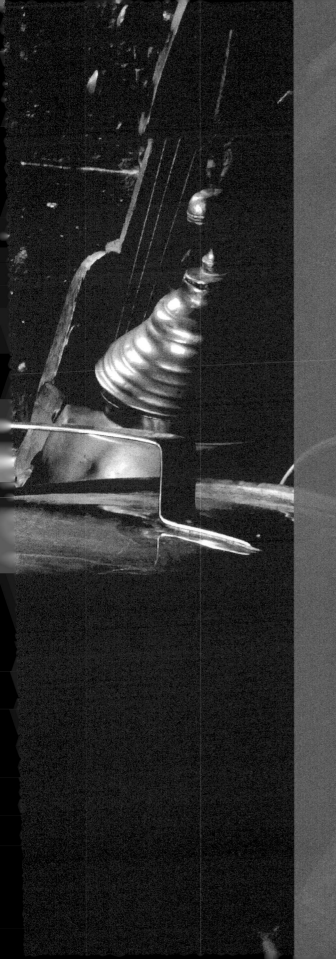

Chapter 7
Tangible Property

- Quick Take-Aways
- Intermediate
- Advanced
- Additional Resources

Tangible Property Quick Take-Aways

by Bryan Clontz

Below are quick take-aways on gifts of tangible property. Tangible property topics are based on Armen Vartian's "Charitable Donations of Art and Collectibles." For quick take-aways on gifts of tangible property, see [Tangible Property Quick Take-Aways](). For a review based on that article, see [Tangible Property Intermediate](). For an in-depth examination adapted and excerpted from the article, see [Tangible Property Advanced](). For further details, see [Tangible Property Additional Resources]().

Tangible property is a highly varied and complex asset class when it comes to charitable giving. There is significant flexibility in both the nature of the item donated, and in the structure of the gift transaction. However, there are also unique considerations and restrictions. Below is a brief overview of the advantages, disadvantages, special considerations, and questions to ask.

Advantages of donations of tangible property include:

- Broad asset category, including collectibles, artwork, vehicles, jewelry, coins and timber (basically, anything you can touch and it will move).
- Flexibility in the transaction's structure, including outright gifts, undivided fractional gifts, vehicles generating an income stream, deferred gifts, etc.
- Fair market value deductions are available for donations meeting certain related-use requirements.
- The charity's use is often a public or educational use, both gratifying to donors.
- For some tangible personal property, the capital gains tax rate is 28 percent, so not recognizing that income is particularly advantageous.

Disadvantages of donating tangible property include:

- Related use and future interest rules limit the availability of fair market value deductions.
- Gift annuities, pooled-income funds, charitable remainder trusts, and charitable lead trusts all require significant evaluation for possible tax issues, marketability and general suitability.
- Tangible property is often difficult to value, and frequently requires a specialist to appraise and evaluate for proper tax substantiation.

- Donors may have an emotional attachment to their collections which may impede the charity's related use or prudent liquidation process.

- For donated artwork, factors such as blockage, buyer's premiums, and independent IRS valuation are relevant to the gift transaction and liquidation, if any.

- Donors may not have basis evidence for inherited property or pieces purchased long ago.

Wrinkles in the process to consider include:

- Payment obligations may require the charity to sell the gift, which is an unrelated use (as would be a charitable auction).

- Bequests may be a more effective way to make the gift, either to retain a lifetime interest or as an alternative bequest should an heir disclaim the gift. However, many planners also suggest donating during life to capture a current charitable income tax deduction (even at basis) which would be lost through the estate. This also eliminates life-time donor expenses like insurance, storage and other holding costs.

- Future interest deduction restrictions do not apply to undivided gifts of fractional interests.

Discovery Questions

Donor Questions

1. What is the donor trying to accomplish with the gift?
2. What is the tangible asset's value and how was that determined (i.e., appraisal or recent transactions)?
3. Legally, who or what owns the asset?

Advisor Questions

1. What is the current tax basis and is it ordinary income or long term gain?
2. What is the likely exit plan for the charity (e.g., auction or private sale)?
3. Does the advisor have an estimate of what a qualified appraisal will cost?
4. Is the asset inventory?

Charity Questions

1. Is the effort worth the expected benefits (i.e., is the juice worth the squeeze)?

2. Has the screening and due diligence process identified any potential problems and can the risks be mitigated (donor restrictions or excessive holding costs—like boat slip fees)?
3. Is there the necessary expertise to accept and manage tangible assets in a timely way?
4. Should indirect gift acceptance be considered, like using external third party foundations or supporting organizations to receive the asset?
5. Is there a clear liquidation plan to maximize the sales proceeds as soon as possible?
6. Can the charity use the assets as part of its charitable mission?
7. How will the charity manage or administer the assets until sale (insurance, transportation, maintenance, storage, etc.)?

Tangible Property Intermediate

by Ryan Raffin

Below is a review on gifts of tangible property. Tangible property topics are based on Armen Vartian's "Charitable Donations of Art and Collectibles." For quick take-aways on gifts of tangible property, see Tangible Property Quick Take-Aways. *For a review based on that article, see* Tangible Property Intermediate. *For an in-depth examination adapted and excerpted from the article, see* Tangible Property Advanced. *For further details, see* Tangible Property Additional Resources.

This review of charitable gifts of tangible property has five parts, beginning with a definition of tangible personal property. It then discusses income tax issues, followed by income-producing gifts. The fourth part analyzes nontax issues, before concluding with practical gift considerations.

Unlike many other types of asset, owners and collectors of tangible personal property often have no idea as to the fair market value of their assets. Correspondingly, they are also commonly unaware of the philanthropic opportunities that such property presents.

Review Part 1: Tangible Personal Property Defined

Tangible personal property comes in many shapes and forms (including vehicles, addressed separately in chapter 9). Jewelry, gems, coins, and artwork such as paintings, prints, sculpture, or photography are all common examples. The general definition is any property you can both touch and move.

It is also a complex area of law that changes slightly with every tax code revision. There are some natural tensions between the players involved, given their different goals. Taxpayers hope to avoid taxes on highly appreciated property, but the IRS wants its share, and nonprofits actively pursuing these donations simply want the gift to be completed.

With these broad motivations as guidance, nonprofits should consider specific assets on a case-by-case basis, paying particular attention to related-use regulations. Those regulations play an important role in determining the size of the deduction, and as a result heavily factor into the donor's plans, and the nonprofit's ability to accept and liquidate the donation.

Review Part 2: Income Tax Considerations

Tangible assets present special issues for income tax charitable deduction purposes. Relevant questions are:

1. Is the property capital gain property?
2. How will the charity use the donated property?
3. Is the charitable organization a public charity or private charity?
4. Is the donation of a fractional interest only?
5. Is the gift of a present or future interest?

If the property is a capital asset which 1) has been held for over a year, and 2) has appreciated in value, it may be deducted at fair market value. If it does not meet these requirements, the donor's deduction is limited to actual basis in the property. Collectible items generally meet these requirements. However, items which are "inventory" do not—items held as part of a trade or business, including creator-owned items. Artwork often falls into this exception: art dealers and artists themselves are both limited to cost basis in artwork they donate.

Additionally, donors may receive a fair market value deduction on gifts of tangible personal property only if the property's use is related to the nonprofit's tax-exempt purpose. What does this requirement mean? The IRS states that an unrelated use is one without connection to the purpose or function constituting the basis of the charitable organization's tax exemption under Section 501. Further, the donor must prove that the use is not unrelated, or must show that it is reasonable to anticipate there will not be an unrelated use. If the use is unrelated, the deduction is limited to the donor's cost basis.

The amount of the deduction also depends on the nature of the charity. A gift to a public charity (receiving over a third of its support from the public) means that the deduction can be up to 50 percent of adjusted gross income—although important caveats usually end up capping the deduction at 30 percent. Similarly, a gift to a private foundation (receiving less than a third of its funding from the public) means that the deduction will be capped at either 20 percent or 30 percent. In any case, the donor will carry over any undeducted amounts for an additional five years beyond the donation year, so long as the charity puts the property to related use.

Donations of fractional interests in artwork—typically to museums—are allowed with certain stipulations:

Tangible Property

1. The donor (or donor and museum together) must own 100 percent of the artwork prior to making the gift.
2. The donor must agree to donate the remaining interest she holds within ten years or on death, and
3. The charity must take physical possession of the work and put it to a related use within that time-frame.
4. Additionally, the deduction is limited to the lesser of originally appraised fair market value or current value—meaning no increased deduction for appreciations in value.

Gifts of a future interest impact the donor's tax deductions as well. The IRS considers the contribution to be made only when earlier or intervening interests in the asset have expired. For tangible property, this usually comes up in a context where the donor reserves a lifetime right to use and possession, and also in the context of charitable remainder trusts. For example, if a lifetime right to possess donated artwork is retained, the contribution will not occur until that interest expires—whether due to the donor's death or relinquishment of the interest.

Review Part 3: Income-Producing Gifts

How do planned giving vehicles which produce income for the donor impact the tangible property gift analysis? Both related use and future interest rules affect planned giving vehicles. Charitable gift annuities, remainder trusts, and pooled-income funds all merit consideration.

When tangible personal property is exchanged for a charitable gift annuity, there is no gift of future interest. This is because the transfer gets part-gift, part-sale treatment. Hence, the donor will not receive a full deduction, but will be able to deduct the gift portion due to the transfer of his present interest, if the charity puts the property to a related use.

Pooled-income funds and charitable remainder trusts satisfy related use requirements when the trust's use would qualify if the nonprofit organization itself was using the property. Since the trust will likely sell the property to meet its obligations, that use is not normally within the tax-exempt purpose of most nonprofits. As a result, related use rules are not met, and the full charitable deduction is not allowable. Further, these gifts to a pooled-income fund or charitable remainder trust are considered gifts of a future interest. But, since the trust is likely to sell the asset in relatively short order, the donor's interest does terminate.

Finally, note one significant exception to the future interest rule. It does not apply to contributions of an undivided fractional interest. This means that when a charity is donated a one-quarter interest in a painting, it has an immediate right to use and possess the painting for the corresponding time period (three months per year, in this case). Since the interest is immediate, the donor gets a corresponding proportionate deduction.

Review Part 4: Nontax Issues

Of course, tax considerations are not the only relevant ones. The tax effects of various planned giving vehicles were discussed above, but there are other factors to discuss when evaluating which charitable vehicle is best for both the nonprofit and the donor.

Charities should carefully evaluate the marketability of the offered property when considering a charitable gift annuity or pooled-income fund. This is because the nonprofit is obligated to make annuity payments regardless of income the asset generates—even if it cannot be sold. As a result, the charity may conservatively value the property to compensate for market risk.

Charitable remainder trusts, meanwhile, are well suited to tangible gifts of property. A flip unitrust in particular is a good structural fit, since the payments can be set to begin only on sale of the asset (with net income before sale—likely zero dollars). A net income unitrust or standard unitrust may also work due to more limited distribution obligations. However, the nonprofit will still need to produce cash at some point to meet its payment obligations. A charitable remainder annuity trust is an unappealing option since they have fixed payment obligations, and cannot receive additional contributions.

A gift of a future interest is not deductible, as discussed above. Further, such a gift will also be taxable for gift and estate purposes. As an alternative, donors should consider donating by bequest, which would preserve the asset for the donor's lifetime use.

Donors can fund charitable lead trusts with tangible property in some cases. However, non-income-producing property will incur a capital gains tax for either the grantor or trust itself. Further, since tangible personal property is difficult to value (and therefore difficult to estimate the income the charity will receive), careful analysis is required before using this particular vehicle.

Finally, even if tangible personal property is left to family members or friends, this does not mean the property will be accepted. Estate tax, insurance, or simple upkeep concerns may result in a refusal. For this reason, the will should include a right to disclaim, with the property going to a specified charity in that case.

Review Part 5: Practical Gift Considerations

Tangible property often involves more emotional attachment than say, interests in LLCs or mineral royalties. If the charity displays the gift, this can be a very gratifying public acknowledgment. Donors and charities alike should be aware that these personal connections can greatly influence the gift for better or for worse, and often in unpredictable ways. For this reason, charities should work with donors and their advisors to plan the gift out as clearly as possible.

These advisors should usually include financial and legal professionals, but should also include an advisor who can help with the valuation and potential sale of the asset. The advisor should be independent (not affiliated with a museum or dealer), and work alongside existing financial or legal planners to structure the transaction plan in a way that best satisfies all interested parties. Two factors that impact the value are the "buyer's premium" which auction houses will charge, and "blockage" reducing the price of collections sold as a unit. The charity's advisor may be the same professional appraiser who values the asset for taxpayer deduction purposes.

Moreover, the nonprofit and donor should work together to ensure compliance with regulations. This includes verifying the nonprofit's tax status, the property's gain character, and planned use, among others. As the value of the donated asset increases, so do IRS valuation and appraisal requirements. Donated art over $20,000 in value must include a copy of the appraisal with the tax return. If it is both over $50,000 and selected for audit, the IRS's Art Advisory Panel must review and make recommendations on the claimed value. The IRS generally defers to the Panel for its official position on value, and rarely alters its initial conclusion.

Conclusion

Tangible personal property is a common and varied noncash asset class. Current tax laws favor donations of these assets to public charities such as museums, often in exchange for income streams. The complexities of the gift often require a specialized appraisal in tandem with other financial and legal advisors. The combined expertise can create an effective gift transaction for all parties involved, while navigating unique requirements such as the related use rule.

# Tangible Property Advanced[1]

by Armen Vartian

Below is an in-depth examination on gifts of tangible property. Tangible property topics are based on Armen Vartian's "Charitable Donations of Art and Collectibles." For quick take-aways on gifts of tangible property, see Tangible Property Quick Take-Aways. For a review based on that article, see Tangible Property Intermediate. For an in-depth examination adapted and excerpted from the article, see Tangible Property Advanced. For further details, see Tangible Property Additional Resources.

Executive Summary

Tangible personal property includes works of art and collectible items such as jewelry, rare coins and stamps, and historical documents. Whether a specific gift of tangible personal property to a charity qualifies as tax deductible, and to what extent, will depend on:

- How the donor holds the property (capital gain or ordinary income property)
- The type of charity (publicly-supported or private)
- Whether the charitable organization can put the property to use, and
- Whether the gift is of present or future interest

Regardless of whether a donation of tangible property provides tax benefits in theory, realizing those benefits involves application of best practices in connection with appraising the values of the property being donated, as well as keeping proper records.

This is an extremely complicated area of law and for three reasons art and collectibles are uniquely difficult assets to deal with in tax planning. First, because art and collectibles can increase greatly in value over time, taxpayers often search for ways to minimize the tax impact of such appreciation when they donate their collections. Second, because public policy deems the study and display of art and collectibles to be in the public interest, tax-exempt organizations such as museums and universities actively pursue donations of such items. Third, because the values of art and collectibles are so subjective, and may differ for different purposes, there is room for serious argument between taxpayers and the IRS.

---

1. This chapter excerpts and adapts Armen R. Vartian, "Charitable Donations of Art and Collectibles" (2016) (on file with author). Thanks to Mr. Vartian for his assistance.

Key Questions

While every taxpayer's situation is different, there are some basic questions to ask when evaluating charitable donations of art or collectibles.

Is the Property Capital Gain Property?

The first question is whether the donor is giving long-term capital gain property. If so, the charitable donor may deduct the full fair market value of the property at the time of the gift, including market appreciation. If not, the donor can deduct only his actual cost basis in the property, which is generally the amount the donor paid for the property. The difference in tax treatment might make the prospective donor consider a testamentary donation rather than one inter vivos. A life-time gift removes the asset from the estate, and effective charitable estate tax deduction as well as provides a current deduction, even at cost basis, which would be lost through an estate gift.

The Internal Revenue Code defines capital gain property in this context as "any capital asset the sale of which at its fair market value at the time of the contribution would have resulted in gain which would have been long-term capital gain."[2] Generally speaking, art or collectibles which owners held over one year will be considered long-term capital gain property.

A major exception, however, applies to items considered "inventory." This includes items an art dealer owned as part of a trade or business. It also includes creators holding their own items, (i.e., artists holding the original works they created). Since the IRS considers an artist's own works "inventory" or "ordinary income property", artists who donate their works to charity may deduct only the value of their "paint and canvas" incorporated into the work. This tax treatment also extends to persons who receive artworks as gifts from their creators. Finally, for collectors or investors who donate property they have held for less than one year, regulations usually limit the deduction to the price they paid for the property, because the IRS considers such property short-term capital gain property.

How Will the Charity Be Using the Donated Item?

The next question is the use to which the charity puts the donated items. Charities sometimes accept gifts for their own use as part of their regular activities, and in other cases charities sell gift

---

2. IRC § 170(b)(1)(C)(iv)

items as part of their fund-raising. According to the Internal Revenue Code, donors may deduct items of tangible personal property which the charity puts to a use "not unrelated" to the charity's tax exempt purpose at their full fair market value, but not items which the charity uses for "unrelated" purposes. Here is the example given by the IRS in Publication 526, entitled "Charitable Deductions":

> "If a painting contributed to an educational institution is used by that organization for educational purposes by being placed in its library for display and study by art students, the use is not an unrelated use. But if the painting is sold and the proceeds are used by the organization for educational purposes, the use is an unrelated use."[3]

The most common "unrelated use" in the art and collectibles field is the charity auction, where collectors donate items for charities to sell for their own benefit. The IRS's example demonstrates the peculiar nature of the "related-unrelated" distinction. A collector choosing between two organizations to which to donate a particular item might well find that one organization would put the item to a related use, while the other would not. If the item is one that has appreciated greatly over time, donating to the former charity might result in a much higher tax deduction.

Practitioners can learn from three Private Letter Rulings the IRS issued to taxpayers contemplating charitable donations of art and collectibles. In one case, the IRS found that a collection of porcelain given to a public charity operating a retirement home was "related" to the charity's exempt purpose, namely creating a comfortable living environment for its residents.[4] Likewise, in another case, the Service found that lithographs donated to a camp for disabled children was "related" to the charity's exempt purpose when the camp used them in connection with an art appreciation program.[5] But in a third case, the IRS found that a classic car donated to a university did not meet the "related use" test, because there was no indication that the organization used the car in connection with any academic program.[6]

Quite often, donors are not in a position to know how charities will use their gifts of property, and charities do not ordinarily know the donor's tax basis in donated property, or whether the donor held the property for more than a year prior to the donation. In other words, neither donor nor charity may be aware of whether or not the gift will result in the maximum tax benefits to the

---

3. IRS Publication 526, "Charitable Contributions," 12 (2015).
4. Private Letter Ruling 8143029 (July 29, 1981).
5. Private Letter Ruling 7751044 (September 22, 1977).
6. Private Letter Ruling 8009027 (November 29, 1979).

donor. Moreover, what happens when a charity displays a gift for a while in its library and then sells? The IRS allows donors who believed in good faith that the charity would use their gifts for "not unrelated" purposes to take their full fair market value deduction, even if the property is ultimately sold, but only if the charity holds the property for one year. Donors may also request a certification from the charity that the donated items will be put to a related use, and such certifications are often conditions precedent to donations.

If the charity sells a donated item within three years of acquiring it, however, the charity must file Form 8282 with the IRS giving the donor's name and the amount for which it sold the item. This enables the IRS to check the "fair market value" deduction the donor took against the actual value the charity received when it sold the item. Pursuant to IRC Sec. 170(e)(7), the donor could be subject to income recapture if such a sale occurs, unless the donor has a written certification of related use from the donee charity.

As with the analysis of whether regulations permit capital gain treatment, artists who donate their own works are limited to the items' cost basis (paint and canvas).

Is the Charitable Organization a Public Charity or Private Charity?

Even if long-term capital gain property is put to a related use, the amount of the deduction can still vary. It depends upon whether the charity is publicly-supported or is a private foundation, and whether the taxpayer wishes to deduct full fair market value in the current year or spread out ("carry over" in IRS parlance) the deduction over up to five years. Taxpayers may deduct gifts to public charities of up to 50 percent of the taxpayer's adjusted gross income in any given year, while donations to private charities are limited to 30 percent and, in some cases, to 20 percent.

A public tax-exempt organization is one that receives at least one-third of its support from the general public; museums, universities and other schools, hospitals and churches are among the institutions that generally qualify. A private tax-exempt organization does not rely on funding from the public. The Ford Foundation is one prominent example, and there are many private foundations which receive funding primarily from specific wealthy individuals.

For donors unsure which category a particular charity falls under, the IRS says to ask them: "You may ask any organization whether it is a 50 percent limit organization, and most will be able to tell you." But gifts of capital gain property are limited to 30 percent regardless of the public recipient, unless the taxpayer elects to deduct only his or her basis, and not any appreciation. If the contributed property satisfies the related-use rule, the taxpayer may elect to increase the 30 percent limitation to 50 percent of his or her adjusted gross income. But if the taxpayer makes that election, the amount of the deduction must be reduced by 100 percent of the appreciation in value of the property. In other words, the IRS limits the deduction to the donor's cost basis.

For example, a collector has an adjusted gross income of $150,000. He contributes to a museum a long-term capital gain visual arts collection with a fair market value of $90,000, and a cost basis of $40,000. If the donor has a qualified appraisal prepared, he has made a gift of $90,000, of which $45,000 (30 percent of $150,000) is deductible in the year of the gift. But if that visual arts collection is donated to a charity but not related to the charitable purposes or functions of that charity, the collector's deduction will be the cost basis of $40,000. That cost basis amount is fully deductible under the 50 percent ceiling, with no carryover.

Is the Donation of a Fractional Interest Only?

Fractional donations of art were once a favorite means for donors working with charities to "have their cake and eat it too," retaining physical possession of their art but obtaining tax benefits as well. But effective August 17, 2006 the rules changed. Donations after that date (with a small exception—see below), must comply with certain requirements that discourage the practice of fractional donations:

- First, the donor or the donor and museum together must own 100 percent of the property immediately before the gift, and the donor must agree to donate the remainder ownership interest within ten years or the donor's death, whichever occurs first.

- Second, the IRS limits the donor, after receiving a qualified appraisal, to a charitable deduction for the fair-market value of the initial fraction donated. He can also carry forward his deduction for five years, but can only deduct an amount up to 30 percent of his gross adjusted income in any given year.

- Third, the subsequent fractions require new appraisals, and the donor may deduct only the lesser of the first appraisal or the current appraisal. In other words, if the value of the art has increased the donor receives no tax benefit, but a decrease in value decreases the tax benefit available to the donor.

- Finally, the charity is legally obligated to take "significant physical possession" of the work and use it for a related use within the ten-year period.

If a donor has given a fraction before the effective date of August 17, 2006, that donor receives one subsequent fractional donation at then-current (possibly higher) fair market value. After that point, any additional donations are valued as the "lesser of" standard applicable after 2006.

Is a Future Interest Involved?

The IRS recognizes charitable contributions of a future interest in tangible personal property, but only if the parties follow some restrictions. All intervening interests in, and rights to the actual possession or enjoyment of, the property must have expired, or persons other than the taxpayer or those in privity with the taxpayer hold those interests. An example of such a future interest donation is where the donor gives tangible personal property to a charitable organization, but has an understanding with the charitable organization that the donor may continue to use, possess, or enjoy of the property.

Outright contributions do not run afoul of the future-interest rule as long as the property is physically delivered to the charitable donee. So a donor who transfers legal title to a painting but retains the right to display the painting in his or her home cannot take a charitable deduction until such time as the charity obtains physical possession of the painting.

Regulations do not consider transfers of tangible personal property in exchange for an immediate or deferred payment charitable gift annuity to be a gift of a future interest because such transfers are considered part outright gift and part sale. Although there are no rulings directly on point, if the donee can put the property to a related use, presumably the donor can claim a deduction with only the factors discussed above limiting it. Furthermore, because the gift portion of the transfer is one of a present interest, the donor could deduct the value of that portion immediately regardless of when the charity eventually sells the property.

This tax treatment is likewise the case for pooled-income funds, where the donor's interest terminates when the fund or trust sells the tangible property to an unrelated party.[7] In one ruling, the taxpayer contributed publicly traded stock and a musical instrument. The IRS allowed deduction of the value of the musical instrument when the charity sold it, reasoning that at that point the taxpayer's interest was no longer in the instrument itself, but rather in the sales proceeds.[8]

Practitioners should be mindful of the potential valuation problems inherent in negotiating deals with charities that require guaranteed future payments. Charities will be reluctant to enter into an annuity arrangement where there is a real possibility of the tangible property declining in value over time to the point where the payouts to the donor are no longer sustainable. Likewise, with a pooled-income fund, if the charity does not believe the property is liquid at an acceptable market

---

7. As with other asset types, transactions between related parties may result in the IRS disallowing any tax deduction.
8. Private Letter Ruling 9452026 (September 29, 1994).

value, it might decline to accept the property so as not to put other participants at risk. Accurate valuation and acceptable liquidity of the asset is important for CGAs and PIFs, because the charity is obligated to make annuity payments.[9] For this reason, charities may conservatively accept the property at a lower value, and sell when able—particularly for PIFs, where all participants are exposed to risk from accepted assets (compare with charitable lead trusts, where the sale of a non-producing asset may result in a capital gains tax burden).[10]

Charitable trusts are the flip side of gift annuities. In this case, the donor places the tangible property in trust with herself as income beneficiary for a period of time (either the donor's lifetime or a fixed term of 20 years or less), and the charity receiving title to the property thereafter. The remainderman can be any qualified charity, including a private foundation the donor created, so this method of charitable donation is popular. Charities also favor it because the payouts from the trust are not necessarily contractually guaranteed, as in the case of an annuity, although providing any payout at all requires that the tangible property be sufficiently liquid to produce income, or must return portions of the asset as distributions.

Charitable remainder annuity trusts are less suitable, for the same liquidity reasons. Unitrusts, particularly a FLIP-CRUT where income distributions only begin after sale of the asset, are a better fit.[11] A net income CRUT also insulates the nonprofit from payment obligations when the asset is nonproducing, but is less appealing "from the perspective of the trustee's ability to reinvest the proceeds from the sale of the property to produce trust accounting (distributable) income."[12]

Generally speaking, the donor may take a charitable deduction for the present value of the remainder interest in the tangible property. However, it may be better to make such gifts by bequest (which would have estate tax benefits). Similarly, testators should include a right to disclaim a gift of tangible property to heirs, with a named charity receiving the gift instead—in addition to possible estate tax benefits, there are no related use concerns in this context.[13]

---

9. Temple, P.T. & Zale, L.C. (January 2005), "Charitable Giving with Tangible Personal Property: A Tax Primer," Journal of Financial Planning, http://www.visualartsadvisory.com/resources/JFPArticle.pdf.
10. Id.
11. Id.
12. Id.
13. Id.

Valuations / Qualified Appraisals

Beyond the complexities of charitable deduction law lies the subjectivity of art and collectibles values, which create problems even where everyone agrees on the nature of the gifts or donations themselves. As discussed above, an executor of an estate will want to understate the values of art and collectibles in the taxable estate while at the same time hoping to get away with overstating the value of items bequeathed to a spouse. Taxpayers also want high valuations for art and collectibles they donate to charity (for their income tax deductions) and low valuations for gifts to nonspouses (to reduce or eliminate gift tax). The IRS, if it reviews the appraised values, will tend toward the opposite positions in each situation (low valuations for charitable gifts, high valuations in estate situations), and it employs art and collectibles experts who often back up its positions. This is an inherent conflict that shows up quite often in evaluating estate tax returns and charitable deductions of art and collectibles.

Beyond these broad valuation issues are questions regarding what market information appraisers do and do not take into account when appraising art and collectibles. For example, a common issue when estates include art and collectibles is whether auction prices for comparable sales which establish value should include the buyer's premium. This 10–25 percent difference can, of course, be significant. It may be advisable to include the buyer's premium because auction buyers generally factor the premium into their bidding calculations. In addition, experts debate the extent to which "blockage", (i.e., the loss of value due to selling a collection as a unit), will affect appraised values for estates or large gifts. A great example of this was the estate of artist Georgia O'Keeffe, in which the IRS and the estate agreed on the total value of some 400 works she bequeathed to various charities and individuals, but were tens of millions of dollars apart on the extent to which blockage and costs of sale reduced their value for tax purposes (a court finally decided upon a 50 percent reduction).

Acknowledgment and Reporting Requirements

In addition to the standard donation substantiation requirements discussed in Appendix A, there are special rules for valuable artwork donations. When donating art valued at over $20,000, the donor must attach the written appraisal itself to IRS Form 8283 and file it with the donor's tax return. For items valued at $50,000 or more, the IRS will (for a fee) provide a statement of value from its Art Advisory Panel, which the taxpayer can use in connection with the tax return.

All taxpayer cases the IRS selected for audit that contain artwork with a claimed value of $50,000 or more per item must be referred to Art Appraisal Services for the Commissioner's Art Advisory Panel to review. The Panel consists of 25 nationally prominent art museum directors, curators, scholars, art dealers, auction representatives, and appraisers. The panel meets once or twice a year for one day, and reviews hundreds of works per session. To ensure objectivity, the panel is not told whether the appraisal was for an income tax charitable contribution deduction or for estate or gift tax purposes.

The panel members, after reviewing photographs or color transparencies, along with relevant documentation provided by the taxpayers and research by the staff appraisers, make recommendations on the acceptability of the claimed values. If unacceptable, the panelists make alternate value recommendations. Such recommendations are advisory only; however, after review by the Office of Art Appraisal Services, these recommendations generally (but not always) become the position of the Service.

If the IRS cannot reach an agreement with the taxpayer, it may request further assistance from the panel and the Office of Art Appraisal Services. The taxpayer may request reconsideration of the return's adjusted claimed value only upon presentation of additional evidence such as comparable sales data or other relevant facts to support the fair market value opinion. These requests for reconsideration almost never result in any change in the IRS's position.

Tangible Property Additional Resources

Below are further details on gifts of tangible property. Tangible property topics are based on Armen Vartian's "Charitable Donations of Art and Collectibles." For quick take-aways on gifts of tangible property, see [Tangible Property Quick Take-Aways](). For a review based on that article, see [Tangible Property Intermediate](). For an in-depth examination adapted and excerpted from the article, see [Tangible Property Advanced](). For further details, see [Tangible Property Additional Resources]().

For an overview of tax and nontax issues in different giving vehicles, see Hoffman, M.D., Temple, P.T. & Zale, L.C. (May 2, 2003), "Technical Report: Tangible Personal Property," Planned Giving Design Center, http://www.pgdc.com/pgdc/tangible-personal-property.

For a discussion of collectors and collectibles, see Breus, A. (September 23, 2010), "Gifts of Tangible Personal Property or How to Find Valuable Donations in Your Donor," Planned Giving Design Center, http://www.pgdc.com/pgdc/gifts-tangible-personal-property-or-how-find-valuable-donations-your-donor.

For practical considerations of the donor's advisors, see Berus, J.G., "The Art of Donating Art: The Charitable Contribution of Art, Antiques, and Collectibles," *Journal of Retirement Planning* 45 (April/May 2008), http://www.pgdc.com/pgdc/art-donating-art-charitable-contribution-art-antiques-and-collectibles.

For an analysis of the law and policy impacting gifts of artwork, see Wieczorek, S.G., "Winokur, Lose, or Draw: Art Collectors Lose an Important Tax Break," *2008 Houston Business and Tax Journal* 90 (2008), http://www.hbtlj.org/v08p1/v08p1wieczorekar.pdf.

For a gift acceptance policy with a particular emphasis on gifts of artwork, see Museum of Modern Art (February 8, 2012), "Gift Acceptance Policies and Guidelines," https://www.moma.org/momaorg/shared/pdfs/docs/about/MoMAGiftAcceptancePolicy.pdf.

IRC § 170(e) (gifts of ordinary income and capital gain property)

IRC § 2503(g) (loans of artwork to charity)

Private Letter Ruling 9452026 (timing of deductions for tangible property)

Private Letter Ruling 9833011 (related use concerns)

Rev. Proc. 96-15, 1996-1 C.B. 627 (instructions on requesting art valuation from the IRS)

Estate of Georgia T. O'Keeffe v. Comm'r, TC Memo 1992-210 (1992) (art valuation discrepancies due to blockage)

Doherty v. Comm'r, 16 F.3d 338 (9th Cir., 1994) (valuation challenges due to questions of authenticity)

Chapter 8
Mineral Interests

- Quick Take-Aways
- Intermediate
- Advanced
- Additional Resources

Mineral Interests Quick Take-Aways

by Bryan Clontz

Below are quick take-aways on gifts of mineral interests. Mineral interest topics are based on Joe Hancock's "Black Gold: Gifts of Oil and Gas Interests Made Simple." For quick take-aways on gifts of real estate, see Mineral Interests Quick Take-Aways. For a review based on that article, see Mineral Interests Intermediate. For an in-depth examination adapted and excerpted from the article, see Mineral Interests Advanced. For further details, see Mineral Interests Additional Resources.

Mineral interests, typically meaning oil and gas, are often an appealing gift for nonprofits. Since these interests can be split into a number of legal interests, the donation can take a variety of forms. Below is a brief summary of the advantages, disadvantages, wrinkles, and questions for nonprofits considering whether they should accept gifts of mineral interests.

Advantages of donations of mineral interests include:

- Standard royalty interests are the most commonly gifted, and involve no potential liability or unrelated business taxable income.
- Interests can produce regular income for your nonprofit over a long period of time.
- Mineral interests are flexible in both the interest conveyed and the transaction structure.

Disadvantages of donating mineral interests include:

- Holding the gift is usually much more lucrative than selling, but requires active management and paying accompanying expenses.
- Gifts of working and operating interests open the nonprofit up to potential liability and UBIT.
- Valuation can be tricky, and it can be tough to even know if an appraisal is necessary.

Potential wrinkles in the gift acceptance process include:

- Gifts which involve an annuity must account for the declining production of mineral interests (consider a charitable remainder unitrust or lead unitrust instead).
- The IRS partial interest rule can disallow a deduction for donations of less than an entire interest, but does not preclude gifts of fractional interests.

- State specific laws can vary and have significant impact on the gift, including recording requirements, marital property, and ownership.
- Qualified appraisers will usually need to be specialized professionals to properly assess and value the current status of the interest and future income streams.

Discovery Questions

Donor Questions

1. What is the donor trying to accomplish with the gift?
2. What is the mineral asset's value and how was that determined (i.e., appraisal, recent transactions, averaging annual prior net income formula)?
3. Legally, who or what owns the asset?
4. What has been the average income received over the previous three years?

Advisor Questions

1. What is the current tax basis?
2. What is the likely exit plan for the charity?
3. Does the advisor have an estimate of what a qualified appraisal will cost?
4. How will the interest be conveyed?

Charity Questions

1. Is the effort worth the expected benefits (i.e., is the juice worth the squeeze)?
2. Has the screening and due diligence process identified any potential problems and can the risks be mitigated (marketability if a small position or issues with liability for working interests)?
3. Is there the necessary expertise to accept and manage mineral assets in a timely way?
4. Should indirect gift acceptance be considered, like using external third party foundations or supporting organizations to receive the asset?
5. If the charity will sell the interest, is there a clear liquidation plan to maximize the sales proceeds as soon as possible?
6. Is the charity prepared to manage the asset over time?

Mineral Interests Intermediate

by Ryan Raffin

Below is a review on gifts of mineral interests. Mineral interest topics are based on Joe Hancock's "Black Gold: Gifts of Oil and Gas Interests Made Simple." For quick take-aways on gifts of real estate, see Mineral Interests Quick Take-Aways. For a review based on that article, see Mineral Interests Intermediate. For an in-depth examination adapted and excerpted from the article, see Mineral Interests Advanced. For further details, see Mineral Interests Additional Resources.

This review of charitable gifts of mineral interests has six parts, starting with definitions of the specialized terminology in this field. Second, is a look at developing acceptance policies and working with donors. Next are valuation considerations, with analysis of compatibility with specific planned giving vehicles coming fourth. Fifth are management and environmental issues. Finally, there are tax considerations, particularly partial interests and unrelated business income.

Part 1: Definitions

A mineral interest is ownership of the right to exploit, mine, or produce minerals lying beneath the surface of the property. The most important types of mineral for the purposes of charitable giving are typically oil and gas. Depending on the state where the minerals are located, the owner of the surface either owns the underlying substances (ownership-in-place), or owns the right to capture those substances using the land (right-to-take or Oklahoma doctrine).

Types of ownership interest include the fee interest (the land owner with both surface and subsurface rights), surface interest (land surface rights only), and the mineral interest (mineral interest / estate / right). If the mineral interest is leased, the lessee has a working interest (sometimes called operating interest), and in exchange, the lessor receives a royalty interest.

Part 2: Acceptance Policies and Working with Donors

As with other asset classes, an ounce of prevention—in the form of a formal acceptance policy—is worth a pound of cure for the nonprofit donee. Provisions to consider include:

1. Setting out a minimum value for gifts of surface rights
2. Setting out a minimum per year royalty

3. Providing for review of liability issues
4. Prohibiting acceptance of working interests
5. Providing for environmental review in order to prevent current or future exposure to environmental liability

Charities will also need an evaluation process when deciding whether to sell or hold donated mineral interests. Relevant considerations include the viability of third-party management, potential environmental liability, carrying costs, and whether the asset is producing.

Charities should avoid working interests as a matter of course. In accepting a gift of this type of interest, the charity also opens itself up to significant potential liability. All liability issues flow to the holder of the working interest, including environmental problems relating to exploration and production. Further, income from working interests is considered unrelated business taxable income.

Determining the nature of the donor's interest is of crucial importance as well. For example, depending on the donor's marital status and state laws, both spouses may need to convey the interest. The key questions the charity will ask are: What does the donor own, and what does the donor want to give? More specifically, the development officer should ask potential donors the following:

1. Is the mineral leased?
2. How was the mineral acquired?
3. What is your understanding of what is owned?
4. What do you want to gift?
5. Are there prior or existing leases? If so, obtain copies.
6. Are there prior division orders? If so, obtain copies.
7. Are there prior transfer orders? If so, obtain copies.
8. Are there check stubs from royalty payments? If so, obtain copies.

How does the actual gift transaction work from a legal perspective? For a charity, this is usually accomplished via conveyance or inheritance. Conveyance transfers ownership by a writing that satisfies certain formal requirements—in the case of oil and gas interests, these transfers occur via deed or lease. Although state law, many do not require recording. It is a good idea for donor and charity alike to have the deed or lease recorded to publicly establish title. When the interest is acquired via inheritance, the interest transfers when the decedent donor's last will and testament is offered for probate.

Part 3: Valuation Considerations

The question of valuation is familiar to any reasonably experienced gift planner, but gifts of mineral interests present a special case given their often literally fluid nature. As with other property types, fair market value is highly relevant to the valuation discussion. Of course, donors will need to substantiate their contributions with a qualified appraisal to receive a deduction over $5,000.

How should donors and gift planners know if an appraisal is necessary? The rule of thumb is that the total value of the interest is approximately four times the annual income it produces. Based on this quick calculation, the donor can decide whether an appraisal is necessary, and the nonprofit can decide whether the gift reaches their minimum threshold value. Conversely, if the interest is nonproducing, both the IRS and the oil and gas industry consider it without value, meaning no deduction for the donor.

Additionally, if the donor is an operator—someone in the business of drilling wells for oil and gas production—the deduction is limited to the cost basis. However, operators may also deduct long-term capital gains on interests treated as trade or business real estate. Finally, gifts where the donor has taken prior deductions for intangible drilling costs or has "carved out" production payments will reduce the amount of the deduction under IRS quid pro quo rules.

Qualified appraisers are discussed in Appendix A, but a few points specific to mineral interests bear mentioning. Although a real estate appraiser may be licensed and certified, this expertise usually applies only to surface interests, not the more specialized task of valuing subsurface mineral interests. The appraiser should be a geologist or petroleum engineer with the expertise necessary to assess current status and project future outputs, including production declines and cash flows. This information has obvious value to the nonprofit receiving the interest, in addition to satisfying IRS requirements for the donor. These estimates often cost between $1,000 and $2,000, but can vary depending on the scope and history of production for the donated interest.

Part 4: Compatibility with Specific Planned Giving Vehicles

Different planned giving vehicles may be compatible with the potential donor's goals. It is important to note that annual production will vary, and will decline over time. Although immediate sale of the interest is an option, often it will be better to retain the interest.

Many planned giving vehicles require regular payments to donors, which the charity often satisfies by use of the production income. Although charitable gift annuities are commonly used for planned giving, the fixed payment obligation makes it a poor match for the varying and declining production of a mineral interest. If it is used, the nonprofit should set the payment obligation at a level significantly below current production.

A donor can also fund a charitable remainder trust with a mineral interest. As with a charitable gift annuity, the structure of the payout provision is key—a charitable remainder annuity trust presents the same fixed-payment issues. Alternatively, a charitable remainder unitrust is much better suited to the income stream of the mineral interest. This is because the trust requires annual revaluation of assets, and the payment is determined as a fixed-percentage of those assets. Charitable lead trusts will invoke the same considerations when deciding between the fixed-payment charitable lead annuity trust and the fixed-percentage charitable lead unitrust.

Finally, a mineral interest may be part of a larger remainder interest in real property such as a personal residence or farm. In this case, the life tenant (typically the donor) retains the use and enjoyment of the property. This means that both the life tenant and the nonprofit remainderman have legally enforceable interests. For example, state law may require both parties to execute a lease for it to be effective. Similarly, different payments on the mineral interest are paid depending on whether they are classified as income (paid to the life tenant) or consumption of corpus (belonging to the remainderman).

Part 5: Management and Environmental Issues

As mentioned previously, a charity is free to sell any donated mineral interests it obtains. However, since these are often purchased for only 1½ to 2 times annual production, it is commonly more lucrative to retain the interest. Since nonprofits usually do not have the resources or expertise to effectively manage these interests, they often retain a third-party to do so. Specialized consulting groups are certainly an option, but many large banks or financial services organizations provide management services as well. Regardless of who manages the interest, the firm should actively manage, review, administer, and negotiate on the nonprofit's behalf to maximize the benefit.

Although management may be an unanticipated expense, incurred environmental liabilities typically will not be. Most prospective gifts of mineral interests do not carry any liability. Should the charity become involved in the production process (by owning a working or operating interest), it would be liable for any environmental problems. A gift acceptance policy that excludes these interests would, of course, avoid liability. However, if the nonprofit does decide to accept a working interest, it should consider its liability protection options, such as potentially creating a limited liability subsidiary organization to hold the interest.

Part 6: Tax Considerations

Partial Interest Rule

If a donor contributes their whole 1/8th interest, in both land and minerals, that donation would be deductible, because it comprises the donor's complete interest in the asset. However, if a donor owns both the surface estate and mineral estate, he cannot receive a deduction on a gift of only the surface interest (even if there is a partition of the surface and mineral estates prior to the gift conveyance). If this gift happens anyways, the charity should restrict surface use rights to prevent drilling and production operations that might interfere with the charity's use.

Unrelated Business Taxable Income

As with other asset types, the potential for unrelated business taxable income (UBTI) can complicate a charity's acceptance of mineral interest gifts. UBTI is income derived from any regularly carried on trade or business and not substantially related to the nonprofit's normal charitable or educational purpose (see the definition on page lxxii). Luckily, some unrelated business activities are excluded from UBTI if they are "passive income" such as royalties.

Most royalty interests that a nonprofit would receive do generate such passive income. However, important exceptions relate to working interests. If a charity owns such an interest (or controls an entity which does), then the income is not passive and is UBTI.

Mineral Interests Advanced[1]

by Joe Hancock

Below is an in-depth examination on gifts of mineral interests. Mineral interest topics are based on Joe Hancock's "Black Gold: Gifts of Oil and Gas Interests Made Simple." For quick take-aways on gifts of real estate, see Mineral Interests Quick Take-Aways. For a review based on that article, see Mineral Interests Intermediate. For an in-depth examination adapted and excerpted from the article, see Mineral Interests Advanced. For further details, see Mineral Interests Additional Resources.

Overview of Mineral Interests

A mineral interest is the ownership of the right to exploit, mine, or produce minerals lying beneath the surface of a property. In the U.S., private owners hold a majority of the minerals, which is particularly good for charitable institutions. Other than oil and gas, coal, iron ore, sulphur, and precious metals are considered minerals. Water, sand and gravel, salt, building stone, limestone, and surface shale are not minerals and belong to the surface owner.

In Texas and many other states, the mineral estate is the dominant estate and allows the owner to use the surface estate in a reasonable manner to exploit, mine, or produce minerals. The mineral owner has the right to lease the interest to others. This right is known as executive rights. The various interests that owners can create using this right are the basis for gift possibilities.

There are two theories related to the ownership of minerals. The "ownership-in-place" theory says that the surface owner owns all substances under the land. Texas, New Mexico, West Virginia, Mississippi, and about half of the other states follow this theory. The "nonownership/exclusive right-to-take" theory says that the surface owner does not own the oil and gas, but merely owns the right to capture oil and gas using the land. After the landowner captures the mineral, that person owns the mineral. This is the Oklahoma doctrine.

Minerals are considered real property until producers extract them. Once extracted, minerals become personal property, and personal property laws then control. The mineral owner bears all costs of producing the mineral and gets all profits, but also bears all risk of loss. Once the owner

---

1. This chapter excerpts and adapts Hancock, J., HighGround Advisors, Dallas, Texas (September 10, 2009), "Black Gold: Gifts of Oil and Gas Interests Made Simple," Oklahoma Planned Giving Council, http://www.okpgc.org/uploads/Joe_Hancock_Black_Gold_9-10-09.pdf.

leases the minerals, the lessee controls the mineral estate subject to the rights the lessor retains under the lease agreement.

Types of Oil & Gas Ownership Interests

If an individual owns all of the private rights in land, including both surface and subsurface rights, he or she is said to own a fee interest. If only the surface interest is owned, then the individual owns a surface interest, and conversely, if the individual only owns the mineral interest, a mineral interest / mineral estate / mineral right is owned. An individual may own all of the mineral interest or may own a percentage. Additionally, an individual may own a certain mineral type.

When the owner of a mineral interest leases the interest to an individual or company, the individual receiving the lease, the lessee, has a leasehold interest. Leasehold interests are typically called working interests or operating interests. In exchange for granting the lease, the lessor typically receives a royalty interest, an initial bonus, delay rental and shut-in royalty. The lessee has the rights to use the surface of the property to obtain the minerals, the right to incur costs of exploration and production of the minerals, and to retain profits subject to the lessor's retained rights, typically the royalty interest. The lessor also holds a reverter in the mineral interest. Upon expiration of the mineral lease, ownership of the minerals revert to the lessor.

A royalty interest is a share in the production of the mineral free of the costs of producing it, when and if there is production on the property. Oil and gas royalties are typically fractions or percentages of the whole production, and owners can create them in different ways. There are landowner's royalty interests, nonparticipating royalty interests, and overriding royalty interests.

The owner generally retains a landowner's royalty interest at the time the oil and gas lease is negotiated. It is the landowner's compensation for granting the lease. A 1/8th royalty was standard from the 1920s through the mid-1980s. Today, many consider a standard royalty to be 3/16th, but prevailing royalty amounts will vary somewhat depending on the level of production in a given area.

A nonparticipating royalty interest is carved out of the mineral interest and entitles the holder to a stated share of production, without regard to the terms of the lease. This can be seen in a situation where a parent conveys a percentage of his or her royalty to children.

An overriding royalty interest is carved out of the lessee's working interest and can be used to compensate landmen, lawyers and geologists who helped structure the drilling operation.

A net profits interest is similar to a royalty interest, but is payable only if there is a net profit. It is important to negotiate what costs the agreement includes in the definition of "net profit."

Gift Acceptance Policies: Identifying Types of Mineral Interests That Charities May Receive

The management and administration of oil and gas assets requires knowledge and expertise. The charity may receive these interests in the conveyance of surface ownership which also includes a mineral interest or the conveyance of the mineral interest alone. Institutions should have acceptance policies addressing mineral gifts. The gift acceptance policies should serve to educate staff and board about the critical issues that gifts of these assets can trigger. There can be valuation issues, environmental issues, unrelated business income issues, and management issues with the acceptance of this asset type.

Many oil and gas acceptance policies across the country include provisions that:
1. Set-out a minimum value for gifts of surface rights
2. Set-out a minimum per year royalty
3. Provide for review of liability issues
4. Prohibit acceptance of working interests
5. Provide for environmental review in order to prevent current or future exposure to environmental liability

Some charities will sell mineral interests as soon as practical, while others will hold and manage them. The question of whether or not to maintain the asset depends upon the charity's ability to effectively manage this asset type. Is the asset of a size that would allow the charity to obtain third party administration / management? Will the charity accept producing and/or nonproducing assets? There are no carrying costs (ad valorem taxes, severance taxes, etc.) for an oil and gas asset that is not in production.

Charities typically do not accept working interests, because of the liability and tax consequences associated with these interests. As mentioned in the definitions above, the working interest holder has the rights to use the surface of the property to obtain the minerals, to incur costs of exploration and production of the minerals, and to retain profits subject to the lessor's retained rights. All liability issues flow to the holder of the working interest. This includes all environmental issues the exploration and production of the asset may cause. IRS regulations classify income a charity derives from working interests as unrelated business income, and therefore is subject to unrelated business income tax.

Working with Donors: Identifying the Donor's Ownership Interest, Objectives and Options

Who owns the mineral interest? Is the donor single or are the donors married? When husband and wife donors approach a charity, the questions are: In what state do the donors reside, and how was the mineral interest obtained?

In nine states, community property statutes presume that each spouse owns a ½ interest in property acquired during marriage except by gift, devise or bequeath. Most states in the U.S. follow the common law property concept—property any spouse acquires in his or her name is property that person owns individually and can be conveyed as such. In states that have homestead protection from creditors, both spouses should sign an oil and gas conveyance.

Does the donor own executive rights or a nonexecutive interest? An executive right gives the holder the power to lease. What does the donor own and what does the owner want to give? The charity must have answers to these questions to fully understand the consequences of a charitable gift of a mineral interest as described below. Knowing the basic questions to ask when a potential donor proposes a mineral interest gift will provide the charity information to make an informed decision on whether or not to accept the gift.

Working with Donors: Facilitating the Gift Transaction

Conveyance, inheritance, judicial action and adverse possession are ways to create and transfer oil and gas interests. A conveyance is a transfer of ownership by an instrument which passes ownership of the land interest to a third party. The instrument must be in writing, contain words of grant, include an adequate description of the property, designate the grantor and grantee (lessor and lessee), and be properly executed. Deed or lease are generally the ways to transfer oil and gas interests. These documents are formal, legal and recordable.

The execution requirements include delivery and acceptance. In an oil and gas context, it is always best to get the deed or lease in hand. Once the charity receives the instrument, it is a good idea to record it. Most states do not require recording the document for it to be legally binding, but practically it is a good idea. Recording protects the charity against claims of subsequent purchasers or creditors. Additionally, several states have marketability title acts or dormant mineral acts which require special recordings or use to preserve the interest beyond the statutory limitation.

Inheritance is another way to acquire oil and gas interests. Transfer of the interest occurs when the executor offers the last will and testament for probate. The executor may or may not prepare an executor's deed transferring the interest. In many cases, if the interest is nonproducing it may or may not be included in the estate inventory, because the executor is often not aware of the existence of the interest. The question of ownership will not surface until such time as someone is interested in leasing the mineral interest.

Valuation of Mineral Interests: General Guidelines

For any asset, including minerals, the fair market value of the contribution is the price at which the property would change hands between a willing buyer and a willing seller, neither being under any compulsion to buy or sell and both having a reasonable knowledge of relevant facts.[2] The IRS has further asserted that the most probative evidence of fair market value is the price at which similar quantities of property are sold in arm's length transactions.[3] Therefore, the donor can calculate fair market value in the market in which the item is most commonly sold to the public.[4]

Valuation of Mineral Interests: Notable Factors

Donors who contribute a royalty interest or a net profits interest may claim a charitable deduction for the fair market value of the interest, if they have held the interest for more than one year.[5] A qualified appraisal must substantiate any such contribution that exceeds $5,000 in value. So, the initial question that all donors and gift planners will face is whether or not the mineral interest would be properly valued in an amount that will necessitate obtaining a qualified appraisal. Fortunately, there is a general rule of thumb that provides that the value of a mineral interest will closely approximate the annual income the interest produces multiplied by a factor of four (annual income x 4).

This helpful guideline provides donors with a reliable estimate of the overall value of the interest before incurring the expense of obtaining a qualified appraisal. Based upon this rule of thumb, donors can then proceed to obtain the appraisal if the interest exceeds the $5,000 threshold. The

---

2. Reg. § 1.170A-1(c)(2); Rev. Rul. 68-69, 1968-1 CB 80.
3. Rev. Rul. 80-69, 1980-1 CB 55.
4. Id.
5. IRC § 170(e).

formal appraisal will be based upon a more sophisticated estimate of the expected future cash flows which will utilize factors such as production history and the number of producing wells, discounted to present value. Both the IRS and the oil and gas industry consider mineral interests not yielding any production to be without any current value. Hence, contributions of such interests result in no deduction for the donor.

Another important distinction among donors is between those that are merely holding a mineral interest as an estate asset or personal investment, and those actively engaged in the business of drilling wells for oil and gas production (i.e., "operators"). Donors who are not operators may contribute a mineral interest and claim a charitable deduction for the full fair market value of the interest, if they held the interest for more than one year.[6] However, regulations limit the deduction for operators who contribute a mineral interest to the operator's cost basis.[7] Notwithstanding this limitation, operators who contribute oil and gas interests may deduct any long-term capital gains, if they can treat the interest as real estate used in a trade or business.[8] Finally, the quid pro quo rules may also apply in certain situations where the donor has taken prior deductions for intangible drilling costs or has "carved out" production payments.

Valuation of Mineral Interests: Obtaining a Qualified Appraisal

Donors who are seeking to gift a mineral interest with a value in excess of $5,000 will need to find a capable appraiser that under the Pension Protection Act of 2006 is qualified to issue a valuation for mineral interests. Specifically, the donor will need to find an appraiser that holds the proper certification, and can demonstrate the necessary education and experience needed for this specialized type of appraisal. Usually real estate appraisers (even though state licensed and certified) do not have expertise that extends to the valuation of subsurface estates and interests. Therefore, for gift substantiation purposes, donors should use a qualified appraiser that can meet the Service's more thorough requirements for the valuation of property other than real property.

Specifically, donors should seek out a geologist or a professional petroleum engineer (or engineering firm) that has at least a bachelor's level degree in their discipline. That person should be able to perform an engineering and economic evaluation of the mineral interest to determine a fair market value. This value should reflect an analysis of historical production data, a calculation of production decline rates, and a review of historical cash flows. The charity can use this information

---

6. Id.
7. Id. at (1)(A).
8. Treas. Reg. § 1.162-1.

to forecast future well performance, calculate remaining oil and gas reserves, and predict future revenues. An estimate of the cost to obtain this type of mineral appraisal is between $1,000 and $2,000, and will vary according to the number of wells to be evaluated, the production history that must be assessed, etc.

Special Considerations: Compatibility with Specific Planned Giving Vehicles

When considering the different planned giving vehicles that may achieve the objectives of a prospective mineral donor, the parties must consider two main issues. First, will the annual income the mineral interest produces be well suited to allow the donor to fully realize the payout feature of a specific planned giving vehicle? Because minerals are a depleting asset, the long-term production is not certain, and the charity must consider this decline in realized income over the life of the mineral interest. Second, what additional other assets may or may not be used to fund the planned gift? These factors will be considered for each of the planned gift vehicles discussed below.

It should also be noted that a charity or trustee could sell a gifted mineral interest immediately upon receiving it in a planned gift context. While selling the interest is an option, charities and trustees will typically realize a greater economic benefit from retaining a mineral interest over the long term. The options for managing versus selling a mineral interest are more fully discussed below in the section entitled "Options for Minerals Management Going Forward."

Perhaps the most popular and most commonly used planned giving vehicle is the qualified charitable gift annuity. While this gift arrangement has the benefit of being relatively straight forward and more familiar to many donors, the gift annuity is not the most compatible planned giving vehicle for gifts of minerals. A gift annuity has a fixed payment obligation that continues for the donor's lifetime(s). For this reason, charities should carefully consider the feasibility of retaining a gifted mineral interest and relying upon its annual production to satisfy the long-term annuity payment obligation. If a charity issues a gift annuity based upon existing production, it is best to set a payout rate that is significantly lower than current income from production, so that a "reserve amount" could accumulate prior to a decline in production.

When considering funding a charitable remainder trust with a mineral interest, the key issue will be the type of payout provision in the trust agreement. For a charitable remainder annuity trust, the very same issues and limitations outlined in the foregoing paragraph dealing with gift annuities will apply. However, the charitable remainder unitrust provides a better option.

Specifically, the annual revaluation of trust assets to determine the payout to the income beneficiaries for the year is the distinctive feature of unitrusts that accommodates mineral interests so well. To determine the amount payable to an income beneficiary under a unitrust, the trustee will calculate the current value of the mineral interest each year based upon the level of production that the interest currently realizes.

The considerations for funding a charitable lead trust with a mineral interest are the same as those discussed above for the charitable remainder trust. As with the charitable remainder unitrust, the variable payment provision of the charitable lead unitrust works very well with the fluctuating nature of future mineral production and the corresponding variations in value. Further, as with qualified charitable gift annuities and charitable remainder annuity trusts, the annuitized payment provision of the charitable lead annuity trust creates a need for more careful consideration before funding a lead annuity trust with a mineral interest.

Finally, it is also possible for a donor to include a mineral interest in a retained interest in a personal residence or farm. This occurs when the donor conveys the remainder interest in both the surface estate and the mineral estate to charity. Because the donor/life tenant retains the full use and enjoyment of the property during the term of the life estate, certain issues regarding the benefits and management of the mineral estate must be addressed.

The common law rules with regard to mineral interests state that the life estate holder and the remainderman both must execute an oil and gas lease for it to be effective. Bonus monies are corpus and therefore should go to the remainderman. Delay rentals are income and are paid to the life estate holder. The common law considers royalties from production to be consumption of the corpus and thus belong to the remainderman, but income from payments that are invested belong to the life estate holder.

A contractual life estate that states that the life estate holder shall receive all of the income and that the life estate holder can execute a mineral lease without the joinder of the remainderman will trump the common law. The open mine doctrine is an exception that provides that if an oil and gas lease is producing at the time the owner creates the life estate, then there is a legal presumption that the party creating the life estate intended the life estate holder to receive all the income.

Special Considerations: Options for Minerals Management Going Forward

Once the charity receives the mineral interests, the charity must then determine how it will effectively manage these interests to ensure that the charity realizes the greatest benefit over the long term. For many smaller charities that receive mineral interests indirectly through an estate or terminating trust, the initial thought is to immediately sell the mineral interest so that the charity can easily deal with the cash proceeds. Although mineral interests may be readily sold through various brokers, the practical reality is that most buyers will only be willing to pay a purchase price of approximately 1½ to 2 times the amount of annual production the interest realizes. As a result, it will most often be in the best interest of the charity to retain ownership of the mineral interest. Regardless of the group the charity selects to manage the mineral interests, it needs to be certain that it will receive active management, administration, and negotiation for all mineral interest so as to realize the greatest possible benefit from its mineral interests.

That having been said, most charitable organizations do not have the resources in-house to effectively manage mineral interests. So, most charitable organizations will need to look outside for a capable minerals management group to assist them with these interests. The most prevalent source for such expertise will be a larger banking organization, an investment manager, or a financial services organization that is large enough to support a minerals management group. However, there may be other smaller organizations or consulting groups that provide this same type of minerals management expertise.

Special Considerations: Environmental Issues

Charities usually will not accept any real property interest which might create liability for environmental problems existing on the property, that could result in significant (or catastrophic) costs to cure. Fortunately, the majority of prospective mineral interest gifts will not create any liability on the part of the charity donee.

Only the owner of an operating interest or a working interest will bear the liability for environmental problems or liability which arise from the surface usage. Royalty interest owners that do not participate in the production process or are not responsible for any expenses of production are not liable for environmental conditions which arise, or any other problems with the use of the surface interest. As discussed earlier in this chapter, many charitable organizations stipulate in their gift acceptance policies that they will not accept any mineral interest that represents an operating interest or a working interest. By adopting a policy that precludes any type of mineral gift other than a royalty interest, charities can safeguard themselves from the potential consequence of an expensive environmental clean-up.

While most charitable organizations choose to avoid owning any type of working interest, there may be circumstances where a charity may wish to make an exception to such a policy and receive one or more working interests. Should a charity wish to do so, the organization should consider an appropriate business structure that would provide the greatest possible liability protection for the charity. For example, some charitable organizations have established wholly-owned for-profit subsidiaries solely for the purpose of holding these types of interests. Should the charitable organization wish to consider such an option, the organization should seek competent legal counsel to ensure that it implements the best structure to provide the necessary liability protection for the charity.

Taxation Issues: Applicability of the Partial Interest Rule

As a general rule, income, gift, and estate tax law limits a donor's ability to claim a deduction for a contribution of less than the donor's entire interest in the property that person contributed.[9] Notwithstanding this general rule, certain exceptions to the "partial interest rule" exist in tax law, including the deductible contribution of an undivided portion of a taxpayer's entire interest in property.[10]

Mineral interests are often owned separately from the surface interest and are often fractional interests of a larger whole. As a result, gift planners must familiarize themselves with the applicability of the partial interest rules to gifts of various types of mineral interests. This is to ensure that the donors will not erroneously make a nondeductible contribution. A contribution of, for example, a 3/16th interest may appear at first glance to pose a partial interest dilemma. However, the partial interest rule does not preclude a deduction for a contribution of such an interest, if the undivided fractional interest represents the donor's entire interest in the property.

One common scenario where prospective donors run into the partial interest rule involves a situation where a donor is the current owner of both the surface estate and the mineral estate. The donor is contemplating a gift of the surface interest to charity, but is planning to retain ownership

---

9. IRC § 170(f)(3)(A), Reg. § 1.170A-7(a)(1); IRC § 2522(c)(2), Reg. § 25.2522(c)-3(c)(1)(i); and IRC § 2055(e)(2), Reg. § 20.2055(c)-2(e)(1)(i).
10. IRC §§ 170(f)(3)(B)(ii), 2522(c)(2), and 2055(e)(2).

of the mineral rights. The retention of the mineral interests in the gifted property will cause the gift to be one of a partial interest for which the IRS will not allow the donor a deduction.[11] For many donors, the realization of this consequence will motivate them to also contribute the mineral interest along with the surface interest.

The applicable tax regulations also deny a charitable deduction for a contribution of a donor's "entire" interest in property immediately following a division of a larger interest for the purpose of creating the contributed portion. The foregoing rule that donors must convey their entire interest to charity in order to receive a deduction will almost always apply. However, the IRS has conceded that a donor will not lose the deduction if the Service deems his retained interest (mineral or otherwise) to be an "insubstantial interest."

In some cases, a donor may elect to retain a substantial mineral interest while contributing the surface ownership to charity (and foregoing a deduction in the process). In these circumstances, the charity receiving the surface interest should restrict the donor's surface use rights so that the owner of the mineral interest could not later begin drilling operations which interfere with the charity's land use, since the mineral estate is the dominant estate. While it is far more typical for the IRS to deny a deduction when the donor retains an underlying mineral interest, it is possible for a donor to realize a charitable deduction in this situation when the gift of the surface interest qualifies as a qualified conservation contribution.

As mentioned above, one of the exceptions to the partial interest rule for a gift of any type of asset allows the donor to realize a deduction for a conveyance of an undivided portion of the taxpayer's entire interest in the property.[12] The applicable regulations require that the undivided portion of the donor's entire interest in the property must:

- consist of a fraction or percentage of each and every substantial interest or right the donor owns in the property, and
- extend over the entire term of the donor's interest in the property and in other property into which the owner may convert the property.[13]

In most cases, the entire mineral interest of many donors will be only a fractional share of a larger interest (example: a 3/8th net royalty interest). When this is true, the donor may still make use of the undivided portion exception to the partial interest rule by conveying a "subfraction" of their

---

11. Rev. Rul. 76-331, 1976-2 CB 52; Priv. Later. Rul. 8429021.
12. IRC §§ 170(f)(3)(B)(ii), 2522(c)(2), and 2055(e)(2).
13. Reg. § 1.170A-7(b)(1)(i).

original fractional interest. For example, a donor who holds a 1/8th net royalty interest may convey half of his 1/8th interest to a charity and receive a deduction for the gift, because it falls within the undivided portion exception. After conveying a mineral deed to the charity, the gift is completed, and the charity and the donor will each own an individual 1/16th net royalty interest. By contrast, however, a donor that holds a working interest in minerals cannot receive a deduction for contributing either an overriding royalty interest or a net profits interest that has been "carved out" of the working interest (since they are not undivided portions of the entire interest).

Taxation Issues: Potential for Unrelated Business Income

Unrelated business taxable income (UBTI) includes "the gross income derived by any organization from any unrelated trade or business … regularly carried on by it […]."[14] The term "unrelated trade or business" means, in the case of any organization taxed under IRC Section 511, any trade or business "which is not substantially related" to the exercise or performance of its charitable, educational or other purpose or function.[15] Tax-exempt organizations are subject to tax on their UBTI at the regular corporate tax rates.[16] Excessive UBTI for a tax-exempt organization can ultimately jeopardize its tax-exempt status.

However, the Code also identifies certain unrelated business activities that, when a tax-exempt organization conducts them, are excluded from UBTI. Tax professionals and advisors often refer to such excluded income as "passive income." The Code provides for one such exclusion for certain types of royalties paid to a tax exempt organization, including payments classified as "shut-in royalties" and "delay rentals."[17]

Most royalty interests that a donor may convey to a charitable organization will constitute passive income, and therefore will not generate unrelated business income tax. However, there are exceptions to this general rule that the gift planner should be aware of. Specifically, if a tax-exempt organization owns a working interest in a mineral property and remains liable for its share of development costs, then the income from the working interest will be subject to unrelated business income taxation.[18] However, the Service also made it clear in an earlier 1969 ruling that it would not allow charities to "disguise" income derived from a working interest that a controlled entity holds.

---

14. IRC § 512(a)(1).
15. IRC § 513(a).
16. IRC § 511.
17. IRC § 512(b)(2).
18. Reg. § 1.512(b)-1(b).

Finally, having determined the applicability of unrelated business income tax to the various types of royalty interests a charity could own, charities will also want to know whether bonus payments from a lessee will be subject to unrelated business income tax. In short, bonus payments a non-profit receives from a royalty interest do not meet the definition of unrelated business taxable income found in IRC Section 512(a)(1), which requires that the charity regularly carries on the income-generating unrelated activity. Bonus payments represent only a one-time payment the royalty interest owner receives at the time a new mineral lease is executed. Accordingly, the IRS classifies bonus payments as passive income, and not subject to the unrelated business income tax.

Mineral Interests Additional Resources

Below are further details on gifts of mineral interests. Mineral interest topics are based on Joe Hancock's "Black Gold: Gifts of Oil and Gas Interests Made Simple." For quick take-aways on gifts of real estate, see Mineral Interests Quick Take-Aways. For a review based on that article, see Mineral Interests Intermediate. For an in-depth examination adapted and excerpted from the article, see Mineral Interests Advanced. For further details, see Mineral Interests Additional Resources.

For a breakdown of different theories and terminology, see Capital University, "Gifts of Mineral Rights: What Do Charities and Donors Need to Know About Gifts of Mineral Rights?," July, 2013, http://www.capconnect.org/file/documents/Oil-and-Gas-Tax-Alert.pdf.

For an examination of mineral production and ownership details, along with case studies and checklists aimed at charities, see Ladendorf, M. and Pittsford, G. (2013), "Charitable Gifts of Mineral Interests," Partnership for Philanthropic Planning, http://my.pppnet.org/library/85127/1/NCPP13_Ladendorf%2CPittsford.pdf.

For a college foundation's policies on gifts of mineral interests, see Harper College Educational Foundation (December 2, 2014), "Mineral Interests – Detailed Gift Description," http://harpercollege.plannedgiving.org/advisors/gift_mineral_detail.

For a discussion of interests, valuation, and planning advice, see Buchanan III, J.W., "Valuation and Taxation of Transfers of Oil and Gas Interests to Charities," 22 *Real Property, Probate and Trust Journal* 561 (1987).

For a historical look at gifts of mineral interests, see Speck, J.K., "Donations of Mineral and Royalty Interests," 8 Proc. Ann. Tul. Tax Inst. 216 (1959).

Rev. Rul. 69-179, 1969-1 C.B. 158 (working interests will generate UBTI)

Rev. Rul. 76-331, 1976-2 C.B. 52 (partial interest rule and retained mineral rights)

Rev. Rul. 88-37, 1988-1 C.B. 97 (IRS analysis of donated royalty interests)

Treas. Reg. § 1.512(b)-1(b) (exclusion of royalties from UBTI)

Private Letter Ruling 9205012 (overriding royalties not partial interests for deduction purposes)

Private Letter Ruling 9318027 (conservation easements with retained mineral rights)

Private Letter Ruling 201142026 (debt of working interest owner not acquisition indebtedness for nonprofits holding net profits interest)

Harding v. Comm'r, TC Memo 1995-216 (May 18, 1995) (donation of an interest in a nonproducing property)

Chapter 9
Vehicles

- Quick Take-Aways
- Intermediate
- Advanced
- Additional Resources

Vehicles Quick Take-Aways

By Bryan Clontz

Below are quick take-aways on gifts of vehicles. Vehicle topics are based on Larry Garrison and Richard Cummings' "New Tax Law Changes the Rules for Donations of Automobiles." For quick take-aways on gifts of vehicles, see <u>Vehicles Quick Take-Aways</u>. For a review based on that article, see <u>Vehicles Intermediate</u>. For an in-depth examination adapted and excerpted from the article, see <u>Vehicles Advanced</u>. For further details, see <u>Vehicles Additional Resources</u>.

Vehicles are a type of tangible personal property that merits special attention, including automobiles, motorcycles, airplanes, and boats. Indeed, both the IRS and Congress have singled out donations of vehicles for special regulations. Below is a brief overview of the advantages, disadvantages, special considerations, and questions to ask before accepting a vehicle.

Advantages of donations of vehicles include:

- Vehicles are often high-demand assets, with strong secondary markets.
- Some vehicles can directly further a charity's exempt purposes, either using them in charitable operations, or providing them to people in need.
- Flexible asset class which can be gifted outright or used to create an income stream (assuming a high enough value).

Disadvantages of donating vehicles include:

- The IRS allows a fair market value deduction only in limited circumstances.
- The charity's use and disposal of the vehicle can affect what sort of specific substantiation information and timing is required.
- Failure to comply with substantiation requirements can result in significant penalties for the charity.

Wrinkles in the process to consider include:

- A nonprofit may use a third-party to receive, sell, and forward the proceeds of donated vehicles, but must properly establish the third-party as its agent.
- State law governs title transfer, and charities must follow these regulations on a state-by-state basis.

- Price guides are only rough indicators of value, and the vehicle's condition can cause significant variation from the posted value.

Discovery Questions

Donor Questions

1. What is the donor trying to accomplish with the gift?
2. What is the vehicle's value and how was that determined (e.g., appraisal, price guide, similar transactions)?
3. Legally, who or what owns the vehicle?

Advisor Questions

1. What is the current tax basis and is it ordinary income or long term gain?
2. What is the likely exit plan for the charity (e.g., auction or private sale)?
3. Is the vehicle inventory?
4. How will the vehicle be conveyed to the charity?

Charity Questions

1. Is the effort worth the expected benefits (i.e., is the juice worth the squeeze)?
2. Has the screening and due diligence process identified any potential problems and can the risks be mitigated (mainly this will be compliance with the IRS substantiation rules and additional disclosure forms)?
3. Is there the necessary expertise to accept and manage vehicle gifts in a timely way?
4. Should indirect gift acceptance be considered, like using external third party foundations or supporting organizations to receive the asset?
5. Is there a clear liquidation plan to maximize the sales proceeds as soon as possible?
6. Does the charity intend to use the vehicle as part of its charitable mission?
7. How will the charity manage or administer the vehicle while sale is pending?

Vehicles Intermediate

By Ryan Raffin

Below is a review on gifts of vehicles. Vehicle topics are based on Larry Garrison and Richard Cummings' "New Tax Law Changes the Rules for Donations of Automobiles." For quick take-aways on gifts of vehicles, see Vehicles Quick Take-Aways. For a review based on that article, see Vehicles Intermediate. For an in-depth examination adapted and excerpted from the article, see Vehicles Advanced. For further details, see Vehicles Additional Resources.

This review of charitable gifts of vehicles has five parts, beginning with an overview. The second part is a look at unique valuation and substantiation issues, before proceeding to discuss considerations for nonprofits. A brief discussion of relevant state law issues is fourth. The fifth and final part is a case study showing how the donor and charity might utilize planned gifts in this context.

Vehicles are popular collector's items, and as such come up frequently in the charitable giving context. This asset class includes automobiles, as well as motorcycles, airplanes, and boats. In the early 2000s, the IRS became concerned about misuse of the charitable deduction for donations of vehicles. The Service believed that deductions were often taken above true fair market value. It issued guidance to both donors and charities, and Congress limited the allowable deduction in certain situations.

Review Part 1: Overview

One area where vehicle donations are different from most other asset classes is in the charity's use of the asset. As with other tangible assets, what the charity does with the asset matters. The contribution must be "to or for the use of" a qualifying tax-exempt organization. "For the use of" typically involves the asset being held in trust, and direct contributions are made "to" the organization itself. In some cases, the nonprofits will use an agent to receive the donation, while still satisfying contribution requirements.

The American Jobs Creation Act of 2004 limits the charitable deduction to the gross sales price that the charity receives for the donated vehicle (cost basis when the vehicle is held in trust). This only applies when the charity sells the donated vehicle, and only if there was no significant intervening use or material improvement to the vehicle. Further, if the charity gives away the vehicle, or sells it well below market price for the purpose of providing aid to the poor or underprivileged, the deduction will be for fair market value.

Review Part 2: Valuation and Substantiation

When fair market value is the appropriate valuation method, popular price guides (such as Kelley Blue Book) are only rough indicators. Indeed, this is why the IRS became concerned about vehicle donations in the first place. The value of the donated vehicle must be the same make, model, year, and condition as the donated vehicle—not just the highest published value for a similar model. The IRS has specifically ruled on two cases where an established price guide was used for valuation. In one case, the donated vehicle was of average condition, so the Service held the pricing guide was acceptable for valuation purposes. In the other, the vehicle was in poor condition, and for that reason, the pricing guide was not allowed for valuation.

In addition to the standard substantiation rules which apply to all asset types, there are some particular requirements for vehicles. These are:

1. Charities must provide a "contemporaneous written acknowledgement," meaning a standard acknowledgement including sale price within 30 days of the vehicle's sale.

2. If the charity intends to use the vehicle or make material improvements, it must provide certification of that within 30 days of the contribution and a guarantee of no sale before completion of the use or improvements.

3. If it intends to give away the vehicle or sell at a deep discount, it must certify such intent within 30 days of the contribution—and verify that the transaction directly furthers the organization's charitable purpose.

Review Part 3: Considerations for Nonprofits

A nonprofit generating income unrelated to its exempt purposes will have to grapple with unrelated business taxable income, and worse, possible loss of exempt status. This is relevant in the vehicle donation context, because nonprofits often partner with a third-party to facilitate the gift and sale transactions. The IRS forbids nonprofits from using earnings to benefit private individuals or shareholders—including payments to insiders that are not reasonable compensation. If the charity uses a third-party agent, it should negotiate reasonable compensation at arm's length. It should be especially sensitive to avoid excessive commissions or other conflicts of interest.

The IRS provides some specific guidance on the possible structures for a charitable used-car donation program. The four charitable program types include:

1. The charity uses or distributes donated cars. The charity would not risk losing its tax-exempt status if it either used the cars or distributed them in furtherance of its charitable purposes. If the cars are given away, they must go to needy individuals.

2. The charity sells donated cars. The charity liquidates the donated vehicles, and uses the proceeds to fund its charitable purposes. This reselling does not affect tax-exempt status, nor does it generate UBTI (compare this with a charity owning a used-car dealership—UBTI would likely be an issue there).

3. The charity uses an agent who receives and sells the cars. It may be easier for a charity to use a third-party to handle the gift and sale transactions. This agent would receive, sell, and forward proceeds to the charity, minus a reasonable commission (see discussion above). So long as the principal-agent relationship is proper, the charity's tax-exempt status will not be in jeopardy.

4. Use of a for-profit entity. Some charities propose an arrangement with a for-profit entity that receives and sells the vehicle in the charity's name. The difference from the agency relationship outlined directly above is that this is more of a licensing relationship. The for-profit pays a transaction fee to the charity in exchange for the use of its name, which the charity uses to further its exempt purposes. Since the charity is not in control of the for-profit entity's activities, there is no principal-agent relationship. The donor's contribution will not be tax deductible, and both the for-profit and charity may be in trouble with the IRS if they state that it is.

Other tripping points that may result in tax penalties include:
- Failing to timely acknowledge the donation
- Failure to sell or give the vehicle away to a needy individual, or
- Sale without significant intervening use or material improvements, after stated intent to do so

The IRS penalty for nonprofits who break these rules depends on the nature of the deduction which the donor claims, but can range from a flat $5,000, to the gross proceeds, to the maximum possible tax avoided by the donor.

Review Part 4: State Law Considerations

One unique issue for vehicles is state laws and regulations on title. The charity should avoid problems with the vehicle's chain of title, particularly any liability issues that might attach. Ensure that donors have properly transferred title with the state department of motor vehicles (or another appropriate agency). Charities should investigate any requirements on the state level, and may consider consulting with state charity officials. The state might also require registration for charities soliciting gifts.

Review Part 5: Case Study

An example might be helpful to illustrate the various considerations involved, and advantages that charities can promote. Imagine the donor owns a collectible vehicle currently valued at $7.5 million, with a basis of $2.9 million (including original purchase price and restoration). Capital gain on the sale would be $4.6 million. At the maximum long-term capital gain tax rate for collectibles of 28 percent, this would mean about $1.3 million in tax due. Net for the donor on sale would be $3.3 million.

Imagine, however, if the donor had used planned giving to dispose of the vehicle. For example, the donor and his spouse could create a flip charitable remainder unitrust (FLIP-CRUT), and transfer the vehicle to the trust. This charitable trust allows a non-income-producing asset to be placed in trust. Then, following a trigger event (usually a sale of the asset), it becomes a charitable remainder unitrust. It distributes income to the beneficiaries based on the proceeds from the sale. Once the lifetime or term of years payments are completed, the charity gets the remaining assets in trust.

From a tax perspective, what does this look like? The charity holds the remainder interest in the asset, and the donor gets a charitable deduction based on this interest. The deduction is calculated based on the projected present value of the remainder interest—based on projections for income it will pay, interest rates (set monthly), and ages of the recipients. The IRS instructs the calculation for the deduction is based on cost basis ($2.9 million in this case), and it is triggered on the FLIP-CRUT's sale of the asset. The deduction is then calculated based on the income to be paid, federal interest rates at the time, and projected life expectancy of income beneficiaries. Assuming a top tax bracket of 37 percent, this could yield tax savings of in the hundreds of thousands of dollars.

This discussion has not yet covered perhaps the biggest advantage of using a charitable trust. The planned giving structure means that no capital gains tax is due on the sale. Sale proceeds can be reinvested freely, and only income distributions are taxable. The asset can be converted to lifetime income streams for the donor—which can lead to significantly more income than the asset was worth, and significant tax savings. This case is just one example, but charities should examine the possibilities of planned giving for each donor rather than jumping immediately to an outright gift.

Vehicles Advanced[1]

By Larry Garrison and Richard Cummings

Below is an in-depth examination on gifts of vehicles. Vehicle topics are based on Larry Garrison and Richard Cummings' "New Tax Law Changes the Rules for Donations of Automobiles." For quick take-aways on gifts of vehicles, see Vehicles Quick Take-Aways. For a review based on that article, see Vehicles Intermediate. For an in-depth examination adapted and excerpted from the article, see Vehicles Advanced. For further details, see Vehicles Additional Resources.

Due to the increase in the number of programs that allow for the donation of used vehicles to charitable organizations, the Internal Revenue Service has become concerned about the misuse of this method of charitable giving. Citing a GAO study, the Service noted that 733,000 income tax returns took charitable contributions for vehicle donations those returns valued at about $2.5 billion. These deductions reduced the taxpayers' combined tax liability by approximately $654 million.[2]

The Service is concerned that taxpayers are deducting fair market values for used vehicles that do not represent the true fair market value of the donation as tax laws require. To address this concern, the Service has issued Publications 4302 and 4303 regarding vehicle donations for both the charity-donee and taxpayer-donor respectively. In addition, the American Jobs Creation Act of 2004 limited the amount of the allowable deduction to the subsequent sale proceeds of the donated vehicle in certain situations. This section discusses issues concerning both the taxpayer's responsibilities when donating a vehicle, and the charitable organization's responsibilities in conducting such a donation program.

Donor and Donee Responsibilities

Donations "To" a Charity: Section 170(a)(1) allows for taxpayers to deduct contributions to IRS-recognized charitable organizations. Section 170(c) states that a charitable contribution includes a contribution or gift to or for the use of "[…a] corporation, trust, or community chest, fund, or foundation that is situated in the United States, and is organized and operated exclusively for religious, charitable, scientific, literary, or educational purposes or for the prevention of cruelty to children or

---

1. Republished with permission of the New York State Society of CPAs, from "New Tax Law Changes the Rules for Donations of Automobiles," Larry R. Garrison and Richard Cummings, *The CPA Journal,* Volume 75, Number 11, November 2015; permission conveyed through Copyright Clearance Center, Inc.
2. IR-2003-139 (December 15, 2003).

animals [...]."[3] The IRS website (www.irs.gov) links to "Exempt Organizations Select Check," allowing taxpayers to verify an organization's eligibility to receive tax-deductible charitable contributions.[4]

Donations of used vehicles may seem to be a contribution "for the use of" a charitable organization. However, as the Davis case notes, a contribution is "for the use of" a qualified organization if a legally enforceable trust or similar arrangement holds the contribution.[5] Since the vehicle donation will generally not be "for the use of" a charity, the donation must qualify under the term "to" rather than "for the use of" the charity.

Generally charitable contributions are made directly "to" the charitable organizations. However, most used vehicle donations are through an agent for the charitable organization. This use of agents to receive donations is acceptable. Therefore, the IRS will consider the donation of a used vehicle through a person or entity acting as an agent to be a donation "to" the employing organization thus satisfying the charitable contribution requirements of Section 170(c).[6]

Valuation of the Donation—General Rules

Regulations state that if a charitable contribution is in the form of property rather than cash, the amount of the donation is the fair market value of the property at the time of the contribution.[7] The general definition for fair market value is the price at which the property would change hands between a willing buyer and a willing seller, neither being under any compulsion to buy or sell and both having reasonable knowledge of the relevant facts.[8]

For vehicles, it is a common practice to refer to a used vehicle pricing guide to determine the value of the used vehicle donation. However, the highest value the pricing guide lists may not be representative of the value of the taxpayer's vehicle. If the donor does use a pricing guide, the value she

---

3. Other allowable recipients include "[a] state or possession of the United States or any subdivisions thereof," "[a] veterans' organization," "[a] fraternal organization operating under a lodge system, or," "[a] cemetery company."
4. Exempt Organizations Select Check (www.irs.gov) replacing IRS Publication 78. This database does not include all qualified charities particularly churches, synagogues, and other religious institutions but assists taxpayers in determining if their donation is to a qualified charity.
5. *Davis v. United States,* 495 US 472 (1990).
6. § 170(c)(2); Reg. § 1.170A-1(b); Rev. Rul. 85-184, 1985-2 CB 84.
7. Reg. § 1.170A-1(c)(1). See also § 170(e)(1) and Reg. § 1.170A-4(a) and § 170(e)(3) and Reg. § 1.170A-4A(c) for possible reductions in value for certain property.
8. Reg. § 1.170A-1(c)(2). See also IRS Publication 561, Determining the Value of Donated Property.

selects must be the same make, model, year, and condition of the donated vehicle. The value must also be representative of the price of the vehicle if a hypothetical owner sold it in the same area.[9]

In Revenue Ruling 2002-67, the Service addressed two donation situations. In the first situation, the taxpayer-donor gave a vehicle of average condition to a qualified charity. An "established used car pricing guide" listed a current sales price of $3,000 for the same make, model, and year of vehicle. The price was for a comparable vehicle someone in the taxpayer's area had sold. The Ruling allowed the taxpayer to use the guide's $3,000 listed price as the amount of their charitable contribution. The Ruling states that the donor could value the vehicle using another "reasonable method."[10]

In the second situation discussed in the Ruling, the facts were the same but the vehicle was in poor condition. Since the established used vehicle pricing guide did not list a sales price for a vehicle in poor condition, the Ruling stated that the donor must use some other reasonable method to determine the fair market value for contribution purposes.

For boats, taxpayers may not estimate fair market value by simply looking at the price of similar size and age of boats.[11] Instead, boats require an individual appraisal. This is because there can be dramatic differences in the value and seaworthiness of boats of the same age and size, making generic valuations less relevant. These rules help to prevent scenarios where it is more profitable to give the item of property than to sell the item of property. For example, if a donor had a boat that had significant issues with rotting and seaworthiness, its actual value may be only a fraction of what a boat in good condition of a similar size and age would sell for. If the donor was allowed to deduct a gift of the boat based upon the typical value of such boats of the same age and size, it could create a situation where the deduction was worth more than what the donor could sell the boat for. This is precisely the situation that tax policy wishes to avoid and hence the reason for requiring individual appraisals for boats.

---

9. Rev. Rul. 2002-67, 2002-2 CB 873. Internet sites including Kelley Blue Book (http://www.kbb.com) can provide valuation using the taxpayer's zip code.
10. Rev. Rul. 2002-67, 2002-2 CB 873.
11. This paragraph's examination of boat donation valuation rules from James III, R. (October 7, 2015), "Visual Planned Giving: An Introduction to the Law and Taxation of Charitable Gift Planning," Chp. 5: Valuing Charitable Gifts of Property, part 2, http://www.pgdc.com/pgdc/5-valuing-charitable-gifts-property-part-2-2.

Valuation of the Donation—Vehicles

The American Jobs Creation Act (AJCA) of 2004 limited the charitable contribution of used motor vehicles (with a claimed value over $500) to the gross sales price the charity receives for the subsequent sale of the donated vehicle instead of fair market value. In addition, the donee organization must provide a contemporaneous written acknowledgement including the gross sales price, and the taxpayer must attach it to his income tax return. The new law applied to donations made after December 31, 2004.[12] The IRS issued Notice 2005-44 to provide guidance regarding the newly enacted Sections 170(f)(12) and 6720(1).[13] The Notice highlights certain exceptions to the general rule limiting the deduction to the sales proceeds.

Exceptions to the Donation Limit of Sales Proceeds

For qualified vehicles the charity sells without significant intervening use or material improvement, the deduction may not exceed the gross proceeds from sale or the fair market value, whichever is lower. However, if the charity makes a significant intervening use or material improvement, the gross proceeds limitation rule does not apply and the deduction amount may be fair market value. In this case, the contemporaneous written acknowledgement (discussed below) must contain 1) a statement certifying that the charity intends to make a significant intervening use or material improvement, 2) a detailed description and duration of the intended intervening use or material improvement, and 3) a statement certifying that the charity will not sell the vehicle before completion of the intervening use or material improvement. [14]

To qualify as significant intervening use, the charity must actually use the vehicle to substantially further its regularly conducted activities, and the use must be considerable. There is no significant intervening use if the charity's use is incidental or not intended at the time of the contribution. A material improvement includes a major repair or improvement that results in a significant increase in the vehicle's value. Cleaning, minor repairs, and routine maintenance are not material improvements. In addition, a material improvement to the vehicle will not qualify if an additional payment from the donor funded the improvement.

---

12. American Jobs Creation Act of 2004, P.L. 108-357 (October 22, 2004). Amending Code at § 170(f)(12). Limitation also applies to donated boats and airplanes with claimed value exceeding $500.
13. Notice 2005-44, 2005-25 IRB 1 (June 3, 2005).
14. Notice 2005-44, § 3.02(1). Also Section 170(f)(12) and Notice 2005-44, § 7.

Another exception to the gross proceeds limitation rule is when the nonprofit sells a donated qualified vehicle at a price significantly below fair market value or gratuitously transfers to a needy individual in direct furtherance of the organization's charitable purpose. The charitable purpose of the organization must relate to "relieving the poor and distressed or the underprivileged who are in need of a means of transportation."[15]

An example in the Notice found an acceptable charitable purpose for a charity who helped unemployed needy individuals develop new job skills, find jobs, and provided transportation to jobs in areas public transportation did not serve. In this case, the contemporaneous written acknowledgement must contain a statement certifying that the charity intends to give or sell the vehicle to a needy individual at a price significantly below fair market value. Further, it must state that the gift or sale directly furthers the charity's charitable purpose of relieving the poor and distressed or the underprivileged who are in need of a means of transportation.[16] Another exception applies if the charity sells the donated vehicle for $500 or less. The donor may claim a deduction for the lesser of the vehicle's fair market value on the date of contribution or $500.

Substantiation and Record Keeping—General Rules

For any deduction for a charitable contribution, the taxpayer must have substantiation. The IRS does not allow a deduction for any individual contribution of $250 or more, unless the taxpayer substantiates the contribution by contemporaneous written acknowledgement from the charitable organization.[17] The acknowledgement must include:

1. The amount of cash and a description (but not value) of any property other than cash,
2. Whether the donee organization provided any goods or services in consideration, in whole or in part, for any property,
3. A description and good faith estimate of the value of any goods or services.[18]

The Service considers the acknowledgement to be contemporaneous if the taxpayer obtains the acknowledgement on or before the earlier of:

1. The date on which the taxpayer files a return for the taxable year of the contribution, or

---

15. Notice 2005-44, § 3.02(3) citing H.R. Conf. Rep. No. 755, 108th Cong., 2d Sess. 750 (2004).
16. Notice 2005-44, § 3.03(4), Example 3.
17. § 170(f)(8)(A).
18. § 170(f)(8)(B).

Vehicles

2. The due date including extensions for filing the return.[19]

Taxpayers are required to maintain records of their charitable contributions. Generally, a taxpayer making a noncash contribution must retain a receipt which includes:

1. The name of the donee,
2. The date and location of the contribution, and
3. A sufficiently detailed description of the property.[20]

The receipt does not have to list the fair market value of the item. The receipt may be in the form of a letter or other written communication from the donee organization acknowledging receipt of the donation. The letter from the donee should include the same information the IRS requires for a receipt listed above.

For noncash donations in excess of $500, the taxpayer must maintain a written record including:

1. The name of the donee,
2. The date and location of the contribution,
3. A sufficiently detailed description of the property,
4. The fair market value of the property at the time of contribution,
5. Method used to determine the fair market value,
6. A statement as to the method used to determine the fair market value, and if applicable, a copy of a signed appraisal.
7. The date and manner of acquisition of the property by the taxpayer,
8. The cost or other basis of the property to the taxpayer.[21]

Substantiation and Record Keeping—Vehicle Donations

The AJCA requires that the donee organization provide a contemporaneous written acknowledgement including the gross sales price, and the taxpayer must attach it to the relevant income tax return. Specifically, a charitable contribution of a qualified vehicle with a taxpayer-claimed value of more than $500 must meet the acknowledgement requirements for being contemporaneous and

---

19. § 170(f)(8)(C). Also Reg. § 1.170A-13(f).
20. Reg. § 1.170A-13(b)(1).
21. Reg. § 1.170A-13(b)(3).

include the required content. In the case of a principal-agent relationship, the agent may satisfy the substantiation requirements of Section 170(f)(8)(B) by providing the written acknowledgement to the donor.[22]

The acknowledgement will be contemporaneous if:

1. The donee organization provides it within 30 days of the sale of the qualified vehicle, or
2. If the donee organization decides to use the vehicle or make a material improvement to the vehicle, then the donee must provide within 30 days of the contribution a) certification of the intended use or material improvement of the vehicle and the duration of such use and b) certification that the vehicle will not be transferred in exchange for money, property, or services before completion of the use or improvement, or
3. If the donee organization intends to sell the vehicle to a needy individual at a price significantly below fair market value or by gratuitous transfer, then the donee must provide within 30 days of contribution a) certification of this intent, and b) that the sale or transfer will be in direct furtherance of the donee organization's charitable purpose of relieving the poor and distressed or the underprivileged who are in need of a means of transportation.[23]

Regulations require the acknowledgement include the following content:

1. The name and taxpayer identification number of the donor,
2. The vehicle identification number or similar number,
3. The date of the contribution, and
4. One of the following:
    a. A statement that the charity provided no goods or services in return for the donation, if that was the case,
    b. A description and good faith estimate of the value of goods or services, if any, that the charity provided in return for the donation, or
    c. A statement that goods or services the charity provided consisted entirely of intangible religious benefits, if that was the case.

---

22. Rev. Rul. 2002-67, 2002-2 CB 873.
23. Section 170(f)(12)(C).

Vehicles

If the donee sells the qualified vehicle for over $500, the acknowledgement must also include:

1. Certification that the sale was an arm's length transaction between unrelated parties,
2. The date the vehicle was sold,
3. The gross proceeds from the sale, and
4. A statement that the deductible amount cannot exceed such gross proceeds.[24]

When the donee sells the qualified vehicle for $500 or less, the acknowledgement includes less information. The acknowledgement must include:

1. Name of the charity,
2. Description, but not the value, of the vehicle, and
3. One of the following:
    a. A statement that no goods or services were provided by the charity in return for the donation, if that was the case,
    b. A description and good faith estimate of the value of goods or services, if any, that the charity provided in return for the donation, or
    c. A statement that goods or services provided by the charity consisted entirely of intangible religious benefits, if that was the case.

While a donee organization may determine the format of the acknowledgement as long as the acknowledgement includes all the required information, the IRS provides a Form 1098-C, "Contributions of Motor Vehicles, Boats, and Airplanes," for use in reporting to the IRS the required information. A donee organization may use Form 1098-C as a contemporaneous written acknowledgement to the donor.[25]

Limitation on Contributions

Generally, the total charitable contribution deductions for an individual taxpayer made to a public charity may not exceed 60 percent of the taxpayer's adjusted gross income, subject to certain limitations for noncash donations. Charitable contributions are listed on Form 1040, Schedule A, itemized deductions.[26]

---

24. Section 170(f)(12)(B).
25. Notice 2005-44. § 8.03.
26. § 170(a)(1); also IRS Publication 526, Charitable Contributions. Limitation percentages of 20 percent and 30 percent apply to certain donations to private foundations.

State Motor Vehicle Registration

The donor should contact the charity or the appropriate state motor vehicle registration office in regards to the transfer of title from the taxpayer to the organization for the donated vehicle. Generally, state charity officials recommend that the donor take responsibility for transfer of title to ensure termination of liability for the vehicle. In most states, this involves filing a form with the state motor vehicle department, which states that the donor has given the vehicle to charity. Before donating the vehicle, the donor should remove the license plates, unless state law requires otherwise. This will help both parties avoid liability problems after the vehicle is transferred.

Prohibition Against Personal Benefit

Tax-exempt organizations may not use their earnings to benefit any private shareholder or individual,[27] meaning a person having a personal and private interest in the activities of the organization.[28] The courts determined that inurement occurs when the tax-exempt organization pays earnings to insiders (excluding reasonable compensation).[29]

For donated vehicles, many charities use a third-party agent to receive and sell the vehicle while transferring part of the proceeds to the charity. The agent receives a percentage of the sales price as a commission or transaction fee. The agency relationship makes the agent a personal or private interest. However, the agency relationship between the third party and the charity would not generally be one the IRS considers to benefit any private shareholder or individual. Revenue Ruling 69-383 identifies several factors that nonprofits should consider in determining if an agreement constitutes inurement of net earnings to private interests.[30] The major factors are:

1. The agreement was negotiated at arm's length,
2. The agent does not participate in management or otherwise have control of the organization,
3. The agreement serves a bona fide business purpose, and
4. The amount received by the agent is reasonable given the services provided.

---

27. § 501(c)(6); also Reg. § 1.501(c)(3)-1(c)(2).
28. Reg. § 1.501(a)-1(c).
29. See *U.S. v. Dykema,* 666 F2d 1096 (7th Cir. 1981); also Unitary Mission Church v. Commissioner, 74 TC 507 (1980).
30. Rev. Rul. 69-383, 1969-2 CB 113.

Regardless, charitable organizations should be aware that the use of third-party agents might increase the possibility of abuses such as excessive commissions or other conflicts of interest.

Unrelated Trade or Business Income

Section 511 imposes a tax on income unrelated to the organization's exempt purpose. An "unrelated trade or business" is any trade or business which is not substantially related (aside from the need for income or use it makes from the profits) to the organization's charitable, educational, or other purpose or function that is the basis for the exemption.[31] A tax-exempt organization may sell merchandise donated to the charity as gifts or contributions and not be considered to have an unrelated trade or business.[32]

The income earned from an unrelated trade or business is "unrelated business taxable income." The Service defines this as the gross income any organization derives from any unrelated trade or business it regularly carries on, less the allowable deductions directly connected with the trade or business.[33] Since the charities receive the proceeds from donated vehicles, the sale of the donated property is not considered unrelated business taxable income from an unrelated trade or business.

IRS Publications 4302 and 4303

The Internal Revenue Service has issued two publications to alert both donees and donors to their responsibilities when donating or receiving used vehicles. They are Publication 4302, "A Charity's Guide to Vehicle Donations,"[34] and Publication 4303, "A Donor's Guide to Vehicle Donations."[35] Publication 4302 discusses the types of vehicle donation programs below. It states any of these arrangements should not adversely impact the charity's tax-exempt status.

1. Charity Uses the Donated Vehicles. In this type of vehicle donation program, the charity uses the donated vehicles for their own charitable activities for a significant period of time to substantially further its charitable programs.

---

31. § 513(a).
32. § 513(a)(3) and Reg. § 1.513-1(e)(3).
33. § 512(a)(1).
34. IRS Publication 4302 (Rev. 01-2015). See also IR-2004-84 (June 29, 2004) and discussion in Private Letter Ruling 200230005 (April 11, 2002).
35. IRS Publication 4303 (Rev. 01-2015). See also IR-2004-84 (June 29, 2004) and discussion in Private Letter Ruling 200230007 (April 11, 2002).

2. **Charity Sells Donated Vehicles.** In this case, the charity receives donated vehicles and then sells them. The charity uses the proceeds exclusively from the vehicle sales to fund their charitable activities.

3. **Charity Sells Donated Vehicles After Making Material Improvement.** Here, the charity receives donated vehicles, makes material improvements, and then sells them. The charity uses the proceeds exclusively from the vehicle sales for their charitable activities.

4. **Charity Distributed Donated Vehicles to Needy Individuals.** In this program, the charity distributes the vehicles at a price significantly below fair market value to needy individuals to further the charitable purpose of relieving the poor, distressed or underprivileged in need of transportation.

The Publication also discusses two alternatives for operating the vehicle donation program if the charity itself does not administer the vehicle donation program.

Charity Hires Agent: Some tax-exempt organizations may find it easier to contract with an outside third-party to receive the donated vehicles, sell them, and forward the proceeds minus a transaction fee to the charity. As discussed above, the organization and third-party must establish a valid principal-agent relationship. The agent performs their duties on behalf of the charitable organization. The charity must maintain oversight regarding the activities carried on by the agent.[36] The tax-exempt status of the organization should not be in jeopardy if the principal-agent relationship is contracted properly under state law.[37]

Use of a For-Profit Entity: Unlike the previous arrangements, the use of a for-profit entity to receive and sell donated vehicles in the charity's name can mean the donor is unable to claim a charitable contribution for the donated property. The charity receives a transaction fee from the for-profit entity, and uses the fee to support its charitable activities. The problem is that the charity does not control the for-profit entity who pays the fee, thus no valid principal-agent relationship exists. As a result, the donor is actually making the donation to a for-profit entity, and therefore is not entitled to a charitable contribution deduction. The Publication cautions that the for-profit entity and the charity may not mislead the public by either stating or inferring that a donation of a used vehicle may be deductible for tax purposes.

---

36. See Private Letter Ruling 200243057 (July 2, 2002) for improper relationship.
37. See example of such an arrangement in Rev. Rul. 2002-67, 2002-2 CB 873.

Penalties

The AJCA imposes significant penalties on the donee-organization for false or fraudulent acknowledgements, or for failure to provide a timely acknowledgment with the required information about the qualified vehicle donation to donor taxpayer. An acknowledgement is false or fraudulent if either 1) the donee does not sell or transfer the vehicle to a needy individual, or 2) the donee sells the vehicle without a significant intervening use or material improvement, when the acknowledgement states in either case that the donee intends to do so.

In the above exceptions allowing for a fair market value deduction rather than the gross proceeds limitation, the penalty for a false or fraudulent acknowledgement is the greater of (1) the product the highest individual tax rate (currently 37 percent) and the claimed value of the qualified vehicle, or (2) $5,000. In normal, gross proceeds cases, the penalty for a false or fraudulent acknowledgement is the greater of (1) the product of the highest individual tax rate and the sales price in the acknowledgement, or (2) the gross proceeds from the sale of the qualified vehicle.[38]

IRS Suggestions

In a consumer alert, the Service suggests that before making a donation of a used vehicle to a charity, the taxpayer should:

1. Check that the Organization is Qualified—Donations must be to an eligible organization or the deduction is not tax deductible.

2. Speak Directly to the Charity—Donors should ask if the charity is soliciting for the donation or if a private fundraiser is acting on behalf of the charity.

3. Examine State Filings—Donors may review state registrations and financial filings for the charity to determine percentage of proceeds spent on charitable programs.

4. Itemize in Order to Benefit—Donors must itemize their deductions rather than take the standard deduction in order to have a charitable contribution deduction.

5. Calculate the Fair Market Value—Donors may refer to IRS Publication 526, "Charitable Deductions," and IRS Publication 561, "Determining the Value of Donated Property," to assist in determining the fair market value of the donation.

6. Deduct Only the Car's Fair Market Value—"Blue Book" value may differ from the fair market value of the actual vehicle being donated.

---

38. See Section 6720; also see Notice 2005-44, § 7.03.

7. Document the Charitable Contribution Deduction—Donors should refer to IRS Publication 526, "Charitable Contributions," to determine recordkeeping requirements.
8. Contact State Charity and IRS Officials When In Doubt—Donors with concerns regarding the charity or solicitation should contact the state charity official generally through the state attorney general's office.[39]

Case Study[40]

Collectors, especially car collectors, frequently occupy the "high net worth" demographic, but they also are uniquely passionate and driven by their hobby. At recent collector car auctions, a rare 1962 Ferrari 250 GT Spyder sold for $7.5 million in less than ten minutes of bidding. In fact, at this particular auction site, twelve cars sold for more than $1 million while the auction average was over $336,000 per vehicle. There were serious financial commitments from all sides of the transactions, indeed.

However, when the passion of the frenzied bidding, the joy of the new acquirer, and of the relieved seller subside, there is personal economic impact to consider. The IRS considers collector cars, and other collectibles, to be tangible personal property. Therefore, when these cars are sold for a profit, the sellers owe capital gains tax. The maximum tax bracket at the federal level is 28 percent while state tax varies depending on the residency of the seller. Because they are so caught up in the fun part of collecting, collectors often do not think about various planning methods to consider prior to the sale to reduce taxes.

As an example, take the $7.5 million Ferrari. The seller purchased the car for $2.3 million and invested another $600,000 in a complete ground-up restoration. That means that before selling costs, his tax basis was $2.9 million and his capital gain was $4.6 million. Following the sale, the seller now owes the federal government the amount of $1.288 million. He nets around $3.3 million and life goes on. However, compare an alternative approach that might make this transaction even more favorable for the seller. Prior to the auction, the 63-year-old seller and his 61-year-old wife transfer their Ferrari to a flip charitable remainder unitrust (FLIP-CRUT). A FLIP-CRUT is a special type of charitable remainder trust that allows the trustee to place nonincome producing assets in trust until a "triggering event" defined in the trust document occurs (in this case, after the car is

---

39. IR-2003-139 (December 15, 2003).
40. This case study is excerpted from Fox, R. (January 25, 2013), "Selling Collectible Cars Without Driving Off the Tax Cliff," Planned Giving Design Center, http://www.pgdc.com/pgdc/collectors-and-fiscal-cliff-ho-hum.

sold). Once this happens, the trust "flips" to a standard charitable remainder unitrust (CRUT) and begins distributing income normally to the husband and wife who established it.

What are the consequences of this transaction to the seller? First, because the balance of the trust will pass to charity at the last to die of the sellers, there is a charitable income tax deduction available. The IRS bases the deduction on the present value of the future gift, and taxpayers calculate it with a formula that considers the fair market value of the car, the amount of income the trust will pay, the number and ages of income recipients, and current interest rates. In this case, because this is tangible personal property, special rules require the taxpayer to calculate the deduction based on the tax basis of the contributed property, not the full fair market value. In this case, the basis was $2.9 million.

This produces a charitable income tax deduction of a little more than $683,000. Even in the 35 percent income tax bracket, this will save almost $240,000 in income taxes. And, like other charitable deductions, the Ferrari sellers have this year and the next five years to utilize the deduction on their income tax return.

Next, there is no capital gains tax due on the sale. FLIP-CRUTs are exempt from income tax and therefore, the sale leaves the entire $7.5 million available for reinvestment. Only the income the trust distributes is subject to income tax. Ultimately, this will produce an income stream for our selling couple that will continue for their lifetimes. Income from a six percent payout trust, which was utilized for this example, begins at $450,000 per year.

If all goes perfectly, the Ferrari sellers will receive over $12 million in income from the trust over their anticipated lifetimes of a little over 26 years based on an assumed trust earnings rate of seven percent. They will save over $1.5 million in income tax through the avoidance of the capital gains tax and their charitable deduction, as well as leaving a charitable gift of close to $10 million to the charities they choose. They will also remove the value of the Ferrari or its sales proceeds from their estates. And, while they have done that, they have also removed it from their children's inheritance. They can resolve that issue with the purchase of life insurance outside of the estate to replace the value of their charitable gift for their children.

NOTE: A simple Sale versus CRUT analysis illustrates that available capital for investment is 20.4 percent higher with the CRUT and income is 17.2 percent higher compared to an outright sale.

While collectors pursue their passionate assets, advisors must position themselves in a way that allows them to keep the collector more informed about the various choices that are available for the ownership and effective disposition of their collectible assets. This may mean millions of dollars to the collector over the course of a collecting lifetime.

Vehicles Additional Resources

Below is an in-depth examination on gifts of vehicles. Vehicle topics are based on Larry Garrison and Richard Cummings' "New Tax Law Changes the Rules for Donations of Automobiles." For quick take-aways on gifts of vehicles, see <u>Vehicles Quick Take-Aways</u>. For a review based on that article, see <u>Vehicles Intermediate</u>. For an in-depth examination adapted and excerpted from the article, see <u>Vehicles Advanced</u>. For further details, see <u>Vehicles Additional Resources</u>.

For basic IRS guidance for charities, see Internal Revenue Service (2015), "Publication 4302: A Charity's Guide to Vehicle Donation," https://www.irs.gov/pub/irs-pdf/p4302.pdf.

For basic IRS guidance for donors, see Internal Revenue Service (2015), "Publication 4303: A Donor's Guide to Vehicle Donation," https://www.irs.gov/pub/irs-pdf/p4303.pdf.

For a more in-depth look at the case study examined here, see Fox, R. (December 13, 2013), "Selling Collectible Cars without Driving Off the Tax Cliff," Planned Giving Design Center, http://www.pgdc.com/pgdc/collectors-and-fiscal-cliff-ho-hum.

For a look at the effect of the mid-2000s changes to the tax treatment of vehicle contributions, see Hrywna, M. (March 15, 2011), "Car Donations Continue to Stall," *The NonProfit Times,* http://www.thenonprofittimes.com/news-articles/car-donations-continue-to-stall/.

IRC § 170(f)(12) (vehicle acknowledgement and use requirements)

Rev. Rul. 2002-67, 2002-47 I.R.B. 873 (use of an agent and pricing guide for vehicle donations)

IRS Notice 2005-44, 2005-25 I.R.B. 1287 (guidance on American Jobs Creation Act of 2004's changes to vehicle donations)

IRS Notice 2006-1, 2006-4 I.R.B. 347 (information on reporting requirements for donees)

Private Letter Ruling 200230005 (charity's use of a third party to receive vehicle donations)

Private Letter Ruling 200512027 (third party accepting, liquidating, and donating a portion of proceeds of boat donations is not tax exempt under 501(c)(3))

Sergeant v. Comm'r, TC Memo 1998-265 (July 20, 1998) (deduction amount for a boat and possible liability for misstatement)

IRS Form 1098-C, Contributions of Motor Vehicles, Boats, and Airplanes (filing of this form is required for both donee and donor alike)

U.S. Gov't Accountability Office, GAO-04-73, "Vehicle Donations: Benefits to Charities and Donors, but Limited Program Oversight," (November 14, 2003) (examining abuses of vehicle donation programs, pre-2004 legislation)

Chapter 10
Virtual Currency

- Quick Take-Aways
- Intermediate
- Advanced
- Additional Resources

Virtual Currency Quick Take-Aways

By Bryan Clontz

Below are quick take-aways on gifts of virtual currency. Virtual currency topics are based on my "Charitable Gifts of Bitcoins: Tax, Appraisal, Legal, and Processing Considerations." For quick take-aways on gifts of virtual currency, see Virtual Currency Quick Take-Aways. For a review based on that article, see Virtual Currency Intermediate. For an in-depth examination adapted and excerpted from the article, see Virtual Currency Advanced. For further details, see Virtual Currency Additional Resources.

As with other types of asset, donations of virtual currencies involve a host of considerations. These include tax questions, regulatory concerns, and practical hurdles. Below is a brief overview of the advantages, disadvantages, and possible wrinkles of virtual currency as a charitable gift.

Advantages of donations of virtual currencies include:

- High ease of transmission after initial setup—a charity could take virtual currency gifts directly from donors, without significant cost or regulation.
- The active market for virtual currencies means that charities can liquidate virtual currency positions with minimal complications and maximum speed.
- The IRS views virtual currencies as property, gifts can qualify for capital asset treatment, so donors of appreciated virtual currencies may receive fair market value deductions.

Disadvantages of donating virtual currencies include:

- The unregulated nature of virtual currencies has led the media to associate them (fairly or not) with nefarious activities.
- Conversely, as regulation increases, owners may become reluctant to donate, since the anonymity of virtual currencies is often their main appeal.
- It may be difficult for donors to find a qualified appraiser if the deduction is over $5,000.

Potential wrinkles in the process include:

- Charities must develop a process to securely receive and liquidate the donated virtual currency, which should be an existing payment processor, or a charity-controlled "wallet."

- The legal and regulatory landscape is in flux, and charities will need to actively monitor changes.
- The value of virtual currencies is even more volatile than the regulatory landscape. The best policy is to sell any Bitcoins or other virtual currencies as soon as possible.

Discovery Questions

Donor Questions

1. What is the donor trying to accomplish with the gift?
2. What is the currency's value and how was that determined (should be able to get fairly accurate real time pricing)?
3. Legally, who or what owns the asset?

Advisor Questions

1. What is the current tax basis and is it ordinary income or long term gain?
2. How was the virtual currency acquired?
3. Has a qualified appraiser been identified and, if so, what is the expected cost?

Charity Questions

1. Is the effort worth the expected benefits (i.e., is the juice worth the squeeze)?
2. Has the screening and due diligence process identified any potential problems and can the risks be mitigated (how quickly can it be sold and any reputational risks to be considered)?
3. Is there the necessary expertise to accept and manage virtual currency assets in a timely way?
4. Should indirect gift acceptance be considered, like using external third party foundations or supporting organizations to receive the asset?

Virtual Currency Intermediate

By Ryan Raffin

Below is a review on gifts of virtual currency. Virtual currency topics are based on my "Charitable Gifts of Bitcoins: Tax, Appraisal, Legal, and Processing Considerations." For quick take-aways on gifts of virtual currency, see Virtual Currency Quick Take-Aways. For a review based on that article, see Virtual Currency Intermediate. For an in-depth examination adapted and excerpted from the article, see Virtual Currency Advanced. For further details, see Virtual Currency Additional Resources.

This review of charitable gifts of virtual currency has five parts. It starts with a high-level overview of how virtual currencies work, and then continues with a look at the unique challenge of IRS appraisal requirements in this context. Following that is a brief examination of the changing legal and regulatory landscape. Finally, there is a discussion of how the actual gift transaction might work, and a brief conclusion.

Bitcoins and other virtual currencies are surely the most futuristic planned gift discussed in this book. Virtual currencies are less than a decade old as of this writing, but have attracted ample media attention. That coverage, combined with a total market capitalization of over $240 billion USD (as of July 13, 2018), means that donors and nonprofits alike are interested in potential charitable giving opportunities.

This section is an intermediate overview of the considerations involved in donating Bitcoin and its counterparts. These considerations include tax, appraisal, regulatory, and transactional issues. The unsettled legal and regulatory landscape for virtual currencies in many ways makes it the most fluid form of noncash gift.

Review Part 1: How Does Virtual Currency Work?

As a primer, consider the nature of virtual currencies ("Bitcoin" is used to represent all virtual currencies throughout this book). They are intended to operate like legal tender (meaning traditional currencies), but no official body in the United States recognizes them as such. One way to think about virtual currencies is that they work like cash, except that they can be exchanged anonymously, and are uncontrolled by any central organization such as the Federal Reserve. Indeed, no traditional financial institutions need be involved in Bitcoin transactions, and the owner of the Bitcoin can have functional anonymity. Transaction costs are exceedingly low, and supply and demand alone determine value.

Virtual Currency

The lack of regulatory oversight does not mean that the Internal Revenue Service is unaware of Bitcoin et al. Indeed, in 2014, the IRS issued a notice providing definitions, tax treatment guidance, and answers to frequently asked questions. The key take-away from this notice is that the IRS treats virtual currencies as property, rather than true currencies. This means that traditional gain and loss principles will apply to this nontraditional noncash gifts.

From a practical perspective, the IRS's position means little to the charity receiving the donated Bitcoin. They are likely to sell it as soon as possible, and since the charity is not taxed on income, any gain or loss during the period of ownership is irrelevant. Conversely, the donor is likely to be very concerned about the character and amount of any gain or loss. Depending on the donor's holding period, the donated Bitcoin may be treated as:

1. A long-term capital asset (meaning an attractive deduction of fair market value),
2. A short-term capital asset (meaning a deduction of only the lesser of cost basis or fair market value), or
3. May receive ordinary gain / loss treatment (again meaning a deduction of only cost basis).

Of course, appreciated virtual currency getting long-term capital asset treatment is very appealing as a prospective donation.

Review Part 2: Appraisal Concerns

Donors, of course, must comply with IRS regulations requiring disclosure and even appraisals for deductions over certain values. For deductions on donations of noncash assets totaling over $500, taxpayers must file Form 8283 disclosing their deductions—even from virtual currency donations. Qualified appraisal requirements similarly apply for deductions over $5,000.

The qualified appraisal may be challenging. The appraiser must qualify by virtue of both expertise and experience in valuing the class of asset. Since virtual currency is a new property type, it may be difficult to find an appraiser who meets these requirements. Even knowing which online marketplace (called an "exchange" for cryptocurrency) to use as an indicator of value can be challenging. Donors should therefore consider the difficulty and cost of meeting this requirement.

Review Part 3: What Is the Legal and Regulatory Landscape?

Simply put, the legal and regulatory landscape remains unsettled. Currently, aside from the IRS position, no federal government body has taken any position on virtual currencies. This means that unlike traditional currencies or securities, there is no federal government guarantee of value or compliance with reporting standards (although in some limited cases the SEC may consider virtual currencies to be securities).

Some state regulatory agencies have moved more quickly than the federal government. New York in particular bears mention. In June of 2015, the New York State Department of Financial Services began regulating virtual currency businesses operating in the state. The regulations require that businesses involved in virtual currency transactions must first be licensed. This entails disclosure of information, making virtual currencies much less anonymous and private than many of its proponents would like.

Although the prospect of increased government oversight may concern potential donors, it may mitigate some acceptance risks. Anti-money laundering and anti-fraud provisions would add an air of legitimacy to an asset the media often associates with the drug trade, money laundering, extortion, and other criminal activities. These unsavory associations would presumably decrease with increased regulation.

Review Part 4: How Does the Transaction Work?

Charities may also wonder how the donation transaction works in practice. It is one thing to decide to accept donations of Bitcoin, but quite another to actually do so. Assuming a sophisticated donor who can comply with the above mentioned appraisal and tax reporting requirements, the charity still needs to be prepared to receive and liquidate the asset. The charity should consider whether it will require donors to provide personal information - some donors may be reluctant to do so.

To receive Bitcoins, the charity will need either to have a "wallet" which allows access to their virtual currency, or work through a payment processor. The latter is likely more appealing, as processors facilitate the donation and liquidate the virtual currency, leaving the charity with the legal tender they want. Both processors and wallets have important access and security considerations, since there is no way to recover stolen Bitcoin. Even if a wallet is used, charities should liquidate the donated virtual currency as soon as possible. The volatility of the market can lead to unintended losses during the "holding period."

Review Part 5: Conclusion

Virtual currencies like Bitcoin present an intriguing development for forward-looking charities. Although a newer type of asset than any other discussed in this book, virtual currencies have attracted much attention during their brief lifespan. While the largely-unregulated status and occasional horror stories may give some charities pause, the ease of donation and liquidation is appealing. For donors, getting a deduction for the donated currency as appreciated capital assets is a big advantage (although the qualified appraisal requirement may put a cap on the total amount donated). Like all other noncash assets, virtual currencies have benefits and drawbacks, and due to their novelty, show a great deal of promise as a vehicle for giving.

Charitable Gifts of Noncash Assets

Virtual Currency Advanced[1]

By Bryan Clontz

Below is an in-depth examination on gifts of virtual currency. Virtual currency topics are based on our "Charitable Gifts of Bitcoins: Tax, Appraisal, Legal, and Processing Considerations." For quick take-aways on gifts of virtual currency, see Virtual Currency Quick Take-Aways. For a review based on that article, see Virtual Currency Intermediate. For an in-depth examination adapted and excerpted from the article, see Virtual Currency Advanced. For further details, see Virtual Currency Additional Resources.

Popular virtual currency Bitcoin has been a news fixture since its introduction in 2009.[2] Bitcoin is the world's leading virtual currency, with a market capitalization over $100 billion.[3] Donors and their advisors are now exploring various charitable giving opportunities using virtual currencies. The Internal Revenue Service (IRS) describes virtual currency as "a digital representation of value that functions as a medium of exchange, a unit of account, and / or a store of value."[4] Its creators designed it to operate like legal tender, and as a medium of exchange, although no governmental body currently recognizes it as legal tender anywhere in the world.[5]

Currently, Bitcoin and other virtual currencies, such as Ethereum and Ripple, represent a total market capitalization of over $240 billion.[6] Many large charities, including large donor-advised funds and community foundations, are eager to tap into this market or have already received virtual donations. For example, United Way Worldwide recently began accepting donations of Bitcoins.[7] Smaller nonprofits have begun accepting the currency as well.[8] This section discusses charitable donations of virtual currencies, including tax, appraisal, legal, and processing considerations.

---

1. This chapter adapts and excerpts Clontz, B. (November 4, 2014), "Charitable Gifts of Bitcoins: Tax, Appraisal, Legal, and Processing Considerations," Planned Giving Design Center, http://www.pgdc.com/pgdc/charitable-gifts-bitcoin-tax-appraisal-legal-and-processing-considerations.
2. Davis, J. (October 10, 2011), "The Crypto-Currency," *The New Yorker,* http://www.newyorker.com/magazine/2011/10/10/the-crypto-currency.
3. Coin Telegraph, Crypto-Currency Market Capitalizations, http://coinmarketcap.com/ (last accessed July 13, 2018).
4. Internal Revenue Service (March 25, 2014), IRS Notice 2014-21, http://www.irs.gov/pub/irs-drop/n-14-21.pdf.
5. Id. Note however, that Germany has recently decided not to tax Bitcoin "when used as a means of payment." De, N. (March 1, 2018), "Germany Won't Tax You for Buying Coffee with Bitcoin," Coindesk, https://www.coindesk.com/germany-considers-crypto-legal-equivalent-to-fiat-for-tax-purposes/
6. Crypto-Currency Market Capitalizations.
7. Vigna, P. & Casey, M.J. (September 15, 2014), "BitBeat: United Way Adds Bitcoin as Conduit for Donations," *Wall Street Journal,* http://blogs.wsj.com/moneybeat/2014/09/15/bitbeat-united-way-adds-bitcoin-as-conduit-for-donations/.
8. Hicks, J. (August 17, 2014), "Safello Enables Charitable Donations with Bitcoins," *Forbes,* http://www.forbes.com/sites/jenniferhicks/2014/08/17/safello-enables-charitable-donations-with-bitcoins/.

Top ten virtual currencies by USD market capitalization (as of July 13, 2018)

1. Bitcoin — $107,681,515,452
2. Ethereum — 44,351,939,390
3. Ripple — 17,289,649,418
4. Bitcoin Cash — 12,106,870,149
5. EOS — 6,377,770,475
6. Litecoin — 4,479,398,375
7. Stellar — 3,529,849,005
8. Cardano — 3,331,110,023
9. IOTA — 2,729,548,769
10. Tether — 2,711,634,199

Tax Considerations

In March of 2014, the IRS issued a Notice on the tax treatment of transactions involving virtual currency.[9] Most importantly, the IRS stated that, for tax purposes, virtual currencies are property and not currency.[10] This means that traditional gain and loss principles will apply therefore treating these assets as securities or business property.[11] A party selling, spending, or otherwise disposing of virtual currency may be subject to capital gains or ordinary income tax. Although the charity will be selling the currency, exempt organizations are not generally taxed on income, even from the sale of appreciated property.[12]

The major tax implications for donations of virtual currency, therefore, involve the donor. The main consideration for donors is the charitable income tax deduction received. The gain can be ordinary, or capital, depending on the source of the virtual currency to the donor. The determination on the type of gain or loss the taxpayer recognizes depends on whether that person held the virtual

---

9. IRS Notice 2014-21.
10. Id.
11. Note, however, that the SEC takes a different approach. In June 2018, SEC Chairman Jay Clayton stated that virtual currencies replacing traditional currencies are not securities. Conversely, tokens, sold through the fundraising process known as an initial coin offering, would be securities in the SEC's eyes. Rooney, K. (June 6, 2018), "SEC Chief Says Agency Won't Change Securities Laws to Cater to Cryptocurrencies," CNBC, https://www.cnbc.com/2018/06/06/sec-chairman-clayton-says-agency-wont-change-definition-of-a-security.html.
12. Internal Revenue Service (August 28, 2014), "Exempt Organizations – Required Filings," http://www.irs.gov/Charities-&-Non-Profits/Exempt-Organizations-Required-Filings.

currency as a capital asset for investment purposes.[13] If the donor did not hold the property as an investment, it would be subject to ordinary gain or loss treatment. This is more likely to be the case if the donor is a so-called "miner" or where the virtual currency is otherwise income paid for services rendered.[14]

These possibilities lead to three potential tax results for donors of virtual currency. First, a donor giving virtual currency held short-term (i.e., less than one year) as a capital asset will be able to deduct the lesser of cost basis or fair market value up to 50 percent of adjusted gross income.[15] However, if the donor held the Bitcoin or other currency for more than a year as a capital asset, the deduction would be the fair market value of the gift up to 30 percent of adjusted gross income.[16] Finally, if the currency is subject to ordinary gain or loss treatment in the hands of the donor, the donor may deduct the cost basis of the gift up to 50 percent of her adjusted gross income.[17] If the donor received Bitcoin as ordinary income as payment for services rendered or property sold, the donor may only deduct the cost basis under the ordinary income reduction rules. The IRS defines the cost basis of the virtual currency as its fair market value when the owner receives it.[18] So if a third-party pays the donor Bitcoin worth $500 for professional services, and that Bitcoin later appreciated to $1,000 USD, the donor's charitable income tax deduction would be limited to $500, or cost basis.

These rules are very favorable to donors holding appreciated virtual currency as capital assets, allowing them to avoid incurring a tax for capital gains on the Bitcoins or other currency.[19] This is especially true following the Tax Cuts and Jobs Act of 2017, which limited Section 1031 exchanges to real estate only, meaning owners of virtual currency could not simply exchange them for other virtual currencies to avoid recognizing gain.[20] Note that this donation would also allow the donor to avoid the potential 3.8 percent Medicare surcharge on investment income.

---

13. Id.
14. Id.
15. Teitell, C. (May 27, 2014), "Charitable Gifts of 'Virtual Currency,'" *Wealth Management,* http://wealthmanagement.com/blog/charitable-gifts-virtual-currency-bitcoins.
16. Id.
17. Id.
18. IRS Notice 2014-21.
19. The rules are also largely the same for corporate donors of virtual currencies, except that the deduction is capped at ten percent of the corporation's contribution base—the "taxable income computed without regard to charitable deductions and certain losses and loss carryovers." Teitell, C.
20. Wood, R.W. (April 9, 2018), "Claiming Bitcoin 1031 Exchanges on Your 2017 Taxes," *Forbes,* https://www.forbes.com/sites/robertwood/2018/04/09/claiming-bitcoin-1031-exchanges-on-your-2017-taxes/#1536d96f4bd2.

Appraisal Considerations

A major concern for potential donors of virtual currencies will be complying with IRS appraisal requirements. The Service requires that donors claiming total deductions of over $500 on noncash donations file Form 8283.[21] Due to the IRS ruling that virtual currency is property, donors of such currencies must therefore file Form 8283 if their deductions exceed the statutory threshold.

More importantly, however, is that the IRS requires a qualified appraisal for donated property over $5,000 in value.[22] Although there is an exception for publicly traded securities, it seems improbable that the Service would deem virtual currency to be qualified appreciated stock. This is because it defines a "publicly traded security" as one that is "listed on a stock exchange in which quotations are published on a daily basis," or "regularly traded in a national or regional over-the-counter market for which published quotations are available."[23] Although there are online virtual currency exchanges, these are not stock exchanges, and hence do not qualify under the first category. The second category is a closer case, because although traders can easily locate price information about virtual currencies online, it is difficult to say that virtual currencies fit within the sort of market described. For example, which one of the approximately 50 exchanges should be used? If exchanges have a higher value, but do not settle inUSD (e.g., Asian exchanges) should that data be excluded? What 24 hour day should be used for pricing? Hence, virtual currencies are probably not within the IRS definition of "publicly traded security" for noncash donation purposes.

This means that persons planning to donate over $5,000 worth of virtual currencies should arrange for an appraisal of the currency's value from a qualified appraiser. This may prove difficult, given the IRS requirements that the appraiser possess "verifiable education and experience in valuing the type of property being appraised."[24] This requirement poses a difficulty to donors thinking about making large gifts of virtual currency, due to the fact that virtual currencies are such a new asset. As a result, finding a qualified appraiser with the requisite education and experience may be difficult. For this reason, potential donors should always either identify a qualified appraiser prior to making their donation or limit their total contributions to all charities in virtual currency form to less than $5,000.[25]

---

21. Internal Revenue Service (December 2013), "Form 8283—Noncash Charitable Deductions," http://www.irs.gov/pub/irs-pdf/f8283.pdf.
22. Internal Revenue Service (April 2007), "Publication 561—Determining the Value of Donated Property," 9, http://www.irs.gov/pub/irs-pdf/p561.pdf.
23. Id.
24. Id. at 10-11.
25. Note that the aggregate donated value of like property is what triggers the IRS qualified appraisal requirement. Even if multiple

Legal Considerations

When examining the legal considerations of virtual currency as a charitable gift, it is important to remember that Bitcoins and any other such currency are—for the moment, at least—simply property in the eyes of the IRS. Although virtual currencies share characteristics with both legal tender and more traditional securities, they lack the regulation that both those forms of property possess. In fact, it may be better to think of the virtual currencies as collectible property which fluctuates—often wildly—in value. This is because the lack of regulatory oversight does not provide the sort of guarantees that exist with currency regulation (a guarantee of value) or securities regulation (a guarantee of compliance with reporting procedures and standards).

However, if charities are not careful, they may have to navigate SEC and state security licensing requirements. The SEC considers virtual currencies to be securities if their owners hold them for investment purposes.[26] Theoretically, this means a charity selling virtual currencies held for investment purposes may have to deal with the potential complications of federal and state securities regulations.[27]

With that basic framework of legal character in mind, the primary legal consideration for donors and charities considering the potential of Bitcoin and its counterparts is the unsettled regulatory environment. As of 2018, states agencies and legislatures have adopted a dizzying patchwork of regulations and guidance, providing little uniformity and inserting a great deal of uncertainty.[28] In 2015, the state of New York, always influential in financial matters, recently enacted regulations for virtual currencies under its Department of Financial Services.[29] Perhaps the biggest change is that the regulations state digital currency companies operating in the state must obtain a license which requires compliance with consumer protection, anti-money laundering, and cybersecurity standards.[30]

---

small gifts of Bitcoin are given to a number of charities, if the sum total is over 5,000 USD, the donor must get the property appraised. Teitell, C.

26. Securities and Exchange Commission (July 2013), "Investor Alert: Ponzi Schemes Using Virtual Currencies," http://www.sec.gov/investor/alerts/ia_virtualcurrencies.pdf.
27. Id.
28.
29. Freifeld, K. and Chavez-Dreyfuss, G. (June 3, 2015), "New York Regulator Issues Final Virtual Currency Rules," Reuters, http://www.reuters.com/article/us-bitcoin-regulation-new-york-idUSKBN0OJ23X20150603.
30. Id.

These regulations may imperil the anonymity of virtual currency transactions, which is the feature that many prize most about them.[31] Should state agencies adopt regulations similar to those in New York (or more stringent requirements), it could drive people away from the currency.[32] Further, it would likely hinder anonymous donations, as the virtual currency exchange operations enabling them would need to be state-licensed and report those transactions.[33]

Conversely, for charities receiving donations of virtual currency, the potential for increasing governmental regulation may assuage some fears about the less-than-legitimate uses the media so often associates the currencies with. Advocates of heavier regulation on virtual currency regulation cite a host of illegal activities publicly tied to Bitcoin and other cryptocurrencies, including the drug trade, money laundering, Ponzi schemes, and theft of the currency itself.[34] Charities wary of accepting virtual currency because of its association with crime may be more willing to accept donations when there is a regulatory framework minimizing the presence of such elements. Fortunately or unfortunately, it appears that increasing regulatory oversight is only a matter of time.[35]

Process Considerations

Most charities have similar questions: What is the donation process? How does the charity convert the virtual currency to cash? What are the acknowledgment, compliance and substantiation requirements? Does the charity require the donor to provide personal information (name, address, Social Security Number, etc.) or other similar Know Your Customer protocols to guard against criminal or fraudulent activity? This section outlines a hypothetical donation of virtual currency from the donor's planning to the charity's liquidation.

Step 1: Donor has decided to donate $50,000 of Bitcoin to charity (recall substantiation thresholds of $5,000 in value). Charity may choose to collect donor personal information at this stage. Some virtual currency donors have shown a reluctance or simply refused to share this information.

---

31. Smith, J., IV. (October 21, 2014), "New York State's Bitcoin Laws Could Ruin Everything Good About Bitcoin," Betabeat, http://betabeat.com/2014/10/new-york-states-bitcoin-laws-could-ruin-everything-good-about-bitcoin/.
32. Indeed, Connecticut enacted regulations in 2015 that require virtual currency businesses to "maintain a surety bond sufficient to account for the potential volatility of the digital currency." Murphy, E., Murphy, M., and Seizinger, M. (October 13, 2015), "Bitcoin: Questions, Answers, and Analysis of Legal Issues," Congressional Research Service, https://www.fas.org/sgp/crs/misc/R43339.pdf.
33. Hajdarbegovic, N. (October 21, 2014), "BitLicense Comment Period Closes with Final Input from Circle, BitPay," Coindesk, https://www.coindesk.com/bitlicense-comment-period-closes-final-input-circle-bitpay/.
34. Hage, J. and Wertman T. (May 21, 2014), "Drugs, Charity and Patio Furniture? How Digital Currencies Are Changing the Way We Look at Money," Thomson Reuters, http://blog.thomsonreuters.com/index.php/drugs-charity-and-patio-furniture-how-digital-currencies-are-changing-the-way-we-look-at-money/.
35. Tillier, M. (September 30, 2014), "Bitcoin Looks More Like a 'Real' Currency Every Day," Nasdaq, http://www.nasdaq.com/article/bitcoin-looks-more-like-a-real-currency-every-day-cm396552.

Step 2: Donor consults with tax/legal advisor to determine the tax characterization of the holding—i.e., a short-term capital asset, a long-term capital asset, or an ordinary income asset. This classification will determine the charitable income tax deduction implications.

Step 3: Donor proceeds with donating Bitcoin to the charity through a processor, like BitPay to immediately convert the donation to cash, or to a "wallet" if they wish to hold the Bitcoin and sell it through an online exchange such as Bitstamp. A virtual currency wallet allows access to virtual currency either through an online platform, a software program (a "hot" wallet), or even offline hardware (a "cold" wallet).[36] The potential problem is that anyone who has the private key to the wallet can access the wallet – and the Bitcoin it holds.[37]

A processor, on the other hand, handles virtual currency transactions for businesses and charities, and will also convert virtual currency to legal tender.[38] This is likely the best and most cost-effective option for charities that wish to accept virtual currencies. Alternatively, the charity could refer its donor to a donor advised fund that accepts virtual currencies and have the donor recommend a grant to the charity.

Similar to receiving publicly traded securities, most Bitcoin gift acceptance policies should encourage automatic conversion because of price volatility. At its highest in early December 2017, the market valued Bitcoin approached $20,000.[39] By comparison, January 2015, the market priced it at only $220, and in April 2016 was around $420.[40] Many payment processors can provide immediate liquidation automatically, including BitPay, and will directly deposit the value of the Bitcoin in the charity's bank account.[41] Otherwise, the charity would have to go through a virtual currency exchange (essentially an online trading platform that works similar to an online stock brokerage platform) to sell the donated Bitcoin in exchange for legal tender, which can be a complicated process.[42]

---

36. Tanzarian, A. (July 7, 2014), "How Businesses Can Start Accepting Bitcoins," Coin Telegraph, http://cointelegraph.com/news/112021/how-businesses-can-start-accepting-bitcoins.
37. Bitcoin Foundation, "Some Bitcoin Words You Might Hear," https://bitcoin.org/en/vocabulary.
38. Tanzarian, A.
39. Coin Telegraph (October 2014), "Crypto-Currency Market Capitalizations – Bitcoin Charts," http://coinmarketcap.com/currencies/bitcoin/#charts.
40. Id.
41. BitPay (August 29, 2011), "Bit-Pay Solutions for Charities and Nonprofits, https://bitpay.com/press/2011-08-29-01.
42. DeMartino, I. (June 7, 2014), "How to Trade Bitcoin," Coin Telegraph, http://cointelegraph.com/news/111717/how_to_trade_bitcoin.

Virtual Currency

Given the appreciation in value of Bitcoin and other cryptocurrencies in 2017, a nonprofit may receive proposals for donations more frequently, or donations of larger amounts, or even proposed gifts of virtual currencies other than Bitcoin. Many charities are seriously considering whether and how to accept virtual currency donations. These conversations should weigh the importance of exchanges, wallets, and security measures, given the high-profile and increased value of virtual currency.

The primary considerations with virtual currency exchanges are:

1. What is the process, information requirements and timeline to open an account?
2. Does the exchange allow charities to trade on their platforms?
3. Does the exchange trade the virtual currencies the charity will receive as donations?
4. Does the exchange allow US-based customers and withdrawals of USD (many large China-based exchanges do not)?
5. Can the charity quickly sell through the donated cryptocurrency and withdraw the USD received in exchange or are there limits?
6. If the virtual currency will take more than a short period of time to sell, is the charity comfortable keeping it in the charity's account on the exchange?

The last question is important for security purposes. The charity may not want to keep the donated virtual currency on the exchange, given that exchanges are frequently the target of hackers. In that case, the charity will need to keep the virtual currency in a wallet. A wallet is a way of storing virtual currency, and can be simply software on a laptop, or even can be stored offline. Prior to accepting gifts of virtual currency, nonprofits should carefully research which solution, if any, will meet their needs. Unfortunately, there have been reports of virtual currency fraud, both phishing and hacking, where the charity was a victim.

Securing unsold virtual currency is extremely important, since theft or other loss cannot be undone, due to the nature of blockchain transactions. Two factor authentication, complex passwords, and separation of duties all merit consideration. Due diligence and research are essential advance tasks if a nonprofit is considering accepting gifts of Bitcoin or other virtual currency.

Each charity, of course, must weigh the convenience (nonprofits can accept Bitcoin from any source worldwide), set-up process, and the legal and tax considerations to determine whether it wishes to receive virtual currency directly or whether they wish to use a third-party charity like a donor advised fund.

Process Considerations in Donation of Virtual Currency

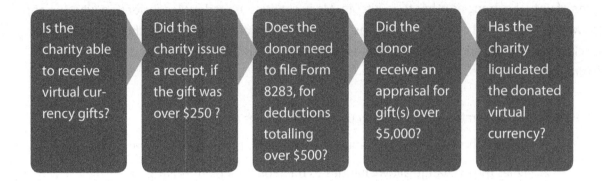

Conclusion

Virtual currencies like Bitcoin represent an exciting possibility for both charities and donors. Although the unsettled legal, tax, and regulatory framework may give some organizations pause, the charitable potential of the currencies is clear. Charities should be open to the speed and ease of donation that virtual currencies allow for once the charity is properly set up to receive these assets, as well as the ability to receive such donations from any source worldwide. Donors, meanwhile, should be aware of the tax advantages that can come with donating appreciated virtual currencies, while remaining mindful of potential filing and appraisal requirements. Even with the situation in a state of flux, the donation process itself is increasingly streamlined, which indicates a promising future for donations of virtual currency.

Virtual Currency Additional Resources

Below are further details on gifts of virtual currency. Virtual currency topics are based on my "Charitable Gifts of Bitcoins: Tax, Appraisal, Legal, and Processing Considerations." For quick take-aways on gifts of virtual currency, see Virtual Currency Quick Take-Aways. For a review based on that article, see Virtual Currency Intermediate. For an in-depth examination adapted and excerpted from the article, see Virtual Currency Advanced. For further details, see Virtual Currency Additional Resources.

For an analysis of the IRS Notice, see Teitell, C. (May 27, 2014), "Charitable Gifts of 'Virtual Currency,'" *Wealth Management*, http://wealthmanagement.com/blog/charitable-gifts-virtual-currency-bitcoins.

For a discussion of charities who have and do accept Bitcoin donations, see Silverman, R.E. (April 12, 2015), "Charities Seek Donations in Bitcoin," *Wall Street Journal*, http://www.wsj.com/articles/charities-seek-donations-in-bitcoin-1428894121.

For a look at Fidelity Investment's charitable fund's policy of Bitcoin acceptance, see Dagher, V. (November 18, 2015), "Bitcoin Can Be Donated to Fidelity Charitable Fund," *Wall Street Journal*, http://www.wsj.com/articles/bitcoin-can-be-donated-to-fidelity-charitable-fund-1447853697.

For an examination of Bitcoin transaction costs in a nonprofit context, see Greenhalgh, H. (December 16, 2015), "Charities Weigh Up Gains in Accepting Bitcoin Donations," *Financial Times*, http://www.ft.com/intl/cms/s/0/cf6644e8-a33f-11e5-bc70-7ff6d4fd203a.html#axzz46xzaiThl.

IRS Notice 2014-21, 2014-16 I.R.B. 938 (the only IRS comment on virtual currencies, at the moment)

N.Y. Comp. Codes R. & Regs. Tit. 23 § 200 et seq. (New York state virtual currency regulations)

Conn. Public Act 15-53, Substitute House Bill No. 6800 (Connecticut state virtual currency licensing regulations)

N.C. Gen. Stat. § 53-208 et seq. (North Carolina state law, including virtual currency in money transmittal regulations)

Press Release, American Institute of Certified Public Accountants, Re: Comments on Notice 2014-21: Virtual Currency Guidance (June 10, 2016) (requesting additional guidance from the IRS on ten unresolved virtual currency issues)

Chapter 11
Intangible Assets

- Quick Take-Aways
- Intermediate
- Advanced
- Additional Resources

Intangible Assets Quick Take-Aways

By Bryan Clontz

Below are quick take-aways on gifts of intangible assets. Intangible asset topics are based on Dennis Walsh's "Donation of Intellectual Property: What Does It Look Like?." For quick take-aways on gifts of intangible assets, see Intangible Assets Quick Take-Aways. For a review based on that article, see Intangible Assets Intermediate. For an in-depth examination adapted and excerpted from the article, see Intangible Assets Advanced. For further details, see Intangible Assets Additional Resources.

Gifts of intangible property can be challenging, but with the proper preparation, are valuable assets for charities which may provide considerable tax benefits for donors. Below is a brief overview of the advantages, disadvantages, special factors to consider, and questions a charity should ask.

Advantages of donations of intangible property include:

- Potential for a strong income stream over an extended time period.
- Flexibility in the charity's use or disposition of the asset—hold for use in operations, have a subsidiary use the asset for profit, or sell the asset.
- Flexibility in the transaction structure—the charity can work to accept the gift in the way that will work best for the donor.

Disadvantages of donating intangible property include:

- Valuation is difficult, and forecasts of future revenues can be highly variable so marketability and liquidity risks are inherent in these donations.
- Reporting requirements are stringent and will frequently apply for many years.
- Tax liability and other liability concerns may attach to the donated asset.

Some special factors to consider for gifts of intangible property include:

- The donor's tax deduction is limited to the lesser of cost basis or fair market value, so the gift might be better accomplished via bargain sale.
- The IRS requires calculation of "qualified donee income," but there is minimal guidance on what is and what is not included in this calculation.

- Intellectual property (including patents, copyrights, trademarks, trade secrets) is the most common class of intangible asset, but it can also include things like franchises, software, or licenses.

Discovery Questions

Donor Questions

1. What is the donor trying to accomplish with the gift?
2. What is the intangible asset's value and how was that determined (e.g., appraisal, recent transactions, cash flow multiple)?
3. Legally, who or what owns the asset?
4. What has been the average annual income for the previous three years?

Advisor Questions

1. What is the current tax basis and is it ordinary income or long term gain?
2. What is the likely exit plan for the charity?
3. Does the advisor have an estimate of what a qualified appraisal will cost?
4. Is the asset inventory?

Charity Questions

1. Is the effort worth the expected benefits (i.e., is the juice worth the squeeze)?
2. Has the screening and due diligence process identified any potential problems and can the risks be mitigated (main risks are marketability and liquidity)?
3. Is there the necessary expertise to accept and manage intangible assets in a timely way?
4. Should indirect gift acceptance be considered, like using external third party foundations or supporting organizations to receive the asset?
5. Is there a clear liquidation plan to maximize the sales proceeds as soon as possible?
6. Is the charity ready, willing and able to manage the asset as well as the IRS substantiation and other reporting requirements?

Intangible Assets Intermediate

By Ryan Raffin

Below is a review on gifts of intangible assets. Intangible asset topics are based on Dennis Walsh's "Donation of Intellectual Property: What Does It Look Like?." For quick take-aways on gifts of intangible assets, see Intangible Assets Quick Take-Aways. For a review based on that article, see Intangible Assets Intermediate. For an in-depth examination adapted and excerpted from the article, see Intangible Assets Advanced. For further details, see Intangible Assets Additional Resources.

This review of charitable gifts of intangible property has six parts, starting with definitions and relevant legislation. Second is an examination of valuation and income calculations for the charity. Following that is a look at reporting, tax, and liability issues. The final three sections deal with donor issues: mitigating the basis limitation, life expectancy, and compliance.

Donation of intangible property is a challenging area. Typically meaning intellectual property assets, the income production and total value of these assets are often difficult to forecast. Although the asset class can be very valuable for nonprofits, they also come with a host of special requirements and factors to consider.

Review Part 1: Definitions and Relevant Legislation

Intellectual property[1] is, simply put, a creation of the mind. It is divided into two categories, 1) industrial property such as patents or trademarks, and 2) copyright such as literary or artistic works. The Internal Revenue Code does not strictly define which assets are included, instead listing common forms with a catch-all provision for unlisted but similar assets. This list includes:

- Computer software
- Patents, inventions, formulae, processes, designs, patterns, trade secrets, or know-how
- Copyrights and literary, musical, or artistic compositions
- Trademarks, trade names, or brand names
- Franchises, licenses, or contracts
- Methods, programs, systems, procedures, campaigns, surveys, studies, forecasts, estimates, customer lists, or technical data

---

1. Used interchangeably with "intangible property" here, although that is a slightly broader category which also includes franchises, licenses, and contracts.

- Other similar items (an item is "similar" if its value comes from intangible properties)

In 2004, Congress limited deductions on donated qualified intellectual property to the lesser of fair market value or adjusted cost basis, intending to prevent exaggerated deductions. Since many donors have zero cost basis, Congress instead allows deductions based on a percentage of annual net income that the donated property produces. This deduction is allowed for up to ten years based on a sliding scale. The donee must file Form 8899 with both the IRS and donor detailing net income received or accrued, if any. The deductible percentage is allowed only to the extent it exceeds any initial deduction, and decreases in graduated intervals from 100 percent of income generated to 10 percent of income generated in the final year.

Review Part 2: Valuation and Income Calculations

Determining the value of the proposed donation is very important for gifts of intangible assets. The nonprofit should determine exactly what the property is, and what rights come with it. The IRS states that the asset should have identifying traits and be subject to private ownership and transfer, while also generating some economic benefit.

The valuation approach can be derived from market, cost, or income approaches. However, the market for these assets is often limited, and cost is not necessarily reasonably related to future revenues. This leaves projected income as the preferred valuation method. One can estimate income either by looking directly to projected revenue based on past production, or by indirect calculation (by taking net earnings and adjusting out other income streams). Either of these approaches should then use a discounted cash flow analysis to calculate overall value for the life of the asset.

Nonprofit donees will also need to calculate the qualified donee income for Form 8899, which goes to both the IRS and donor as described above. "Qualified donee income" means net income derived from the intellectual property, instead of income from activities in which the property is merely used. However, the Service does not provide guidance on how distinguish between the two sources of income. The best approach may be to allocate based on use.

The IRS also does not explicitly answer the question of whether proceeds from sale should be included, and the legislative history is unclear. However, including sale proceeds in qualified donee income would seem consistent with the original Congressional intent of preventing deductions based on speculative value. Practically speaking, excluding sales proceeds complicates reporting, particularly when the disposition of a partial interest is involved.

Review Part 3: Reporting, Tax, and Liability Issues

Other reporting hurdles are more common, and the charity should not overlook the potential administrative burden. For example, Form 8899 must be provided within 30 days of the nonprofit's fiscal year end, and no filing extension is available. If the asset requires the sort of cost allocation described above, this may prove difficult, and additional reporting could be necessary. In the event that the net income attributable to the assets is used directly for production of income, the nonprofit will likely need to complete its annual 990 before the 8899.

The possibility of unrelated business taxable income (UBTI) can emerge in an intangible property context as well. Receipt of royalties are exempt from UBTI, except in the case of debt-financed royalties. However, income from operation of a trade or business activity that is not related to the nonprofit's exempt purpose is considered UBTI. Note further that the income which the assets generate may be allocated proportionally between exempt activities and commercial, UBTI-generating activities (meaning that it is not an either/or situation).

The donee organization should assess whether the intangible asset's income is unrelated, and should consider the staff time and resources necessary for these activities. In some cases, it may be wiser to operate the unrelated business as a separate legal entity, so as to clearly delineate between the exempt organization's activities and the unrelated activities. This would maintain the nonprofit's exempt status, and still allow it to receive dividends from the unrelated activities as passive, non-UBTI income.

Donors should help charities consider any known and unknown liability issues that may attach to donated intangible property, including contract, tort, or environmental liabilities. As with other asset classes involving ongoing business activities, due diligence is key. The form of legal entity which will hold the intangible property is important as well. Insulating the nonprofit from liability is one consideration, as is maintaining the nonprofit's exempt status.

Review Part 4: Mitigating the Basis Limitation

Since the basis in intangible assets is typically very low, thereby limiting the deduction, the donor could consider a bargain sale to the nonprofit. This sale should be at a price that is equivalent to the tax savings that would be realized on a fair market value deduction. This would both benefit the donor through savings above the basis deduction, and potentially give the charity a considerable return on an initially modest investment.

However, since this would be a bargain sale, the donor would have to allocate basis between the gift and sale elements. It is unclear whether this part-gift, part-sale treatment would also apply to the deductible percentage based on the income generated. However, it is plausible that the donor would only be able to deduct income the property generates to the extent it was a gift. Although both valuation and application of bargain sale rules are the responsibility of the donor, the non-profit should endeavor to work with the donor to determine what the amounts are and how they should be reported.

There is also a strong possibility that the intangible asset would qualify for long-term capital asset treatment in the event of an arm's-length, fair market value transaction. Any gain in this circumstance would receive a favorable capital gains tax rate. The original owner could then make a donation from the proceeds, which would be deducted at the donor's normal income tax rate. Of course, this would not allow for future deductions based on income the asset generates, so donors should weigh the immediate tax savings against long-term tax savings.

Review Part 5: Life Expectancy

Another important consideration in the context of the 10-year income-based deduction is donor life expectancy. Also relevant are marital status, future tax rates, and future income. In the event of the donor's death during the deduction period, the IRS will not allow a transfer to the estate or an heir. For this reason, if the donor is married, joint ownership prior to donation is advisable.

If the intangible asset owner is of advanced age and there are no estate tax issues, the owner may consider "gifting" the income tax deductions to a beneficiary of the estate. This would be done by leaving the asset to a beneficiary who would in turn donate it. The advantage here is that the basis steps up to fair market value on transfer, possibly leading to a much larger deduction for the beneficiary. Further, a high-income beneficiary might benefit more from the deductions than the original owner would have. Regardless, an appraisal will be necessary to support the deduction, given that it would have a stepped-up value and therefore be more likely to draw IRS attention.

Review Part 6: Donor Compliance

As with other asset types, no deduction is available for a donation of a partial interest in intangible property. In the specific context of intangible property, this can come up in a context where the donor retains some interest in or right to derive value from the donated asset. For example, if the donor retained a right to manufacture goods that the patent covers, this would be a nondeductible partial interest.

Another requirement is that deductions over $5,000 have a qualified appraisal (discussed separately in Appendix A). Since intangible property is limited to the lesser of cost or fair market value, the donor in certain cases will need to substantiate that the fair market value exceeds cost basis.

Conclusion

Even with the limitation on deduction, donations of intangible property are appealing for donors who might prefer a multi-year deduction rather than the additional income produced. Charities receiving such gifts may have a lucrative income stream, although the earnings often have some degree of uncertainty. When combined with the possibility of liability attaching and UBTI, charities are well-advised to evaluate what is being offered, including both risks and value.

Intangible Assets Advanced[2]

By Dennis Walsh

Below is an in-depth examination on gifts of intangible assets. Intangible asset topics are based on Dennis Walsh's "Donation of Intellectual Property: What Does It Look Like?." For quick take-aways on gifts of intangible assets, see Intangible Assets Quick Take-Aways. For a review based on that article, see Intangible Assets Intermediate. For an in-depth examination adapted and excerpted from the article, see Intangible Assets Advanced. For further details, see Intangible Assets Additional Resources.

Prior to 2004, Congress became increasingly interested in the valuation of charitable contributions of intellectual property rights. High values which donors claimed for contributions frequently resulted in significant tax benefits, but little or no actual benefit to the charities. Many donations of patents, copyrights, software, and other forms of intellectual property assets turned out to be worthless or produced far less revenue than projected. Congress felt that actual revenue the property generated, instead of predictions, would provide a more accurate measure of the value eligible for a charitable income tax deduction.

This section explains opportunities for the charitable transfer of intellectual property assets, identifies practical issues for donors and donee organizations, and illustrates the potential cumulative tax benefits from particular intellectual property asset donations.

What Is Intellectual Property?

Intellectual property (IP) refers to creations of the mind—inventions, literary and artistic works, symbols, names, images, and designs used in commerce. IP is conceptually divided into two categories: industrial property, which includes patents, utility models, trademarks, industrial designs and geographical indications of source; and copyright, which includes literary and artistic works.[3]

In the federal tax law context, intellectual property is a variant of intangible property. Due to the diverse and evolving nature of IP, the Internal Revenue Code does not provide an all-inclusive definition of assets within this class. Rather, the Code and other guidance lists common forms of IP, along with a catch-all provision for similar types of assets it does not specifically list.

---

2. This chapter excerpts and adapts Walsh, D. (January 20, 2015), "Donation of Intellectual Property: What Does It Look Like?," Planned Giving Design Center, http://www.pgdc.com/pgdc/donation-intellectual-property-what-does-it-look.
3. World Intellectual Property Organization (WIPO) Publication 943, 2013.

Charitable Gifts of Noncash Assets

In particular, Internal Revenue Manual (IRM) guidance provides examples of intangible property that the Service may also classify as intellectual property depending on specific asset characteristics. The IRM states that intangible property includes, but is not limited to:

- Computer software
- Patents, inventions, formulae, processes, designs, patterns, trade secrets, or know-how
- Copyrights and literary, musical, or artistic compositions
- Trademarks, trade names, or brand names
- Franchises, licenses, or contracts
- Methods, programs, systems, procedures, campaigns, surveys, studies, forecasts, estimates, customer lists, or technical data
- Other similar items

An item is similar if it derives its value not from physical attributes, but from its intellectual content or other intangible properties.[4] Added in 2004, Internal Revenue Code Section 170(e)(1)(B)(iii) provides that for purposes of this charitable contribution provision,[5] qualified intellectual property is any:

- Patent
- Copyright (other than as described in Section 1221(a)(3) or 1231(b)(1)(C))[6]
- Trademark
- Trade name
- Trade secret
- Know-how
- Software (other than as described in Section 197(e)(3)(A)(i))[7]
- Similar property and applications or registrations of such property (emphasis added)

---

4. IRM 4.48.5.1 (07-01-2006).
5. IRC § 170(e)(1)(B)(iii).
6. A copyright described in IRC § 1221(a)(3) or § 1231(b)(1)(C) is a copyright held by a taxpayer whose personal efforts created the property, or in whose hands the basis of the property is determined, for purposes of determining gain from a sale or exchange, in whole or in part by reference to the basis of the property in the hands of a taxpayer whose personal efforts created the property.
7. Software described in IRC § 197(e)(3)(A)(i) is software readily available for purchase by the general public, subject to a nonexclusive license, that has not been substantially modified.

2004 Changes

Congress addressed its concern with donor-inflated deductions of corporate patents in particular by the enactment of Section 170(e)(1)(B)(iii) in October 2004. This legislation added the donation of IP as a situation where any long-term capital gain that the donor would otherwise realize if the property were sold at its fair market value at the time of the contribution instead reduces the deductible amount of a charitable contribution of property.

This provision effectively limits a deduction for the contribution of qualified intellectual property that would otherwise be eligible for a fair market value deduction to the lesser of fair market value or the donor's adjusted basis. Thus, for a contribution of such property made after 2004, a donor receives no deduction for any excess of fair market value over basis.

This is a disincentive to charitable gifts of valuable, income-producing IP. The deduction is minimal, since many owners will have little or no basis as a result of having previously deducted developmental costs. These deductions could come in the form of ordinary and necessary business expenses (Section 162), research and experimental expenditures (Section 174), or as amortization under Section 197 in the case of an intellectual asset the donor acquired and held in connection with a trade or business. In addition, qualified creative expenses of freelance writers, photographers, and artists[8] are exempt from the uniform capitalization rules and are typically deducted in the year incurred under Section 162. Also, no increase in basis is allowable for the value of a developer's time for a self-created asset.

To help remedy the basis disincentive, the 2004 amendments created a new Section 170(m). It authorizes a donor of qualified intellectual property to a charity, other than a private nonoperating foundation, to deduct a percentage of annual net income which the asset produces for up to ten years, on a sliding percentage scale (see the table below).

To be eligible for future charitable deductions, the donor must provide notice to the donee organization at the time of the donation that includes:[9]

1. The name, address, and taxpayer identification number of the donor
2. A description of the qualified intellectual property in sufficient identifying detail
3. The date of the contribution

---

8. As defined in IRC § 263A(h)(2) (2005).
9. IRC § 170(m)(8)(B).

4. A statement that the donor intends to treat the contribution as a qualified intellectual property contribution for purposes of Sections 170(m) and 6050L

Tax year	Deductible percentage
1	100%
2	100%
3	90%
4	80%
5	70%
6	60%
7	50%
8	40%
9	30%
10	20%
11	10%
12	10%

The donee organization must file an annual return for any taxable year in which the donee receives or accrues net income from the property.[10] The charity must file the information to the Internal Revenue Service on Form 8899, Notice of Income from Donated Intellectual Property, and is due 30 days after the end of the donee's tax year. The donee must file Form 8899 and provide a copy to the donor for any donee organization tax year that includes any portion of the ten-year period beginning with the date of the contribution.[11]

But Form 8899 is not provided for any part of a year after the date of the expiration of the legal life of the property, if occurring prior to the tenth anniversary of the date of the contribution.[12] Also, if the qualified intellectual property fails to produce net income for the donee's tax year, the IRS does not require the organization to file Form 8899.

To determine the Section 170(m) additional deduction for a particular year, the donor multiplies the amount of qualified donee income reported on Form 8899 by the applicable percentage shown in the table. However, the additional deduction for any year is allowable only to the extent that the aggregate amount of net income from the property since donation, with adjustments for

---

10. Treas. Reg. § 1.6050L–2(a).
11. IRC § 170(m)(5).
12. IRC § 170(m)(6).

the annual percentage limitations, exceeds the amount of any deduction allowable to the donor for the initial contribution of the property.[13]

Although the allowable period of additional contributions is ten years, the table provides for twelve separate taxable years. The additional years are necessary due to potential for a donee to have a fiscal year other than the calendar year, as well as the possibility of an additional short tax year resulting from a donee's change in accounting period.

As the joint committee indicates with the decreasing percentages, the further in time from the date of a gift, the more likely it will be that the value inuring to the charity from its use of the property is attributable to value the charity adds since the time of the contribution.

Examples

The following examples illustrate the donation of an intellectual property asset, including some of the nuances associated with the donation of a copyright in particular. For each situation, assume that the fair market value of a copyright Sandy donated to XYZ Charity, arising from a book manuscript, is $100,000 and that book sales are generating $10,000 per year in royalties.

Example (1): Sandy authored the manuscript and her basis is $1,000, consisting of legal fees and costs associated with registration and protection of the copyright. Under Section 170(e)(1)(B)(iii), the donation does not qualify as a contribution of qualified intellectual property, because the holder created it through personal efforts, as described in Section 1221(a)(3)(A).[14] Accordingly, Sandy is not eligible for additional contribution deductions under Section 170(m) for any royalties XYZ Charity subsequently received. The copyright is not a capital asset in Sandy's hands and remains ordinary income property regardless of her holding period, since she created it through her personal efforts. Her charitable deduction is therefore $1,000—the copyright fair market value of $100,000, less $99,000 of ordinary income,[15] effectively limiting her charitable deduction to her basis.

Example (2): Sandy purchased all rights and interests in the manuscript and the related copyright as an investment for $75,000 three years ago. The copyright is qualified intellectual property and Sandy provides the IRS-required notice to XYZ Charity that she intends to treat the donation as

---

13. IRC § 170(m)(2), (7).
14. IRC § 170(e)(1)(B)(iii).
15. Id. at (A).

such. Sandy's initial deduction is $75,000, consisting of the copyright fair market value of $100,000, minus $25,000 of long-term capital gain that she would realize if she had sold it instead, limiting her charitable deduction to her basis.[16] She may also annually deduct a portion of net royalty income which XYZ Charity subsequently received in excess of her initial deduction, until the 10th anniversary of her contribution.

Example (3): Sandy acquired the copyright by gift from her mother prior to her mother's death. Her mother authored the manuscript and had a basis of $1,000. Under Section 1015, Sandy's carryover basis in the gift property is her mother's basis. Under Section 170(e)(1)(B)(iii), the donation does not qualify as a contribution of qualified intellectual property. This is because Sandy can calculate her basis for determining gain from a sale or exchange by reference to the basis in the hands of a taxpayer whose personal efforts created the property, as provided in Section 1221(a)(3)(C).[17] Accordingly, Sandy is not eligible for additional contribution deductions under Section 170(m) for royalties XYZ Charity subsequently receives. Sandy's charitable contribution for donation of the copyright is $1,000 as computed in example (1).

Example (4): Sandy acquired ownership of the manuscript and related copyright by specific bequest from her mother's estate. Accordingly, her basis under Section 1014 is $100,000, representing the fair market value in the decedent's estate, and the asset is long-term capital gain property upon Sandy's receipt. The copyright is qualified intellectual property and Sandy provides the IRS-required notice to XYZ Charity that she intends to treat the donation as such. Sandy's initial deduction is $100,000, consisting of the copyright fair market value of $100,000, which is the same as her basis, and therefore regulations do not require a reduction to fair market value in determining the deductible amount of her contribution. She is also eligible to annually deduct, as additional charitable contributions, a portion of net royalty income XYZ Charity subsequently receives in excess of her initial deduction, until the 10th anniversary of her contribution.

Valuation

Since IP can take many forms, the planning process for assigning value should start with an analysis of what constitutes the property and its associated rights. As Internal Revenue Manual guidance provides, the property should:[18]

- Be subject to specific identification and a recognizable description

---

16. Id.
17. Id.
18. IRM 4.48.5.2.3 (07-01-2006).

- Be subject to legal existence and protection, which owners may incorporate within a larger entity
- Be subject to private ownership and be legally transferable
- Generate some measurable amount of economic benefit
- Potentially enhance the value of assets with which owners associate it

A market, cost, or income based approach is typically used to identify one or more specific methodologies for valuing IP. The frequent lack of an active market involving comparable property will often render a market-based approach inapplicable for valuation of an IP asset. Identifying and quantifying costs necessary to create or reproduce a unique IP asset result in practical difficulties for the cost approach as well, which does not account for the value of future earnings. However, the cost approach may provide a good basis for determining a value ceiling.

The charity may directly estimate an asset's value by reference to comparable royalty rates using projected revenue, or costs that ownership of an IP asset could save, such as by relief from royalty payments. Alternatively, the organization may estimate an asset's value indirectly from net earnings of the whole entity, after adjustment for reasonable return on other assets. This approach imputes a value to IP by estimating excess earnings resulting from its addition to the acquiring entity.

Use of the above direct or indirect income method in conjunction with discounted cash flow techniques may be the best way to value the earnings potential of an IP asset. Discounted cash flow analysis is forward looking: it considers both the asset's expected net cash flows generated over its remaining economic life, and the risks associated with achieving the cash flow through the selection of an appropriate discount rate.

Qualified Donee Income

In addition to a donor's potential charitable income tax deduction for a gifted IP asset, she may deduct additional amounts in later years as charitable contributions, based on the amount of qualified donee income, consisting of royalties or other net income the donee accrued or received during such years.[19] For this purpose, "qualified donee income" (QDI) includes net income deriving

---

19. IRC § 170(m)(1).

from, and properly allocable to, the intellectual property itself. It does not include any and every activity in which the intellectual property is simply used.[20]

In determining QDI, neither the Code nor Regulations provide any guidance or safe harbor provisions for distinguishing net income attributable to the intellectual property versus an activity within which the property is used. Presumably, accounting for net income from such property should adopt the unrelated business income activity approach. This should include identification of revenue, assignment of direct costs, and allocation of indirect expenses of the donee organization in the same manner as for unrelated business income, whether or not the donee so classifies it.

In such case, where facilities and personnel are used both to carry on exempt activities and to conduct unrelated trade or business activities, the donee organization must allocate costs between the two uses on a reasonable basis. It should proportionally divide expenses such as depreciation, salaries, and similar items of overhead attributable to such facilities and personnel in this manner.[21] Common allocation bases include time spent, square footage of facilities, miles driven, and units of output.

Congress authorized the issuance of future regulations or other guidance on determining net income from qualified intellectual property in situations where the charitable donee organization uses the property for the direct accomplishment of its exempt purposes, as distinguished from a separate commercial activity.[22]

A question arises as to whether qualified donee income within the meaning of Section 170(m)(3) should include the proceeds from a nonprofit's subsequent sale or disposition of qualified intellectual property. The February 2004 Joint Committee on Taxation description of the revenue provisions of H.R. 4520, the American Jobs Creation Act, states that additional deductions are based on royalties or other revenue from the property. It also clarifies that other revenue for this purpose includes the donee's sales proceeds and net income derived from, and properly allocable to, the property.[23] However, later pre-enactment reports do not contain such a reference to sale proceeds, nor is this reference contained in the enacted Statute, or in Regulations or authoritative guidance issued to date.

---

20. IRC § 170(m)(3), IRS Notice 2005-41 (Internal Revenue Bulletin June 6, 2005).
21. Treas. Reg. § 1.512(a)-1(c).
22. IRC § 170(m)(10)(D)(ii).
23. Description of Revenue Provisions Contained in the President's Fiscal Year 2005 Budget Proposal, Prepared by the Staff of the Joint Committee on Taxation, February 2004.

The inclusion of sale proceeds as qualified donee income seems consistent with the intent of Congress in limiting a charitable contribution of IP to value that a seller can realize in a market transaction, as opposed to a speculative appraisal. Practically speaking, making a distinction between net income and sale proceeds could raise a myriad of interpretive issues with the disposition of less than all of a donee's rights and interests in an IP asset, such as where the owners sever the income rights from ownership of the underlying asset. Would the IRS view the proceeds from the sale of such rights as qualified donee income or as from a disposition not reportable to the donor on Form 8899? Further guidance in this area appears to be needed.

Reporting Issues

When considering the acceptance of a gift of intellectual property, the charitable donee should not overlook the potential administrative burden that may result from the requirement that it provide Form 8899 to a donor within 30 days after the end of the organization's fiscal year.[24] There is no opportunity for a filing extension with Form 8899. Depending on the accounting complexities of the asset and need for determination of indirect costs properly allocable to the income it produces, it may be simply impractical for a charity to comply with this reporting requirement in such a short time frame. Penalties relating to the reporting requirements set forth at Section 6050L and the related Form 8899 are found at Sections 6721 through 6724.[25]

In many situations, timely and accurate determination of qualified net income the charity receives from an IP asset will not be difficult to determine, such as when a donee's licensing of an asset to another party creates revenue. On the other hand, attributing net income to an IP asset that is used within a broader activity, such as from the trademark of a going business the organization subsequently operates, may pose a more formidable challenge. This situation likely would require concurrent completion of the annual IRS Form 990 and Form 990-T (when required) prior to providing Form 8899 to a donor.

Unrelated Business Income

The nonprofit's receipt of royalties, less all deductions directly connected with such income, is exempt from treatment as unrelated business income, except to the extent that the asset is debt-financed.[26] However, when the operation of a trade or business activity is unrelated to the organiza-

---

24. Treas. Reg. § 1.6050L-2(d)(2).
25. IRC §§ 6721–6724 (2015).
26. IRC § 512(b)(2).

tion's exempt purposes, the donee organization will report the unrelated business income on IRS Form 990-T, and compute corporate income tax on net earnings just like a C corporation.

Before undertaking such an activity, the nonprofit should evaluate whether the IRS might consider the income from an unrelated business to be substantial in relation to its exempt activities, taking into account the staff time and other resources it applied to the respective activities. It may be prudent to operate an unrelated business as a separate legal and taxable entity to safeguard the tax exempt status of the donee organization. In this case, after-tax earnings of the business may be passed to the parent exempt organization as dividends exempt from unrelated business income tax.[27]

Other Donee Concerns

The nonprofit's counsel also should consider liability issues, including the potential assumption of the donor's known and unknown liabilities (e.g., for contracts, torts, and environmental issues) that may attach to transferred assets. It should also consider the form of legal entity within which the donee organization will operate the business. This decision will involve multiple factors, with legal liability and protection of tax-exempt status of primary concern.

Form of Asset Transfer

Donors should evaluate the tax effect of the transfer of the individual assets to assure that the projected tax benefits meet expectations. For example, consider a contribution of depreciable personal property which the donor used in a trade or business, such as equipment. Generally, this offers limited tax benefits to a charitable donor, because of the property's typical lack of economic appreciation and short depreciable tax life. Prior depreciation deductions reduce the cost basis of the property, and any gain the donor realizes upon sale results in ordinary income to the extent of the previous deductions. This ordinary income element reduces the fair market value the donor uses for a charitable deduction.

Mitigating the Basis Limitation

When an individual donor has minimal basis in a qualified IP asset, consider a bargain sale to the charity. The pre-tax price should result in the donor receiving total consideration equivalent to the tax savings if the IRS allowed a fair market value deduction for an outright donation. In this

---

27. IRC § 512(b)(1).

way, a donor may receive a more substantial benefit from the charitable transfer of an IP asset than what the individual would realize from tax saved through a basis deduction alone, in addition to receiving contribution deductions in later years. And a donee organization may enjoy a generous return on its bargain investment.

In determining the amount of an initial charitable deduction and any taxable gain to be recognized from a bargain sale, however, the donor must allocate basis between the gift and sale elements. Bargain sale rules provide that the calculation is based on the respective ratios of the gift value and sale price to the total fair market value of the asset.[28]

A question arises as to whether a donor would also need to bifurcate additional charitable contributions from net income the donee receives in subsequent years between the gift and sale portions. The parties could calculate this in two ways. The first is the nonprofit organization determines the amount of qualified donee income reportable to the donor on IRS Form 8899, Notice of Income from Donated Intellectual Property. The second has the donor calculate the amount prior to application of the annual percentage reductions for additional contributions under Section 170(m)(7). Unfortunately, current guidance does not address this situation.

Despite the lack of guidance, it is reasonable that Treatment as a qualified intellectual property contribution would not apply to the extent that the donor transfers property in exchange for consideration. In addition, valuation of a charitable donation of property and application of the bargain sale rules when regulations require is a responsibility of the donor. Planners for the donor and donee organization should have a documented understanding of how they will determine and report qualified donee income.

When an individual's sale of a qualified IP asset would result in long-term capital gain, that donor might also consider a fair market value sale followed by contribution of the cash proceeds to the charity. The deduction would be subject to the annual 60 percent of adjusted gross income limitation, with a five-year carryover of unused amounts. Under current law, long-term capital gain is taxed at a rate lower than the rate applied to ordinary income. The donor could then deduct a charitable contribution of the proceeds at her higher marginal rate for ordinary income, creating a potential net tax savings from the rate differential.

However, deductions for future contributions arising from net income which the asset produces will not be available in such case. Therefore, the donor should compare tax savings from the

---

28. IRC § 170(e)(2), IRC § 1011(b), examples at Treas. Reg. § 1.1011-2(c).

contribution of cash realized from a fair market value sale, in excess of tax paid on the capital gain, with the estimated tax savings from the sum of the initial contribution and the present value of additional contributions in evaluating this alternative. In some cases, projections may forecast that the asset will produce greater tax savings if donated, particularly when it realizes revenue from the asset primarily in the early part of the ten-year period. If this is the case, it is more likely that the present value of tax savings from a donation will exceed the tax benefit available from a sale of the asset followed by donation of the net proceeds.

Life Expectancy

Because additional charitable contributions arising from qualified donee income can span a period of up to ten years, the parties should consider an individual donor's life expectancy, projected taxable income, marginal tax rates, and the resulting likelihood that a donor will fully benefit from the additional deductions during lifetime. There is no provision for a donor's estate or a beneficiary of the estate to take additional deductions in the event that a donor dies before the end of the ten-year period. Married persons should consider joint ownership of the asset prior to donation to reduce this risk. A transfer of a property interest between married individuals is eligible for unlimited exemption from gift tax.

When an IP asset owner is of advanced age and estate tax is not in play, an opportunity for enhancing income tax deductions may arise for a beneficiary of the estate by delaying charitable donation of the asset until after the owner's death. By bequeathing the asset to a beneficiary with charitable goals similar to those of the decedent, the Section 1014 basis adjustment to fair market value by the estate may result in a much larger initial deduction for a subsequent gift by the beneficiary.

In addition, a high-income beneficiary may realize greater tax savings from the additional contribution deductions than the decedent would have realized if he had gifted the asset to charity during life. An expert appraisal will be essential to support the value the estate assigns, and withstanding an IRS valuation challenge is not guaranteed.

Donor Compliance

With certain exceptions, Section 170(f)(3) provides that no charitable contribution deduction is allowed for a transfer to a charity of less than the taxpayer's entire interest in property.[29] For

---

29. IRC § 170(f)(3) (2015).

example, if a donation agreement states that a transfer of the taxpayer's interests in a patent is subject to a right retained by the taxpayer to manufacture or use any product covered by the patent, the taxpayer has transferred a nondeductible partial interest in the patent.[30]

The IRS specifically exempts donation of qualified intellectual property from the requirement for a qualified appraisal for the donation of noncash property valued at more than $5,000.[31] However, the donor must attach a statement to her tax return showing how the deductible amount was determined, and must complete specific sections of IRS Form 8283. The taxpayer must also obtain the nonprofit's acknowledgment of the donation in Part IV of Form 8283 to claim a deduction for the initial contribution.

Since the amount deductible for the contribution of a qualified IP asset cannot exceed the donor's adjusted basis, a donor must be able to substantiate, when reasonable, that the value of the asset exceeds its basis at the time of the contribution. In no case can an income tax deduction for the charitable contribution of noncash property exceed the property's fair market value.

In contrast, the donee organization is responsible for the determination of additional contributions reported annually to a donor on Form 8899. Accordingly, advisors for the donor and nonprofit alike should have an advance understanding of how qualified donee income will be calculated and assure that the organization has the ability to undertake this determination.

Conclusion

The 2004 amendments to Section 170 created a potentially valuable opportunity for a gift of intellectual property, particularly for high marginal rate donors who do not need the income such produces. A donor may experience satisfaction from enhancing the sustainability of a favored charity by providing a future income stream to the charity while enjoying both current and future income tax savings as a result.

However, an IP asset derives value only from the expectation of future cash flow from specific rights. The inherent uncertainty of earnings from such rights requires careful timing of asset valuation and transfer in order to maximize both cash flow to the charity and tax benefits to the donor. In addition, the donor must relinquish all substantial rights in the property, possibly meaning no certainty of future income to the charity and no additional tax savings to the donor.

---

30. IRS Notice 2004-7 (Internal Revenue Bulletin January 20, 2004).
31. IRS Publication 561, IRS Form 8283 instructions.

Therefore, the donee organization should assess whether it has the capacity to exploit the asset and manage production of income in accordance with its contemplated use. It should also evaluate whether it can meet accounting and reporting requirements in an accurate, timely, and sufficiently transparent manner that is likely to satisfy the donor. Other key indicators in evaluating a charitable gift, versus an alternative donation of cash the donor realized from the sale or continuing operation of the asset include:

- Donor's basis relative to asset value
- Expected duration of asset value
- Life expectancy of the donor
- Projected estate value

For individual donors in particular, the complexities of intellectual property rights valuation, projection of income and estate tax effects, and other charitable and estate goals combine to require a team planning approach. The expected charitable and tax benefits should justify planning and gift administration costs.

Intangible Assets Additional Resources

Below are further details on gifts of intangible assets. Intangible asset topics are based on Dennis Walsh's "Donation of Intellectual Property: What Does It Look Like?." For quick take-aways on gifts of intangible assets, see Intangible Assets Quick Take-Aways. For a review based on that article, see Intangible Assets Intermediate. For an in-depth examination adapted and excerpted from the article, see Intangible Assets Advanced. For further details, see Intangible Assets Additional Resources.

For analysis of intangible asset valuation, see Wishing, K.J. & Reilly, R.F. (2012), "The Cost Approach and the Intangible Asset Valuation Assignment," *Willamette Management Insights*, http://www.willamette.com/insights_journal/12/autumn_2012_1.pdf.

For an examination of the underlying theories and policies governing gifts of intellectual property, see Nguyen, X.T. & Maine, J.A., "Giving Intellectual Property," 39 U.C. Davis L. Rev. 1723 (June 2006), http://digitalcommons.mainelaw.maine.edu/faculty-publications/31/.

For a look at corporate donations of patents, see Feder, B.J. (November 17, 2002), "Patent Donations Are Novel Corporate Gift," *N.Y. Times,* http://www.nytimes.com/2002/11/17/business/17PATE.html?pagewanted=all.

For a comprehensive review of intellectual property rights, transfers, and tax consequences to donors and donees, see Drennan, W.A. (2002), "It Does Not Compute: Copyright Restriction on Tax Deduction for Developer's Donation of Software," Planned Giving Design Center, http://www.pgdc.com/pdf/It_Does_Not_Compute.pdf.

For an investigation of how lawmakers give effect to underlying tax policies, and defense of the fair market value deduction, see Drennan, W.A., "Charitable Donations of Intellectual Property: The Case for Retaining the Fair Market Value Tax Deduction," 2004 Utah L. Rev. 1045 (2004).

For an example of a college's intellectual property gift acceptance policies, see North Carolina State University (November 20, 2000), "REG 10.00.01 - Donations of Intellectual Property to NC State University," https://policies.ncsu.edu/regulation/reg-10-00-01.

IRC § 170(m) (laying out the graduated deduction and other special rules for donating IP assets)

IRC § 6050L(b) (donee reporting requirements)

Rev. Rul. 2003-28, 2003-1 C.B. 594 (variations on the gift transaction, including donor-retained rights)

IRS Notice 2004-7, 2004-3 I.R.B. 310 (situations arising out of intellectual property donations that will be closely scrutinized)

IRS Form 8899, Notice of Income from Donated Intellectual Property (the form nonprofit donees must use to report to both the donor and the IRS the income which donated IP assets generate)

Internal Revenue Manual 4.48.5 (July 1, 2006), "Intangible Property Valuation Guidelines" (IRS procedures for its agents to value intangible assets)

Chapter 12

Life Income Assets

- Quick Take-Aways
- Intermediate
- Advanced
- Additional Resources

Life Income Interests Quick Take-Aways

By Bryan Clontz

Below are quick take-aways on gifts of life income interests. Life income interest topics are based on Michael Parham's "I Want It Now! Early Termination of Charitable Remainder Trusts." For quick take-aways on gifts of life income interests, see Life Income Interests Quick Take-aways. For a review based on that article, see Life Income Interests Intermediate. For an in-depth examination adapted and excerpted from the article, see Life Income Interests Advanced. For further details, see Life Income Interests Additional Resources.

Income interests are generally donated to the charity who holds the remainder interest, so that the charity then owns the underlying asset outright. These gifts most often involve a charitable gift annuity, charitable remainder trust, or pooled-income fund. Below is a brief overview of the advantages, disadvantages, unique considerations, and questions to ask.

Advantages of donations of life income interests include:

- The charity typically already holds the remainder or residuum interest—there is a pre-existing relationship with the donors, and after the life income donation, the charity owns the entire underlying asset outright.
- If the charity does not hold the underlying asset already (meaning some third-party does), it will instead get a simple income interest for the life of the donor.
- Deductions are usually available for the projected present value of the income stream and may be partial terminations as well (e.g., 50 percent of the life income may be donated or assigned).
- In some cases, it may be possible for the charity to buy the donor's interest for full or less than full consideration.

Disadvantages of donating life income interests include:

- Spendthrift provisions make transfer difficult in trusts where the creator, lifetime beneficiary, and trustee are not all the same person.
- Complex contractual or trust agreements usually govern these income interests, as well as state contract law, so charities will likely need professional advice.
- Percentage-based income interests may have negligible distributions.

Wrinkles in the process to consider include:

- Donations must still be of an entire, undivided interest (most relevant for charitable remainder trusts, and pooled-income funds).
- If there are multiple income interests, the charity will need to determine exactly how the proposed gift will impact the other interests.
- The deduction for unitrusts can vary depending on interest rates.
- The deduction rules on charitable gift annuity life income terminations has not been clarified. One school of thought suggests that it is more like a trust and therefore allows a deduction for the present value of life income relinquished. Another school of thought suggests the deduction is limited to the unrecovered basis similar to a commercial annuity contract.
- Substantiation rules still apply and an appraisal is necessary if the value is greater than $5,000.

Discovery Questions

Donor Questions

1. What is the donor trying to accomplish with the gift?
2. Is the life income interest being considered a charitable remainder trust, charitable gift annuity or a pooled-income fund?
3. Does the donor wish to donate the entire interest or some smaller undivided interest?
4. Does the donor wish to receive any lump sum or periodic payment for the life income interest or is it a gift?

Advisor Questions

1. How will the interest be valued and appraised, if necessary?
2. Has the advisor reviewed any state law or trust issues that may complicate the transaction?
3. Does the advisor understand the process and paperwork necessary to complete the transaction?

Charity Questions

1. Is the effort worth the expected benefits (i.e., is the juice worth the squeeze)?

2. Has the screening and due diligence process identified any potential problems and can the risks be mitigated (mainly contract law, valuation, deduction approach and whether any consideration is being requested)?

3. Should indirect gift acceptance be considered, like using external third party foundations or supporting organizations to receive the asset?

Life Income Interests   Intermediate

By Ryan Raffin

Below is a review on gifts of life income interests. Life income interest topics are based on Michael Parham's "[I Want It Now! Early Termination of Charitable Remainder Trusts](#)*." For quick take-aways on gifts of life income interests, see* [Life Income Interests Quick Take-aways](#)*. For a review based on that article, see* [Life Income Interests Intermediate](#)*. For an in-depth examination adapted and excerpted from the article, see* [Life Income Interests Advanced](#)*. For further details, see* [Life Income Interests Additional Resources](#)*.*

This review of gifts of income interests has six parts, beginning with an overview of the transaction generally. It then examines how the gift works in the context of a number of different planned giving vehicles, beginning with charitable remainder trusts. Next is charitable QTIPs, followed by charitable gift annuities. After this is a short discussion of the unusual case of bequests of charitable lead trusts. Finally, the review finishes with a look at gifts of income interests in pooled-income funds.

Review Part 1: Overview

Like other assets, income interests can be given to charity. However, distinct from most other intangible assets, they are typically only a portion of a larger asset and arrangement. Similar to royalty interests, a gift of an income interest is a gift of revenue derived from some underlying asset. In many cases, there will be also be a party holding a remainder interest—often the charity in question. In these situations, the donation is referred to as a "split-interest gift."

One important legal concept in this area is the merger doctrine. For split interests in assets, there is often a lifetime income interest in one party, and a remainder interest in another. These are called equitable or beneficial interests. The trustee who holds the asset has the legal interest. If one party has both the equitable / beneficial interest(s) and the legal interest, the separate interests "merge." As a result of the merger, the party holding the interests owns the underlying property free and clear of the trust.

For charities, if they are already the trustee and remainder beneficiary, the only "piece" preventing merger is the lifetime interest. When the owner of the lifetime income interest donates it, the interests merge and the charity owns the underlying assets outright.

Review Part 2: Gift of an Income Interest in a Charitable Remainder Trust

In the case of a charitable remainder trust, the donor creates a trust with both a standard income interest and remainder interest. For the purposes of these asset gifts, the donor is typically (although not always) the income beneficiary, and a designated charity is the remainderman. As with a charitable gift annuity, the donor receives an income stream, either for life or a set term of years. On death or the end of the term of years, the remaining amount in trust is distributed to the designated charity. The donor gets an immediate deduction in the amount of the present value of the assets which pass to charity. This is calculated as the present value of the amount transferred minus the present value of income distributable to the income beneficiaries.

In the event that the donor decides they no longer need the income, they can accelerate the remainder by contributing their income interest to charity. That amount will be the present value of the remaining life interest. The donor should sign a document assigning the income interest to the remainder beneficiary. Further, if the donor reserved the right to change the remainder beneficiary, that right should be removed, rescinded, or assigned to the charity as a matter of course to avoid any future confusion.

As with gifts of other types of assets, the donor must donate his entire, undivided interest to receive a deduction. As a result, there are three ways to terminate a charitable remainder trust—total termination, partial termination, and pro-rata distribution termination. Total termination refers to a situation where the trust is (with the consent of all beneficiaries) dissolved and all assets are distributed. Partial termination is when only a portion of the overall trust is terminated, while the remainder continues as originally planned. Pro rata distribution termination is a division of actuarial present values—basically a sale of the interests to charity.

For total termination, the donors must relinquish or exercise discretionary powers such that the charity is the sole, irrevocable remainder beneficiary. Once the income interest is transferred, the charity will hold all interests and may terminate the trust. The donors could also exchange their income interest for a charitable gift annuity—a result which the IRS has approved.

The donor can partially terminate the trust either by assignment of a portion of the donor's income interest, or by dividing the trust. In either case, the donor can choose the proportion that she wishes to give to charity. If the charitable remainder beneficiary is irrevocable, then any donated portion of the lifetime interest will meet this requirement, since the charity is already entitled to the remainder interest. For example, the IRS ruled in 2012 that the donor-trustee of a charitable remainder trust could assign half of the income interest to charity and receive a deduction. Note however, that the donor-trustee also had to irrevocably designate the charity as a 50 percent remainder beneficiary (presumably to achieve a merger, as discussed above).

For the purpose of donating an income interest, the donated interest being in a CRUT or CRAT can matter. Interest rates in particular can have more of an effect on donated CRATs. In a low interest rate environment, the remainder value is low compared to the present value of the annuity. This makes donating the income interest very appealing, since the deduction is based on the (comparatively higher) present value of income due to the income beneficiary. It is unclear whether this treatment would also apply to a CRUT.

The above paragraphs deal with cases where the creator of the remainder trust is also the income beneficiary, and either the charity or the creator-beneficiary is the trustee. This may always not be the case. If the beneficiary in this instance wishes to donate her interest, she may not be able to. If the trust is a spendthrift trust, the beneficiary may not donate her interest barring cooperation from the donor and all other beneficiaries (or court permission in some states).

Review Part 3: Gift of an Income Interest in a Charitable QTIP Trust

A qualified terminable interest property trust (QTIP trust) is an estate planning tool for spouses, and offers flexibility for charitable planning. A charitable QTIP trust means that the remainder is left to charity; the surviving spouse will have the lifetime income interest. The IRS has approved a transaction where the trustee would divide the trust and assign one of the resulting income interests to charity. Since the charity already has the remainder interest, it gets all of the underlying assets for that portion of the divided trust.

In the event where the donor divides a charitable QTIP and partially gifts it to charity, the donation does not render the remaining trusts ineligible for QTIP treatment. Further, it is not considered a transfer of a fractional interest, but is instead a transfer of an undivided portion, since the entire trust is divided, and a whole portion goes to charity. Of course, the donor's gift is deductible for both gift tax and income tax purposes.

Review Part 4: Gift of an Income Interest in a Charitable Gift Annuity

A charitable gift annuity (CGA) is a contractual agreement between a donor and charity, whereby the donor receives a fixed annuity from the charity and an immediate income tax deduction (equal to the present value of the life income interest) in return for cash or other assets. To qualify as a CGA, the agreement must leave ten percent of the present value of contributed assets to charity, calculated from interest rates and mortality tables at the time the annuity is created.

The IRS views the arrangement as being a bargain sale, meaning part-gift, part-sale treatment. Any basis and gain is allocated proportionally between the gift and sale portions of the CGA.

If the holder of an annuity from a CGA no longer needs the income, she may donate the right to some or all of the annuity payments. Even without contractual provisions restricting transfer of the income stream to a third party, the natural impulse for a potential donor would be to say to the charity, essentially "I do not need this, you have it all." However, in many cases, the agreement will include language restricting the transfer of the interest—to any party other than the charity. Thankfully, this simplifies the analysis by limiting the total number of parties involved to the original donor and the original CGA-issuing charity.

From the charity's perspective, the gift is easy to assess—it gets everything, since it was already due to get any amounts left following the donor's death. For the donor, the situation is not as clear. Although the donor will get a charitable deduction for the gift of the income interest, how to calculate the amount is less clear.

Unlike charitable remainder trusts, there is little in the way of IRS guidance on the tax consequences of assigning a donor interest in a CGA to charity. Based on applicable regulations, a portion of each annuity payment is ordinary income. For this reason, many commentators agree that the deduction may be less than the amount of the gift—likely the unreturned investment in the contract (which would be the adjusted cost basis). Some argue, however, that the interest is a capital asset and therefore can appreciate, which would mean that the deduction would be increased to gain plus adjusted cost basis.

Review Part 5: Bequest of an Income Interest in a Charitable Lead Trust

A charitable lead trust (CLT) is in many ways the reverse of a charitable remainder trust—the charity gets income for a term of years, with the remainder going to a third party. For this reason, existing income interests are not donated to charity. However, an income-generating asset may be suitable for a CLT, if the trust is created as part of a bequest. This would have the benefit of allowing an estate tax charitable deduction.

Like a remainder trust, the CLT can be an annuity (CLAT) or unitrust (CLUT). However, unlike the CRT, there are no minimum or maximum payout thresholds. This is appealing to both charities and donors, since it allows a significant degree of flexibility in planning. Very wealthy donors should be alerted to this gift transaction format, since it can be structured to remove assets from the estate and defer transfer to heirs. In particular, under certain conditions the CLT can be set up as a deferred generation-skipping transfer with no transfer tax regardless of value.

Review Part 6: Gift of an Income Interest in a Pooled-Income Fund

Like the other forms of split-interest gift, pooled-income funds (PIFs) involve an asset transfer and payment of income to the donors. The PIF is a trust that a public charity administers, and as its name suggests, pools donations (more often, donation proceeds), and provides the resulting income to donors. Those donors receive income in proportion to their interest in the pooled fund. On the death of the income beneficiaries for each interest, the charity receives the remainder. The donor receives a deduction on transfer in the present value of that remainder interest.

In the event that the donor decides to donate his income interest, the deduction will be similar to the other split-interest gifts. The tax deduction is equal to the present value of remaining income stream. For the charity, it will usually already be holding the assets and PIF; this donation would simply accelerate their ownership of the entire interest. Theoretically, a donor could donate its interest to a different charity, but the deduction would be the same. And a charity receiving income from an unrelated PIF would simply treat the amount like any other donated income stream, such as an annuity.

Charitable Gifts of Noncash Assets

Life Income Interests Advanced[1]

By Michael Parham

Below is an in-depth examination on gifts of life income interests. Life income interest topics are based on Michael Parham's "I Want It Now! Early Termination of Charitable Remainder Trusts." For quick take-aways on gifts of life income interests, see Life Income Interests Quick Take-aways. For a review based on that article, see Life Income Interests Intermediate. For an in-depth examination adapted and excerpted from the article, see Life Income Interests Advanced. For further details, see Life Income Interests Additional Resources.

Most other chapters in this book address noncash asset gifts which have a determinable value. The owners donate these assets to a qualifying nonprofit, and oftentimes receive an income stream in return—typically the asset-funded vehicle pays that amount through the income which the asset generates. Imagine instead if the donor already owned an income stream, meaning that the individual had a right or interest in receiving payments for some period of time. This period of time could be for a set number of years, or more likely, for life. What if the donor did not need the income interest, and decided to donate it to charity? How would the parties complete the gift?

This section examines a number of different types of income interest, including charitable remainder trusts, gift annuities, charitable lead trusts, and pooled-income funds. It discusses how they are structured, and how the donor and charity might go about completing the gift together. It also addresses the all-important tax aspects of these gifts.

Donation of Income Interests By Early Termination of Charitable Remainder Trusts

Quick Refresher—What is a Charitable Remainder Trust?

A charitable remainder trust is a trust that holds assets and pays an amount for a term of years or lifetime to an income recipient. The income recipient can be the person who donated the assets to the trust, the donor's spouse, or a third party. The donor receives a charitable income tax deduction at the time the trust is funded, and if the payments end at the donor's death, there is no estate tax liability. At the end of the trust term, whatever assets remain in the trust pass to charity. The donor can name the charity in the trust or can designate it in some other way.

---

1. This chapter excerpts and adapts Parham, M. (2009), "I Want It Now! Early Termination of Charitable Remainder Trusts," 13 *Journal of Gift Planning* 5, http://my.pppnet.org/library/000/000/23/s1.pdf.

The payments can be a set amount each year—either a fixed dollar amount or percentage of the value of the assets on transfer to the trust. This type of charitable remainder trust is known as a charitable remainder annuity trust (CRAT). The payments can also be based on the value of the trust assets as of a certain day each year. This type of charitable remainder trust is known as a charitable remainder unitrust (CRUT).

A third option is for the trust to pay the lesser of the net income or a fixed percentage of the trust assets as valued on a certain day each year. The trust can also contain a provision that allows for increased payments, if the income generated for a certain year exceeds the fixed percentage amount. This type of charitable remainder trust is known as a net income with make-up charitable remainder unitrust (NIMCRUT).

Another variation is the flip charitable remainder unitrust (FLIP-CRUT). In this case, the trust only begins operating as a CRUT following a predetermined trigger event. Typically, this will be the sale of the underlying asset placed in trust. After the trust receives the proceeds from sale, it distributes income to the named beneficiaries just as a normal CRUT would, and the nonprofit receives the remainder interest. See the case study in chapter 9 for an example of a FLIP-CRUT funded with an automobile.

Why Terminate Charitable Remainder Trusts Early

There are two basic motivations for terminating a charitable remainder trust early. The first is when the remainder charity needs money immediately. The assets contained in a charitable remainder trust are a good source of funds that a charity can tap without requiring the donor to write a check. The second case is when the income beneficiaries no longer need some or all of the income, or conversely, wish to receive their portion as a lump sum immediately. By terminating a NIMCRUT, a beneficiary who had only been receiving the net income from the trust each year could instead receive one lump-sum payment.

There are several tax issues related to the early termination of charitable remainder trusts. In addition, charitable remainder trusts are subject to the private foundation rules. Because of this, the rules relating to the termination of private foundations come into play.

Income tax issues include the value of the charitable deduction, if any, that the person terminating the trust will receive. If the person is going to receive a lump-sum payment, there is also the question of how the IRS will tax the payment: as ordinary income or capital gain. Gifts to charity qualify for the gift tax charitable deduction under Code Section 2522. When the parties terminate a trust, there is the question of whether this would generate any gift tax.

If the parties only terminate a portion of the trust, there is the question of whether the remainder of the trust would continue to qualify as a charitable remainder trust. Also, the private foundation rules bring up the questions of whether the partial termination would require payment of the excise tax under Code Section 507, whether the self-dealing rules under Code Section 4941 and following would apply, and whether the partial interest rule under Code Section 170(f) would be violated.

Different Ways to Terminate

There are two main ways to terminate a charitable remainder trust to donate the existing income interest, in part or in whole. For purposes of these materials, they will be referred to as total termination and partial termination. The parties to a charitable remainder trust can also terminate it on a pro rata basis, but this simply means that beneficiaries all receive the present value of their existing interest—so the charity is not actually receiving a gift of an income interest.

- Total termination refers to the situation where the donor or income beneficiary agrees with the trustee and charitable remainder beneficiaries to completely shut down the trust and distribute any remaining assets to the charities.
- Partial termination happens when the donor or income beneficiary agrees with the trustee and charitable remainder beneficiaries that only a portion of the trust will be terminated and that the remainder of the trust will continue to make payments as before. The partial termination means smaller distributions since a portion of the trust assets have been transferred to charity.

Total Termination

In 1986, the IRS issued Revenue Ruling 86-60, which subsequent private letter rulings frequently reference in dealing with terminations of charitable remainder trusts.[2] To qualify for the deductions, the donors must either relinquish or exercise any discretionary powers they may hold. For example, if the donor has the power to change the charitable remainder beneficiary, he will have

---

2. Revenue Rulings and Private Letter Rulings addressing total termination include: Rev. Rul 86-60, Private Letter Ruling 9529039 (April 28, 1995), Private Letter Ruling 9721014 (February 19, 1997), Private Letter Ruling 200152018 (September 26, 2001) (CRT terminated in exchange for gift annuity), Private Letter Ruling 200633011 (April 14, 2006), Private Letter Ruling 200631006 (April 14, 2006), and Private Letter Ruling 200802024 (September 14, 2007).

to irrevocably name a charity as the beneficiary. If he has the power to revoke the income interest of a successor income beneficiary, he will have to exercise this power.

What kind of income tax deduction will there be? Depending on how much the value of assets in the trust appreciate and what the 7520 rate will be at the time the donors terminate the trust, the combined value of the two deductions could total more than the amount of the original gift.[3]

A wrinkle on this method was set forth in Private Letter Ruling 200152018. In this case, the donor (Taxpayer) established a CRUT with trust assets distributed to Academy upon Taxpayer's death. Later, Taxpayer proposed to transfer his unitrust interest in the trust to Academy in exchange for a charitable gift annuity. The IRS approved this transaction, with some interesting tax results.

The IRS ruled that Taxpayer would be entitled to a charitable income tax deduction to the extent that the present value of Taxpayer's unitrust interest on the transfer date exceeded the present value of the annuity payments made by Academy on the same date. It also allowed a charitable gift tax deduction on the excess value of the unitrust interest on the date of transfer over the value of the annuity payments on the date of transfer.

However, the IRS ruled that upon the transfer of his unitrust interest in the trust to Academy in exchange for the annuity, the Taxpayer would have long-term capital gain in the amount of the value of the annuity. In other words, the Service would treat termination of the CRUT in exchange for the gift annuity as a sale of a capital asset (although undistributed capital gains on trust assets were not included in income). The Taxpayer's basis would be deemed zero pursuant to Code section 1001(e)(1).

Partial Termination

Termination of a charitable remainder trust does not have to be an all-or-nothing deal. The IRS has allowed the partial termination of a trust which would allow for the donation to charity of a portion of a charitable remainder trust, with the balance continuing as before.[4] By terminating a portion of

---

3. For example, if Donor established a one-life CRAT at age 75 with $1 million with a 5 percent payout with a 7520 rate of 4.2 percent, his charitable income tax deduction would be $594,680. If he transferred his remaining annuity interest to charity five years later, at age 80, assuming that the current balance of the CRAT was $750,000 and the 7520 rate was still 4.2 percent, his charitable deduction would then be $244,807. Between the two contributions, he would receive a total of $839,487 in charitable income tax deductions. In the meantime, he had received $250,000 in payouts.
4. Private Letter Rulings addressing total termination include: Private Letter Ruling 8805024 (November 5, 1987), Private Letter Ruling 9550026 (September 18, 1995), Private Letter Ruling 200140027 (June 29, 2001), Private Letter Ruling 200205008 (February 1,

the charitable remainder trust, the charity who was the remainder beneficiary received immediate dollars.

The partial terminations are carried out in two basic ways. One method is for the donor to assign an undivided percentage of the trust to the charity. Another method is to divide the trust into two separate trusts with the donor then disclaiming the unitrust interest. Both methods are discussed in this section.

Assignment Method

A good example of the "assignment" method is Private Letter Ruling 9550026. In this case, a married couple were the income beneficiaries of a NIMCRUT which made unitrust payments to the husband and wife jointly and would continue to make payments to the survivor of them. Upon the death of the survivor, the trust would distribute its assets to University. Each spouse had the right by will to revoke the other spouse's interest in trust as to his or her community property interest in the trust.

Six years after establishment of the trust, University needed ready cash, so the couple proposed to make a gift of a 20 percent undivided partial interest in the unitrust payment to University. Each spouse would disclaim his or her contingent right to receive the other's unitrust interest after the spouse's death by executing a valid disclaimer. Then, the couple would make a gift of a 20 percent undivided interest in the unitrust payment to University by execution and delivery of an irrevocable assignment valid under state law. The gifted 20 percent interest would merge with the remainder interest, leaving University with a 20 percent undivided interest in the entire trust assets, and an undivided remainder interest in the other 80 percent of the trust.

The IRS ruled that the couple were entitled to charitable income and gift tax deductions for the value of the undivided interest in the unitrust payment transferred to University. The IRS stated that although the couple did not contribute their entire interest in the property, the gift still qualified as an undivided portion of the entire interest since they contributed 20 percent of their income interest in the trust. The IRS also said that the taxpayers' statement that they did not divide their interest in the property to avoid the partial interest rules was creditable, in part because of the six-year period between their creation of the trust and the proposed contribution.

2002), Private Letter Ruling 200207026 (February 26, 2002), Private Letter Ruling 200524014 (June 17, 2005), Private Letter Ruling 200525008 (June 24, 2005), and Private Letter Ruling 200808018 (February 22, 2008).

In addition, the IRS ruled that the gift of the undivided partial interest in the unitrust would not disqualify the trust as a unitrust. Also, they ruled that the couple would not realize capital gain and that the value of the gift under Code Section 170 (for income tax purposes) and Section 2522 (for gift tax purposes) would be the present value of the right to receive annual payments per the terms of the trust.

Division Method

A good example of the "division" method is found in Private Letter Ruling 200140027. Taxpayer had established a standard unitrust which provided that on the death of the Taxpayer, the trustee was to distribute all principal and income of the trust among certain charities it named. However, Taxpayer reserved the right to change the amounts or percentages which the trust would distribute or could designate other charitable organizations for distributions.

The trustee proposed to divide the trust into two separate trusts, Trust A and Trust B, on a fractional basis of 85 percent and 15 percent respectively. The provisions of the trust would govern both Trust A and Trust B. Taxpayer would irrevocably designate a charity as the remainder beneficiary of Trust B. Taxpayer would then assign to the charity his unitrust interest in the assets segregated as Trust B.

Under local law, Taxpayer's release of his unitrust interest accelerated the charity's succeeding interest. Under state law, the segregation of assets into Trust B, the designation of charity as the remainder beneficiary of Trust B, and the assignment to charity of the unitrust interest in Trust B would result in a merger of the unitrust and remainder interests in Trust B. Hence, the charity would be entitled to an outright distribution of the Trust B corpus.

The IRS allowed a charitable deduction and stated that the value of the gift would be the present value of the right to receive unitrust payments. Upon the irrevocable designation, the Taxpayer's transfer of the remainder in Trust B became a completed gift. The Service allowed a charitable gift tax deduction, because the Taxpayer's transfer to charity was a transfer, not in trust, of every interest and right the Taxpayer owned in the property. Finally, the IRS ruled that although Trust B terminated, Trust A would continue to qualify as a charitable remainder unitrust.

Self-Dealing

Charitable remainder trusts are subject to the same rules as private foundations. One of those rules is the one against "self-dealing." Before the IRS will approve, they must determine whether the early termination could result in a greater allocation of trust assets to the income beneficiary, to the detriment of the charitable beneficiary, than would a termination at the income beneficiary's death as the trust agreement provides.

The IRS will not allow early termination unless the donors can show that the early termination cannot be reasonably expected to cause the charity to receive less than it would have if the trust had remained in effect for the duration. Although there is no way to answer this question definitively, the IRS has stated that the question can still be answered in a positive manner. To do this, the income beneficiary must demonstrate he has no knowledge of a medical condition or other circumstance likely to result in a shorter life expectancy than that set forth in Table V of Section 1.72-9 of the Regulations.[5]

In a number of Private Letter Rulings, the income beneficiaries provided sworn evidence that they had no physical condition that would cause them to have a shorter than normal life expectancy. Affidavits of this type appear in all of the relevant Private Letter Rulings. Basically, the income beneficiary has to be in decent health. If the income beneficiary has, or has had, any condition that could shorten his or her life expectancy, then the IRS will not allow early termination with a pro rata distribution. The penalty for early termination that does not meet IRS approval would be the enforcement of a "termination tax." Code Section 507 imposes the termination tax on certain private foundation terminations.

Private Letter Ruling 200324035 stated, in language that has been repeated in later Private Letter Rulings, that the donor's proposed early termination would not constitute an act of self-dealing because all of the following factors were present: state law allowed the early termination; all beneficiaries favored the early termination; the trustees would use the regulations formula for determining the present values of the income and remainder interests in a charitable remainder trust; the income beneficiaries' physicians had conducted examinations of the income beneficiaries and stated under penalty of perjury that they found no medical conditions expected to result in shorter than average longevity (under Section 1.72-9); the income beneficiaries had signed similar statements; and any distribution of assets in kind would be made in a pro rata manner.[6]

---

5. 26 C.F.R. 1.72-9
6. Here is a list of Private Letter Rulings that deal with pro rata distribution: (standard valuation) – 200127023 (July 6, 2001), 200314021 (April 4, 2003), 200324035 (June 13, 2003), 200403051 (January 16, 2004), 200616035 (April 21, 2006), (NIMCRUTs—old valuation method) – 200208039 (November 29, 2001), 200304025 (January 24, 2003) (distribution of portion of trust with continuation of remainder), 200310024 (December 12, 2002), 200408031 (November 25, 2003), 200525014 (June 24, 2005) (later revoked by Private Letter Ruling 200614032 (April 7, 2006)), (NIMCRUTs—new valuation method) – 200725044 (June 22, 2007), 200733014 (August 17, 2007), 200817039 (April 25, 2008), and 200833012 (August 15, 2008).

Early Termination of Charitable QTIP Trust

A charitable QTIP trust for married couples can be more flexible than charitable remainder trust planning. A charitable QTIP is simply a QTIP trust that has a charity as the remainder beneficiary. A spouse can establish it either during life or at death for the benefit of the other spouse. The trust pays no less than the net income to the spouse for life. It could also contain a provision for distribution of principal to the spouse in the trustee's discretion. The trust would meet all the rules to qualify as a QTIP trust, but does not have to qualify as a charitable remainder trust, because the trust qualifies for both the unlimited marital deduction during the spouse's life and the charitable deduction at the spouse's death.[7]

An example may be helpful. Decedent died, survived by Spouse. During her life, Decedent and Spouse transferred their respective 50 percent interests in certain community property to a revocable trust which terminated on Decedent's death. On termination of the trust, Decedent's 50 percent interest in the trust passed to Trust B, a trust which Decedent created during her lifetime. Under Decedent's will, the residue of her estate was likewise distributable to Trust B.

Trust B provided that the trustee was to distribute the trust residue to a "Marital Trust." However, there was a provision that any part of the Marital Trust for which the trustee did not make a QTIP election would pass to a third trust (Trust C).

Under the terms of the Marital Trust, Spouse was to receive for his life the net income of the trust and as much principal as the trustee distributed in the trustee's discretion for the Spouse's support and medical care. On Spouse's death, the trust would distribute certain tangible assets to designated persons and organizations, with the balance of the Marital Trust property passing to charity.

Spouse was the trustee of the Marital Trust as well as executor of Decedent's estate. The Spouse proposed that he, as trustee of the Marital Trust, petition the local probate court for an order dividing the Marital Trust into two trusts, Marital Trust 1 and Marital Trust 2. In all respects, the terms of Marital Trust 1 and Marital Trust 2 would be identical to the terms of the Marital Trust. Marital Trust 1 would receive all tangible personal property, all of the business, and possibly some cash and marketable securities.

---

7. There are two Private Letter Rulings that deal with the early termination of a portion of a Charitable QTIP: 200122025 (June 1, 2001) and 200438028 (September 17, 2004).

Marital Trust 2 would receive only publicly traded securities and cash. The division order would not transfer a fractional interest in any asset to Marital Trust 2. The Spouse would make a QTIP election over all property of Marital Trust 1 and Marital Trust 2.

The court order would provide that if Spouse transferred his income interest in Marital Trust 2 to charity, that Marital Trust 2 would terminate and the Marital Trust 2 property would be distributed outright to charity. Accordingly, Spouse would then give his income interest in Marital Trust 2 to charity.

The IRS ruled as follows:

1. For estate tax purposes, the court's division of the Marital Trust into two trusts funded with specific assets would not make either Marital Trust 1 or Marital Trust 2 ineligible for Spouse's QTIP election.

2. For estate tax purposes, both Marital Trust 1 and Marital Trust 2 were eligible for the QTIP election, and would not lose eligibility as a result of the court order authorizing Spouse to make a gift of his income interest in Marital Trust 2 to charity.

3. For gift tax purposes, Spouse's gift of his income interest in Marital Trust 2 qualifies for the gift tax charitable deduction.

4. For gift tax purposes, the Spouse would be treated as making a gift of the remainder interest in Marital Trust 2 when he makes a gift of his income interest in Marital Trust 2 and Spouse's gift of the remainder interest would qualify for the gift tax charitable deduction.

5. For gift tax purposes, Spouse's gift of his income interest in Marital Trust 2 would not result in gift tax treatment of any part of Marital Trust 1.

6. For income tax purposes, Spouse's gift of his income interest in Marital Trust 2 would qualify for an income tax charitable deduction.

The IRS also ruled that dividing the Marital Trust into Marital Trust 1 and Marital Trust 2 and contributing the spouse's interest in Marital Trust 2 was not a transfer of a fractional interest, but was a transfer of an undivided portion of his entire interest in the Marital Trust.

Charitable Gift Annuities Structure and Timing

When considering donations of income interests in charitable gift annuities, there is one key structural consideration. CGAs usually make distributions for the lifetime of one or two annuitants, although income for a term of years can be contractually arranged with a "commuted" annuity that squeezes lifetime payments into a shorter time period.[8] Regardless of whether there are one or two annuitants, the CGA has a basis which regulations allocate between gift and sale portion (meaning it gets bargain sale treatment). The gift amount creates the immediate tax deduction, while the sale portion is deductible only if and when the annuitant gives income to charity.[9]

To qualify as a CGA, the agreement must leave at least ten percent of the present value of contributed assets to charity.[10] The American Council on Gift Annuities recommends rates that leave a projected average of 50 percent to charity.[11] The charity calculates present value based on interest rates and mortality tables at the time the parties create the annuity. Regulations exist in the form of state securities and insurance laws, as well as best practices and guidance that the ACGA publishes. These regulations and guidelines typically mean that the donor should utilize a qualified advisor's services in creating a CGA.

Donation of Charitable Gift Annuity Income Interest

Oftentimes, the CGA contract will limit the ability of the annuitant to transfer or otherwise assign the income interest to any party other than the charity. This makes the donation of the income interest somewhat simpler, since there is only one possible charitable recipient. Of course, an annuitant could simply donate annuity distributions as she receives them, and then deduct the donated amounts. However, this is a somewhat clunky arrangement and, and the donor would have to repeat it with each year's tax return. Hence many donors would prefer to simply donate the entire interest.

Donation of the CGA income stream is simple from the recipient charity's point of view. It gets to keep whatever funds were left. This means the unreturned amounts of the initial contribution, along with any excess amount the annuity generated (interest, dividends, appreciation).

To complete the transaction, the charity should first enter into an agreement with the donor, and then give the donor written acknowledgement of the donation.[12] The parties should

---

8. Kallina II, E.J. and Koenig, E. (2010), "Gift of an Income Interest in a Charitable Gift Annuity," Partnership for Philanthropic Planning 1, https://www.charitableplanning.com/library/documents/1791195.
9. Id. at 2.
10. Id.
11. See the American Council on Gift Annuities, "Gift Annuity Rates," http://www.acga-web.org/gift-annuity-rates (describing rates and underlying assumptions).
12. Memorandum from J. Thomas MacFarlane, Esq. to the Council on Michigan Foundations at 2 (July 14, 2009), https://www.michiganfoundations.org/sites/default/files/resources/Legal%20Opinion_Termination%20of%20CGA%20Contract%20Payments.pdf.

reduce the agreement to writing with the donor assenting to the termination of payments and acknowledging that the charity will retain the remaining amounts. The acknowledgement should contain the present value of the annuity payments, and should indicate that regulations may limit the donor's deduction to unreturned investment (which typically should be lower than the present value).

As the charity's acknowledgement suggests, the donor and former annuitant's calculation of her tax deduction is less clear. Although a deduction is certainly available, the IRS has not clearly established which amounts the donor should consider including.[13] It is tempting to simply treat the deduction the same way as a gift of a CRT income interest, but the IRS views annuity income amounts differently. The Service treats portions of the distributions above the donor's proportionate basis as ordinary income.[14] As a result, many advisors will limit donor deductions to unreturned investment in the contract.

Despite this limitation, Tax Court holdings have long held that annuity contracts are capital assets, which suggests the deduction may be more than simply unreturned investment.[15] Indeed, "a portion of the increase in the FMV of the annuity may be attributable to factors other than the accrual of interest or a buildup in the underlying value of the annuity."[16] These include changes to interest rates, mortality assumptions, credit condition, and other external factors. Arguably the donors should characterize these amounts as capital gain; donors should consult with their tax advisors to determine the appropriate deductible amounts.

Bequest of Income Interest in a Charitable Lead Trust

A charitable lead trust (CLT) is similar to a CRT, but with the donor and charity reversing roles. As a result, there is no lifetime income interest for the donor to contribute—the charity already is the income beneficiary. This means that to donate an income interest, the setup must be different than with CRTs or CGAs.

From the charity's perspective, it should approach donors with a proposal for a bequest that creates a CLT, ideally funding the trust with income-producing assets. Very wealthy donors in particular may be amenable to this gift structure, for two important reasons. First, CLTs remove assets

---

13. Fogt, A. (October, 2013), "Turning Planned Gifts in Current Dollars," Partnership for Philanthropic Planning 9, http://my.pppnet.org/library/85161/1/NCPP13_Fogt.pdf.
14. Kallina II, E.J. and Koenig, E. at 2.
15. Id. at 3.
16. Id. at 2.

from the estate, which lowers the estate tax by creating a tax deduction.[17] Secondly, the assets in the remainder can pass to the CLT's named beneficiaries (typically the donor's heirs) tax free. Indeed, the Waltons use CLTs for this purpose, as did the late Jacqueline Kennedy Onassis.[18]

The charity should work with the donor to create the CLT in the donor's will, putting it either in annuity or unitrust form (CLAT or CLUT—again similar to remainder trusts). The term of the trust should generally run for 10, 15, or 20 years.[19] The charity will receive annuity payments for that time period, either in a set dollar amount or as a set percentage amount. Unlike CRTs, the CLT does not have any minimum or maximum payout requirements. Nonetheless, the trust will still owe the charity annuity payments of some sort, so the asset will either need to be income-producing or the trustee must sell and reinvest it. In both cases, the donor will likely want trust assets to produce a return that beats the governmental applicable federal rate (AFR). Arranged correctly, with favorable interest rates and sufficient appreciation, the CLT can be a winning vehicle for all parties involved.

Pooled-Income Funds

The oft-ignored pooled-income fund (PIF) is another possible source for donations of income interests. In some ways, it may actually be better suited to donation than the others discussed above. PIFs are a split-interest gift, where the donor transfers underlying assets to a public charity. The charity pools those assets together with others donated to the fund, splitting management costs and income produced proportionally among members of the PIF.[20] On the death of each beneficiary, their proportionate remainder passes to the charity. Donors receive a tax deduction when they first transfer the assets for the present value of the projected remainder interest—calculated from the beneficiary's actuarially-determined remaining lifespan.

If a donor decides he no longer needs the income interest, one option is to donate the income outright.[21] PIF income interests have a significant advantage here, particularly over CGAs—the income interest is a capital asset with zero basis. This means that the income tax deduction the donor receives will be the full present value of the interest minus the deduction he already took.

---

17. Toce Jr., J.P. et al, Tax Economics of Charitable Giving, 26-8 – 26-12 (2003).
18. Mider, Z.R. (September 11, 2013), "How Wal-Mart's Waltons Maintain Their Billionaire Fortune: Taxes," Bloomberg, http://www.bloomberg.com/news/articles/2013-09-12/how-wal-mart-s-waltons-maintain-their-billionaire-fortune-taxes.
19. Houston, M. (May 11, 2000), "The Charitable Lead Trust: Don't Forget the Donor!," Planned Giving Design Center, http://www.pgdc.com/pgdc/charitable-lead-trust-dont-forget-donor.
20. Newman, D.W. (May 5, 2003), "Pooled-Income Fund," Planned Giving Design Center, http://www.pgdc.com/pgdc/pooled-income-fund.
21. Newman, D.W. (January 8, 2000), "Terminating a Pooled-Income Fund," Planned Giving Design Center, http://www.pgdc.com/pgdc/terminating-pooled-income-fund.

The charity will likely need to enter into a written agreement with the donor, and provide an acknowledgement, as described for CGA income donations above. The charity will then own the donor's interest in the PIF outright via the income and remainder interests merging.

Of course, rather than an outright gift of the income interest, the donor may want a differently structured income stream—either in CRT or CGA form.[22] A CRT may be impractical from the charity's perspective, since PIFs tend to have lower account values than CRTs. This may make it difficult to justify administrating a CRT which the donor funds with income from a PIF.

However, a CGA may work. One major hurdle to converting the income from a PIF to a CGA is that the recommended ACGA rates (discussed above) will result in a significant drop in income for donors. As a result, the charity may need to issue the CGA at rates much higher than the ACGA recommends. The charity must carefully weigh whether it can depart from normal CGA best practices, and whether it is advisable to do so given the risk. However, in the event that the charity does issue a CGA or even CRT, it must comply with normal regulations on those planned giving vehicles.

---

22. Id.

Life Income Assets

Life Income Interests   Additional Resources

Below are further details on gifts of life income interests. Life income interest topics are based on Michael Parham's "I Want It Now! Early Termination of Charitable Remainder Trusts." For quick take-aways on gifts of life income interests, see Life Income Interests Quick Take-aways. For a review based on that article, see Life Income Interests Intermediate. For an in-depth examination adapted and excerpted from the article, see Life Income Interests Advanced. For further details, see Life Income Interests Additional Resources.

For a discussion of practical considerations pertaining to early termination, see Fogt, A. (October, 2013), "Turning Planned Gifts in Current Dollars," Partnership for Philanthropic Planning 9, http://my.pppnet.org/library/85161/1/NCPP13_Fogt.pdf.

For a broad analysis of many remainder trust and gift annuity issues, see Teitell, C. (2010), "Charitable Giving Tax Pitfalls: Avoiding; Climbing Out; Cyanide Capsule?," Partnership for Philanthropic Planning, http://my.pppnet.org/library/41711/1/NCPP2010_teitell.pdf.

For a legal examination of the termination of charitable gift annuities, see J. Thomas MacFarlane, Esq. to the Council on Michigan Foundations (July 14, 2009), https://www.michiganfoundations.org/sites/default/files/resources/Legal%20Opinion_Termination%20of%20CGA%20Contract%20Payments.pdf.

For a discussion of remainder trust administration and early termination, see Katzenstein, L. (2012), "Charitable Remainder Trusts: Charity Can Begin at Home," American Bar Association, http://www.americanbar.org/content/dam/aba/events/real_property_trust_estate/step/2012/materials/rpte_step_2012_07_13_Katzenstein_01_CRATs_and_CRUTs.authcheckdam.pdf.

For analysis of recent legislative changes to early termination of NICRUTs and NIMCRUTs, see Fox, R.L. (January 25, 2016), "Protecting Americans from Tax Hikes (PATH) Act of 2015 Amends IRC Section 664(e) to Disregard Net Income Limitation Upon Early Termination of NICRUTs and NIMCRUTs; Long-Awaited Change Negates IRS Ruling Position," Planned Giving Design Center, http://www.pgdc.com/pgdc/protecting-americans-tax-hikes-path-act-2015-amends-irc-section-664e-disregard-income-limitatio.

IRC § 170(f)(2)(B) (allowing income tax deductions for gifts of certain income interests)

IRC § 2522(c) (allowing gift tax deductions for transfers of interests in the form of remainder interests or annuities)

Rev. Rul. 86-60, 1986-1 C.B. 302 (approving a deduction after assignment of a lifetime CRAT income interest to charity)

Private Letter Ruling 200140027 (approving proposed division of income interest in CRT and assignment to charitable remainderman)

Private Letter Ruling 200438028 (approving early termination of a charitable QTIP)

Estate of Washburn, 11 Cal.App. 735 (Cal. Ct. App. 1909) (discussion of merger doctrine)

Appendix

- Valuation, Appraisals, and Substantiation

- Charitable Estate Settlement

- At Least a Day Late and Perhaps Many Dollars Short – The Top Seven Post-Transaction Creative Charitable Planning Ideas

- Unique Gift Annuity Planning Opportunities with S-Corp Stock and Real Estate

Appendix A:
Valuation, Appraisals, and Substantiation[1]

By Russell James III

To begin the topic of valuing charitable gifts of property, consider why this topic is so important. The vast majority of wealth in this country is not held in cash, savings accounts, checking accounts, or money market accounts. Consequently, if fundraisers wish to ask for gifts of wealth, then, generally they must ask for gifts of property. In other words, if fundraisers want to ask from the "big bucket" of wealth, then they need to ask for gifts of property, meaning any type of noncash asset. A fundamental requirement is an understanding of how such gifts are valued for tax purposes. Correspondingly, donors and their advisors must evaluate whether these gifts will achieve the charitable goals in an optimized way. As described below, this is no small issue.

Different types of assets in various types of transactions may generate dramatically differently values for taxation purposes. To learn how to ask for noncash gifts, it is essential to have a basic understanding of how property gifts are valued. A fundraiser or advisor who suggests a charitable gift of property—while being unaware that the deduction in that particular case would be far less than the value of the property—is creating serious potential problems. For the same reason, the donor will want to know exactly what sort of tax benefit she will receive. This reading reviews the rules for valuing charitable gifts of property.

Charities, donors, and their advisors may only be familiar with cash gifts to charity, so the valuation issues may be new. Cash gifts include all cash equivalent transactions such as checks, currency, or credit cards. Gifts of cash require no valuation. The value is simply the amount of the gift. Because the valuation is simple, calculating the deduction is also simple. Although cash gifts are simple, the donor rarely holds the bulk of her wealth in cash. Understanding gifts of noncash assets opens up the possibility for many more sophisticated and beneficial conversations with donors.

The simplicity of valuation with cash or cash equivalent gifts contrasts with the complexity of valuing several kinds of property gifts. An initial cause of this complexity may come from the difficulty inherent in valuing certain property types. Additionally, there are special tax rules for

---

1. This reading is an adaptation of James III, R. (October 7, 2015), "Visual Planned Giving: An Introduction to the Law and Taxation of Charitable Gift Planning," Chp. 5: Valuing Charitable Gifts of Property, parts 1 and 2, http://www.pgdc.com/pgdc/5-valuing-charitable-gifts-property-part-1-2; http://www.pgdc.com/pgdc/5-valuing-charitable-gifts-property-part-2-2.

charitable gifts of certain kinds of property which can themselves alter the valuation of the property for tax purposes.

These rules have at times been put in place to curb abuses of the charitable gift tax deduction. Because Congress and the IRS created many of these rules in a reactive fashion—responding to particular individual abuses—it has resulted in a hodgepodge of rules that are not always consistent. Consequently, because so many specialized exceptions have arisen over the years, it is not always enough to know a single approach to the valuation of charitable gifts of property. Nevertheless, there are some general principles that apply to most gifts of property.

Property Valuation Overview

Despite the variety of rules and exceptions, the most typical valuations fall into three categories.[2] With a few exceptions, the value for tax deduction purposes of a charitable gift of property will be (1) the fair market value of the property, (2) the cost basis of the property (only where such basis is less than the fair market value), or (3) nothing. Notice that the most advantageous valuation that a donor can receive under any circumstances is the fair market value of property.

Donors almost universally expect that the charitable gift will generate a charitable deduction equivalent to the value of the property, but those three categories show that is simply not the case. Asking for property gifts that generate no deduction or a much reduced deduction without understanding that reality in advance places the fundraiser or advisor in a highly unfavorable position. Thus, as a prerequisite to suggesting charitable transactions involving property, the fundraiser or advisor must be familiar with the rules for deducting such property gifts to avoid embarrassment, financial loss, and broken relationships.

One of the common valuation options for charitable gifts of property is the property's "cost basis," or what tax professionals refer to more technically as "adjusted basis." The term cost basis is used here because, in most cases, the adjusted basis is simply the amount the donor paid for the item (i.e., its cost to the donor). So, if a donor paid $100 for an item that is now worth $200, the deduction for giving that item to charity will be $100 if the gift's value is based on its cost basis.

Note that the cost basis valuation of charitable gifts of property is not used when the cost basis is greater than the property's fair market value. Cost basis valuation of gifts of property can only

---

2. For a general guide to IRS valuation and appraisal rules, see IRS Publication 561 (April 2007), Determining the Value of Donated Property, https://www.irs.gov/publications/p561/index.html.

lower the gift's value compared with its fair market value, not raise it. The property's cost basis can include other items besides the initial purchase price. For example, if a person purchases a house for $100,000 and then spends $30,000 on an addition to the house, his basis in the home is $130,000. So, the basis of a property includes both its initial purchase price and any subsequent capital expenditures.

Calculating the basis of property becomes more complex if it involves depreciation deductions. Not all property is subject to depreciation deductions. However, this is common with property the donor used for business purposes. A depreciation deduction allows a person to claim that the property has become less valuable, because it is wearing out. For example, if someone purchases a $5,000 computer for her business, she can claim that after one year of use the computer is worth $4,000. Consequently, she will have a depreciation deduction of $1,000. She can do this for each of the first five years that she uses the computer in her business until, after five years, she has completely depreciated it. If after five years she has taken depreciation deductions of $5,000, her basis is $0.

Depreciation deductions affect charitable deductions for gifts of property, because a taxpayer cannot deduct the same item twice. So, if a $5,000 computer purchase has already generated $5,000 of depreciation deductions, the taxpayer cannot then give it to charity and generate another $2,000 deduction (even if it is truly worth $2,000). As a result, any depreciation deductions that the donor has already taken may reduce the value of property for purposes of determining the charitable deduction. If it is real property, however, the donor still may take a fair market value deduction even if the property has been depreciated, assuming a straight line schedule. Of course, donors cannot depreciate all property—it is not a concern in most property gift transactions. But, it is an important concept to keep in mind for those cases when it does arise (primarily physical items used in business operations).

Charitable gifts of property can also be given their current "fair market value." The IRS indicates that fair market value is the price that property would sell for on the open market. It is the price that a willing buyer and a willing seller would agree on, with neither being required to act, and both having reasonable knowledge of the relevant facts. It is easiest to think of fair market value as simply the answer to the question, "What could you normally sell it for?" or, "What is it worth?"

When valuing an item of property to be given as a charitable gift, the initial issue is, for almost all transactions, "Which of these three valuation approaches apply?" How will the item be valued for purposes of the charitable tax deduction? Will the donor be able to deduct its fair market value, its basis, or nothing at all? The next section reviews the basic framework that determines which of these deduction amounts the donor can use.

Determining Deduction Amounts

When property sales proceeds would be ordinary income if the donor had sold the property (rather than given it to a charity), then the donor may deduct only his or her basis in the property. For example, if a cobbler received $100 for selling a pair of his shoes, this money is ordinary income. Selling shoes is his ordinary business. If the cobbler gave a pair of shoes that normally sells for $100 to a charity, the IRS limits his deduction to his cost basis in the shoes (i.e., cost of materials). Similarly, if an artist painted a painting and gave it to a charity, her deduction would be the cost of the canvas and paint she used in the painting. Just as with the cobbler selling shoes, if the artist had sold the painting, the IRS would tax the money from the sale as ordinary income to the artist.

The cost basis valuation also applies to any property the donor held for one year or less. If the donor sold this property for a profit, that profit would have been short-term capital gain. The IRS values all such short-term capital gain property at its basis for purposes of the charitable deduction. Any property that generates a loss on sale would not be valued at its basis because, in that case, the basis would be higher than the fair market value. The IRS never allows the donor to use basis for valuation if it is higher than fair market value.

The only type of noncash property that may receive fair market value for a charitable deduction is long-term capital gain property. Start with the assumption that long-term capital gain property can be valued at its fair market value for charitable tax deduction purposes. However, several circumstances can cause long-term capital gain property to instead have cost basis valuation.

The first scenario where long-term capital gain property would be subject to cost basis deduction is if the property is given to a private foundation, rather than to a public charity. Although here there is an exception to the exception, because if the gift is "qualified stock," defined as publicly traded stock, then the donor can still deduct it at fair market value. Another reason that long-term capital gain property does not receive fair market value treatment for tax deduction purposes is if the donor has made a "special election" to accept the lower valuation in exchange for a higher charitable deduction income limitation.

A third circumstance when long-term capital gain property receives cost basis treatment is when it is "unrelated use" tangible personal property.[3] "Unrelated use" tangible personal property is property that the charity does not intend to use in furtherance of its charitable purposes. If, for example, the charity intends to simply sell the gifted item, then the item is "unrelated use" property. Note that this is true even though the charity will use cash from the sale of the item to further the charitable purposes of the organization.

Capital Loss Property

Capital loss property is property that is worth less at its sale than the owner originally paid for it. In that case, the fair market value would be less than the cost basis of the property. If the fair market value is less than the cost basis of the property, then the donor cannot deduct the fair market value regardless of what kind of property he gives. If the donor is contributing loss property, short-term or long-term makes no difference for gift valuation.

In practice, donors should likely never give capital loss property. Instead they should realize the loss and deduct it upon the sale of the property. For example, if a donor bought a share of stock for $110 and it is now worth $10, it is better for the donor to sell the share and then give the proceeds to charity, rather than to give the share directly to the charity. If he sells the share, he will recognize a loss of $100 ($110 purchase price less the $10 sale price). This loss can offset other gains that he might otherwise have to recognize. But if he gives the share directly to a charity, he loses the ability to recognize that loss, and so he loses a valuable tax benefit. The charitable tax deduction is the same whether he gives the share directly to the charity or sells the share and then gives the proceeds to the charity (i.e., $10).

Appraisal Considerations[4]

The best way to minimize valuation problems is to employ a professional appraiser who follows guidelines set forth in IRS Publication 561, "Determining the Value of Donated Property." These guidelines require appraisals to include references to sales of comparable items, such as other works by the same artist, as well as some statement regarding the present market in the type of item being appraised. They also limit who can act as an appraiser in this context. The first requirement is that the appraiser must have an appraisal designation from a recognized professional

---

3. It is easiest to think of tangible personal property as movable physical property. This would not include immovable real estate such as land or anything permanently attached to the land, like a building, or intangible personal property, such as shares of stock or bonds.
4. This section was written by Armen Vartian ("Charitable Donations of Art and Collectibles" (2016) (on file with author)).

appraiser organization, or otherwise must have met certain minimum education and experience requirements. The second requirement is that they must have demonstrated verifiable education and experience in valuing specific type of property in question.

A dealer from whom a collector purchased the item in question, any expert who derives 50 percent of his appraisal income from appraisals for the collector or the charity, and any family member of such persons cannot perform appraisals for tax purposes. Make sure the appraiser applies USPAP, the Uniform Standards of Professional Appraisal Practice. Under IRS Notice 2006-96, the IRS recognizes this standard, "…[t]he Appraisal will be treated as satisfying generally accepted appraisal standards if, for example, the appraisal is consistent with substance and principles of USPAP."[5] Additionally, the appraiser must also be aware of the extra IRS requirements for charitable contribution appraisal reports that are required in addition to the USPAP requirements.

Applications

Consider some examples that demonstrate how these rules function with specific gifts:

Stock: Suppose that a donor owns a share of closely held C corporation stock that he paid one dollar for in 1990, which today is worth $25. He gives that share of stock to a public charity. How much could he deduct for that charitable gift? Notice that the stock is long-term capital gain property. Why? First, it has appreciated in value, therefore, so it is gain property. Second, the donor has owned it since 1990. This means he has owned it for more than 12 months and, therefore, it is long-term capital property.

Because it is long-term capital gain property, this means that the donor can deduct its fair market value (in this case, $25), unless one of the three exceptions applies. In this case, none of the three exceptions apply. The donor is not giving the property to a private foundation, but instead is giving it to a public charity. The donor has not made a special election to reduce the valuation, so that exception does not apply. And finally, this is intangible personal property, therefore, the third exception, which relates to tangible personal property, does not apply. Because none of the three exceptions apply, the donor can deduct this gift at its fair market value of $25.

Farmland: Now suppose the donor has farmland that he purchased for $600 an acre in 1990, which is now worth $1,800 an acre. He contributes this farmland as a gift to a private foundation. How much per acre can he deduct for this gift? As before, we begin by recognizing that this is long-term

---

5. Notice 2006-96, 2006-46 I.R.B. 902.

capital gain property. First, it has enjoyed capital appreciation. Second, the donor has owned it for more than 12 months.

Because this is long-term capital gain property, the donor can normally deduct its fair market value, unless one of the exceptions applies. The donor has not made a special election to lower his gift's valuation, so that exception does not apply. Similarly, this is not tangible personal property—it is real property. Therefore, the tangible personal property exception does not apply either. However, the donor has made this gift to a private foundation. Consequently, he will not be able to deduct its fair market value, unless it is "qualified stock." Clearly, this is not stock, it is real property. So, this exception to the exception is not relevant. As a result of making this gift to a private foundation (since it is not "qualified stock"), the donor's deduction for the charitable gift of land will be statutorily limited to cost basis. In this case, that means that the donor's deduction will be limited to $600 per acre.

Antique Toy Car, Part I: Next, consider an example involving a different kind of property. Suppose a donor purchased an antique toy car six weeks ago for $1. This was quite a good purchase, because today the value of the antique toy car is $25. The donor's plan is to give the toy car to a toy museum that is recognized as a public charity. The charity is interested in the car for its historical value and intends to display the car in its museum collection. How much can the donor deduct for the gift of the antique toy car she gives to the public charity?

The answer to this question is actually simpler than it may seem at first. Since the donor has owned the antique toy car for only six weeks, it is short-term capital gain. Because it is short-term capital gain, the rules concerning "related use" or "unrelated use" tangible personal property become irrelevant. The gift's value is the lower of fair market value or basis regardless of the charity's use. These exceptions are irrelevant because, as short-term capital gain property, the donor may value this item only at cost basis. As always, valuing at cost basis assumes that the cost basis is less than fair market value. Here, the cost basis of $1 is less than the fair market value of $25.

Antique Toy Car, Part II: Now consider a slightly different example. Suppose that the donor purchased the antique toy car, not six weeks ago, but in 1990. How does this change the result? Since the donor has owned the property for more than 12 months and it has appreciated in value, this property is long-term capital gain.

Because this is long-term capital gain property, there is the potential to deduct the full fair market value of the gifted property, rather than only its cost basis. Of course, this is true only if none of the exceptions apply. The first exception does not apply, because this is not a gift to a private foundation. It is a gift to a public charity—a toy museum. Next, there was no mention of a special election, so this exception does not apply either. Finally, this is tangible personal property and consequently the unrelated use exception could apply. However, in this case, the charity will actually be using the gifted item in furtherance of its charitable purposes. Thus, this property is related use property, not unrelated use property.

As none of the exceptions apply, the IRS allows the donor to deduct the full fair market value of the property donated to the charity. In this case, it is important that the charity "intended" to use the item in its charitable operations by displaying the toy in its collection. How can the IRS prevent abuse of this rule by charities that might say they "intend" to use gifts of property, but then simply sell the gifted property?

Recapture Rule

The recapture rule limits abuse of the related use regulations. If a charity sells (or otherwise transfers) the property item within three years, the valuation could change from fair market value to cost basis. Such a change of valuation would require the donor to amend his or her tax return to reflect the lower deduction. This recapture rule applies only to tangible personal property worth more than $5,000. For these larger gifts, the charity's transfer or sale of the property within three years will lead to the donor reducing the charitable deduction. This occurs unless the charity certifies that it made substantial related use of the property prior to sale or that the intended use became impossible.

For example, if the donor's toy car was worth $25,000 (instead of $25) and the charity sold the toy three months later, then the original deduction would be subject to recapture. However, if the reason the charity sold the car was because their museum location was destroyed, making it impossible to display the car as the organization originally intended, then the IRS would likely not require recapture (assuming that the charity certified that the original intended use became impossible). Alternatively, if the charity had displayed the car for 2½ years in its collection prior to the sale of the item and was willing to certify this substantial related use, this certification could also prevent recapture.

Obviously, the simplest and cleanest way to avoid recapture is to make sure the charity does not sell the item for at least three years. If the charity does sell within three years, but it also certifies that one of these two exceptions applies, that will also avoid recapture. However, this certification must be accurate. The charity must sign under penalty of perjury, and there is a $10,000 fine if the charity provides false information.

So, what happens if the charity does not use the item, but instead simply sells it soon after receiving it? In this case the donor gives his antique toy car to a public charity that displays toys in its museum, but the charity does not want to display the donor's toy. The charity just wants to sell it. So, after the donor has given the toy to the charity, the charity sells the toy at its annual benefit auction. What happens then?

Once again, this is still long-term appreciated capital gain property because the donor has owned it since 1990, so there is the possibility that it could receive fair market value treatment unless one of the exceptions applies. In this case, one of the exceptions does indeed apply, because this is unrelated use tangible personal property. It is unrelated use property, because the charity did not use it. Instead, the charity simply sold the car. It is tangible personal property because it is a moveable physical item. Thus, since the charity is selling this tangible personal property instead of using it, the exception to fair market valuation does apply. Because one of the exceptions applies, the donor cannot use the fair market value for calculating the deduction. Instead, the valuation must drop down to the cost basis valuation. So, the gift of an item worth $25 generates a deduction of only $1.

Qualified Stock

An exception to the exception is the rule on "qualified stock." Qualified stock is typically publicly traded stock but usually does not include other publicly traded securities like bonds or publicly traded partnerships. That is, stocks that trade on an exchange such that market quotations are regularly available. For example, any stock traded on the New York Stock Exchange can be qualified stock. In addition to being a publicly traded stock, the private foundation cannot have more than ten percent of the entire company when counting all family member transfers together.

The intent is to avoid giving special benefit to large, closely held, insider transactions. Consider the case of a family-owned business where family members transfer most shares of the business to their own private family foundation. This transaction has some potential for abuse. The family members controlled the asset before the gift. And now, as board members of the private family foundation, they control the asset after the gift (at least until the foundation sells it). Determining the fair market value of shares in a family-owned business may be quite difficult. This is especially true for closely held corporations where other investors may be uninterested in owning a minority share when the family still controls all aspects of the business. Because the donor or the donor's family often control private family foundations, these transfers are generally less desirable, from a policy-makers perspective, than gifts to traditional public charities

The exception is allowed for cases in which the property given is almost like cash. It is almost like cash because the shares are regularly traded and have an easily identifiable value. It is also like cash because it is not a very large share of the total ownership of the corporation (even when considering all family members' transfers together). Given the cash-like nature of the transfer, there is less concern about inappropriate or abusive transactions, making a fair market value deduction more appropriate. Consider an example of the mechanics of this kind of transaction.

Suppose a donor owns 10,000 shares of Microsoft Corporation (a publicly traded corporation), which she originally paid $1 per share for and is today worth $25 per share. The donor gives these 10,000 shares to a private foundation. What is her deduction for this gift?

Initially, it is useful to note that this is long-term capital gain property. This is true because the donor has owned it for more than 12 months and it has appreciated. Since it is long-term capital gain, there is at least the potential that the donor can deduct its fair market value, unless one of the exceptions apply. In this case, the donor is giving the property to a private foundation, so one of the exceptions to a fair market value deduction does apply, unless the donor qualifies for the exception to the exception.

Because the donor is giving qualified stock, the normal rule for private foundations does not apply. As a result, the IRS allows the donor to deduct the fair market value of the shares of stock. Thus, the donor's deduction is $25 per share ($250,000) rather than $1 per share ($10,000). The property is "qualified stock" because it was publicly traded (meaning that market quotations are available) and because 10,000 shares is nowhere close to a ten percent ownership interest in the corporation (given that it has billions of shares).

Special Cases: Taxpayer Abuses and Congressional Responses

From time to time there have been special kinds of property that have been used in significant tax abuses. As a result, Congress has acted to create special rules that apply only to specific types of property, usually in response to these tax abuses. For these special kinds of property, it modifies the normal rules. Special charitable donation rules apply to clothing, household items, cars, boats, airplanes, taxidermy, inventory, patents, and other intellectual property.

Considering the complexity of the "standard" rules reviewed above, why would Congress add these special rules for specific assets? The answer is that Congress reacted to ongoing abuses that fit the normal rules, but which it still considered to be inappropriate.

There is always a special potential for abuse in the area of deductions for gifts of property when the property has an uncertain valuation. Consider a taxpayer at the top federal tax rate of 37 percent, and at the top state tax rate in a state like California, where the top rate is 13.3 percent. A deduction for this taxpayer is worth more than half of the value of the gifted property, considering that the donor will likely already have reached the cap for federal deductions of state and local taxes. A property may be difficult to value or difficult to sell, but the donor can immediately convert it into a tax benefit worth nearly fifty cents of every appraised dollar. This can make such transfers highly attractive, even to those with little or no charitable intent. If a difficult-to-value item of property can be appraised for two or three times what the owner could actually sell it for in an immediate sale, it may be more profitable to donate the property, rather than to sell it. Such financial incentives make gifts of difficult-to-value assets ripe for abuse.

Taxpayer Abuses

What do the abuses that led to special rules look like? For example, a person might have old clothes that she would otherwise throw in the trash, because they have little or no resale value. Instead of throwing them away, the person could give them away and generate a charitable deduction. Perhaps the person may attempt to value the deduction based on the original cost of the clothing or some "estimated" value based on a percentage of the original cost, when in reality the poor quality clothing has little or no resale value.

Another abuse could result from gifts of automobiles where the automobile has some defect that reduces its value below the normal resale value for that model and year of car. Even though in reality the automobile may be worth nothing, except in a junkyard, taxpayers may be tempted to donate the vehicle and deduct the standard value for a vehicle of that age, make and model (i.e., the "blue book" value). For an in-depth discussion of vehicle valuation issues, see Chapter 9.

A particularly egregious abuse occurred in the area of donating stuffed animals to a wildlife museum. In this scheme, the taxpayer would go on safari to hunt exotic animals, have a taxidermist stuff the animals, and then donate the animals to a wildlife museum. An appraisal firm would provide a high valuation for exotic stuffed animals (a valuation which might be difficult to disprove given the rarity of transactions and the high cost of acquiring new exotic stuffed animals). A few small wildlife museums were willing to accept these donations (often taking in thousands of animals). The donor would then deduct his cost basis in the stuffed animal, including all of the costs of acquiring the animal, such as the entire expense of the safari travel. Thus, the tax code was essentially funding a substantial portion of safari tourism intended to kill exotic animals.

A different problem arose with copyrights and other intellectual property not simply because of the risk of fraud, but also because of the enormous difficulty in valuing such intellectual property in advance. If a best-selling author wrote a new book and immediately donated the copyright of the book to charity, such a donation would be enormously valuable. If a less well-known author did the same, the donation could be highly valuable or it could be worth nothing. The difficulty is that it may be impossible to tell at the time of the donation how much the gift is worth. No amount of sophistication, education, experience, or integrity of any appraiser will be able to correct that problem.

Congressional Responses

Because of the wide variety of problems and issues with these special kinds of property, each of them has their own special rule.

Clothing and household items typically get no deduction unless they are in "good used condition or better." The purpose of requiring "good used condition" is to exclude worn out clothes. An exception to this rule is if the donor gives more than $500 of clothing and the donor includes a qualified appraisal of the clothing with the tax return. Thus, small donations of clothing in poor condition are not deductible. Large donations of such clothing may be deductible, but only if there is a qualified appraisal.

This same rule applies not only to clothing, but to other household items. The term "household items" does not include art, antiques, jewelry or collections. Instead, it refers to items like furniture, electronics, appliances, linens and the like. The donor may not deduct these household items unless they are in "good used condition or better," or where there is an accompanying qualified appraisal indicating a value in excess of $500 for the entire donation.

To address the problem of taxpayer financed safari trips, Congress limited deductions for taxidermy property to the cost of stuffing the animal only. Thus, none of the other costs of acquiring the animal may be deducted.

Deducting charitable gifts of copyright (or other intellectual property, such as patents and trademarks) is not simply a problem of fraud or abuse, but is fundamentally a problem of accurately valuing the property in advance. To resolve this issue, Congress allowed for special deduction rules, discussed in depth in Chapter 11. However, note that, as in all other forms of charitable property deductions, the cost basis is deductible only if such basis is less than fair market value. Thus conceptually, it may still be necessary to estimate the fair market value of an intellectual property right in advance. However, in practice, many such rights have little or no cost basis. For example, an author's cost basis would include only some paper and ink, and would not take into account his or her time spent in producing the work.[6]

Another exception to the standard valuation rules involves an unusual compromise. The normal rule for gifts of inventory is that only the cost basis of inventory is deductible. However, the tax code provides a special increase in the deduction for specific types of inventory gifts. If the donor is a standard corporation (a C corporation, as opposed to an S corporation), it can receive a higher deduction. To do so, it must be giving inventory to a public charity for care of ill individuals, needy individuals, or infants, or it is giving qualified research materials to an institution of higher education or other scientific institution. This higher deduction will be the average of basis and fair market value.

Thus, the Corporation receives neither the most favored status (which would be fair market value) nor the less favored status (which would be cost basis), but instead receives something in the middle. However, regulations still limit this deduction to no more than double the cost basis in the gifted items. This is to prevent a scenario where the deduction was worth more than the cost of manufacturing the property.

General Reporting Requirements[7]

The burden of defending the value claimed for a deduction rests with the donor. In order to claim a charitable deduction over $5,000 for any noncash asset other than publicly traded stock, the donor must secure a qualified independent appraisal, with a qualified appraiser completing a qualified appraisal under IRC 170(f)(11).[8] The appraisal must be dated within sixty days of the gift, or by the donor's tax return filing date for the year of the gift. Further, in order to claim the deduction, the donor must file IRS Form 8283, and for any noncash asset gift over $5,000, the Form must

---

6. Note that time and effort are excluded from cost basis in other areas as well. For example, if a taxpayer purchases a dirty car for $5,000 and then spends three months cleaning and detailing it, his basis in the car is still only $5,000.
7. This section was written by Phil Purcell.
8. See IRS Publication 561, "Determining the Value of Donated Property," for a helpful summary of IRS appraisal requirements.

be signed by the appraiser, as well as a representative of the charitable organization. Failure to follow these appraisal rules can result in denial of the charitable deduction.[9]

If the charity sells or disposes of the donated asset within three years, then it must file IRS Form 8282 reporting the sale price. If there is a significant discrepancy between the sale price it lists on Form 8282 and the original deduction claimed by the donor as reported on the Form 8283, then this could trigger an IRS audit review. There is no "bright line" standard of how much difference between the deduction and a reduced sale price would threaten the claim of a deduction, but tax counsel should be aware of the discrepancy.

Special Valuation Requirements

Although not exceptions to the general rules, some items can be hard to value and consequently, the IRS requires a special kind of valuation for these items. For example, when valuing gifts of clothing, the valuation must be what the used clothing would sell for in a consignment or thrift shop, not what it sells for new in a retail environment. Of course, the difference between what an Armani suit sells for in an upscale retail environment and what a used Armani suit would sell for in a thrift shop is dramatic.

Finally, for gifts of large quantities of individual items, donors must determine the valuation from the value of the entire lot of items. The IRS does not permit donors to estimate the value of a single item and multiply that by the total number of items gifted. For example, suppose a donor found a box of 1,000 beanie babies on sale online for $1,000. If the donor purchased these, then gave them to an orphanage over a year later for use in their charitable activities, the donor could be legally entitled to a deduction of fair market value (long-term capital gain related use personal property). However, even if the fair market value for a single beanie baby toy was $5, the donor could not claim a fair market value for the gift of $5,000 ($5 x 1,000). Instead, the fair market value would be the value of the entire lot of 1,000 such beanie babies in a single lot sale.

If, during an audit, the IRS determines that the taxpayer overvalued a charitable gift, there will be distinctly adverse results. First, the donor must reduce the deduction to an appropriate value, and consequently will need to pay for additional taxes and any interest accrued since the due date for those taxes. In addition to this repayment and interest, there can be penalties for overvaluing a charitable gift. Those penalties depend upon the amount of the gift and the degree of overvaluation. If the taxpayer valued the gift at greater than 50 percent of its true value and, as a

---

9. See *Mohamed v. Commissioner*, T.C. Memo. 2012-152 (May 29, 2012).

result, there was more than $5,000 in underpayment of tax, then the taxpayer must pay not only the taxes due, but also an additional 20 percent of the unpaid taxes. If in the previous case, the valuation was more than double the item's true value, then the penalty would be an additional 40 percent of the unpaid taxes. Finally, if the misstatement of value was due to fraud, the penalty would be an additional 75 percent of the unpaid taxes, regardless of the amount of underpayment or the degree of over valuation.[10]

The IRS often requires the donor to obtain an appraisal to deduct gifts of property. Can the taxpayer avoid the penalties discussed above if the taxpayer had a qualified appraisal for the amounts reported? The answer is: it depends.

There will be no penalty if the taxpayer's valuation was based upon a qualified appraisal, the donor made a good-faith investigation of value, and the valuation was less than double the actual value of the item. This exception would not apply if the appraisal was not a qualified appraisal under IRS guidelines. Even if the appraisal was a qualified appraisal, the IRS still requires the donor to have made a good-faith investigation of the value of the item, besides simply relying upon the appraisal. But if both of those conditions apply, and the appraised value was less than double the actual value, then no penalty will apply. However, the donor still must remit any unpaid tax resulting from the overvaluation and any interest due.

What are the penalties to the appraiser for making an excessive appraisal of an item of property gifted to a charity? If the valuation was more than 50 percent greater than the actual value of the item, the appraiser's penalty will be the greater of $1,000 or 10 percent of the tax underpayment. This penalty could be potentially catastrophic for appraisers who appraise items of extremely high value. Recognizing that such a rule would prevent even legitimate appraisers from functioning, the tax code limits the penalty for appraisers to 125 percent of the appraiser's fee for making the appraisal. For example, an appraiser charges $1,000 and values a piece of artwork at $10 million when it was actually worth only $5 million and this error results in a $1.5 million tax underpayment. The appraiser's penalty will therefore not be $150,000 (10 percent of the tax underpayment), but instead would be 125 percent of the appraisal fee, or $1,250.

One interesting case that illustrates the sometimes unusual results from property valuation is that involving a work of art called "Canyon." This work of art was a bequest to the heirs of an estate. The IRS appraised the value of the artwork at $65 million and charged $29.2 million in estate taxes on

---

10. Tax fraud can lead not only to financial penalties, but also to imprisonment.

the item. The IRS based this valuation upon its definition of fair market value, which is the price that property would sell for on the open market.

The problem in this case was not the valuation in itself, but that the artwork incorporated the use of a taxidermied eagle. Federal law prohibits the sale of such taxidermied eagle feathers or parts. Consequently, the IRS required the estate to pay a large tax on an item that it could not sell. This is an interesting example of what could happen with items where the law restricts sale, but the valuation is the price that the item would sell for on the open market. In this case, the heirs would have been much better off if the decedent had gifted the artwork to a charity, rather than left it to them. In the final settlement, the IRS allowed the heirs to retroactively donate the artwork, treating it as if the estate made the gift, thus generating no net estate taxes on the donated artwork.

Charitable Gifts of Noncash Assets

Appendix B:
Charitable Estate Settlement[11]

By Gary Snerson, Laura Peebles, and Bryan Clontz

Below is an in-depth examination on charitable estate settlement. Charitable estate settlement topics are based on Snerson, G., Peebles, L., and Clontz, B., "Charitable Estate Settlement: A Primer from the Charity's Perspective." For further details, see Charitable Estate Settlement Additional Resources.

Introduction[12]

As charitable bequests and legacy gifts continue to rise, an increasing number of charities are either anticipating or reacting to the estate settlement process. If the estate settlement is not handled properly, gifts may create direct and indirect liabilities, shrink, be delayed, result in litigation, or be impossible to administer.

This reading aims to outline the charitable estate settlement process from the perspectives of the donor, the charity, and even the donor's surviving family.[13] It first considers the form of the gift and resulting tax implications—the actual estate planning. Then it discusses consequences of these gifts to charities. It then outlines a model procedure for donors. Finally, it lists eight potential pitfalls in the charitable estate settlement process.

Estate Planning

There are two main considerations during the charitable gift planning process to consider with the settlement process in mind. The first is the how the donor owns the assets that are destined for charity, which can affect whether there will be any need for probate before the transfer to charity. The second is the tax implications of the chosen gift, both relating to estate and gift taxes, and lifetime and estate income taxes. This section discusses bequests in wills or revocable trusts, beneficiary designations, charitable remainder trusts (CRTs), and charitable gift annuities (CGAs).

---

11. This reading is an adaptation of Snerson, G., Peebles, L., and Clontz, B. (February 17, 2016), "Charitable Estate Settlement: A Primer from the Charity's Perspective," Planned Giving Design Center, http://www.pgdc.com/pgdc/charitable-estate-settlement-primer-charitys-perspective; http://www.pgdc.com/pgdc/charitable-estate-settlement-primer-charitys-perspective-part-2-2.
12. All authors are associated with Charitable Solutions LLC, Jacksonville Florida, charitablesolutionsllc.com.
13. This reading does not include any of the special estate administration and tax rules applicable to private foundations.

The simplest, and most obvious, gift from an estate planning perspective is the charitable bequest. This form of gift simply leaves property to a charity the donor names in the will or revocable trust.[14] This is by far the most common way to leave a charitable legacy—around 80 percent of planned gifts are will bequests.[15] Much of their appeal comes from their relative simplicity, as well as their flexibility. Only assets the donor did not use during life are committed, and even then the gift is revocable and modifiable.[16] Should the donor's estate be subject to the estate tax, the bequest will reduce the size of the taxable estate.[17] However, the donor gets no tax benefit during his or her lifetime, unlike some other forms of gift.[18]

Another simple form of gift is the beneficiary designation, which the contract may describe as a gift. This is easy for donors to make, because they do not even need to include the gift in a will.[19] Indeed, a will provision cannot override or affect a beneficiary designation. Therefore, these gifts avoid the probate process. Donors can make beneficiary designations on financial devices as diverse as retirement plans, IRAs, life insurance contracts, and pay-on-death bank accounts, among others.[20]

Depending on the asset, beneficiary designations can reduce estate taxes using the estate tax charitable deduction and avoid income taxes because the charitable beneficiary is income tax exempt.[21] There is no impact on the donor's assets during life, and the charity simply receives the remaining balance or a predetermined amount on death. For a beneficiary designation on life insurance, an estate tax deduction is available, but not against lifetime taxable income (unless the donor also transfers ownership of the policy to the charity before death).[22] IRAs and retirement plans can allow tax deductions on both estate and income taxes, but these deductions are much more complex.[23] It is crucial to determine if the plan permits the owner to name a charitable

---

14. Throughout this chapter, "will" should be read to include a revocable trust used as a testamentary substitute.
15. PG Calc. (Feb. 2011). "Bequest-Like Gifts That Don't Require a Will." Retrieved from http://www.pgcalc.com/about/featured-article-february-2011.htm.
16. Id.
17. Silverman, R.E. (2011, October 1). "The Quest for the Right Bequest." *Wall Street Journal.* Retrieved from http://www.wsj.com/articles/SB10001424052970204010604576594790543894476.
18. Id.
19. PG Calc, supra note 279.
20. Id.
21. Midura, T.S. (2009). "Handling Charitable Bequests and Charitable Trusts." Illinois Estate Administration, p. 8. Retrieved from http://www.timothymidura.com/uploads/Charitable_Bequest_Administration_-_Midura.pdf.
22. Dagher, V. (2013, September 18). "Donating a Life-Insurance Policy to a Charity." *Wall Street Journal.* Retrieved from http://www.wsj.com/articles/SB10001424127887323608504579022743817392368.
23. *American Institute for Cancer Research.* (2014). "Tips and Traps on Retirement Accounts and Other Charitable Beneficiary Designations," p. 6-7. Retrieved from http://www.aicr.org/assets/docs/pdf/estateplanner/2014-tips-traps-on-retirement-accounts-tra.pdf. See also *The Harvard Manual on Tax Aspects of Charitable Giving,* Ninth Edition, 2011, p. 166-167.

beneficiary. In addition, for married donors, all qualified plans are subject to one of two forms of federal spousal rights, but the nonparticipant spouse can waive those to allow a full or partial charitable designation.

If the donor wishes to give the charity a gift in the most tax-efficient manner, the most likely asset to use is an IRA or qualified plan. If the plan distributes those assets to a noncharitable beneficiary, the recipient generally will pay income tax on them. Therefore, most planners recommend designating a charity as the beneficiary of an IRA as a means of fulfilling a charitable gift. However, over time, the value of those accounts may shrink due to investment losses, required minimum distributions, and the donor's own voluntary withdrawals from the account. Therefore, if the donor wants the charity to receive a certain amount, a back-up clause in his or her will may be necessary. For example, "to the extent that Charity does not receive at least $1 million from my IRA accounts, I hereby bequeath to Charity the difference between $1 million and the date of death value of my IRA accounts, to be funded by assets selected by my executor."

It may be wise to back up that designation with a bequest of the IRA under the donor's will. Due to the number of bank mergers and changes in custodianship of IRAs over time, the custodian may misplace the charitable beneficiary designation. Although not as efficient for tax or administrative purposes as an outright beneficiary designation, passing the IRA through the estate and on to the charity is better than losing out entirely.

If a donor has an outstanding charitable pledge, and that pledge is enforceable under state law, then the charity has standing as a creditor, rather than as a beneficiary under the will or trust. This generally will result in quicker payment of the amount remaining on the pledge, as the estate must pay creditors before even specific legacies.[24]

Pay-on-death accounts have limited tax benefits, but are deductible in calculating the taxable estate as a charitable bequest. Pay-on-death accounts can backfire on the donor and the charity if the account does not properly name the charity. In such a case, the noncharitable beneficiaries may claim that the gift was not complete. Such a claim is likely if the debts, taxes and expenses of the estate exceed the available liquid assets in the probate estate or substantially impact the beneficiaries taking through the probate estate.

CRTs are more complex instruments, both from planning and tax perspectives. They require carefully prepared documents that comply with Internal Revenue Service regulations, to ensure the

---

24. Beckwith and Allan, 839-2nd T.M. Estate and Gift Tax Charitable Deductions IV.A.5.

most favorable tax treatment. They come in two flavors—inter vivos and testamentary. Essentially, an inter vivos CRT works by transferring assets in trust during the donor's lifetime.[25] The donor retains a life annuity or unitrust interest, and receives distributions from the trust.[26] Married donors often give their surviving spouse a successor life interest. Donors can also establish CRTs at death through a will or trust provision with the spouse or another individual as a beneficiary. Upon the death of the last income beneficiary (or the term of the trust for term CRTs), the trustee transfers the assets to the charitable remainderman subject to the terms of the trust document.

CGAs are contracts between the donor and the charity. The assets the donor used to create the CGA belong to the charity upon transfer. Therefore, there is no transfer on the death of the donor unless the donor's will creates the CGA. If the donor created the CGA during his lifetime, which is usually the case, the death of the donor relieves the charity of any further responsibility to make future payments. The exception would be when the CGA is a joint and survivor annuity and the spouse survives the donor. Because of the timing of the payments by the charity, and possible delays in the charity becoming aware of the annuitant's death, it is possible that the decedent's estate may owe the charity a portion of the payment already made or charity may owe the estate a portion of the payment to be made. In either case the charity should make the executor aware of these circumstances.

Consequences to Charities

How do charities treat gifts left to them as part of estate planning? The answer depends on the form of the gift (discussed above for donors), as well as the nature of the gift. These factors combine to inform both how (the value) and when (the recognition) the charity reports the gift. Further, although charities are exempt from income taxes due to their 501(c)(3) status, tax issues relating to settlement of the whole estate in which they have an interest may still impact the non-profit legatees.

Determining the value of gifts is an important task for charities. Not only can they sometimes have difficulty immediately ascertaining the true value of an outright gift, deferred gifts such as CRTs can also have uncertain values. Add to this revocable gifts such as POD accounts or life insurance beneficiary designations, and it is sometimes unclear whether the donor has made a completed gift at all. Even if a beneficiary designation on a policy is irrevocable, if there are future premiums

---

25. Gessaman, P.H. (1996). "Charitable Remainder Trusts and Charitable Annuities as Estate Planning Tools." NebFacts. Retrieved from http://digitalcommons.unl.edu/cgi/viewcontent.cgi?article=1679&context=extensionhist.
26. Id.

Appendix

due, failure of the donor to pay the future premiums could cause the gift value to diminish or vanish. Therefore, determining the value of a gift can be a complex task.

The other factor charities must consider is when they should recognize the gift. For example, if a donor has irrevocably pledged life insurance (with the charity as the policy beneficiary), the charity may easily determine the value of that gift, but when it should recognize the gift is not immediately clear. As indicated above, charities should consider requiring the donor to transfer ownership of the policy along with the beneficial interest at the time of the gift. If the donor did not fully pay up the policy at the time of the gift, arrangements must be made for future premium payments, or conversion to a paid-up policy, to avoid a policy lapse. If the donor pays the premiums after the charity owns the policy, the IRS allows the donor to take additional tax deductions for the amount paid. As a baseline, consider an inter vivos gift of cash, which clearly would not be part of any estate settlement process. This outright gift can be "recognized as revenues … in the period received."[27]

Generally, charities should recognize contributions when they receive them. FASB recommends that charities recognize "unconditional promises to give" as received when the donor makes the promise, rather than the asset actually received.[28] However, "to be recognized in financial statements there must be sufficient evidence in the form of verifiable documentation that a promise was made and received."[29]

Usually this recognizable promise takes the form of an irrevocable pledge binding the donor and the donor's estate. For assets the testator pledges in a bequest that was revocable during the testator's lifetime, once the donor dies, the charity can recognize the value of those assets before the assets become available. This recognition is permissible, because the bequest is irrevocable once the testator-donor dies (see comment above). The charity could take a similar approach for a pay-on-death bank account or life insurance. For CRTs (whether inter vivos or testamentary) and CGAs, the charities receive the assets when the irrevocable document or trust comes into effect (although the valuation question is more difficult, as discussed above).

Another consideration for the recipient charities is the interaction between taxes during estate administration and bequests to the charities. These taxes can include both the estate tax and

---

27. *Financial Accounting Standards Board*, p. 6.
28. Id.
29. Id. Further, if no clear promise was made, the gift may still be considered received if there is an unconditional intention that is legally binding.

income taxes. Although estates (and some trusts) can deduct from income amounts they distribute to charities, the charitable beneficiaries should work with estate executors to ensure that they receive everything the donor intended.[30] Charities should be similarly careful with regard to the estate tax, when the estate apportions that tax to a charitable residue.[31] They should review estate tax clauses and returns to make sure that any tax payments the executor makes were in accordance with the donor's expressed intent.[32] Suggestions for specific due diligence are discussed in the next section.

Recommended Procedure

This section broadly outlines how a charity should go about contributing to a smooth and equitable estate settlement process. This process includes estate planning, post-mortem communication with the executor, investigation of non-probate gifts, and working with the executor, the professionals, and surviving family on administration issues. Maintaining open lines of communication with all parties is essential to not only individual estates, but to good relationships with the community and potential donors in general.

Depending on the size and experience of the charity, it may have more experience with charitable estate administration than the executor and his or her accountants and attorneys.

Recommendations During the Estate Planning Process

The parties lay the groundwork for smooth estate settlement during the planning process. When a potential donor approaches the charity about a gift, the nonprofit should help determine the form and extent of the donor's charitable intent.[33] This includes figuring out what the donor wishes to accomplish, and how much and when he or she wants to give.[34] Once the donor has decided to give, the charity should engage with the donor's professional advisors—his or her attorneys, accountants, and investment advisors, among others. Such due diligence can avoid complications when the donor dies and his or her intentions are no longer discernable.

---

30. Katzenstein, L.P. (2011). "Estates with Charities as Beneficiaries: How Do We Protect Their Interests?." Saint Louis Planned Giving Council, p. 1. Retrieved from http://www.slpgc.org/files/Handouts_2011/SLPGC_Lunch_Handout-estates_011311.pdf.
31. Id., p. 5-11.
32. Id., p. 9.
33. Livingston, R. (2005). "Charitable Giving Methods: What Nonprofits Need to Know – And Need to Tell Their Donors." Colorado Planned Giving Roundtable, p. 2. Retrieved from http://www.cpgr.org/lal/files/File/uploads/Methods.pdf.
34. Id.

Appendix

Family dissatisfaction with the estate plan can lead to disagreements during the probate process and often costly litigation.[35] The goal of all parties should be "to maximize the tax benefits and impact of the donation on [the donor's] estates, families, and the philanthropic causes they wish to support."[36] Ideally, the donor, the donor's family, the advisors, and the charity should all be fully informed and ready to proceed when the time comes for the actual gift transfer to occur.

Part of the planning process is to confirm that the assets are the type that the charity wants to receive, and is able to accept under their gift acceptance policy. If the estate includes assets that the charity does not want, but that have value, the time to deal with that issue is during the planning process if at all possible. Perhaps the will or trust should include instructions to the executor for the disposition of the assets during estate administration. Alternative dispositions to family members or other charities merit consideration. Assets a charity does not want to receive may vary depending on the size and type of charity, but mortgaged real estate, collectibles, and family business interests are typically not gifts nonprofits prefer.

Another advantage of charitable involvement in the planning process is to discuss with the donor the possibility of lifetime gifts of some of the assets. Generally, there will be an income tax advantage of lifetime gifts over testamentary gifts.

Of course, not all donors involve the charity in the planning process. Perhaps the testator does not want contact from the charity during her lifetime, or perhaps she wants to be able to quietly change the charity up to the last minute without making a permanent commitment to her chosen charity or charities. Whatever the reason, it is typical for the charity to find out about the bequest only after the death of the donor. Despite major charitable efforts to identify and catalogue potential bequest donors, most bequests come from donors who either the charity did not know, or that the charity knew but never indicated an intention to make a bequest. Normally, the executor informs the charity, but sometimes the information becomes public even before that person contacts the charity.

Actions Immediately Following the Donor's Death

The next phase of the process begins when the charity receives notice of the donor's death. For charities, the next steps involve "reviewing documents, providing needed information, monitoring

---

35. Brill, B. (2002). "Incorporating Philanthropic Planning Adds Value to Your Client Services and Makes Good Business Sense to You." The Journal of Practical Estate Planning. Retrieved from http://www.pgdc.com/pgdc/incorporating-philanthropic-planning-adds-value-your-client-services-and-makes-good-business-sense-you.
36. Herzberg, P.

progress, and stewardship."[37] Ultimately, the charity's goal is "ensuring your nonprofit receives the amount it is entitled to, as quickly as possible."[38] Abatement—when the estate is insufficient to pay all legacies in the will—may reduce the charitable gift, if the testator makes it from the residuary estate or a general legacy of cash.[39] Ademption—where the specific asset that the decedent bequeathed no longer exists—can eliminate the charitable gift entirely.

Typically, the estate's executor[40] notifies the charity that the donor has died, and has left a bequest to the charity.[41] In probate estates, the law often requires such notification. The charity should obtain a copy of the will, or if applicable, the trust agreement. Once the executor files the will, it is a public document available for inspection in the probate court for the county in which the donor last lived. If the donor had a revocable trust, it may be inappropriate to request a copy of the full trust document, at least initially, but it would be common for the executor to at least provide an excerpt that shows the gift. Depending on the size and nature of the gift, the complexity of the estate, the impact of taxes, and the donor's family situation, the charity may need to see other provisions of the document, especially clauses allocating taxes and administrative costs among the beneficiaries. The charity and its counsel should immediately review the relevant documents.

If the bequest is a fixed amount (a pecuniary bequest), these are some of the subjects for discussion:

   a. Does the executor expect there will be sufficient liquid assets to fund the bequest without waiting for the estate to sell illiquid assets?

   b. Are there expected to be any challenges to the estate documents, or to the specific bequest?

   c. If there are sufficient liquid assets, and no expected challenges, then the charity should make a general inquiry as to when it might expect a full or partial payment. If the estate is large enough that the executor must file federal (and state) inheritance tax returns, the executor may be unwilling to pay any bequests until she receives a federal and/or state closing letter. Alternatively, if there is no estate tax audit, the executor may delay payment until the applicable statute of limitations has run (up to

---

37. O'Carroll, A. (2013, July 19). "Bequests – Stewardship and Administration." Northwest Planned Giving Roundtable, p. 14. Retrieved from http://www.nwpgrt.org/Mbrmtg/7.13_Handout_BequestsStewardshipAndAdminPaper.pdf.
38. Id.
39. Katzenstein L.P., p. 24.
40. Executor also refers to the successor trustee under the decedent's formerly revocable trust.
41. Boedecker, A.S. (2012, May 1). "What to Do When the Donor Dies – Understanding Estate Administration Rights and Responsibilities of Charitable Beneficiaries." Sharpe Group. Retrieved from http://sharpenet.com/give-take/donor-dies-understanding-estate-administration-rights-responsibilities-charitable-beneficiaries/.

Appendix

four years and three months after the date of death). Given that the IRS may personally charge executors if they pay bequests while leaving insufficient funds in the estate for any taxes, this reluctance is understandable.[42] If the charity has substantial net worth it should offer to sign a receipt, release, and refunding agreement in order to achieve early partial or full payment so as to minimize any opportunity cost from delayed payment. State law typically provides for interest on delayed payment of bequests.

d. Offer to provide any relevant paperwork, such as a copy of the IRS exemption letter or any state registration that might facilitate the executor's work.

e. If the bequest is a fixed amount of money less any payments made under a pledge agreement prior to the date of death, the charity should review its records and provide its list of relevant payments, as the executor will need that information before making the payment under the will.

f. If the executor indicates that the estate is composed primarily of illiquid assets, or there are other reasons to delay full payment, then the charity should retain experienced local probate counsel to advise it of its rights under the relevant state law and the documents. Reasons the estate may delay full payment include expected IRS disputes over valuation, litigation with heirs, assets with unclear title or environmental issues, or potentially insufficient assets to fund all specific bequests.

g. If the decedent's estate is composed of illiquid assets, gain an understanding of the executor's plan for valuation and liquidation of those assets. If the appraised value of those assets is equal or greater than the amount of the bequest, the charity should consider taking them in lieu of cash if there is the perception that a hasty liquidation may decrease the value of the bequest. If the bequest is relatively small compared to the overall estate, then there is less concern with those issues than if the bequest is such that the net realizable value of the assets would affect the ability to fully fund the bequest. Any in-kind settlement agreement may require a court or state charity official's approval so it is prudent to consult counsel.

If the bequest is either all, or a portion, of the residue of the estate, there are additional issues that should concern the charity. Discerning the quality of the bequest is important in determining what its treatment should be during the settlement process, and can have economic implications for all beneficiaries, not just the charity.[43]

---

42. *United States v. Stiles*, No. 13-138, 2014 BL 338556 (W.D. Pa. Dec. 2, 2014).
43. Midura, T.S. (2009). "Handling Charitable Bequests and Charitable Trusts." Illinois Estate Administration, p. 8. Retrieved from http://www.timothymidura.com/uploads/Charitable_Bequest_Administration_-_Midura.pdf.

a. What is the executor's plan for distribution of the assets in the estate? Unless the will or trust instructs otherwise, the executor may want to value the assets, and then distribute them to the charity (and possibly other heirs) in kind in the interest of closing the estate promptly. If that is the plan, a close review of the assets is in order. If the estate is composed of marketable securities and a condominium, this might be acceptable. On the other hand, if the estate contains assets that would generate unrelated business taxable income for the charity (such as leveraged real estate, publicly traded partnerships, Subchapter S corporations), the net after-tax proceeds to the charity are likely to be greater if the executor can sell those assets in the estate or trust. Generally, estates are not subject to the unrelated business income tax.

If the estate includes assets that the charity would not typically accept under their gift acceptance policy, significant negotiations may be necessary to avoid that outcome. These include assets such as hedge funds, leveraged real estate, closely held business interests, mineral interests, general partnership interests, complex financial instrument contracts, undeveloped real estate, tangible personal property, undivided interests, timber, and art that is unaccessionable. The charity should engage counsel to review the documents to determine if the charity can insist that the executor liquidate the assets before closing the estate. If the documents restrict the executor's actions or the executor is unwilling to exercise her powers to liquidate the problematic assets and distribute the proceeds to the charity, local counsel should explore the possibility of asking the probate court for an order expanding the executor's powers under applicable state laws or entering an order forcing the executor to act.

If liquidation before distribution is not possible, then plans should be made well in advance for disposition of the unwanted assets. It may be desirable to ask the executor to transfer the assets to a single member LLC. This would avoid placing the charity in the direct chain of title if there is real estate or mineral properties in the estate assets that will go to the charity. Another alternative is to transfer the illiquid assets to a dedicated fund at a donor-advised fund with experience in liquidating such assets. After liquidation, the executor transfers net proceeds minus taxes and fees to the charity. Certain donor-advised funds minimize the income tax that would be due on disposition of assets subject to the unrelated business income tax. If the estate assets include Subchapter S stock,[44] debt-financed property of any kind,[45] or other assets subject to

---

44. IRC § 512(e).
45. IRC § 514.

the tax,[46] it will generally be worthwhile to use a donor-advised fund for this purpose, as the tax savings can be substantial.

b. Valuation.[47] Valuation is as much an art as a science, and if the estate contains substantial hard-to-value assets, the charity should satisfy itself that the executor is being diligent in valuing them. Especially when the charity is the residual beneficiary, executors might be tempted to use cheaper but less accurate appraisals since the value would not affect any estate taxes, and the IRS has no incentive to challenge the valuations. If only a portion of the residuary is going to charity there may be a conflict between the recipients with one desiring a higher appraisal and the other a lower one. If the estate will be subject to state or federal estate taxes, the heirs would generally prefer a lower appraisal.

Applying common sense here is essential. An "appraisal" using a real estate valuation website might be perfectly appropriate for a vacation condo unit where there are many similar units, or using various websites to value general personal property.[48] But if an interest in a closely held business is included in the estate, and the interest is to be sold to a related party, a more in-depth and perhaps costlier appraisal may be necessary. Valuation and net realizable value can also be affected by any shareholders' agreements. Such agreements are common in closely held companies, and may give either the shareholders or the company the right, or the obligation, to purchase the stock. Many, but not all, agreements also set the price at which the sale may, or must, be made. If the agreement allows the purchaser to buy the stock at less than fair market value, there may be estate tax consequences to that agreement. Those issues are discussed below.

c. Volatility. Are there assets in the estate that carry a larger than average risk of loss in value during administration? To reduce the risk from volatility, professional fiduciaries commonly sell them immediately. They then put the proceeds in an insured or extremely safe account, such as a bank CD or a money market account (this may not be practical if the charity is not the full residual beneficiary, as other beneficiaries may not have the same philosophy). Cars, planes, and boats depreciate quickly, generally produce no income, and can be costly to insure and maintain. In some situations, a quick sale at a lower than "market" price may be better than holding out for a higher price, but absorbing the carrying costs and the risks of loss.

---

46. IRC §§ 511-515 generally.
47. Kelley, 830-3rd T.M., Valuation: *General and Real Estate*.
48. Ebay.com or craigslist.com for personal property, kbb.com for vehicles, alibris.com for books.

If the estate includes a closely held business and the decedent was the key person, the business value may evaporate quickly.[49] If the decedent traded in complex financial instruments, gaining an understanding of the estate's financial positions and if they should be unwound promptly is important to both the executor and the charity. Decedent's personal property should be inventoried as soon as possible, and compared to his or her insurance listings. In most situations, it will be prudent for the executor to obtain a third party appraisal of the decedent's personal property.

If the charity is sharing the residue, perhaps the executor can allocate such items to the family share, with the charity taking more of the other assets (assuming the executor has that discretion under the will—otherwise, a settlement agreement may be required). If the charity has the full residue, and the decedent did not leave specific bequests of these items to family members, the charity should consider encouraging the executor to sell those items to the family promptly at an appropriately fair price. If the family is not interested, prompt disposition of tangible personal property is in order, through live or on-line auctions, consignment, or a local company specializing in estate sales. Obviously, if the estate includes valuable art or collectibles, an expert appraisal and disposition through an auction house is recommended. Since some types of auctions occur only seasonally, there may be storage and insurance costs, but those are generally worthwhile for such valuable items.[50]

d. What are the lines of communication between the executor and the charity? Later meetings can be by phone, but the initial meeting is key to setting the tone of the estate administration, and should always occur in person if possible. This initial meeting is also the perfect opportunity to express gratitude for the bequest—after all, the family members in attendance might have otherwise received those funds. The charity should keep the lines of communication open with the executor—asking about progress in the administration process, and checking what information the executor might need from the charity.[51] Regular meetings help keep the administration moving, especially if the executor is a family member who is assuming this responsibility in addition to their family and business duties. The executor owes a fiduciary duty to the charity as a beneficiary, but it is in the best interest of all parties to keep the process as collegial as possible.

---

49. Bekerman, 804-2nd T.M. Probate and Administration of Decedent's Estates XII.C.3.b.
50. Value, like beauty, is in the eye of the beholder. An executor will balance the cost of storage and insurance with the additional value that could be obtained by waiting for an auction.
51. Id.

Appendix

As part of the initial meeting, the charity should also inquire about any beneficiary designations. Unlike estate assets, there are less likely to be any administrative or tax impediments to an immediate payment of assets directed to the charity through a beneficiary designation. Also, there is less likely to be hard-to-administer or hard-to-value assets in IRAs, qualified plans, or life insurance contracts, which are the most typical contracts with beneficiary designations.

If the decedent was a beneficiary of a CRT that terminates at his or her death, the CRT trustee has a duty to contact the charity as well,[52] wind up the trust and transfer the remaining assets to the charity. If the decedent left a surviving spouse, often the spouse is a successor beneficiary, so not every CRT will terminate at the death of the first spouse to die. In many CRTs, the settlor of the trust retains the right to change the charity during their lifetime or through their will. If the settlor included that provision in a CRT, the decedent's death causes the charitable remainder beneficiary to become irrevocable, so the charity may now have rights under the document and state law regarding the administration of the trust.

If the trustee of the CRT is a family member without trustee experience, the charity might gently encourage the family member to retain appropriate professional guidance for investment management, valuation, tax, and legal matters of the trust. Where the trustee is a bank or other corporate fiduciary the charity should carefully check the amounts the trustee charges to wind up the trust and make final distributions. If the CRT was created with a predecessor bank or fiduciary the contract which the bank or fiduciary inherited may not have provided any additional fees for these tasks.

There may be tax issues if the bequest is a split-interest gift that is not in the standard form of a CRT, CGA, CLT (charitable lead trust), or remainder interest in a home or farm.[53] For example, there is no deduction for a trust that pays income to the decedent's sister for life, with the remainder to charity. However, a CRT for her benefit would allow an estate tax charitable deduction for the value of the remainder interest. Only split interest bequests in those listed formats are deductible for federal estate tax purposes. If a will or trust includes a nondeductible split interest bequest, and federal taxes may therefore decrease the amount passing to the charity, the charity should consult counsel immediately to see if the court can reform the bequest to obtain the estate tax charitable deduction. Reformation proceedings may be costly, especially if it is necessary to obtain a Private

---

52. Boedecker, A.S.
53. Midura, T.S., p. 8-9.

Letter Ruling from the IRS. However, if the estate's tax saved is substantial, the cost in time and dollars will probably be worthwhile.

Taxes and Other Administration Issues

As mentioned above, the estate settlement process can be daunting, especially if the executor is inexperienced. As a preliminary matter, the charity should obtain a copy of the inventory and valuation list, which will give the charity a better idea of exactly what property the will entitles it to, especially if it is a residuary beneficiary.[54] Often the inability or reluctance of the executor or attorney to supply a proper inventory and valuations within the first six months after the death of the decedent is the first indication of problems. If this situation persists local counsel may be necessary to prompt the fiduciaries into action. The charity should work with the executor, if at all possible, to ensure it receives the full amount to which it is entitled. Gifts of specified dollar amounts, percentages, or residue can have some effect on other beneficiaries, based on where in the estate the property in question is drawn from.[55]

Often, receiving the full amount the donor bequeathed to charity means delving into complex tax regulations. One example is ensuring that the executor takes deductions both for income the estate actually distributes and reserves for future distribution to the charity.[56] However, to qualify for these deductions, the estate's amount distributed or reserved must be from "gross income pursuant to the terms of the will (or trust)."[57]

If the charity is a partial or full residuary beneficiary, it would be prudent to ask the executor for an opportunity to review the estate's income tax filing (Form 1041 and related state returns) while the returns are still in draft form. The executor may or may not agree to this. If the estate is reporting net income on the return, typically the IRS will allow a "charitable set-aside" for the estate's income that it will eventually distribute to the charity. If the charity is a full residuary beneficiary, this set-aside may reduce the taxable income to zero, thus preserving more assets for the eventual distribution. If the charity is to receive less than all of the residue, the estate should expect a partial set-aside.

Due to the complexities of the fiduciary income tax rules and the Alternative Minimum Tax, the charitable income tax deduction may not completely offset the income, especially in the initial

---

54. O'Carroll, A., p. 16.
55. Midura, T.S., p. 8., Pennell 834-2nd T.M. Transfer Tax Payment and Apportionment I.B.3.a.
56. Katzenstein, L.P., p. 1.
57. Midura, T.S., p. 26.

year of the estate. If a family accountant prepares the return, that person may have little experience in fiduciary income taxation and the charitable set-aside. As a result of that inexperience, the return may overlook or miscalculate the set-aside deduction. If the executor is reluctant to share the returns in draft form before filing them, it is still worth requesting copies of the returns as the executor filed them, either from the fiduciary or even from the IRS.[58] If, after review, it appears the estate paid tax in error, it can amend the returns.

If the charitable transfer is made via a beneficiary designation, any related income will generally not appear on the estate's fiduciary income tax return. For example, if the decedent named the charity as the beneficiary of his or her IRA, neither the income nor the offsetting deduction would appear on the income tax return (both will appear only on the estate tax return). However, if the decedent named his or her estate as the IRA's beneficiary, and then made a specific bequest of the IRA to the charity in the estate documents, both the income and a completely offsetting income tax deduction should appear on the return.[59] For tax and administrative efficiency, the direct beneficiary designation is preferable, and the charity should encourage it if possible during the planning process.

Note: If the charitable bequest is a pecuniary bequest or a bequest of a specific asset, rather than a share of the residual estate, the IRS will not allow an income tax deduction on the estate's income tax return.[60] If state law or the document allocates income from a specific asset to the charity, then there would be a deduction, but only for the amount of income.

Estate taxes are also a concern. This happens primarily when the charity is a residuary beneficiary, but the will directs that the executor pay estate taxes from that same residuary interest. This creates a circular calculation (albeit one whose final result most spreadsheet software or estate planning software can calculate) where the tax reduces the charitable deduction, which increases the tax, etc.[61]

If the will contains this error, the charity should investigate whether state law might exempt the charitable bequest from paying estate taxes through the state tax apportionment statutes.[62] Sometimes it is clear from the documents that the testator intended for the charity to share the burden

---

58. IRC § 6103(e)(1)(E), § 6103(e)(1)(F).
59. IRC § 642(c).
60. Crestar Bank, DC Va., 99-1 USTC ¶50,545.
61. Katzenstein, L.P., p. 5-8.
62. Id., p. 8-11., Pennell 834-2nd T.M. Transfer Tax Payment and Apportionment III.D.

of the taxes; typically the document provisions will override the default state law provisions.[63] Administration expenses can reduce charitable gifts as well, either by virtue of the donor's directions, or by equitable apportionment according to state and federal law.[64]

Unexpected increases in estate taxes can occur in many situations, but most of them involve closely held business interests. The first potentially problematic situation involves buy-sell agreements. Many buy-sell agreements allow related parties, or the company itself, to purchase the decedent's interest in the company for less than full fair market value. In accordance with the Treasury Regulations,[65] many of these agreements are not binding for tax valuation purposes, although they are still binding for legal purposes. The Service only allows a charitable estate tax deduction for the amount actually passing to the charity.

If the market values a business at $30 million, but the family can buy it for $17 million, then the maximum possible charitable deduction would be the $17 million that the estate would receive, thus leaving a $13 million taxable difference between the value on the estate tax return and the allowable charitable deduction (assuming a bequest of 100 percent of the estate to charity). Even assuming the maximum $11.18 million[66] estate tax exemption, there would still be a $1.82 million taxable estate generating a tax of $728,000. That $728,000 would further reduce the charitable bequest of $17 million, thus triggering the circular calculation discussed above.

The second possible problem with closely held business interests involves valuation discounts. Assume the estate includes an 80 percent interest in a business, with the decedent bequeathing half of that to the US citizen surviving spouse and half to a charity. One would assume that there would be no estate tax, given the availability of the marital and charitable estate tax deductions.

Unfortunately, the math does not work out as expected. An 80 percent interest in a closely held business is subject to a valuation discount for lack of marketability, simply because the business is closely held. But the spouse and the charity each receive a 40 percent interest in the business. Each 40 percent is subject to a minority interest discount in addition to the estate-level discount for lack of marketability. This is an example of the whole being more than the sum of the parts. Assuming an additional 10 percent discount for a minority interest, the two 40 percent deductible bequests

---

63. Bekerman, 804-2nd T.M. Probate and Administration of Decedent's Estates XVI.C.
64. Midura, T.S., p. 22., Beckwith and Allan, 839-2nd T.M. Estate and Gift Tax Charitable Deductions VII.B.
65. Treas. Reg. § 25.2703-1
66. Internal Revenue Service, "Estate Tax," https://www.irs.gov/businesses/small-businesses-self-employed/estate-tax.

only add up to 72 percent of the estate, thus leaving 8 percent taxable (and also subject to the circular calculation problem[67]).

No matter what the charity's interest is in the estate, the charity will want to know when the estate accountant files the federal estate tax return. The executor may be waiting for the federal closing letter before distributing estate assets. In a wholly charitable estate, the nonprofit may receive the closing letter fairly quickly after the filing of the return ("fairly quickly" means three to six months). Unless the estate cannot settle its tax issues through the audit and appeals process and ends up in Tax Court, it should receive the closing letter within three years of the filing of the Form 706 estate tax return. If there are state estate tax returns, those may have different deadlines and different administrative processes.

Nontax administrative issues exist as well. There can be complications involving the payment of interest on a legacy when there are delays in funding testamentary trusts, including CRTs and CLTs.[68]

A final note should be made on the split-interest gift. The executor may deduct the value of the charity's remainder interest from the taxable estate, but the value of assets allocated to income beneficiaries may not be (unless the sole lifetime beneficiary is the donor's US citizen spouse).[69] CRTs and CGAs are examples of such a gift, although they can also take the form of property interests such as a remainder interest in a home or a farm.[70]

In the case of such a remainder interest gift, the charity should strongly consider entering into an agreement with the life tenant spelling out the rights and responsibilities of both parties. Such an agreement will address such matters as insurance, the definition of "repairs" vs. "improvements," and who is responsible for paying for them. The agreement should also discuss disposition of the property before the end of the life term. This is especially important if the life tenant is a surviving spouse who may need to sell the property at some point to move to a warmer climate or an assisted living facility. Typically, the agreement will allocate proceeds of the sale based on the actuarial life expectancy of the life tenant, but the parties should reach an understanding regarding which life tables they will use, since state and federal tables may differ. The time to reach this

---

67. *Ahmanson Foundation v. United States* [81-2 USTC ¶13,438], 674 F.2d 761 (9th Cir. 1981).
68. Katzenstein, L.P., p. 4-5.
69. Bourland, M.V. & Myers, J.N. (1999, August 17). "The Charitable Remainder Trust." Planned Giving Design Center. Retrieved from http://www.pgdc.com/pgdc/charitable-remainder-trust.
70. Indiana University Foundation. (2012). "Charitable Bequests and Different Aspects of Testamentary Giving." Retrieved from https://options.iuf.indiana.edu/spring-2012#split-interest.

agreement is during the estate administration period—not when the septic tank needs replacement or the condo association board issues a special assessment.

Regardless of the form of the gift, the charity with the remainder interest should make sure that it stays in touch with both the lifetime beneficiary and whoever is responsible for care of the assets (the trustee in the case of CRTs). This is because the caretaker has responsibilities (typically codified under state law in the case of trusts) to both beneficiaries.[71] This means the charity should again take care to ensure it is receiving the full amount to which it is entitled.

Potential Pitfalls

This section aims to outline a number of possible mistakes a charity might make in navigating the estate settlement process.

1. Failure to communicate with the donor's advisors

Although the charity may have a good understanding of what and how the donor wants to give, the donor's professional advisors may have no idea. This can cause countless problems during the settlement process, all because the donor did not keep the advisors apprised of what he and the charity discussed and what commitments he made. There is "little doubt that candor will greatly benefit the long-term health of every nonprofit organization."[72]

2. Failure to account for reactions of surviving family

Similar to the point above, charities should keep the other beneficiaries, if any, in mind. In a worst case scenario, the donor's family members might be bitter or resentful due to being "passed over" in favor of the charity, which could even lead to litigation. And when there are split-interest gifts, the assets will likely tie the charity and lifetime beneficiary together until all the remaining noncharitable interests have expired. Maintaining good relationships with the donor's family during all phases of the process is essential, and can aid the flow of information to the charity.

---

71. Comstock, P.L. (1998, December 4). "Investment Strategies for Fiduciaries of Split-Interest Trusts." Planned Giving Design Center. Retrieved from http://www.pgdc.com/pgdc/investment-strategies-fiduciaries-split-interest-trusts.
72. Livingston, R., p. 8.

Appendix

3.   Failure to have gift-acceptance guidelines in place

The charity receives surprise notice that an unexpected donor has bequeathed it the mineral rights to a patch of land. This sounds great, but what if the charity has no experience with such gifts? How should it know if the cost is worth the benefit? What about potential environmental liability risks? How would the charity go about liquidating the asset? It is important to have policies for evaluating which gifts to accept, particularly when it comes to nontraditional gifts.[73] Any time environmental risks are a concern, the charity and its counsel should review both state law and any relevant documents to see if they provide any additional protection.

4.   Failure to follow proper tax and accounting procedures

As described in earlier sections. These problems can range from wrongful payment of income or estate taxes from the assets the decedent bequeathed to charity, to the charity recognizing receipt of the gift in the wrong period (or in the wrong amount). These are problems which can start small, by simply neglecting to fill out or obtain paperwork, but can end up costing the charity real money by adding to the tax or administrative costs to the estate.

5.   Failure to thank surviving family

This can be easy to forget. Once the settlement process is over (or the charity has received its remainder interest), its formal involvement with the donor's estate is over. But an appropriate token of appreciation can go a long way, and "ongoing stewardship of surviving family members can result in tremendous long-term benefits for your organization."[74] Not only can the surviving family potentially become donors, but a show of gratitude can go a long way towards building strong relationships with the community.

6.   Failure to comply with regulatory rules

Aside from maintaining 501(c)(3) status under federal law, there are also state compliance issues. The charity will in all likelihood already be registered with at least one state office, but there may be additional registration requirements relating to estate settlement. For example, Illinois requires

---

73. See Hancock, J., p. 6-8 (describing gift acceptance considerations for gifts relating to mineral interests); KeyBank. "Managing Nontraditional Donations." Retrieved from https://www.key.com/business/programs/managing_nontraditional_donations.jsp (describing potential maintenance, insurance, appraisal, and liquidation concerns for nontraditional donations).
74. Slawson, D.M. (2006, July 1). "After the Bequest – Estate Administration Tips." Sharpe Group. Retrieved from http://sharpenet.com/give-take/bequest-estate-administration-tips/.

that all estates and trusts holding assets for charity over $4,000 be register with it. This can lead to potential headaches when working with inexperienced executors.[75] If the estate establishes a charitable gift annuity (an admittedly rare occurrence), the charity must be sure it is registered in all relevant states.

7. Failure to accurately tailor restrictions on the gift

Restrictions on the gift in the governing document—typically relating to use of the gift—can cause problems for both the charity and the estate. For example, if the donor earmarks the gift "for a noncharitable purpose, or even a charitable purpose that is outside of the donee organization's charitable mission, the gift is not deductible."[76] From the charity's perspective, it might lose the gift entirely if it does not comply with conditions, if there is a reverter clause or a "gift over" clause that would transfer the property to another charity.[77] Hence, there should be careful planning when the decedent creates restrictions, and both the estate and the charity should keep those restrictions in mind when it comes to distribution and use of the gift.[78]

8. Potential conflicts of interest

The final potential issue is one of professional ethics. Professional advisors must take care not to represent both parties in the process, which would constitute a conflict of interest.[79] This can happen, for example, when a potential donor's attorney is also on the charity's board. Although it may seem convenient to all parties involved, it is nonetheless an ethics violation. The charity must ensure that its representation is independent of the donor and estate.

Conclusion

This article has discussed estate settlement for charities, from the groundwork the parties lay during the planning process through final distribution of the gift. It discussed the practical and legal implications of various forms of gifts, and recommended steps to take to ensure the process goes smoothly. It also highlighted various issues that might arise if the parties involved do not take

---

75. Midura, T.S., p. 28-30.
76. Rothschild, A.F., Jr. (2007). "Planning and Documenting Charitable Gifts." American Bar Association. Retrieved from https://www.americanbar.org/newsletter/publications/law_trends_news_practice_area_e_newsletter_home/planningcharitablegifts.html.
77. Id.
78. Gary, Susan N, The Problems with Donor Intent: Interpretation, Enforcement, and Doing the Right Thing. *Chicago-Kent Law Review* Volume 85 Issue 3, January 2010.
79. Id.

proper care. Leaving a bequest to charity is a wonderful way to support countless worthy causes, and, even though it can be a daunting and complex process, everyone with the means to do so should consider it. But charities and their advisors have a responsibility to effectively navigate the estate settlement process, so that the charitable gift and its impact can be maximized.

Appendix B:
Charitable Estate Settlement Additional Resources

Below are further details on charitable estate settlement. Charitable estate settlement topics are based on Snerson, G., Peebles, L., and Clontz, B., "Charitable Estate Settlement: A Primer from the Charity's Perspective." For an in-depth examination adapted and excerpted from the article, see Charitable Estate Settlement.

For an introduction to the probate process, see Moran, M.C. (2010), "Dream Gift or Dickensian Nightmare? Probate Fundamentals for Estate Administrators," 14 *Journal of Gift Planning* 18, http://my.pppnet.org/library/000/000/0d/TJGPv14n1_moran.pdf.

For a look at the interests and possible pitfalls of being a charitable beneficiary to an estate, see Katzenstein, L.P. (2011). "Estates with Charities as Beneficiaries: How Do We Protect Their Interests?." Saint Louis Planned Giving Council, http://my.pppnet.org/library/92872/1/Katzenstein_FINAL.pdf.

For an overview of the estate administration process from the charity's perspective, see Blitz, A.H. and Franey, J.W. (October 24, 2003), "Implementing An Effective Estate Administration Program to Increase Your Bottom Line," Partnership for Philanthropic Planning 507, http://my.pppnet.org/library/85914/1/NCPGC2003s17.pdf.

For tips on how to optimize the bequest and settlement process, see Prosser, T.J. (2012), "Getting the Most from Charitable Bequests," *Journal of Gift Planning*, http://my.pppnet.org/library/75925/1/NCPP12_Prosser.pdf.

For an examination of legal standing and enforcement issues in the charitable estate context, see Brody, E. (2007), "From the Dead Hand to the Living Dead: The Conundrum of Charitable Donor Standing," 41 *Ga. L. Rev.* 1183, http://scholarship.kentlaw.iit.edu/fac_schol/119.

For an analysis of the tension between heirs and charities, see Carter, Elizabeth Ruth (June 15, 2013), "Tipping the Scales in Favor of Charitable Bequests: A Critique," Pace Law Review, Forthcoming, http://papers.ssrn.com/sol3/papers.cfm?abstract_id=2279911.

For cautionary tales illustrating the importance of clear donor intent, see Manterfield, E.A. (June 23, 2010), "Perfecting Donor Intent on Gifts to Charity - The Gift Agreement (From the Charity)," Planned Giving Design Center, http://www.pgdc.com/pgdc/perfecting-donor-intent-gifts-charity-gift-agreement-charity.

Appendix

For guidance on developing gift acceptance policies, see Miree, K.W. (August 18, 2000), "Understanding and Drafting Nonprofit Gift Acceptance Policies," Planned Giving Design Center, http://www.pgdc.com/pgdc/understanding-and-drafting-nonprofit-gift-acceptance-policies.

For an example gift acceptance policy, see Oregon State University (December 10, 2010), "Gift Acceptance Policy and Guidelines," http://my.pppnet.org/library/55863/1/Revised%20Gift%20Acceptance%20Policy.pdf.

For an example of a college's bequest declaration of intent, see University of Michigan (October 1, 2013), "Planned Giving: Declaration of Intent," http://my.pppnet.org/library/81610/1/10-21-13%20EDITABLE%20Declaration%20of%20Intent%20Form.pdf.

Private Letter Ruling 200024016 (bequest creating charitable trust intended to perform charitable functions in a non-US country)

Private Letter Ruling 201342011 (examination of unusually large bequests which may put the nonprofit beneficiary out of compliance with public support requirements)

Private Letter Ruling 201446024 (bequest creates possible self-dealing with trust and private foundation beneficiary)

Appendix C: At Least a Day Late and Perhaps Many Dollars Short

The Top Seven Post-Transaction Creative Charitable Planning Ideas

For many noncash donations, some donors miss the window of opportunity to make a charitable donation. Once there is a legally binding contract to sell, it is usually too late under the assignment of income doctrine. For a charitably-inclined donor, this can be very disappointing news.

Nonetheless, there are still a number of tax-effective planning opportunities while still achieving the donor's charitable goals. This is particularly true when the donor must recognize a large capital gain as a result of the original transaction.

Below is an examination of the top seven post-transaction charitable planning ideas. It discusses seven different techniques for tax advantaged charitable contributions post-sale. When the donor and charity properly plan and execute the post-transaction donation, the gift can still be beneficial for both parties.

Planning Idea #1: Donate the sale proceeds

This is the simplest option – the taxpayer simply donates the proceeds of the transaction. The donation can be as much or as little as the donor wishes to give. The drawback to this simplicity is that the donor will be paying taxes on dollars she has given away, without any replacement income. Although the options discussed in the following sections may also fund planned giving vehicles with the proceeds, so some life income may be provided to the donor.

Consider the following example of how this transaction might work. An unmarried taxpayer, age 75, earns $250,000 in wage income and sells non-collectible long term capital assets with a gain of $250,000 in 2018. Adjusted gross income is $500,000. The calculations utilize the IRS's "Qualified Dividends and Capital Gains Tax Worksheet" in calculating taxable income. Further, the examples assume the taxpayer lives in a state without individual income tax. Net investment income tax (NIIT) is an additional $9,500 in all cases.

With no donation and a standard deduction, this leaves taxable income of $488,000. Her total tax with NIIT, including income and capital gains, is $109,100. With a donation of the entire sales proceeds, the taxpayer significantly lowers her tax bill (the benefits would be smaller for a donation of only part of the proceeds). The tradeoff is that her post-gift, post-tax income is only $68,490 – wages minus taxes paid. The donor may be perfectly happy with this, but if she wanted some income stream or future return, she has better options.

	No gift made	**$250,000 gift made**
Wages	250,000	250,000
Capital gain	250,000	250,000
Deduction	12,000	250,000
Taxable income	488,000	250,000
Tax paid, including $9,500 NIIT	109,100	68,490
Taxes saved	0	40,610
Cost of gift	0	209,390
Net 2018 income	390,900	181,510

Planning Idea #2: Donate other long term capital gain property

Another intuitive option is simply to donate other highly-appreciated capital gain property. The goal for the donor is to maximize the deduction. Doing so will counteract the capital gains tax due from the original transaction. A charitable income tax deduction will reduce the donor's taxable income, meaning the tax benefit will come at standard income tax bracket rates, rather than at capital gains rates. Effectively, the donor is lowering her non-gain taxable income.

In this instance, she should consider giving long-term capital gain property with a low cost basis and a high fair market value. Ideally, the donated asset should be some form of corporate stock, business interest, or real estate. These asset classes avoid limitations such as related use regulations for tangible property, which may reduce the value of the deduction to cost basis. Those assets are also not subject to the specialized deduction rules for intellectual property like copyrights and patents which may sharply limit the immediately available deduction.

An advantage of this approach is that it does not require the donor to commit any cash. Instead, the donor avoids capital gains tax by donating an appreciated asset, which presumably would incur taxes on sale or transfer at some point. Further, it is relatively simple, since it is an outright donation and does not involve any advanced planning techniques. Indeed, this gift is so simple it could possibly be completed without the involvement of specialized professional advisors (e.g., donation of publicly-traded stock as an example).

Disadvantages of the approach are readily apparent. It requires additional appreciated long term capital property, which the donor is willing to donate. Any income from the original transaction is not used at all.

Now, consider the same unmarried taxpayer (this time 70 years old) with $250,000 each of wages and capital gains, but this time having donated publicly traded stock worth $100,000 (exempt from appraisal requirements for noncash donations). She is able to deduct $100,000. This reduces taxable income to $400,000. Her new total tax with NIIT is $74,410. These tax savings mean that the $100,000 gift essentially costs the taxpayer only $65,310.

	No gift made	$100,000 stock gift made
Wages	250,000	250,000
Capital gain	250,000	250,000
Deduction	12,000	100,000
Taxable income	488,000	400,000
Tax paid, including $9,500 NIIT	109,100	74,410
Taxes saved	0	34,690
Cost of gift	0	65,310
Net 2018 income	390,900	425,590

Sources:

Hoffman, M. (May 2, 2003), "Privately Held Business Interests," Planned Giving Design Center, http://www.pgdc.com/pgdc/privately-held-business-interests.

Hoffman, M. et al (May 2, 2003), "Tangible Personal Property," Planned Giving Design Center, http://www.pgdc.com/pgdc/tangible-personal-property.

Hoffman, M. (May 2, 2003), "Publicly Traded Securities," Planned Giving Design Center, http://www.pgdc.com/pgdc/publicly-traded-securities.

Planning Idea #3: Establish a deferred charitable gift annuity

Another option is to use the proceeds from the transaction set up a deferred charitable gift annuity (DCGA). This is a slightly more complex option than simply donating appreciated capital property. However, it has some noteworthy benefits. It can utilize the proceeds of the original transaction, and it can lead to a future income stream after the deferral period. Further, like all CGAs, it generates an immediate tax deduction.

As a quick refresher, a charitable gift annuity is a contractual agreement between the donor and the donee charity. The donor donates property to the charity, which in turn agrees to make regular payments to the donor for life. The IRS prescribes part-gift, part-sale treatment for this arrangement (i.e., installment bargain sale). The gift portion is calculated as the value transferred, minus the value of the life annuity. Since the donor's date of death is unknown, the annuity value is based on the present value of actuarial projections for the total payments starting after the deferral period. The donor receives a current charitable income tax deduction for the amount given to charity above that calculated annuity value.

A popular option for donors is a joint income CGA. Typically established for married couples, the payment period is for two lives – a "joint and survivor" annuity. The donee charity will make payments first to both spouses, and then continue full payments to the surviving spouse. For example, the couple might receive a $5,000 annuity, and later, the surviving spouse would continue to receive the $5,000 amount for life. Actuarial projections and resulting deductions are adjusted based on the additional life.

The simplest CGA variant begins the annuity payments immediately, but this is not ideal from the perspective of a donor trying to mitigate recognized capital gains. A deferred annuity will delay the payments until a future date, which must be more than one year after the contribution date. This deferral reduces the projected actuarial life expectancy, which in turn lowers the life-time annuity value and increases the deduction. The longer the deferral, the higher the charitable deduction. Further, deductions grow depending on the initial age of the donor. For example, the deduction will be higher for a 70-year-old donor deferring for five years compared to a 55-year-old donor with payments beginning immediately.

A flexible deferred gift annuity may better suit the donor's needs. The donor chooses a target start date range for annuity payments, and calculates the income tax deduction based on the earliest date. The annuity payments are reduced or increased as necessary depending on the actual date they begin to maintain the original deduction.

Compare the two cases below, with both an immediate annuity and a five-year deferred annuity. In both cases, the donor, age 70, transfers $100,000 to charity in exchange for a quarterly payout stream.

Charitable Gifts of Noncash Assets

	Immediate single life annuity	Deferred single life annuity
Input Assumptions		
Date of transfer	August 01, 2018	August 01, 2018
Fair market value of property transferred	$100,000.00	$100,000.00
Date of first payment	August 31, 2018	August 01, 2023
Annuity starting date (payment period before 1st payment)	August 01, 2018	June 01, 2023
Annual annuity rate for immediate annuity	5.6%	7.4%
Payment frequency	Quarterly	Quarterly
Deferred annuity interest adjustment factor	--	1.0155
Annual annuity rate adjusted for deferral	--	7.5%
IRC Sec. 7520(a) election to use 8/2018 discount rate of	3.4%	3.4%
Nearest age of Mr. Jones on the date of the gift is	70	70
Present Value of Remainder Interest		
Net fair market value paid for annuity	$100,000.00	$100,000.00
Age nearest to annuity starting date	70	75
Age nearest to date of transfer	70	70
Annual annuity rate	5.6%	7.4%
Annuity amount payable on an annual basis	$5,600.00	$7,400.00
Present value of annuity	$59,841.04	$47,414.28
Minimum value of annuity	$59,841.04	$47,414.28
Present value of remainder interest – Charitable Deduction	$40,158.96	$52,585.72

Under this example, a deferral period of only five years increases the deduction by over $12,000 – a nearly 30% increase. Note that the IRS 7520 interest rate used to calculate present value is 3.4%. This rate is set on a monthly basis, and the rate used was for August 2018 - lower rates mean higher deductions. Additionally, with the deferral, the annuity amount payable increases from $5,600 to $7,400, a 32% increase.

Refer back to the case of the taxpayer making no gift to offset the capital gains. A $100,000 deferred CGA leads to tax savings of $19,997. Better yet, this donation will produce lifetime income once the deferral period ends, unlike an outright gift of an appreciated capital asset.

Appendix

	No gift made	$100,000 deferred CGA
Wages	250,000	250,000
Capital gain	250,000	250,000
Deduction	12,000	52,586
Taxable income	488,000	447,414
Tax paid, including $9,500 NIIT	109,100	89,103
Taxes saved	0	19,997
Cost of gift	0	80,003
Net income	390,900	319,997

Sources:

Hoffman, M. (April 7, 2008), "Charitable Gift Annuity," http://www.pgdc.com/pgdc/charitable-gift-annuity.

American Council on Gift Annuities, "Promoting Responsible Philanthropy: Suggested Gift Annuity Rates, Quality Training Opportunities, and Consumer Protection Advocacy," http://www.acga-web.org/ (last accessed September 7, 2016).

Planning Idea #4: Join a new pooled income fund

A fourth option is to join a newly-formed pooled income fund (PIF). The fund must be less than three years old to realize the maximum tax benefits. In that case, regulations prescribe that the deduction is calculated using favorable Applicable Federal Rates.

How does the PIF work? In many ways, it is similar to a charitable remainder trust. The donor transfers assets to the fund, and the administering charity pools those assets together with others in the fund for investment. The donors receive their prorated share of the PIF's income annually, and the charity receives the remainder interest in the assets. The donor's income tax deduction is the present value of the remainder interest.

The deduction is calculated using the highest rate of return for the prior three years, but funds in existence for less than three years have special rules. Instead, they calculate the deduction using the following IRS-prescribed method:

"[T]he highest rate of return is deemed to be the interest rate (rounded to the nearest two-tenths of one percent) that is 1 percent less than the highest annual average of the monthly section 7520 rates for the 3 calendar years immediately preceding the calendar year in which the transfer to the pooled income fund is made. The deemed rate of return for transfers to new pooled income funds is recomputed each calendar year using the monthly section 7520 rates for the 3-year period immediately preceding the calendar year in which each transfer to the fund is made until the fund has been in existence for 3 taxable years." Treas. Reg. § 1.642(c)-6(e)(4).

This means that, in a low interest rate environment, the present value of the remainder interest will be very high. Indeed, it can be much larger than a comparable contribution to a charitable remainder trust. Assuming the 70-year-old donor gives $100,000 of her capital gains to a new PIF, the deduction is calculated as follows:

Current Applicable Federal Rate (2018):	1.4%
Age of donor at time of gift:	70
Single Life Remainder Factor (IRS Table S):	0.82473
Amount to PIF:	$100,000
Present value of remainder interest:	$82,473

This means that the total income tax deduction is $82,473. The low Applicable Federal Rate largely drives this high deduction, and therefore only PIFs less than three years old are suitable, if this is the desired effect.

Appendix

	No gift made	$100,000 PIF
Wages	250,000	250,000
Capital gain	250,000	250,000
Deduction	12,000	82,473
Taxable income	488,000	417,527
Tax paid, including $9,500 NIIT	109,100	78,616
Taxes saved	0	30,484
Cost of gift	0	69,516
Net 2018 income	390,900	321,384

This example creates a deduction almost as valuable as the outright gift of appreciated assets. Further, the PIF provides lifetime income for the donor, which can make the gift worthwhile from a practical perspective, even with a 70-year-old donor and a 5% annual return.

Sources:

Hoffman, M. (May 2, 2003), "Pooled Income Fund," Planned Giving Design Center, http://www.pgdc.com/pgdc/pooled-income-fund.

Treas. Reg. § 1.642(c)-6 (2011), https://www.law.cornell.edu/cfr/text/26/1.642(c)-6.

Planning Idea #5: Create a grantor charitable lead annuity trust

A charitable lead trust is similar to a charitable remainder trust, but with the interests of both the donor and nonprofit donee swapped. The trust assets pay income to the nonprofit, usually for a term of years. After the term expires, the assets revert back either to the donor, or to a party named in the trust instrument. Since the charity gets an income interest, the donor's income tax deduction, if any, is based on the value of that interest.

The difference between a reversionary and non-reversionary charitable lead trust merits further explanation for estate planning purposes. This section deals primarily with reversionary lead trusts, where the donor will hold the remainder interest, meaning that the donor will eventually regain outright ownership of the property. This is an appealing option for the donor when they have a spike in income which they need to offset with a charitable income tax deduction. However, non-reversionary charitable lead trusts can be very advantageous in planning inter-generational wealth transfers. This is because the trust assets are outside of the donor's estate (the donor is not the trustee in this case), so the donor can assign the remainder interest to any future heirs. From an estate tax perspective, this can be a significant advantage for donors with large estates.

The best way to utilize this vehicle with the aim of maximizing the present period deduction is a grantor charitable lead annuity trust ("CLAT"). Since the IRS treats the grantor (usually meaning the donor) as owning all trust income, that income is taxable to the grantor as if the trust did not exist. This disadvantage is offset by the accelerated deduction. The donor gets a larger deduction in the first year, equaling the present value of the income interest. Since the donor determines the value of that interest in the trust instrument, this deduction can be as large or small as desired. Also, due to the annuity income payment feature (rather than the "fixed proportion of assets" of a unitrust), the deduction amount is easily calculated.

Another lead trust variant that may meet the donor's needs is the defective non-grantor lead trust (sometimes called "super trusts"). The donor intentionally drafts this vehicle with a defect that leads to grantor trust treatment, including the "up front" income tax deduction described above. This result is due to an apparent inconsistency in the tax code's rules for grantor trust treatment. Drafters of defective non-grantor lead trusts typically include a defective provision that allows for substitution of trust property or trustees.

To better illustrate this option, imagine again the 70-year-old donor with $250,000 each of normal wages and realized capital gains. This time, she wishes to create a $100,000 charitable lead trust, either as a grantor CLAT or defective non-grantor lead trust. In either case, she will receive an income tax deduction equal to the present value of the nonprofit's income interest. Assuming a 5% annual payout (perhaps funded from municipal or state bonds), and a 10-year term for the income interest, the deduction is calculated as below:

Appendix

	Assumptions
Value of assets transferred into CLAT	$100,000
Annual payout to nonprofit holding income interest	$5,000 (5%)
Length of income interest term	10 years
§7520 rate (August 2018)	3.4%
Term certain annuity factor (IRS Table B)	8.3587
Income tax deduction	$42,324

Holding the payout amount constant, the main factors driving the deduction are the §7520 rate and the term length of the income interest. For example, holding the assets and payout constant:

	Short term CLAT	Long term CLAT	High §7520 rate
Length of income interest term	5 years	20 years	10 years
§7520 rate	3.4%	3.4%	8.0%
Term certain annuity factor (IRS Table B)	4.5279	14.3419	6.7101
Income tax deduction	$22,927	$72,620	$33,551

Taking the original assumptions, and the resulting deduction of $42,324, the taxpayer sees the following benefits:

	No gift made	$100,000 CLAT
Wages	250,000	250,000
Capital gain	250,000	250,000
Deduction	12,000	42,324
Taxable income	488,000	457,676
Tax paid, including $9,500 NIIT	109,100	92,900
Taxes saved	0	16,200
Cost of gift	0	83,800
Net 2018 income	390,900	307,100

The deduction here is smaller than the gift structures outlined above. However, unlike those gifts, there is a significant remainder interest which the donor retains. Not only should the initial principal be returned assuming an investment return at least equal to the payout rate, it is possible that the remainder may actually appreciate in value if it grows faster than the payout rate.

Sources:

McKeever, M. (May 3, 2003), "Charitable Lead Trust," Planned Giving Design Center, http://www.pgdc.com/pgdc/charitable-lead-trust.

James III, R. (June 29, 2016), "Charitable Lead Trusts," Planned Giving Design Center, http://www.pgdc.com/pgdc/13-charitable-lead-trusts.

Lindquist, P.M. et al (July 11, 2012), "Drafting Defective Grantor Trusts," American Bar Association, http://www.americanbar.org/content/dam/aba/events/real_property_trust_estate/step/2012/materials/rpte_step_2012_07_11_Lindquist_Grantor_Trusts_The_Basics_Speech_Outline.authcheckdam.pdf.

Planning Idea #6: Specialized Small Business Investment Company

This alternative is one that only works in specific circumstances – when the donor has capital gain from sale of publicly traded stock. The Small Business Administration allows donors to roll over capital gain, up to $50,000 per year, with a lifetime cap of $500,000. The donor can use the sales proceeds to invest in a licensed small business investment company ("SBIC"), but must do so within 60 days of the sale. Note however, that the basis in the SBIC is reduced by the deferred capital gain.

There is a simple way to incorporate a charitable outlook into this strategy. The donor transfers the SBIC investment with a low, deferred-gain basis to a charitable remainder trust, or donates it outright. In either case, the donor escapes the capital gains, and receives a deduction for donating the capital asset (of the sort described in the first section). If a charitable remainder trust holds the SBIC interest, it can even generate income for the donor.

Sources:

Teitell, C. (2007), "Charitable Planning," Practising Law Institute at 37, http://www.pli.edu/emktg/toolbox/Charit_Plng37.PDF.

Appendix

Planning Idea #7: Qualified charitable distributions from a traditional IRA

For donors over age 70 ½ with a traditional IRA, a qualified charitable distribution ("QCD") can offset ordinary income with recognized capital gains at a lower tax rate. Traditional IRAs in particular (rather than a Roth IRA) work well here, since owners are required to take minimum distributions beginning at that age. A QCD will count towards the minimum distribution, and therefore lower adjusted gross income.

Taxpayers should therefore direct their IRA trustees to make donations equal to their required minimum distributions. From a practical perspective, it is the trustee who makes the donation, but otherwise, acknowledgement requirements are the same as any other charitable contribution. Also, note that the maximum annual QCD exclusion is $100,000. Additionally, only public charities are eligible to receive these donations (private foundations and donor-advised funds are not), and the gift must be made outright.

Required minimum distributions are calculated based on remaining life expectancy and the IRA account balance. This means that the minimum distributions will be higher with large accounts and short remaining life expectancies. However, regardless of the size of the exclusion, the taxpayer should always consider a QCD if she has sufficient income from capital gains. Essentially, a QCD equal to the required minimum distribution will mean no income from the IRA reported on the taxpayer's return.

Sources:

IRS Publication 590-B (Jan. 4, 2016), "Distributions from Individual Retirement Arrangements (IRAs)," 13, https://www.irs.gov/pub/irs-pdf/p590b.pdf.

James III, R. (August 2, 2016), "Donating Retirement Assets: Part 1 of 2," Planned Giving Design Center, http://www.pgdc.com/pgdc/15-donating-retirement-assets-part-1-2.

Factoring in Donor Age: Two Examples

For the major planned gifts discussed here (CGA, PIF, CLAT), donor age is a major factor. Projected remaining lifespan can have a significant impact on both the deduction allowed and on the income received. Similarly, an older donor is more likely to need an income stream, due to current or impending retirement. This section discusses how donor age can impact the method of giving.

Imagine two donors, aged 55 and 75, each with identical income and capital gains of $250,000. The older donor is retiring after this year, and the younger donor plans to retire in 20 years. Both decide to utilize a planned giving vehicle to make a donation while generating some return. Which planned giving vehicle is best? The table below outlines the alternatives in a qualitative format.

	55-year-old donor	**75-year-old donor**
Immediate CGA	• Lower annuity rate • Lower deduction • Income stream less useful while working	• Lower annuity rate • Lower deduction • Donor can use the immediate income stream
Deferred CGA	• Higher annuity rate • Higher deduction • Donor can defer the income until closer to retirement	• Higher annuity rate • Higher deduction • Deferral may mean few annuity payments received
New PIF	• Lower deduction, even with low federal rate • Uncertain income less relevant while donor is working	• Higher deduction, even with a higher federal rate • Uncertain income may not be desirable
Short term CLAT	• Low deduction • Donor can still put assets to productive use after income interest ends	• Lower deduction, when compared to long term CLAT • Donor can still put assets to productive use after income interest ends
Long term CLAT	• High deduction • Donor likely to get the assets back before or during retirement	• High deduction • Donor less likely to get the assets back

Appendix D: Unique Gift Annuity Planning Opportunities with S-Corp Stock and Real Estate

Introduction

Even though an asset is very common, this does not mean it will be easy to donate. In fact, sometimes the most commonplace assets are more difficult to dedicate toward charitable purposes. This is particularly true for gifts of subchapter S corporations and real estate.

In both cases, there are liquidity and marketability problems. Additionally, each is significantly regulated, which may make ownership and transfer challenging. Nonetheless, there are options for donors who wish to give these assets to charity. Even a planned giving vehicle which typically requires significant liquidity, such as a charitable gift annuity, will work with some ingenuity and additional creativity.

Background

A brief discussion of the definitions, risks, and structure of these planned giving transactions may be useful.

Real estate likely needs no explanation, but instead should be highlighted as the largest source of U.S. privately-held wealth. Its total value far exceeds more traditionally-donated assets such as equities, life insurance, and cash. Since it can appreciate significantly in value over time, it is an appealing donation for the charity and donor alike. The charity, of course, receives a valuable gift. The donor both avoids realizing capital gain and receives a charitable deduction.

Similarly, S corporations are the largest type of privately-held business entity. In fact, there are more S corps than C corps and LLCs combined. S corps usually have a very low adjusted tax basis in the shares, but also may have low cost basis assets (like real estate) inside the entity which can also provide charitable giving opportunities.

Despite real estate and S corps having obvious upsides as charitable gifts, there are still material risks for nonprofits considering accepting them. Generally speaking, these involve liquidity and marketability. Both classes of asset can be difficult to sell, whether because of a limited pool of buyers or otherwise. Additionally, both can lead to tax problems for the nonprofit, in the form of unrelated business taxable income ("UBTI"). This section outlines those risks for each asset type.

S corporations are closely-held businesses which meet certain IRS requirements, and in doing so, qualify for pass-through treatment. Beginning in 1998, Congress allowed charities to own interests in S corporations, whereas previously only individuals, estates, and certain trusts were permitted. This is particularly helpful since, as of 2018, over 4.8 million S corporations exist, with a proportionately small pool of owners – in 2016, less than eight million.

Charitable gift annuities ("CGAs") are the primary planned giving vehicle this article focuses on. Unlike charitable trusts, CGAs are a contract between the donor and the charity, wherein the donor transfers some consideration (cash or otherwise) to the charity in exchange for an annuity. However, that CGA contract can be arranged in many ways. It can pay either a single person or couple for life, it can begin payments immediately or defer them until some future start date. These considerations all affect the value of the annuity, which in turn affects the allowable deduction.

Charitable remainder trusts ("CRTs") are a common planned giving vehicle. They are a form of charitable trust where the donor-grantor transfers some asset into the trust. The trustee administers the CRT for the income beneficiary (usually the donor) and the remainder beneficiary (the charity). Once the income interest expires, usually after either a pre-determined term of years or the donor's death, the charity receives the remaining trust assets.

Real Estate

This section discusses the risks of holding donated real estate, and standard mitigation techniques which nonprofits might utilize. It also suggests some lesser-known techniques that could work well, including option agreements and a unique CGA contract.

Real Estate Risks

Real estate has a reputation for being a sometimes-difficult gift to accept, considering environmental liability, property management, and an array of other potential headaches. Assuming a nonprofit has done its due diligence, these sorts of troublesome real property will not be in the charity's portfolio. Even if it is only holding "good" real estate, there can still be some risk exposure. In the planned giving context of CGAs and CRTs, this usually comes in the related forms of liquidity and marketability, as well as UBTI in some circumstances. Each is discussed in turn below.

Liquidity is important in the CGA and CRT context, because of the payment obligations the donee charity assumes (or that the trustee assumes on the charity's behalf). The charity or trustee must make payments to the annuitants or income beneficiaries. For example, imagine some very illiquid real estate – say, an undeveloped rural tract. How will the nonprofit make payments to the donors? If the tract is not generating any regular income without tenants, and until sale, there is no cash on hand. This is clearly an issue the nonprofit will need to address.

Marketability is a related concern. Some real estate is very attractive to potential buyers and will spend little time on the market. However, more time spent on the market means more time without cash proceeds and on-going holding period costs from the property. As described above, this means a potential liquidity crunch, given planned giving vehicle payment obligations.

UBTI is a problem in some circumstances, due to some unique tax rules for real estate. If the real estate represents an unrelated business or has debt-financed income, then there will be UBTI. For CRTs holding real estate, this leads to a 100 percent excise tax.

Traditional Real Estate Risk Mitigation

How do charities mitigate these risks when the real estate is not going to sell quickly (or if was supposed to but didn't)? Traditionally, they use one – or more – of the following strategies. First, for CGAs, they can defer the annuity payment start date. Next, again for CGAs, they can use a discounted annuity rate, based on the suggested American Council on Gift Annuities ("ACGA") rates. For CRTs, nonprofits/trustees can consider using a so-called "flip" unitrust, or FLIP-CRUT. Below, each option is explained briefly.

A deferred CGA is common, even when there is no real estate risk. It is often used to increase the charitable deduction in the current period, since the deferral means fewer expected payments based on actuarial projections of life expectancy. This makes it even more advantageous to donors of risky real estate. The deferral allows the charity time to liquidate the property, and the donor gets a higher deduction than she otherwise would.

Another common option is for the charity to simply discount the annuity rate – 15-25 percent is quite common. Rather than defer or otherwise rearrange the CGA contract, they simply pay less. Donors may not prefer this, but the tradeoff is that they receive an increased deduction, as with the deferred CGA. The charity simply hedges on the risk of an extended sale process, or receiving settlement proceeds less than the appraised fair market value, by paying the annuitant less. This approach would work in the same manner for a Charitable Remainder Annuity Trust (CRAT), although the income must be paid from the trust, meaning the charity cannot simply pay the income beneficiary out of its reserves. Also note that a CRAT may not defer payments more than a year which lead many advisors to recommend against using a CRAT for any kind of illiquid asset.

A better mitigation alternative exists for Charitable Remainder Unitrusts (CRUTs) holding real estate. A FLIP-CRUT is well-tailored to gifts of real estate, since it only begins paying a percentage of trust assets to the income beneficiary after a specified trigger event occurs. Prior to that event, the CRUT simply pays the lesser of a stated fixed percentage or net income. For real estate not producing income, this is a natural fit though it is still important to have enough liquidity to pay pre-sale expenses. The FLIP-CRUT is simply set up so that the real estate's sale is the trigger event, and the charity pays the net income (of zero dollars) to the income beneficiary until it occurs.

Special Techniques

An innovative approach is to fund special deferred CGAs with real estate or other illiquid assets. The way this works is by adjusting the payments after the donee charity liquidates the donated real estate, based on the difference between any expected and actual principal. The deferred CGA can be single or joint life.

An example of this special CGA arrangement may be useful. A donor with real estate appraised at $500,000 gives the property to a charity in exchange for a CGA. The annuity pays 5% per year, with a one-year deferral period. The charity has two years after the deferral period to sell the property. If the deferral period has ended and payments are now due, but there has not been a sale, the 5% payment is based on the $500,000 appraised value. One year passes by, and the real estate sells for $450,000 in net proceeds. Going forward, the 5% annuity will use that amount as principal. Since that amount is the true principal, the payor (meaning the donee charity) will recapture the "extra" payment amounts above what was payable on the actual amount of net proceeds. Of course, if the net sales proceeds are above the appraised price, the reverse will be true.

This arrangement has significant advantages for illiquid and difficult-to-market real estate, even when compared to standard deferred CGAs. First, it provides additional time for the donee charity to sell the property. Second, if the property is (or must be) sold for less than the appraised value, it allows recapture through reduced annuity payments. It also makes the CGA more appealing to potential donors, since there need not be a discount on standard rates due to the mitigated liquidity concerns. Of course, the caveat for the nonprofit issuing the CGA is that it must have the cash on hand to pay once the deferral period ends, even if it is still holding the property.

Another iteration is where the owner/donor gives the charity an option to purchase. In a planned giving context, this would be in exchange for a CGA, which could be deferred until exercise. The charity could sell the option contract to a third-party buyer, who would pay the difference between the real estate's fair market value and the exercise price. The charity would need to ensure that the option contract price was sufficient to make the projected annuity payments.

Charities have used CRTs in the past to accept debt-financed real estate while avoiding UBTI. The way this worked was by granting an option to purchase the property to the CRT, which sold the option to a third party for an amount slight less than the difference between fair market value and the exercise price. This worked best when the third-party was a charity. However, in the mid-1990s, the IRS issued private letter rulings which disallowed these gift structures. Thus, their continuing validity is uncertain at best, and such transactions may result in an IRS challenge.

S Corporations

S corporations present somewhat different issues as charitable gifts. Nonetheless, there are still some appealing options for planned giving, particularly considering their nature as closely-held businesses, usually having only one or two owners. This section outlines the risks, standard charitable mitigation tactics, and special techniques which merit consideration.

S Corporation Risks

S corporations are closely-held businesses with special regulations, and therefore have some risks. UBTI is a major concern for charities accepting these interests, particularly in a planned giving context. Marketability may also be an issue. This section outlines the risks associated with planned giving and S corporations.

Charities holding S corporation interests can trigger UBTI regulations in more than one way. First, they must report their share of income as UBTI for every day they own the interest, including passive investment income. Worse still, this income is taxable whether distributed or not. This all means that planned giving vehicles should usually liquidate their interests as soon as possible. Additionally, sale of appreciated S corporation stock will create UBTI on all capital gain above the donor's adjusted tax basis, and is taxed at corporate or trust rates.

Current laws do not even allow CRTs to hold S corporation stock. Further, "[e]ven if a charitable remainder trust could be an eligible shareholder, the UBIT from the S corporation could revoke the tax-exempt status of the trust."[80] CRTs can receive donated S corporation assets, however.

---

80. Hoyt, Christopher, "Charitable Gifts of Subchapter S Stock: How to Solve the Practical Legal Problems," Planned Giving Design Center, http://www.pgdc.com/pgdc/charitable-gifts-subchapter-s-stock-how-solve-practical-legal-problems.

A serious practical concern with S corporation interests is marketability. The simple fact is that S corporations are always closely held, typically with not more than a few owners (they are legally limited to 100 shareholders). This means that the pool of potential buyers is often limited to an entity acquiring the entire business, the few other owners, or the S corporation itself (a redemption). Without a buyer, the charity will be holding an interest which literally may generates UBTI on a daily basis.

Traditional S Corporation Risk Mitigation

As mentioned above, a common planned giving technique with S corporations is to donate corporate assets to the CRT instead of an interest. The shareholder will still qualify for a charitable income tax deduction, since S corporation transactions flow through to the shareholders. Of course, the charity will then have to liquidate the asset.

Rules barring ownership of S corporation stock only apply to charitable remainder trusts – a donor-advised fund ("DAF") organized as a trust can hold S corporation stock. This means that the S corporation income is taxed at trust rates rather than corporate rates, which is particularly appealing for long-term capital gains, where the rate is currently only 20 percent. Indeed, if the DAF trust donates the proceeds from sale of the S corporation, the IRS allows a full deduction, up to 60 percent of adjusted gross income. Effectively, this means that the net federal long term capital gains rate would be only 8 percent. The trust would also be exempt for the Net Investment Income Tax as well as potentially no state income tax for a share sale.

For example, see the table below, showing the result where a top bracket California taxpayer donates an S corporation interest worth $1 million and zero basis.

	Dollars ($)
Value of donated S corp stock	1,000,000
Federal tax savings in 37% bracket	370,000
State tax savings in 13.3% bracket	133,000
Total federal and state tax savings	**503,000**
Taxable gain for trust form DAF	1,000,000
Charitable deduction for trust form DAF	600,000
Tax paid at 20% trust rate + fee from charity	100,000
Total amount for charitable giving	900,000

Appendix

Special Techniques

One possibility for younger donors is to donate S corporation interests to a charity in exchange for a CGA with a lengthy deferral period. This route provides significant flexibility. Not only can it provide an income stream in the future (typically well over a decade ahead), the deferred interest is itself an asset. Simply put, the donors can receive charitable deductions before the deferral period ends.

To illustrate this, begin with two married donors, making a million-dollar S corporation gift at age 45. Not needing income for many years, they settle on a 20-year deferral period. As outlined in the table above, the charity will still be subject to tax on gain from the S corporation interest – ideally at the 8% rate allowed by the combination of trust form and charitable deduction.

	Dollars ($)
Value of donated S corp stock	1,000,000
Available charitable deduction for trust form DAF	600,000
Tax paid at 20% trust rate + fee from charity	100,000
Total amount for CGA	900,000
Deferral period	20 years
Annuity value	622,276
Annual payment	83,700
Present value of remainder interest / deduction amount*	377,724
Present value calculated using the August 2018 7520 rate of 3.4%.	

On making the gift, the donors receive a significant deduction, but further still, have a $622,276 annuity for potential future gifts and charitable deductions. This bonus deduction works by the donors relinquishing or otherwise assigning some portion of their annuity interest to the donee charity which issued the CGA. They would generally receive a deduction for the then-present value of the portion relinquished back to the charity (some experts suggest that this is limited to the unrecovered cost in the contract). Donors should defer to their tax advisor's recommendation on deciding what the deduction amount should be. No additional deduction is allowed for the remainder interest, since the donors already took a deduction for that amount.

As an example, imagine the same married donors decide to make a donation by relinquishing all of their annuity back to the donee charity. They do this halfway through the deferral period.

Charitable Gifts of Noncash Assets

	Dollars ($)
Value of donated annuity interest / unrecovered cost in the contract	622,276
Taxable ordinary income portion of annuity	48,044
Taxable portion of the gift (present value of 24.9 expected annuity payments)	887,756
Remaining value of annuity	0

This allows a large deduction several years down the line (regardless of whether the donor takes the present value of the annuity or the amount invested in the contract), but, of course, comes at the cost of eliminating the annuity entirely. Imagine now that the same donors gave only half of their interest in the CGA at the 10 year mark of the deferral, rather than the entire interest.

	Dollars ($)
Value of donated annuity interest	311,138
Taxable ordinary income portion of annuity	24,022
Taxable portion of the gift (present value of 24.9 expected annuity payments)	443,878
Remaining value of annuity	311,138
New annuity amount payable	41,850

Hence, the deferred interest acts as a sort of charitable spigot (also called a charitable deduction suspension or stretch account), which can be used as the donors see fit. Of course, if they need the income, they can hold onto as much of the interest as they wish. This is particularly effective when donors are unable to use the full planned charitable deduction over the six year period. Note however, that this typically requires a high-value CGA for the deduction to be worth the effort.

The "recapture" deferred CGA described in the real estate section above works in the S corporation gift context as well. Since S corps often have marketability concerns, the deferral and sale periods can provide a significant buffer for nonprofits attempting to sell their donated interest. However, that same time period is one where UBTI will accumulate over time. To counteract that, the CGA contract could also include UBTI in the recapture language, so that the charity recovers any tax paid.

Made in the USA
Coppell, TX
19 December 2020